PROFESSIONAL NoSQL

D0840305

PROFESSIONAL

NoSQL

Shashank Tiwari

WILEY

John Wiley & Sons, Inc.

Professional NoSQL

Published by
John Wiley & Sons, Inc.
10475 Crosspoint Boulevard
Indianapolis, IN 46256
www.wiley.com

Copyright © 2011 by John Wiley & Sons, Inc., Indianapolis, Indiana

Published simultaneously in Canada

ISBN: 978-0-470-94224-6

Manufactured in the United States of America

10 9 8 7 6 5 4 3 2 1

For general information on our other products and services please contact our Customer Care Department within the United States at (877) 762-2974, outside the United States at (317) 572-3993 or fax (317) 572-4002.

Wiley also publishes its books in a variety of electronic formats. Some content that appears in print may not be available in electronic books.

Library of Congress Control Number: 2011930307

I would like to dedicate my work on this book to my parents, Mandakini and Suresh Tiwari.

Everything I do successfully, including writing this book, is a result of the immense support of my dear wife, Caren and my adorable sons, Ayaan and Ezra.

CREDITS

EXECUTIVE EDITOR
Robert Elliot

PROJECT EDITOR
Sydney Jones

TECHNICAL EDITORS
Stefan Edlich
Matt Ingenthron

PRODUCTION EDITOR
Daniel Scribner

COPY EDITOR
Kim Coffer

EDITORIAL DIRECTOR
Robyn B. Siesky

EDITORIAL MANAGER
Mary Beth Wakefield

FREELANCER EDITORIAL MANAGER
Rosemarie Graham

MARKETING MANAGER
Ashley Zurcher

PRODUCTION MANAGER
Tim Tate

VICE PRESIDENT AND EXECUTIVE GROUP PUBLISHER
Richard Swadley

VICE PRESIDENT AND EXECUTIVE PUBLISHER
Barry Pruett

ASSOCIATE PUBLISHER
Jim Minatel

PROJECT COORDINATOR, COVER
Katherine Crocker

PROOFREADER
Scott Klemp, Word One

INDEXER
Robert Swanson

COVER DESIGNER
LeAndra Young

COVER IMAGE
© René Mansi

ABOUT THE AUTHOR

 SHASHANK TIWARI is an experienced software developer and technology entrepreneur with interests in the areas of high-performance applications, analytics, web applications, and mobile platforms. He enjoys data visualization, statistical and machine learning, coffee, deserts and bike riding. He is the author of many technical articles and books and a speaker at many conferences worldwide.

Learn more about his company, Treasury of Ideas, at www.treasuryofideas.com. Read his blog at www.shanky.org or follow him on twitter at @tshanky. He lives with his wife and two sons in Palo Alto, California.

ABOUT THE TECHNICAL EDITORS

PROF. DR. STEFAN EDLICH is a senior lecturer at Beuth HS of Technology Berlin (U.APP.SC) with a focus on NoSQL, Software-Engineering and Cloud Computing. Beside many scientific papers and journal articles, he is a continuous speaker at conferences and IT events concerning enterprise, NoSQL, and ODBMS topics since 1993.

Furthermore, he is the author of twelve IT books written for Apress, OReilly, Spektrum/Elsevier, Hanser, and other publishers. He is a founding member of OODBMS.org e.V. and started the world's First International Conference on Object Databases (ICOODB.org) series. He runs the NoSQL Archive, organizes NoSQL events, and is constantly writing about NoSQL.

MATT INGENTHRON is an experienced web architect with a software development background. He has deep expertise in building, scaling and operating global-scale Java, Ruby on Rails and AMP web applications. Having been with Couchbase, Inc. since its inception, he has been a core developer on the Open Source Membase NoSQL project, a contributor to the Memcached project, and a leader for new developments in the Java spymemcached client. Matt's NoSQL experiences are widespread though, having experience with Hadoop, HBase and other parts of the NoSQL world.

ACKNOWLEDGMENTS

THIS BOOK REPRESENTS the efforts of many people, and I sincerely thank them for their contribution.

Thanks to the team at Wiley. You made the book possible!

Thanks to Matt and Stefan for the valuable inputs and the technical review.

Thanks to my wife and sons for encouraging and supporting me through the process of writing this book. Thanks to all the members of my family and friends who have always believed in me.

Thanks to all who have contributed directly or indirectly to this book and who I may have missed unintentionally.

—SHASHANK TIWARI

CONTENTS

INTRODUCTION

THE GROWTH OF USER-DRIVEN CONTENT has fueled a rapid increase in the volume and type of data that is generated, manipulated, analyzed, and archived. In addition, varied newer sets of sources, including sensors, Global Positioning Systems (GPS), automated trackers and monitoring systems, are generating a lot of data. These larger volumes of data sets, often termed *big data*, are imposing newer challenges and opportunities around storage, analysis, and archival.

In parallel to the fast data growth, data is also becoming increasingly semi-structured and sparse. This means the traditional data management techniques around upfront schema definition and relational references is also being questioned.

The quest to solve the problems related to large-volume and semi-structured data has led to the emergence of a class of newer types of database products. This new class of database products consists of column-oriented data stores, key/value pair databases, and document databases. Collectively, these are identified as NoSQL.

The products that fall under the NoSQL umbrella are quite varied, each with their unique sets of features and value propositions. Given this, it often becomes difficult to decide which product to use for the case at hand. This book prepares you to understand the entire NoSQL landscape. It provides the essential concepts that act as the building blocks for many of the NoSQL products. Instead of covering a single product exhaustively, it provides a fair coverage of a number of different NoSQL products. The emphasis is often on breadth and underlying concepts rather than a full coverage of every product API. Because a number of NoSQL products are covered, a good bit of comparative analysis is also included.

If you are unsure where to start with NoSQL and how to learn to manage and analyze big data, then you will find this book to be a good introduction and a useful reference to the topic.

WHO THIS BOOK IS FOR

Developers, architects, database administrators, and technical project managers are the primary audience of this book. However, anyone savvy enough to understand database technologies is likely to find it useful.

The subject of big data and NoSQL is of interest to a number of computer science students and researchers as well. Such students and researchers could benefit from reading this book.

Anyone starting out with big data analysis and NoSQL will gain from reading this book.

WHAT THIS BOOK COVERS

This book starts with the essentials of NoSQL and graduates to advanced concepts around performance tuning and architectural guidelines. The book focuses all along on the fundamental concepts that relate to NoSQL and explains those in the context of a number of different NoSQL products. The book includes illustrations and examples that relate to MongoDB, CouchDB, HBase, Hypertable, Cassandra, Redis, and Berkeley DB. A few other NoSQL products, besides these, are also referenced.

An important part of NoSQL is the way large data sets are manipulated. This book covers all the essentials of MapReduce-based scalable processing. It illustrates a few examples using Hadoop. Higher-level abstractions like Hive and Pig are also illustrated.

Chapter 10, which is entirely devoted to NoSQL in the cloud, brings to light the facilities offered by Amazon Web Services and the Google App Engine.

The book includes a number of examples and illustration of use cases. Scalable data architectures at Google, Amazon, Facebook, Twitter, and LinkedIn are also discussed.

Towards the end of the book the discussion on comparing NoSQL products and polyglot persistence in an application stack are explained.

HOW THIS BOOK IS STRUCTURED

This book is divided into four parts:

➤ **Part I:** Getting Started
➤ **Part II:** Learning the NoSQL Basics
➤ **Part III:** Gaining Proficiency with NoSQL
➤ **Part IV:** Mastering NoSQL

Topics in each part are built on top of what is covered in the preceding parts.

Part I of the book gently introduces NoSQL. It defines the types of NoSQL products and introduces the very first examples of storing data in and accessing data from NoSQL:

➤ **Chapter 1** defines NoSQL.
➤ Starting with the quintessential Hello World, **Chapter 2** presents the first few examples of using NoSQL.
➤ **Chapter 3** includes ways of interacting and interfacing with NoSQL products.

Part II of the book is where a number of the essential concepts of a variety of NoSQL products are covered:

➤ **Chapter 4** starts by explaining the storage architecture.
➤ **Chapters 5 and 6** cover the essentials of data management by demonstrating the CRUD operations and the querying mechanisms. Data sets evolve with time and usage.

➤ **Chapter 7** addresses the questions around data evolution. The world of relational databases focuses a lot on query optimization by leveraging indexes.

➤ **Chapter 8** covers indexes in the context of NoSQL products. NoSQL products are often disproportionately criticized for their lack of transaction support.

➤ **Chapter 9** demystifies the concepts around transactions and the transactional-integrity challenges that distributed systems face.

Parts III and IV of the book are where a select few advanced topics are covered:

➤ **Chapter 10** covers the Google App Engine data store and Amazon SimpleDB. Much of big data processing rests on the shoulders of the MapReduce style of processing.

➤ Learn all the essentials of MapReduce in **Chapter 11**.

➤ **Chapter 12** extends the MapReduce coverage to demonstrate how Hive provides a SQL-like abstraction for Hadoop MapReduce tasks. **Chapter 13** revisits the topic of database architecture and internals.

Part IV is the last part of the book. Part IV starts with **Chapter 14**, where NoSQL products are compared. **Chapter 15** promotes the idea of polyglot persistence and the use of the right database, which should depend on the use case. **Chapter 16** segues into tuning scalable applications. Although seemingly eclectic, topics in Part IV prepare you for practical usage of NoSQL. **Chapter 17** is a presentation of a select few tools and utilities that you are likely to leverage with your own NoSQL deployment.

WHAT YOU NEED TO USE THIS BOOK

Please install the required pieces of software to follow along with the code examples. Refer to Appendix A for install and setup instructions.

CONVENTIONS

To help you get the most from the text and keep track of what's happening, we've used a number of conventions throughout the book.

 The pencil icon indicates notes, tips, hints, tricks, and asides to the current discussion.

As for styles in the text:

➤ We *italicize* new terms and important words when we introduce them.

➤ We show file names, URLs, and code within the text like so: `persistence.properties`.

> ➤ We present code in two different ways:

```
We use a monofont type with no highlighting for most code examples.
We use bold to emphasize code that is particularly important in the present
context or to show changes from a previous code snippet.
```

SOURCE CODE

As you work through the examples in this book, you may choose either to type in all the code manually, or to use the source code files that accompany the book. All the source code used in this book is available for download at www.wrox.com. When at the site, simply locate the book's title (use the Search box or one of the title lists) and click the Download Code link on the book's detail page to obtain all the source code for the book. Code that is included on the website is highlighted by the following icon:

Available for download on Wrox.com

Listings include the filename in the title. If it is just a code snippet, you'll find the filename in a code note such as this:

Code snippet filename

 Because many books have similar titles, you may find it easiest to search by ISBN; this book's ISBN is 978-0-470-94224-6.

Once you download the code, just decompress it with your favorite compression tool. Alternately, you can go to the main Wrox code download page at www.wrox.com/dynamic/books/download .aspx to see the code available for this book and all other Wrox books.

ERRATA

We make every effort to ensure that there are no errors in the text or in the code. However, no one is perfect, and mistakes do occur. If you find an error in one of our books, like a spelling mistake or faulty piece of code, we would be very grateful for your feedback. By sending in errata, you may save another reader hours of frustration, and at the same time, you will be helping us provide even higher quality information.

To find the errata page for this book, go to www.wrox.com and locate the title using the Search box or one of the title lists. Then, on the book details page, click the Book Errata link. On this page, you can view all errata that has been submitted for this book and posted by Wrox editors. A complete book list, including links to each book's errata, is also available at www.wrox.com/misc-pages/booklist.shtml.

If you don't spot "your" error on the Book Errata page, go to www.wrox.com/contact/techsupport.shtml and complete the form there to send us the error you have found. We'll check the information and, if appropriate, post a message to the book's errata page and fix the problem in subsequent editions of the book.

P2P.WROX.COM

For author and peer discussion, join the P2P forums at p2p.wrox.com. The forums are a Web-based system for you to post messages relating to Wrox books and related technologies and interact with other readers and technology users. The forums offer a subscription feature to e-mail you topics of interest of your choosing when new posts are made to the forums. Wrox authors, editors, other industry experts, and your fellow readers are present on these forums.

At p2p.wrox.com, you will find a number of different forums that will help you, not only as you read this book, but also as you develop your own applications. To join the forums, just follow these steps:

1. Go to p2p.wrox.com and click the Register link.

2. Read the terms of use and click Agree.

3. Complete the required information to join, as well as any optional information you wish to provide, and click Submit.

4. You will receive an e-mail with information describing how to verify your account and complete the joining process.

 You can read messages in the forums without joining P2P, but in order to post your own messages, you must join.

Once you join, you can post new messages and respond to messages other users post. You can read messages at any time on the Web. If you would like to have new messages from a particular forum e-mailed to you, click the Subscribe to this Forum icon by the forum name in the forum listing.

For more information about how to use the Wrox P2P, be sure to read the P2P FAQs for answers to questions about how the forum software works, as well as many common questions specific to P2P and Wrox books. To read the FAQs, click the FAQ link on any P2P page.

PART I
Getting Started

NoSQL: What It Is and Why You Need It

WHAT'S IN THIS CHAPTER?

➤ Defining NoSQL

➤ Setting context by explaining the history of NoSQL's emergence

➤ Introducing the NoSQL variants

➤ Listing a few popular NoSQL products

Congratulations! You have made the first bold step to learn NoSQL.

Like most new and upcoming technologies, NoSQL is shrouded in a mist of fear, uncertainty, and doubt. The world of developers is probably divided into three groups when it comes to NoSQL:

➤ **Those who love it** — People in this group are exploring how NoSQL fits in an application stack. They are using it, creating it, and keeping abreast with the developments in the world of NoSQL.

➤ **Those who deny it** — Members of this group are either focusing on NoSQL's shortcomings or are out to prove that it's worthless.

➤ **Those who ignore it** — Developers in this group are agnostic either because they are waiting for the technology to mature, or they believe NoSQL is a passing fad and ignoring it will shield them from the rollercoaster ride of "a hype cycle," or have simply not had a chance to get to it.

 Gartner coined the term hype cycle to represent the maturity, adoption, and application of a technology. Read more at http://en.wikipedia.org/wiki/Hype_cycle.

I am a member of the first group. Writing a book on the subject is testimony enough to prove that I like the technology. Both the groups of NoSQL lovers and haters have a range of believers: from moderates to extremists. I am a moderate. Given that, I intend to present NoSQL to you as a powerful tool, great for some jobs but with its set of shortcomings, I would like you to learn NoSQL with an open, unprejudiced mind. Once you have mastered the technology and its underlying ideas, you will be ready to make your own judgment on the usefulness of NoSQL and leverage the technology appropriately for your specific application or use case.

This first chapter is an introduction to the subject of NoSQL. It's a gentle step toward understanding what NoSQL is, what its characteristics are, what constitutes its typical use cases, and where it fits in the application stack.

DEFINITION AND INTRODUCTION

NoSQL is literally a combination of two words: No and SQL. The implication is that NoSQL is a technology or product that counters SQL. The creators and early adopters of the buzzword *NoSQL* probably wanted to say *No RDBMS* or *No relational* but were infatuated by the nicer sounding NoSQL and stuck to it. In due course, some have proposed *NonRel* as an alternative to NoSQL. A few others have tried to salvage the original term by proposing that NoSQL is actually an acronym that expands to "Not Only SQL." Whatever the literal meaning, NoSQL is used today as an umbrella term for all databases and data stores that don't follow the popular and well-established RDBMS principles and often relate to large data sets accessed and manipulated on a Web scale. This means NoSQL is not a single product or even a single technology. It represents a class of products and a collection of diverse, and sometimes related, concepts about data storage and manipulation.

Context and a Bit of History

Before I start with details on the NoSQL types and the concepts involved, it's important to set the context in which NoSQL emerged. Non-relational databases are not new. In fact, the first non-relational stores go back in time to when the first set of computing machines were invented. Non-relational databases thrived through the advent of mainframes and have existed in specialized and specific domains — for example, hierarchical directories for storing authentication and authorization credentials — through the years. However, the non-relational stores that have appeared in the world of NoSQL are a new incarnation, which were born in the world of massively scalable Internet applications. These non-relational NoSQL stores, for the most part, were conceived in the world of distributed and parallel computing.

Starting out with Inktomi, which could be thought of as the first true search engine, and culminating with Google, it is clear that the widely adopted relational database management system (RDBMS) has its own set of problems when applied to massive amounts of data. The problems relate to efficient processing, effective parallelization, scalability, and costs. You learn about each of these problems and the possible solutions to the problems in the discussions later in this chapter and the rest of this book.

CHALLENGES OF RDBMS

The challenges of RDBMS for massive Web-scale data processing aren't specific to a product but pertain to the entire class of such databases. RDBMS assumes a well-defined structure in data. It assumes that the data is dense and is largely uniform. RDBMS builds on a prerequisite that the properties of the data can be defined up front and that its interrelationships are well established and systematically referenced. It also assumes that indexes can be consistently defined on data sets and that such indexes can be uniformly leveraged for faster querying. Unfortunately, RDBMS starts to show signs of giving way as soon as these assumptions don't hold true. RDBMS can certainly deal with some irregularities and lack of structure but in the context of massive sparse data sets with loosely defined structures, RDBMS appears a forced fit. With massive data sets the typical storage mechanisms and access methods also get stretched. Denormalizing tables, dropping constraints, and relaxing transactional guarantee can help an RDBMS scale, but after these modifications an RDBMS starts resembling a NoSQL product.

Flexibility comes at a price. NoSQL alleviates the problems that RDBMS imposes and makes it easy to work with large sparse data, but in turn takes away the power of transactional integrity and flexible indexing and querying. Ironically, one of the features most missed in NoSQL is SQL, and product vendors in the space are making all sorts of attempts to bridge this gap.

Google has, over the past few years, built out a massively scalable infrastructure for its search engine and other applications, including Google Maps, Google Earth, GMail, Google Finance, and Google Apps. Google's approach was to solve the problem at every level of the application stack. The goal was to build a scalable infrastructure for parallel processing of large amounts of data. Google therefore created a full mechanism that included a distributed filesystem, a column-family-oriented data store, a distributed coordination system, and a MapReduce-based parallel algorithm execution environment. Graciously enough, Google published and presented a series of papers explaining some of the key pieces of its infrastructure. The most important of these publications are as follows:

➤ Sanjay Ghemawat, Howard Gobioff, and Shun-Tak Leung. "The Google File System"; pub. 19th ACM Symposium on Operating Systems Principles, Lake George, NY, October 2003. URL: http://labs.google.com/papers/gfs.html

➤ Jeffrey Dean and Sanjay Ghemawat. "MapReduce: Simplified Data Processing on Large Clusters"; pub. OSDI'04: Sixth Symposium on Operating System Design and Implementation, San Francisco, CA, December 2004. URL: http://labs.google.com/papers/mapreduce.html

➤ Fay Chang, Jeffrey Dean, Sanjay Ghemawat, Wilson C. Hsieh, Deborah A. Wallach, Mike Burrows, Tushar Chandra, Andrew Fikes, and Robert E. Gruber. "Bigtable: A Distributed Storage System for Structured Data"; pub. OSDI'06: Seventh Symposium on Operating System Design and Implementation, Seattle, WA, November 2006. URL: http://labs.google.com/papers/bigtable.html

➤ Mike Burrows. "The Chubby Lock Service for Loosely-Coupled Distributed Systems"; pub. OSDI'06: Seventh Symposium on Operating System Design and Implementation, Seattle, WA, November 2006. URL: `http://labs.google.com/papers/chubby.html`

 If at this stage or later in this chapter, you are thoroughly confused and over-whelmed by the introduction of a number of new terms and concepts, hold on and take a breath. This book explains all relevant concepts at an easy pace. You don't have to learn everything right away. Stay with the flow and by the time you read through the book, you will be able to understand all the important concepts that pertain to NoSQL and big data.

The release of Google's papers to the public spurred a lot of interest among open-source developers. The creators of the open-source search engine, Lucene, were the first to develop an open-source version that replicated some of the features of Google's infrastructure. Subsequently, the core Lucene developers joined Yahoo, where with the help of a host of other contributors, they created a parallel universe that mimicked all the pieces of the Google distributed computing stack. This open-source alternative is Hadoop, its sub-projects, and its related projects. You can find more information, code, and documentation on Hadoop at `http://adoop.apache.org`.

Without getting into the exact timeline of Hadoop's development, somewhere toward the first of its releases emerged the idea of NoSQL. The history of who coined the term *NoSQL* and when is irrelevant, but it's important to note that the emergence of Hadoop laid the groundwork for the rapid growth of NoSQL. Also, it's important to consider that Google's success helped propel a healthy adoption of the new-age distributed computing concepts, the Hadoop project, and NoSQL.

A year after the Google papers had catalyzed interest in parallel scalable processing and non-relational distributed data stores, Amazon decided to share some of its own success story. In 2007, Amazon presented its ideas of a distributed highly available and eventually consistent data store named Dynamo. You can read more about Amazon Dynamo in a research paper, the details of which are as follows: Giuseppe DeCandia, Deniz Hastorun, Madan Jampani, Gunavardhan Kakulapati, Avinash Lakshman, Alex Pilchin, Swami Sivasubramanian, Peter Vosshall, and Werner Vogels, "Dynamo: Amazon's Highly Available Key/value Store," in the Proceedings of the 21st ACM Symposium on Operating Systems Principles, Stevenson, WA, October 2007. Werner Vogels, the Amazon CTO, explained the key ideas behind Amazon Dynamo in a blog post accessible online at `www.allthingsdistributed.com/2007/10/amazons_dynamo.html`.

With endorsement of NoSQL from two leading web giants — Google and Amazon — several new products emerged in this space. A lot of developers started toying with the idea of using these methods in their applications and many enterprises, from startups to large corporations, became amenable to learning more about the technology and possibly using these methods. In less than 5 years, NoSQL and related concepts for managing big data have become widespread and use cases have emerged from many well-known companies, including Facebook, Netflix, Yahoo, EBay, Hulu, IBM, and many more. Many of these companies have also contributed by open sourcing their extensions and newer products to the world.

You will soon learn a lot about the various NoSQL products, including their similarities and differences, but let me digress for now to a short presentation on some of the challenges and solutions around large data and parallel processing. This detour will help all readers get on the same level of preparedness to start exploring the NoSQL products.

Big Data

Just how much data qualifies as big data? This is a question that is bound to solicit different responses, depending on who you ask. The answers are also likely to vary depending on when the question is asked. Currently, any data set over a few terabytes is classified as big data. This is typically the size where the data set is large enough to start spanning multiple storage units. It's also the size at which traditional RDBMS techniques start showing the first signs of stress.

DATA SIZE MATH

A byte is a unit of digital information that consists of 8 bits. In the International System of Units (SI) scheme every 1,000 (10^3) multiple of a byte is given a distinct name, which is as follows:

➤ Kilobyte (kB) — 10^3

➤ Megabyte (MB) — 10^6

➤ Gigabyte (GB) — 10^9

➤ Terabyte (TB) — 10^{12}

➤ Petabyte (PB) — 10^{15}

➤ Exabyte (EB) — 10^{18}

➤ Zettabyte (ZB) — 10^{21}

➤ Yottabyte (YB) — 10^{24}

In traditional binary interpretation, multiples were supposed to be of 2^{10} (or 1,024) and not 10^3 (or 1,000). To avoid confusion, a parallel naming scheme exists for powers of 2, which is as follows:

➤ Kibibyte (KiB) — 2^{10}

➤ Mebibyte (MiB) — 2^{20}

➤ Gibibyte (GiB) — 2^{30}

➤ Tebibyte (TiB) — 2^{40}

➤ Pebibyte (PiB) — 2^{50}

➤ Exbibyte (EiB) — 2^{60}

➤ Zebibyte (ZiB) — 2^{70}

➤ Yobibyte (YiB) — 2^{80}

Even a couple of years back, a terabyte of personal data may have seemed quite large. However, now local hard drives and backup drives are commonly available at this size. In the next couple of years, it wouldn't be surprising if your default hard drive were over a few terabytes in capacity. We are living in an age of rampant data growth. Our digital camera outputs, blogs, daily social networking updates, tweets, electronic documents, scanned content, music files, and videos are growing at a rapid pace. We are consuming a lot of data and producing it too.

It's difficult to assess the true size of digitized data or the size of the Internet but a few studies, estimates, and data points reveal that it's immensely large and in the range of a zettabyte and more. In an ongoing study titled, "The Digital Universe Decade – Are you ready?" (http://emc.com/ collateral/demos/microsites/idc-digital-universe/iview.htm), IDC, on behalf of EMC, presents a view into the current state of digital data and its growth. The report claims that the total size of digital data created and replicated will grow to 35 zettabytes by 2020. The report also claims that the amount of data produced and available now is outgrowing the amount of available storage.

A few other data points worth considering are as follows:

➤ A 2009 paper in ACM titled, "MapReduce: simplified data processing on large clusters" — http://portal.acm.org/citation.cfm?id=1327452.1327492&coll=GU IDE&dl=&idx=J79&part=magazine&WantType=Magazines&title=Communications% 20of%20the%20ACM — revealed that Google processes 24 petabytes of data per day.

➤ A 2009 post from Facebook about its photo storage system, "Needle in a haystack: efficient storage of billions of photos" — http//facebook.com/note.php?note_id=76191543919 — mentioned the total size of photos in Facebook to be 1.5 pedabytes. The same post mentioned that around 60 billion images were stored on Facebook.

➤ The Internet archive FAQs at archive.org/about/faqs.php say that 2 petabytes of data are stored in the Internet archive. It also says that the data is growing at the rate of 20 terabytes per month.

➤ The movie *Avatar* took up 1 petabyte of storage space for the rendering of 3D CGI effects. ("Believe it or not: Avatar takes 1 petabyte of storage space, equivalent to a 32-year-long MP3" — http://thenextweb.com/2010/01/01/avatar-takes-1-petabyte-storage-space-equivalent-32-year-long-mp3/.)

As the size of data grows and sources of data creation become increasingly diverse, the following growing challenges will get further amplified:

➤ Efficiently storing and accessing large amounts of data is difficult. The additional demands of fault tolerance and backups makes things even more complicated.

➤ Manipulating large data sets involves running immensely parallel processes. Gracefully recovering from any failures during such a run and providing results in a reasonably short period of time is complex.

➤ Managing the continuously evolving schema and metadata for semi-structured and un-structured data, generated by diverse sources, is a convoluted problem.

Therefore, the ways and means of storing and retrieving large amounts of data need newer approaches beyond our current methods. NoSQL and related big-data solutions are a first step forward in that direction.

Hand in hand with data growth is the growth of scale.

DISK STORAGE AND DATA READ AND WRITE SPEED

While the data size is growing and so are the storage capacities, the disk access speeds to write data to disk and read data from it is not keeping pace. Typical above-average current-generation 1 TB disks claim to access data at the rate of 300 Mbps, rotating at the speed of 7200 RPM. At these peak speeds, it takes about an hour (at best 55 minutes) to access 1 TB of data. With increased size, the time taken only increases. Besides, the claim of 300 Mbps at 7200 RPM speed is itself misleading. Traditional rotational media involves circular storage disks to optimize surface area. In a circle, 7200 RPM implies different amounts of data access depending on the circumference of the concentric circle being accessed. As the disk is filled, the circumference becomes smaller, leading to less area of the media sector being covered in each rotation. This means a peak speed of 300 Mbps degrades substantially by the time the disk is over 65 percent full. Solid-state drives (SSDs) are an alternative to rotational media. An SSD uses microchips, in contrast to electromechanical spinning disks. It retains data in volatile random-access memory. SSDs promise faster speeds and improved "input/output operations per second (IOPS)" performance as compared to rotational media. By late 2009 and early 2010, companies like Micron announced SSDs that could provide access speeds of over a Gbps (`www.dailytech.com/UPDATED+Micron+Announces+Worlds+First+Native+6Gbps+SATA+Solid+State+Drive/article17007.htm`). However, SSDs are fraught with bugs and issues as things stand and come at a much higher cost than their rotational media counterparts. Given that the disk access speeds cap the rate at which you can read and write data, it only make sense to spread the data out across multiple storage units rather than store them in a single large store.

Scalability

Scalability is the ability of a system to increase throughput with addition of resources to address load increases. Scalability can be achieved either by provisioning a large and powerful resource to meet the additional demands or it can be achieved by relying on a cluster of ordinary machines to work as a unit. The involvement of large, powerful machines is typically classified as vertical scalability. Provisioning super computers with many CPU cores and large amounts of directly attached storage is a typical vertical scaling solution. Such vertical scaling options are typically expensive and proprietary. The alternative to vertical scalability is horizontal scalability. Horizontal scalability involves a cluster of commodity systems where the cluster scales as load increases. Horizontal scalability typically involves adding additional nodes to serve additional load.

The advent of big data and the need for large-scale parallel processing to manipulate this data has led to the widespread adoption of horizontally scalable infrastructures. Some of these horizontally scaled infrastructures at Google, Amazon, Facebook, eBay, and Yahoo! involve a very large number of servers. Some of these infrastructures have thousands and even hundreds of thousands of servers.

Processing data spread across a cluster of horizontally scaled machines is complex. The MapReduce model possibly provides one of the best possible methods to process large-scale data on a horizontal cluster of machines.

Definition and Introduction

MapReduce is a parallel programming model that allows distributed processing on large data sets on a cluster of computers. The MapReduce framework is patented (`http://patft.uspto.gov/` `netacgi/nph-Parser?Sect1=PTO1&Sect2=HITOFF&d=PALL&p=1&u=/netahtml/PTO/srchnum.` `htm&r=1&f=G&l=50&s1=7,650,331.PN.&OS=PN/7,650,331&RS=PN/7,650,331`) by Google, but the ideas are freely shared and adopted in a number of open-source implementations.

MapReduce derives its ideas and inspiration from concepts in the world of functional programming. Map and reduce are commonly used functions in the world of functional programming. In functional programming, a map function applies an operation or a function to each element in a list. For example, a multiply-by-two function on a list [1, 2, 3, 4] would generate another list as follows: [2, 4, 6, 8]. When such functions are applied, the original list is not altered. Functional programming believes in keeping data immutable and avoids sharing data among multiple processes or threads. This means the map function that was just illustrated, trivial as it may be, could be run via two or more multiple threads on the list and these threads would not step on each other, because the list itself is not altered.

Like the map function, functional programming has a concept of a reduce function. Actually, a reduce function in functional programming is more commonly known as a fold function. A reduce or a fold function is also sometimes called an accumulate, compress, or inject function. A reduce or fold function applies a function on all elements of a data structure, such as a list, and produces a single result or output. So applying a reduce function-like summation on the list generated out of the map function, that is, [2, 4, 6, 8], would generate an output equal to 20.

So map and reduce functions could be used in conjunction to process lists of data, where a function is first applied to each member of a list and then an aggregate function is applied to the transformed and generated list.

This same simple idea of map and reduce has been extended to work on large data sets. The idea is slightly modified to work on collections of tuples or key/value pairs. The map function applies a function on every key/value pair in the collection and generates a new collection. Then the reduce function works on the new generated collection and applies an aggregate function to compute a final output. This is better understood through an example, so let me present a trivial one to explain the flow. Say you have a collection of key/value pairs as follows:

```
[{ "94303": "Tom"}, {"94303": "Jane"}, {"94301": "Arun"}, {"94302": "Chen"}]
```

This is a collection of key/value pairs where the key is the zip code and the value is the name of a person who resides within that zip code. A simple map function on this collection could get the names of all those who reside in a particular zip code. The output of such a map function is as follows:

```
[{"94303":["Tom", "Jane"]}, {"94301":["Arun"]}, {"94302":["Chen"]}]
```

Now a reduce function could work on this output to simply count the number of people who belong to particular zip code. The final output then would be as follows:

```
[{"94303": 2}, {"94301": 1}, {"94302": 1}]
```

This example is extremely simple and a MapReduce mechanism seems too complex for such a manipulation, but I hope you get the core idea behind the concepts and the flow.

Next, I list some of the most well-known NoSQL products and categorize them in terms of their features and attributes.

SORTED ORDERED COLUMN-ORIENTED STORES

Google's Bigtable espouses a model where data in stored in a column-oriented way. This contrasts with the row-oriented format in RDBMS. The column-oriented storage allows data to be stored effectively. It avoids consuming space when storing nulls by simply not storing a column when a value doesn't exist for that column.

Each unit of data can be thought of as a set of key/value pairs, where the unit itself is identified with the help of a primary identifier, often referred to as the primary key. Bigtable and its clones tend to call this primary key the row-key. Also, as the title of this subsection suggests, units are stored in an ordered-sorted manner. The units of data are sorted and ordered on the basis of the row-key. To explain sorted ordered column-oriented stores, an example serves better than a lot of text, so let me present an example to you. Consider a simple table of values that keeps information about a set of people. Such a table could have columns like first_name, last_name, occupation, zip_code, and gender. A person's information in this table could be as follows:

```
first_name: John
last_name: Doe
zip_code: 10001
gender: male
```

Another set of data in the same table could be as follows:

```
first_name: Jane
zip_code: 94303
```

The row-key of the first data point could be 1 and the second could be 2. Then data would be stored in a sorted ordered column-oriented store in a way that the data point with row-key 1 will be stored before a data point with row-key 2 and also that the two data points will be adjacent to each other.

Next, only the valid key/value pairs would be stored for each data point. So, a possible column-family for the example could be name with columns first_name and last_name being its members. Another column-family could be location with zip_code as its member. A third column-family could be profile. The gender column could be a member of the profile column-family. In column-oriented stores similar to Bigtable, data is stored on a column-family basis. Column-families are typically defined at configuration or startup time. Columns themselves need no a-priori definition or declaration. Also, columns are capable of storing any data types as far as the data can be persisted to an array of bytes.

So the underlying logical storage for this simple example consists of three storage buckets: `name`, `location`, and `profile`. Within each bucket, only key/value pairs with valid values are stored. Therefore, the `name` column-family bucket stores the following values:

```
For row-key: 1
first_name: John
last_name: Doe
For row-key: 2
first_name: Jane
```

The `location` column-family stores the following:

```
For row-key: 1
zip_code: 10001
For row-key: 2
zip_code: 94303
```

The `profile` column-family has values only for the data point with row-key 1 so it stores only the following:

```
For row-key: 1
gender: male
```

In real storage terms, the column-families are not physically isolated for a given row. All data pertaining to a row-key is stored together. The column-family acts as a key for the columns it contains and the row-key acts as the key for the whole data set.

Data in Bigtable and its clones is stored in a contiguous sequenced manner. As data grows to fill up one node, it is spilt into multiple nodes. The data is sorted and ordered not only on each node but also across nodes providing one large continuously sequenced set. The data is persisted in a fault-tolerant manner where three copies of each data set are maintained. Most Bigtable clones leverage a distributed filesystem to persist data to disk. Distributed filesystems allow data to be stored among a cluster of machines.

The sorted ordered structure makes data seek by row-key extremely efficient. Data access is less random and ad-hoc and lookup is as simple as finding the node in the sequence that holds the data. Data is inserted at the end of the list. Updates are in-place but often imply adding a newer version of data to the specific cell rather than in-place overwrites. This means a few versions of each cell are maintained at all times. The versioning property is usually configurable.

HBase is a popular, open-source, sorted ordered column-family store that is modeled on the ideas proposed by Google's Bigtable. Details about storing data in HBase and accessing it are covered in many chapters of this book.

Data stored in HBase can be manipulated using the MapReduce infrastructure. Hadoop's MapReduce tools can easily use HBase as the source and/or sink of data.

Details on the technical specification of Bigtable and its clones is included starting in the next chapter. Hold on to your curiosity or peek into Chapter 4 to explore the internals.

Next, I list out the Bigtable clones.

The best way to learn about and leverage the ideas proposed by Google's infrastructure is to start with the Hadoop (http//hadoop.apache.org) family of products. The NoSQL Bigtable store called HBase is part of the Hadoop family.

A bullet-point enumeration of some of the Bigtable open-source clones' properties is listed next.

HBase

➤ **Official Online Resources** — http://hbase.apache.org.

➤ **History** — Created at Powerset (now part of Microsoft) in 2007. Donated to the Apache foundation before Powerset was acquired by Microsoft.

➤ **Technologies and Language** — Implemented in Java.

➤ **Access Methods** — A JRuby shell allows command-line access to the store. Thrift, Avro, REST, and protobuf clients exist. A few language bindings are also available. A Java API is available with the distribution.

 Protobuf, short for Protocol Buffers, is Google's data interchange format. More information is available online at http://code.google.com/p/protobuf/.

➤ **Query Language** — No native querying language. Hive (http://hive.apache.org) provides a SQL-like interface for HBase.

➤ **Open-Source License** — Apache License version 2.

➤ **Who Uses It** — Facebook, StumbleUpon, Hulu, Ning, Mahalo, Yahoo!, and others.

WHAT IS THRIFT?

Thrift is a software framework and an interface definition language that allows cross-language services and API development. Services generated using Thrift work efficiently and seamlessly between C++, Java, Python, PHP, Ruby, Erlang, Perl, Haskell, C#, Cocoa, Smalltalk, and OCaml. Thrift was created by Facebook in 2007. It's an Apache incubator project. You can find more information on Thrift at http://incubator.apache.org/thrift/.

Hypertable

➤ **Official Online Resources** — www.hypertable.org.

➤ **History** — Created at Zvents in 2007. Now an independent open-source project.

➤ **Technologies and Language** — Implemented in C++, uses Google RE2 regular expression library. RE2 provides a fast and efficient implementation. Hypertable promises performance boost over HBase, potentially serving to reduce time and cost when dealing with large amounts of data.

➤ **Access Methods** — A command-line shell is available. In addition, a Thrift interface is supported. Language bindings have been created based on the Thrift interface. A creative developer has even created a JDBC-compliant interface for Hypertable.

➤ **Query Language** — HQL (Hypertable Query Language) is a SQL-like abstraction for querying Hypertable data. Hypertable also has an adapter for Hive.

➤ **Open-Source License** — GNU GPL version 2.

➤ **Who Uses It** — Zvents, Baidu (China's biggest search engine), Rediff (India's biggest portal).

Cloudata

➤ **Official Online Resources** — `www.cloudata.org/`.

➤ **History** — Created by a Korean developer named YK Kwon (`www.readwriteweb.com/hack/2011/02/open-source-bigtable-cloudata.php`). Not much is publicly known about its origins.

➤ **Technologies and Language** — Implemented in Java.

➤ **Access Methods** — A command-line access is available. Thrift, REST, and Java API are available.

➤ **Query Language** — CQL (Cloudata Query Language) defines a SQL-like query language.

➤ **Open-Source License** — Apache License version 2.

➤ **Who Uses It** — Not known.

Sorted ordered column-family stores form a very popular NoSQL option. However, NoSQL consists of a lot more variants of key/value stores and document databases. Next, I introduce the key/value stores.

KEY/VALUE STORES

A HashMap or an associative array is the simplest data structure that can hold a set of key/value pairs. Such data structures are extremely popular because they provide a very efficient, big O(1) average algorithm running time for accessing data. The key of a key/value pair is a unique value in the set and can be easily looked up to access the data.

Key/value pairs are of varied types: some keep the data in memory and some provide the capability to persist the data to disk. Key/value pairs can be distributed and held in a cluster of nodes.

A simple, yet powerful, key/value store is Oracle's Berkeley DB. Berkeley DB is a pure storage engine where both key and value are an array of bytes. The core storage engine of Berkeley DB doesn't attach meaning to the key or the value. It takes byte array pairs in and returns the same back to the calling client. Berkeley DB allows data to be cached in memory and flushed to disk as it grows. There is also a notion of indexing the keys for faster lookup and access. Berkeley DB has existed since the mid-1990s. It was created to replace AT&T's NDBM as a part of migrating from BSD 4.3 to 4.4. In 1996, Sleepycat Software was formed to maintain and provide support for Berkeley DB.

Another type of key/value store in common use is a cache. A cache provides an in-memory snapshot of the most-used data in an application. The purpose of cache is to reduce disk I/O. Cache systems could be rudimentary map structures or robust systems with a cache expiration policy. Caching is a popular strategy employed at all levels of a computer software stack to boost performance. Operating systems, databases, middleware components, and applications use caching.

Robust open-source distributed cache systems like EHCache (`http://ehcache.org/`) are widely used in Java applications. EHCache could be considered as a NoSQL solution. Another caching system popularly used in web applications is Memcached (`http://memcached.org/`), which is an open-source, high-performance object caching system. Brad Fitzpatrick created Memcached for LiveJournal in 2003. Apart from being a caching system, Memcached also helps effective memory management by creating a large virtual pool and distributing memory among nodes as required. This prevents fragmented zones where one node could have excess but unused memory and another node could be starved for memory.

As the NoSQL movement has gathered momentum, a number of key/value pair data stores have emerged. Some of these newer stores build on the Memcached API, some use Berkeley DB as the underlying storage, and a few others provide alternative solutions built from scratch.

Many of these key/value pairs have APIs that allow get-and-set mechanisms to get and set values. A few, like Redis (`http://redis.io/`), provide richer abstractions and powerful APIs. Redis could be considered as a data structure server because it provides data structures like string (character sequences), lists, and sets, apart from maps. Also, Redis provides a very rich set of operations to access data from these different types of data structures.

This book covers a lot of details on key/value pairs. For now, I list a few important ones and list out important attributes of these stores. Again, the presentation resorts to a bullet-point-style enumeration of a few important characteristics.

Membase (Proposed to be merged into Couchbase, gaining features from CouchDB after the creation of Couchbase, Inc.)

➤ **Official Online Resources** — `www.membase.org/`.

➤ **History** — Project started in 2009 by NorthScale, Inc. (later renamed as Membase). Zygna and NHN have been contributors since the beginning. Membase builds on Memcached and supports Memcached's text and binary protocol. Membase adds a lot of additional features on top of Memcached. It adds disk persistence, data replication, live cluster reconfiguration, and data rebalancing. A number of core Membase creators are also Memcached contributors.

➤ **Technologies and Language** — Implemented in Erlang, C, and C++.

➤ **Access Methods** — Memcached-compliant API with some extensions. Can be a drop-in replacement for Memcached.

➤ **Open-Source License** — Apache License version 2.

➤ **Who Uses It** — Zynga, NHN, and others.

Kyoto Cabinet

➤ **Official Online Resources** — `http://fallabs.com/kyotocabinet/`.

➤ **History** — Kyoto Cabinet is a successor of Tokyo Cabinet (`http://fallabs.com/tokyocabinet/`). The database is a simple data file containing records; each is a pair of a key and a value. Every key and value are serial bytes with variable length.

➤ **Technologies and Language** — Implemented in C++.

➤ **Access Methods** — Provides APIs for C, C++, Java, C#, Python, Ruby, Perl, Erlang, OCaml, and Lua. The protocol simplicity means there are many, many clients.

➤ **Open-Source License** — GNU GPL and GNU LGPL.

➤ **Who Uses It** — Mixi, Inc. sponsored much of its original work before the author left Mixi to join Google. Blog posts and mailing lists suggest that there are many users but no public list is available.

Redis

➤ **Official Online Resources** — `http://redis.io/`.

➤ **History** — Project started in 2009 by Salvatore Sanfilippo. Salvatore created it for his startup LLOOGG (`http://lloogg.com/`). Though still an independent project, Redis primary author is employed by VMware, who sponsor its development.

➤ **Technologies and Language** — Implemented in C.

➤ **Access Methods** — Rich set of methods and operations. Can access via Redis command-line interface and a set of well-maintained client libraries for languages like Java, Python, Ruby, C, C++, Lua, Haskell, AS3, and more.

➤ **Open-Source License** — BSD.

➤ **Who Uses It** — Craigslist.

The three key/value pairs listed here are nimble, fast implementations that provide storage for real-time data, temporary frequently used data, or even full-scale persistence.

The key/value pairs listed so far provide a strong consistency model for the data it stores. However, a few other key/value pairs emphasize availability over consistency in distributed deployments. Many of these are inspired by Amazon's Dynamo, which is also a key/value pair. Amazon's Dynamo promises exceptional availability and scalability, and forms the backbone for Amazon's distributed fault tolerant and highly available system. Apache Cassandra, Basho Riak, and Voldemort are open-source implementations of the ideas proposed by Amazon Dynamo.

Amazon Dynamo brings a lot of key high-availability ideas to the forefront. The most important of the ideas is that of eventual consistency. Eventual consistency implies that there could be small intervals of inconsistency between replicated nodes as data gets updated among peer-to-peer nodes.

Eventual consistency does not mean inconsistency. It just implies a weaker form of consistency than the typical ACID type consistency found in RDBMS.

 This book covers a lot of details on the building blocks of eventually consistent data stores like Amazon Dynamo. No discussion is included in this very first chapter because a little context and technical build-up is necessary to present the ideas appropriately.

For now I will list the Amazon Dynamo clones and introduce you to a few important characteristics of these data stores.

Cassandra

➤ **Official Online Resources** — http://cassandra.apache.org/.

➤ **History** — Developed at Facebook and open sourced in 2008, Apache Cassandra was donated to the Apache foundation.

➤ **Technologies and Language** — Implemented in Java.

➤ **Access Methods** — A command-line access to the store. Thrift interface and an internal Java API exist. Clients for multiple languages including Java, Python, Grails, PHP, .NET. and Ruby are available. Hadoop integration is also supported.

➤ **Query Language** — A query language specification is in the making.

➤ **Open-Source License** — Apache License version 2.

➤ **Who Uses It** — Facebook, Digg, Reddit, Twitter, and others.

Voldemort

➤ **Official Online Resources** — http://project-voldemort.com/.

➤ **History** — Created by the data and analytics team at LinkedIn in 2008.

➤ **Technologies and Language** — Implemented in Java. Provides for pluggable storage using either Berkeley DB or MySQL.

➤ **Access Methods** — Integrates with Thrift, Avro, and protobuf (http://code.google.com/p/protobuf/) interfaces. Can be used in conjunction with Hadoop.

➤ **Open-Source License** — Apache License version 2.

➤ **Who Uses It** — LinkedIn.

Riak

➤ **Official Online Resources** — http://wiki.basho.com/.

➤ **History** — Created at Basho, a company formed in 2008.

➤ **Technologies and Language** — Implemented in Erlang. Also, uses a bit of C and JavaScript.

➤ **Access Methods** — Interfaces for JSON (over HTTP) and protobuf clients exist. Libraries for Erlang, Java, Ruby, Python, PHP, and JavaScript exist.

➤ **Open-Source License** — Apache License version 2.

➤ **Who Uses It** — Comcast and Mochi Media.

All three — Cassandra, Riak and Voldemort — provide open-source Amazon Dynamo capabilities. Cassandra and Riak demonstrate dual nature as far their behavior and properties go. Cassandra has properties of both Google Bigtable and Amazon Dynamo. Riak acts both as a key/value store and a document database.

DOCUMENT DATABASES

Document databases are not document management systems. More often than not, developers starting out with NoSQL confuse document databases with document and content management systems. The word *document* in *document databases* connotes loosely structured sets of key/ value pairs in documents, typically JSON (JavaScript Object Notation), and not *documents* or *spreadsheets* (though these could be stored too).

Document databases treat a document as a whole and avoid splitting a document into its constituent name/value pairs. At a collection level, this allows for putting together a diverse set of documents into a single collection. Document databases allow indexing of documents on the basis of not only its primary identifier but also its properties. A few different open-source document databases are available today but the most prominent among the available options are MongoDB and CouchDB.

MongoDB

➤ **Official Online Resources** — www.mongodb.org.

➤ **History** — Created at 10gen.

➤ **Technologies and Language** — Implemented in C++.

➤ **Access Methods** — A JavaScript command-line interface. Drivers exist for a number of languages including C, C#, C++, Erlang. Haskell, Java, JavaScript, Perl, PHP, Python, Ruby, and Scala.

➤ **Query Language** — SQL-like query language.

➤ **Open-Source License** — GNU Affero GPL (http://gnu.org/licenses/agpl-3.0.html).

➤ **Who Uses It** — FourSquare, Shutterfly, Intuit, Github, and more.

CouchDB

➤ **Official Online Resources** — http://couchdb.apache.org and www.couchbase.com. Most of the authors are part of Couchbase, Inc.

➤ **History** — Work started in 2005 and it was incubated into Apache in 2008.

➤ **Technologies and Language** — Implemented in Erlang with some C and a JavaScript execution environment.

➤ **Access Methods** — Upholds REST above every other mechanism. Use standard web tools and clients to access the database, the same way as you access web resources.

➤ **Open-Source License** — Apache License version 2.

➤ **Who Uses It** — Apple, BBC, Canonical, Cern, and more at `http://wiki.apache.org/couchdb/CouchDB_in_the_wild`.

A lot of details on document databases are covered starting in the next chapter.

GRAPH DATABASES

So far I have listed most of the mainstream open-source NoSQL products. A few other products like Graph databases and XML data stores could also qualify as NoSQL databases. This book does not cover Graph and XML databases. However, I list the two Graph databases that may be of interest and something you may want to explore beyond this book: Neo4j and FlockDB:

Neo4J is an ACID-compliant graph database. It facilitates rapid traversal of graphs.

Neo4j

➤ **Official Online Resources** — `http://neo4j.org`.

➤ **History** — Created at Neo Technologies in 2003. (Yes, this database has been around before the term NoSQL was known popularly.)

➤ **Technologies and Language** — Implemented in Java.

➤ **Access Methods** — A command-line access to the store is provided. REST interface also available. Client libraries for Java, Python, Ruby, Clojure, Scala, and PHP exist.

➤ **Query Language** — Supports SPARQL protocol and RDF Query Language.

➤ **Open-Source License** — AGPL.

➤ **Who Uses It** — Box.net.

FlockDB

➤ **Official Online Resources** — `https://github.com/twitter/flockdb`

➤ **History** — Created at Twitter and open sourced in 2010. Designed to store the adjacency lists for followers on Twitter.

➤ **Technologies and Language** — Implemented in Scala.

➤ **Access Methods** — A Thrift and Ruby client.

➤ **Open-Source License** — Apache License version 2.

➤ **Who Uses It** — Twitter.

A number of NoSQL products have been covered so far. Hopefully, it has warmed you up to learn more about these products and to get ready to understand how you can leverage and use them effectively in your stack.

SUMMARY

This first chapter introduced the very notion of NoSQL. A little history and a tour of the basics started the exploration. After that, a few essentials of sorted ordered column-oriented stores, key/value pairs, eventually consistent databases, and document stores were covered. Apart from the fundamentals, a list of products with their core attributes was also included.

NoSQL is not a solution for all problems and certainly has its shortcomings. However, most products scale well when data grows to a very large size and needs to be distributed out to a number of nodes in a cluster. Processing large data is equally challenging and needs newer methods. You learned about MapReduce and its capabilities, and you will see its usage patterns in the chapters to come.

The current generation of developers has grown up with RDBMS and adopting NoSQL is as much a behavioral change as it is a new technology adoption. This means as a developer you need to look at NoSQL and understand it well before you make your decision on its suitability. Further, many ideas in NoSQL apply well to solving large-scale scalability issues and can be applied in all types of applications.

In the next chapter, you start getting a hands-on and conceptual introduction to the building blocks of column-oriented stores, key/value pairs, and document databases. All effort is made to provide all relevant information but the coverage is not exhaustive by any means. Not all products are covered in each category; rather, only representatives are selected from each. If you read the book from beginning to end you will be ready to leverage NoSQL effectively in your application stack. So good luck and start by rolling your sleeves up!

2

Hello NoSQL: Getting Initial Hands-on Experience

WHAT'S IN THIS CHAPTER?

➤ Tasting NoSQL technology

➤ Exploring MongoDB and Apache Cassandra basics

➤ Accessing MongoDB and Apache Cassandra from some of the popular high-level programming languages

This chapter is a variation of the quintessential programming tutorial first step: Hello World! It introduces the initial examples. Although elementary, these examples go beyond simply printing a hello message on the console and give you a first hands-on flavor of the topic. The topic in this case is NoSQL, which is an abstraction for a class of data stores. NoSQL is a concept, a classification, and a new-generation data storage viewpoint. It includes a class of products and a set of alternative non-relational data store choices. You are already familiar with some of the essential concepts and pros and cons of NoSQL from Chapter 1. This is where you start seeing it in action.

The examples in this chapter use MongoDB and Cassandra so you may want to install and set up those products to follow along. Refer to Appendix A if you need help installing these products in your development environment.

WHY ONLY MONGODB AND APACHE CASSANDRA?

The choice of MongoDB and Cassandra to illustrate NoSQL examples is quite arbitrary. This chapter intends to provide a first flavor of the deep and wide NoSQL domain. There are numerous NoSQL products and many offer compelling features and advantages. Choosing a couple of products to start with NoSQL was not easy. For example, Couchbase server could have been chosen over MongoDB and HBase could have been used instead of Cassandra. The examples could have been based on products like Redis, Membase, Hypertable, or Riak. Many NoSQL databases are covered in this book, so read through and you will learn a lot about the various alternative options in the NoSQL space.

FIRST IMPRESSIONS — EXAMINING TWO SIMPLE EXAMPLES

Without further delay or long prologues, it's time to dive right into your first two simple examples. The first example creates a trivial location preferences store and the second one manages a car make and model database. Both the examples focus on the data management aspects that are pertinent in the context of NoSQL.

A Simple Set of Persistent Preferences Data

Location-based services are gaining prominence as local businesses are trying to connect with users who are in the neighborhood and large companies are trying to customize their online experience and offerings based on where people are stationed. A few common occurrences of location-based preferences are visible in popular applications like Google Maps, which allows local search, and online retailers like Walmart.com that provide product availability and promotion information based on your closest Walmart store location.

Sometimes a user is asked to input location data and other times user location is inferred. Inference may be based on a user's IP address, network access point (especially if a user accesses data from a mobile device), or any combination of these techniques. Irrespective of how the data is gathered, you will need to store it effectively and that is where the example starts.

To make things simple, the location preferences are maintained for users only in the United States so only a user identifier and a zip code are required to find the location for a user. Let's start with usernames as their identifiers. Data points like "John Doe, 10001," "Lee Chang, 94129," "Jenny Gonzalez 33101," and "Srinivas Shastri, 02101" will need to be maintained.

To store such data in a flexible and extendible way, this example uses a non-relational database product named MongoDB. In the next few steps you create a MongoDB database and store a few sample location data points.

Starting MongoDB and Storing Data

Assuming you have installed MongoDB successfully, start the server and connect to it.

You can start a MongoDB server by running the mongod program within the bin folder of the distribution. Distributions vary according to the underlying environment, which can be Windows, Mac OS X, or a Linux variant, but in each case the server program has the same name and it resides in a folder named bin in the distribution.

The simplest way to connect to the MongoDB server is to use the JavaScript shell available with the distribution. Simply run mongo from your command-line interface. The mongo JavaScript shell command is also found in the bin folder.

When you start the MongoDB server by running mongod, you should see output on your console that looks similar to the following:

```
PS C:\applications\mongodb-win32-x86_64-1.8.1> .\bin\mongod.exe
C:\applications\mongodb-win32-x86_64-1.8.1\bin\mongod.exe
--help for help and startup options
Sun May 01 21:22:56 [initandlisten] MongoDB starting : pid=3300 port=27017
   dbpath=/data/db/ 64-bit
Sun May 01 21:22:56 [initandlisten] db version v1.8.1, pdfile version 4.5
Sun May 01 21:22:56 [initandlisten] git version:
a429cd4f535b2499cc4130b06ff7c26f41c00f04
Sun May 01 21:22:56 [initandlisten] build sys info: windows (6, 1, 7600, 2, '')
   BOOST_LIB_VERSION=1_42
Sun May 01 21:22:56 [initandlisten] waiting for connections on port 27017
Sun May 01 21:22:56 [websvr] web admin interface listening on port 28017
```

This particular output was captured on a Windows 7 64-bit machine when mongod was run via the Windows PowerShell. Depending on your environment your output may vary.

Now that the database server is up and running, use the mongo JavaScript shell to connect to it. The initial output of the shell should be as follows:

```
PS C:\applications\mongodb-win32-x86_64-1.8.1> bin/mongo
MongoDB shell version: 1.8.1
connecting to: test
>
```

By default, the mongo shell connects to the "test" database available on localhost. From mongod (the server daemon program) console output, you can also guess that the MongoDB server waits for connections on port 27017. To explore a possible set of initial commands just type help on the mongo interactive console. On typing help and pressing the Enter (or Return) key, you should see a list of command options like so:

```
> help
        db.help()                       help on db methods
        db.mycoll.help()                help on collection methods
        rs.help()                       help on replica set methods
```

```
help connect              connecting to a db help
help admin                administrative help
help misc                 misc things to know
help mr                   mapreduce help

show dbs                  show database names
show collections          show collections in current database
show users                show users in current database
show profile              show most recent system.profile entries
                              with time >= 1ms
use <db_name>             set current database
db.foo.find()             list objects in collection foo
db.foo.find( { a : 1 } )  list objects in foo where a == 1
it                        result of the last line evaluated;
                              use to further iterate
DBQuery.shellBatchSize = x  set default number of items to display
                              on shell
exit                      quit the mongo shell
>
```

CUSTOMIZING THE MONGODB DATA DIRECTORY AND PORT

By default, MongoDB stores the data files in the `/data/db` (`C:\data\db` on Windows) directory and listens for requests on port 27017. You can specify an alternative data directory by specifying the directory path using the `dbpath` option, as follows:

```
mongod --dbpath  /path/to/alternative/directory
```

Make sure the data directory is created if it doesn't already exist. Also, ensure that `mongod` has permissions to write to that directory.

In addition, you can also direct MongoDB to listen for connections on an alternative port by explicitly passing the port as follows:

```
mongod --port 94301
```

To avoid conflicts, make sure the port is not in use.

To change both the data directory and the port simultaneously, simply specify both the `--dbpath` and `--port` options with the corresponding alternative values to the `mongod` executable.

Next, you learn how to create the preferences database within the MongoDB instance.

Creating the Preferences Database

To start out, create a preferences database called `prefs`. After you create it, store tuples (or pairs) of usernames and zip codes in a collection, named `location`, within this database. Then store the available data sets in this defined structure. In MongoDB terms it would translate to carrying out the following steps:

1. Switch to the `prefs` database.

2. Define the data sets that need to be stored.

3. Save the defined data sets in a collection, named `location`.

To carry out these steps, type the following on your Mongo JavaScript console:

```
use prefs
w = {name: "John Doe", zip: 10001};
x = {name: "Lee Chang", zip: 94129};
y = {name: "Jenny Gonzalez", zip: 33101};
z = {name: "Srinivas Shastri", zip: 02101};
db.location.save(w);
db.location.save(x);
db.location.save(y);
db.location.save(z);
```

That's it! A few simple steps and the data store is ready. Some quick notes before moving forward though: The `use prefs` command changed the current database to the database called `prefs`. However, the database itself was never explicitly created. Similarly, the data points were stored in the `location` collection by passing a data point to the `db.location.save()` method. The collection wasn't explicitly created either. In MongoDB, both the database and the collection are created only when data is inserted into it. So, in this example, it's created when the first data point, `{name: "John Doe", zip: 10001}`, is inserted.

You can now query the newly created database to verify the contents of the store. To get all records stored in the collection named `location`, run `db.location.find()`.

Running `db.location.find()` on my machine reveals the following output:

```
> db.location.find()
{ "_id" : ObjectId("4c97053abe67000000003857"), "name" : "John Doe",
    "zip" : 10001 }
{ "_id" : ObjectId("4c970541be67000000003858"), "name" : "Lee Chang",
    "zip" : 94129 }
{ "_id" : ObjectId("4c970548be67000000003859"), "name" : "Jenny Gonzalez",
    "zip" : 33101 }
{ "_id" : ObjectId("4c970555be6700000000385a"), "name" : "Srinivas Shastri",
    "zip" : 1089 }
```

The output on your machine should be similar. The only bit that will vary is the `ObjectId`. `ObjectId` is MongoDB's way of uniquely identifying each record or document in MongoDB terms.

> *MongoDB uniquely identifies each document in a collection using the* ObjectId. *The* ObjectId *for a document is stored as the* _id *attribute of that document. While inserting a record, any unique value can be set as the* ObjectId. *The uniqueness of the value needs to be guaranteed by the developer. You could also avoid specifying the value for the* _id *property while inserting a record. In such cases, MongoDB creates and inserts an appropriate unique id. Such generated ids in MongoDB are of the BSON, short for binary JSON, format, which can be best summarized as follows:*
>
> ➤ BSON Object Id is a 12-byte value.
>
> ➤ The first 4 bytes represent the creation timestamp. It represents the seconds since epoch. This value must be stored in big endian, which means the most significant value in the sequence must be stored in the lowest storage address.
>
> ➤ The next 3 bytes represent the machine id.
>
> ➤ The following 2 bytes represent the process id.
>
> ➤ The last 3 bytes represent the counter. This value must be stored in big endian.
>
> ➤ The BSON format, apart from assuring uniqueness, includes the creation timestamp. BSON format ids are supported by all standard MongoDB drivers.

The find method, with no parameters, returns all the elements in the collection. In some cases, this may not be desirable and only a subset of the collection may be required. To understand querying possibilities, add the following additional records to the location collection:

➤ Don Joe, 10001

➤ John Doe, 94129

You can accomplish this, via the mongo shell, as follows:

```
> a = {name:"Don Joe", zip:10001};
{ "name" : "Don Joe", "zip" : 10001 }
> b = {name:"John Doe", zip:94129};
{ "name" : "John Doe", "zip" : 94129 }
> db.location.save(a);
> db.location.save(b);
>
```

To get a list of only those people who are in the 10001 zip code, you could query as follows:

```
> db.location.find({zip: 10001});
{ "_id" : ObjectId("4c97053abe67000000003857"), "name" : "John Doe",
```

```
          "zip" : 10001 }
{ "_id" : ObjectId("4c97a6555c760000000054d8"), "name" : "Don Joe",
          "zip" : 10001 }
```

To get a list of all those who have the name "John Doe," you could query like so:

```
> db.location.find({name: "John Doe"});
{ "_id" : ObjectId("4c97053abe67000000003857"), "name" : "John Doe",
          "zip" : 10001 }
{ "_id" : ObjectId("4c97a7ef5c760000000054da"), "name" : "John Doe",
          "zip" : 94129 }
```

In both these queries that filter the collection, a query document is passed as a parameter to the find method. The query document specifies the pattern of keys and values that need to be matched. MongoDB supports many advanced querying mechanisms beyond simple filters, including pattern representation with the help of regular expressions.

Because a database includes newer data sets, it is possible the structure of the collection will become a constraint and thus need modification. In traditional relational database sense, you may need to alter the table schema. In relational databases, altering table schemas also means taking on a complicated data migration task to make sure data in the old and the new schema exist together. In MongoDB, modifying a collection structure is trivial. More accurately, collections, analogous to tables, are schema-less and so it allows you to store disparate document types within the same collection.

Consider an example where you need to store the location preferences of another user, whose name and zip code are identical to a document already existing in your database, say, another {name: "Lee Chang", zip: 94129}. Intentionally and not realistically, of course, the assumption was that a name and zip pair would be unique!

To distinctly identify the second Lee Chang from the one in the database, an additional attribute, the street address, is added like so:

```
> anotherLee = {name:"Lee Chang", zip: 94129, streetAddress:"37000 Graham Street"};
{
        "name" : "Lee Chang",
        "zip" : 94129,
        "streetAddress" : "37000 Graham Street"
}
> db.location.save(anotherLee);
```

Now getting all documents, using find, returns the following data sets:

```
> db.location.find();
{ "_id" : ObjectId("4c97053abe67000000003857"), "name" : "John Doe",
          "zip" : 10001 }
{ "_id" : ObjectId("4c970541be67000000003858"), "name" : "Lee Chang",
          "zip" : 94129 }
{ "_id" : ObjectId("4c970548be67000000003859"), "name" : "Jenny Gonzalez",
          "zip" : 33101 }
```

```
{ "_id" : ObjectId("4c970555be6700000000385a"), "name" : "Srinivas Shastri",
    "zip" : 1089 }
{ "_id" : ObjectId("4c97a6555c760000000054d8"), "name" : "Don Joe",
    "zip" : 10001 }
{ "_id" : ObjectId("4c97a7ef5c760000000054da"), "name" : "John Doe",
    "zip" : 94129 }
{ "_id" : ObjectId("4c97add25c760000000054db"), "name" : "Lee Chang",
    "zip" : 94129, "streetAddress" : "37000 Graham Street" }
```

You can access this data set from most mainstream programming languages, because drivers for those exist. A section titled "Working with Language Bindings" later in this chapter covers the topic. In a subsection in that section, this location preferences example is accessed from Java, PHP, Ruby, and Python.

In the next example, you see a simple data set that relates to car make and models stored in a non-relational column-family database.

Storing Car Make and Model Data

Apache Cassandra, a distributed column-family database, is used in this example. Therefore, it would be beneficial to have Cassandra installed before you delve into the example. That will allow you to follow along as I proceed. Refer to Appendix A if you need help installing and setting up Cassandra.

Apache Cassandra is a distributed database, so you would normally set up a database cluster when using this product. For this example, the complexities of setting up a cluster are avoided by running Cassandra as a single node. In a production environment you would not want such a configuration, but you are only testing the waters and getting familiar with the basics for now so the single node will suffice.

A Cassandra database can be interfaced via a simple command-line client or via the Thrift interface. The Thrift interface helps a variety of programming languages connect to Cassandra. Functionally, you could think of the Thrift interface as a generic multilanguage database driver. Thrift is discussed later in the section titled "Working with Language Bindings."

Moving on with the car makes and models database, first start Cassandra and connect to it.

Starting Cassandra and Connecting to It

You can start the Cassandra server by invoking `bin/cassandra` from the folder where the Cassandra compressed (tarred and gzipped) distribution is extracted. For this example, run `bin/Cassandra -f`. The `-f` option makes Cassandra run in the foreground. This starts one Cassandra node locally on your machine. When running as a cluster, multiple nodes are started and they are configured to communicate with each other. For this example, one node will suffice to illustrate the basics of storing and accessing data in Cassandra.

On starting a Cassandra node, you should see the output on your console as follows:

```
PS C:\applications\apache-cassandra-0.7.4> .\bin\cassandra -f
Starting Cassandra Server
 INFO 18:20:02,091 Logging initialized
 INFO 18:20:02,107 Heap size: 1070399488/1070399488
 INFO 18:20:02,107 JNA not found. Native methods will be disabled.
 INFO 18:20:02,107 Loading settings from file:/C:/applications/
    apache-cassandra-0.7.4/conf/cassandra.yaml
 INFO 18:20:02,200 DiskAccessMode 'auto' determined to be standard,
    indexAccessMode is standard
 INFO 18:20:02,294 Deleted \var\lib\cassandra\data\system\LocationInfo-f-3
 INFO 18:20:02,294 Deleted \var\lib\cassandra\data\system\LocationInfo-f-2
 INFO 18:20:02,294 Deleted \var\lib\cassandra\data\system\LocationInfo-f-1
 INFO 18:20:02,310 Deleted \var\lib\cassandra\data\system\LocationInfo-f-4
 INFO 18:20:02,341 Opening \var\lib\cassandra\data\system\LocationInfo-f-5
 INFO 18:20:02,388 Couldn't detect any schema definitions in local storage.
 INFO 18:20:02,388 Found table data in data directories. Consider using JMX to call
    org.apache.cassandra.service.StorageService.loadSchemaFromYam
l().
 INFO 18:20:02,403 Creating new commitlog segment /var/lib/cassandra/commitlog\
    CommitLog-1301793602403.log
 INFO 18:20:02,403 Replaying \var\lib\cassandra\commitlog\
    CommitLog-1301793576882.log
 INFO 18:20:02,403 Finished reading \var\lib\cassandra\commitlog\
    CommitLog-1301793576882.log
 INFO 18:20:02,419 Log replay complete
 INFO 18:20:02,434 Cassandra version: 0.7.4
 INFO 18:20:02,434 Thrift API version: 19.4.0
 INFO 18:20:02,434 Loading persisted ring state
 INFO 18:20:02,434 Starting up server gossip
 INFO 18:20:02,450 Enqueuing flush of Memtable-LocationInfo@33000296(29 bytes,
    1 operations)
 INFO 18:20:02,450 Writing Memtable-LocationInfo@33000296(29 bytes, 1 operations)
 INFO 18:20:02,622 Completed flushing \var\lib\cassandra\data\system\
    LocationInfo-f-6-Data.db (80 bytes)
 INFO 18:20:02,653 Using saved token 63595432991552520182800882743159853717
 INFO 18:20:02,653 Enqueuing flush of Memtable-LocationInfo@22518320(53 bytes,
    2 operations)
 INFO 18:20:02,653 Writing Memtable-LocationInfo@22518320(53 bytes, 2 operations)
 INFO 18:20:02,824 Completed flushing \var\lib\cassandra\data\system\
    LocationInfo-f-7-Data.db (163 bytes)
 INFO 18:20:02,824 Will not load MX4J, mx4j-tools.jar is not in the classpath
 INFO 18:20:02,871 Binding thrift service to localhost/127.0.0.1:9160
 INFO 18:20:02,871 Using TFastFramedTransport with a max frame size of
    15728640 bytes.
 INFO 18:20:02,871 Listening for thrift clients...
```

The specific output is from my Windows 7 64-bit machine when the Cassandra executable was run from the Windows PowerShell. If you use a different operating system and a different shell, your output may be a bit different.

ESSENTIAL CONFIGURATION FOR RUNNING AN APACHE CASSANDRA NODE

Apache Cassandra storage configuration is defined in `conf/cassandra.yaml`. When you download and extract a Cassandra stable or development distribution that is available in a compressed `tar.gz` format, you get a `cassandra.yaml` file with some default configuration. For example, it would expect the commit logs to be in the `/var/lib/cassandra/commitlog` directory and the data files to be in the `/var/lib/cassandra/data` directory. In addition, Apache Cassandra uses log4j for logging. The Cassandra log4j can be configured via `conf/log4j-server .properties`. By default, Cassandra log4j expects to write log output to `/var/log/ cassandra/system.log`. If you want to keep these defaults make sure that these directories exist and you have appropriate permissions to access and write to them. If you want to modify this configuration, make sure to specify the new folders of your choice in the corresponding log files.

Commit log and data directory properties from `conf/cassandra.yaml` in my instance are:

```
# directories where Cassandra should store data on disk.
data_file_directories:
    - /var/lib/cassandra/data

# commit log
commitlog_directory: /var/lib/cassandra/commitlog
```

The path values in `cassandra.yaml` need not be specified in Windows-friendly formats. For example, you do not need to specify the commitlog path as `commitlog_directory: C:\var\lib\cassandra\commitlog`. The log4j appender file configuration from `conf/log4j-server.properties` in my instance is:

```
log4j.appender.R.File=/var/log/cassandra/system.log
```

The simplest way to connect to the running Cassandra node on your machine is to use the Cassandra Command-Line Interface (CLI). Starting the command line is as easy as running `bin/ Cassandra-cli`. You can pass in the host and port properties to the CLI as follows:

```
bin/cassandra-cli -host localhost -port 9160
```

The output of running `cassandra-cli` is as follows:

```
PS C:\applications\apache-cassandra-0.7.4> .\bin\cassandra-cli -host localhost
    -port 9160
Starting Cassandra Client
Connected to: "Test Cluster" on localhost/9160
Welcome to cassandra CLI.

Type 'help;' or '?' for help. Type 'quit;' or 'exit;' to quit.
[default@unknown]
```

To get a list of available commands type `help` or `?` and you will see the following output:

```
[default@unknown] ?
List of all CLI commands:
?                                                      Display this message.
help;                                                    Display this help.
help <command>;                        Display detailed, command-specific help.
connect <hostname>/<port> (<username> '<password>')?; Connect to thrift service.
use <keyspace> [<username> 'password'];              Switch to a keyspace.
describe keyspace (<keyspacename>)?;                   Describe keyspace.
exit;                                                             Exit CLI.
quit;                                                             Exit CLI.
describe cluster;                         Display information about cluster.
show cluster name;                             Display cluster name.
show keyspaces;                              Show list of keyspaces.
show api version;                            Show server API version.
create keyspace <keyspace> [with <att1>=<value1> [and <att2>=<value2> ...]];
                  Add a new keyspace with the specified attribute(s) and value(s).
update keyspace <keyspace> [with <att1>=<value1> [and <att2>=<value2> ...]];
                  Update a keyspace with the specified attribute(s) and value(s).
create column family <cf> [with <att1>=<value1> [and <att2>=<value2> ...]];
           Create a new column family with the specified attribute(s) and value(s).
update column family <cf> [with <att1>=<value1> [and <att2>=<value2> ...]];
                Update a column family with the specified attribute(s) and value(s).
drop keyspace <keyspace>;                           Delete a keyspace.
drop column family <cf>;                        Delete a column family.
get <cf>['<key>'];                              Get a slice of columns.
get <cf>['<key>']['<super>'];              Get a slice of sub columns.
get <cf> where <column> = <value> [and <column> > <value> and ...] [limit int];
get <cf>['<key>']['<col>'] (as <type>)*;         Get a column value.
get <cf>['<key>']['<super>']['<col>'] (as <type>)*;   Get a sub column value.
set <cf>['<key>']['<col>'] = <value> (with ttl = <secs>)*;       Set a column.
set <cf>['<key>']['<super>']['<col>'] = <value> (with ttl = <secs>)*;
                                                                Set a sub column.
del <cf>['<key>'];                                        Delete record.
del <cf>['<key>']['<col>'];                              Delete column.
del <cf>['<key>']['<super>']['<col>'];                Delete sub column.
count <cf>['<key>'];                         Count columns in record.
count <cf>['<key>']['<super>'];         Count columns in a super column.
truncate <column_family>;                  Truncate specified column family.
assume <column_family> <attribute> as <type>;
              Assume a given column family attributes to match a specified type.
list <cf>;                                  List all rows in the column family.
list <cf>[<startKey>:];
             List rows in the column family beginning with <startKey>.
list <cf>[<startKey>:<endKey>];
          List rows in the column family in the range from <startKey> to <endKey>.
list ... limit N;                          Limit the list results to N.
```

Now that you have some familiarity with Cassandra basics, you can move on to create a storage definition for the car make and model data and insert and access some sample data into this new Cassandra storage scheme.

Storing and Accessing Data with Cassandra

The first place to start is to understand the concept of a keyspace and a column-family. The closest relational database parallels of a keyspace and a column-family are a database and a table. Although these definitions are not completely accurate and sometimes misleading, they serve as a good starting point to understand the use of a keyspace and a column-family. As you get familiar with the basic usage patterns you will develop greater appreciation for and understanding of these concepts, which extend beyond their relational parallels.

For starters, list the existing keyspaces in your Cassandra server. Go to the cassandra-cli, type the show keyspaces command, and press Enter. Because you are starting out with a fresh Cassandra installation, you are likely to see output similar to this:

```
[default@unknown] show keyspaces;
Keyspace: system:
  Replication Strategy: org.apache.cassandra.locator.LocalStrategy
    Replication Factor: 1
  Column Families:
    ColumnFamily: HintsColumnFamily (Super)
    "hinted handoff data"
      Columns sorted by: org.apache.cassandra.db.marshal.BytesType/
    org.apache.cassandra.db.marshal.BytesType
      Row cache size / save period: 0.0/0
      Key cache size / save period: 0.01/14400
      Memtable thresholds: 0.15/32/1440
      GC grace seconds: 0
      Compaction min/max thresholds: 4/32
      Read repair chance: 0.0
      Built indexes: []
    ColumnFamily: IndexInfo
    "indexes that have been completed"
      Columns sorted by: org.apache.cassandra.db.marshal.UTF8Type
      Row cache size / save period: 0.0/0
      Key cache size / save period: 0.01/14400
      Memtable thresholds: 0.0375/8/1440
      GC grace seconds: 0
      Compaction min/max thresholds: 4/32
      Read repair chance: 0.0
      Built indexes: []
    ColumnFamily: LocationInfo
    "persistent metadata for the local node"
      Columns sorted by: org.apache.cassandra.db.marshal.BytesType
      Row cache size / save period: 0.0/0
      Key cache size / save period: 0.01/14400
      Memtable thresholds: 0.0375/8/1440
      GC grace seconds: 0
      Compaction min/max thresholds: 4/32
      Read repair chance: 0.0
      Built indexes: []
    ColumnFamily: Migrations
    "individual schema mutations"
      Columns sorted by: org.apache.cassandra.db.marshal.TimeUUIDType
      Row cache size / save period: 0.0/0
```

```
      Key cache size / save period: 0.01/14400
      Memtable thresholds: 0.0375/8/1440
      GC grace seconds: 0
      Compaction min/max thresholds: 4/32
      Read repair chance: 0.0
      Built indexes: []
    ColumnFamily: Schema
    "current state of the schema"
      Columns sorted by: org.apache.cassandra.db.marshal.UTF8Type
      Row cache size / save period: 0.0/0
      Key cache size / save period: 0.01/14400
      Memtable thresholds: 0.0375/8/1440
      GC grace seconds: 0
      Compaction min/max thresholds: 4/32
      Read repair chance: 0.0
      Built indexes: []
```

System keyspace, as the name suggests, is like the administration database in an RDBMS. The system keyspace includes a few pre-defined column-families. You will learn about column-family, via example, later in this section. Keyspaces group column-families together. Usually, one keyspace is defined per application. Data replication is defined at the keyspace level. This means the number of redundant copies of data and how these copies are stored are specified at the keyspace level. The Cassandra distribution comes with a sample keyspace creation script in a file named schema-sample.txt, which is available in the conf directory. You can run the sample keyspace creation script as follows:

```
PS C:\applications\apache-cassandra-0.7.4> .\bin\cassandra-cli -host localhost
   --file .\conf\schema-sample.txt
```

Once again, connect via the command-line client and reissue the show keyspaces command in the interface. The output this time should be like so:

```
[default@unknown] show keyspaces;
Keyspace: Keyspace1:
  Replication Strategy: org.apache.cassandra.locator.SimpleStrategy
    Replication Factor: 1
  Column Families:
    ColumnFamily: Indexed1
      Columns sorted by: org.apache.cassandra.db.marshal.BytesType
      Row cache size / save period: 0.0/0
      Key cache size / save period: 200000.0/14400
      Memtable thresholds: 0.2953125/63/1440
      GC grace seconds: 864000
      Compaction min/max thresholds: 4/32
      Read repair chance: 1.0
      Built indexes: [Indexed1.birthdate_idx]
      Column Metadata:
        Column Name: birthdate (626972746864617465)
          Validation Class: org.apache.cassandra.db.marshal.LongType
          Index Name: birthdate_idx
          Index Type: KEYS
    ColumnFamily: Standard1
      Columns sorted by: org.apache.cassandra.db.marshal.BytesType
```

```
  Row cache size / save period: 1000.0/0
  Key cache size / save period: 10000.0/3600
  Memtable thresholds: 0.29/255/59
  GC grace seconds: 864000
  Compaction min/max thresholds: 4/32
  Read repair chance: 1.0
  Built indexes: []
ColumnFamily: Standard2
  Columns sorted by: org.apache.cassandra.db.marshal.UTF8Type
  Row cache size / save period: 0.0/0
  Key cache size / save period: 100.0/14400
  Memtable thresholds: 0.2953125/63/1440
  GC grace seconds: 0
  Compaction min/max thresholds: 5/31
  Read repair chance: 0.0010
  Built indexes: []
ColumnFamily: StandardByUUID1
  Columns sorted by: org.apache.cassandra.db.marshal.TimeUUIDType
  Row cache size / save period: 0.0/0
  Key cache size / save period: 200000.0/14400
  Memtable thresholds: 0.2953125/63/1440
  GC grace seconds: 864000
  Compaction min/max thresholds: 4/32
  Read repair chance: 1.0
  Built indexes: []
ColumnFamily: Super1 (Super)
  Columns sorted by: org.apache.cassandra.db.marshal.BytesType/
org.apache.cassandra.db.marshal.BytesType
  Row cache size / save period: 0.0/0
  Key cache size / save period: 200000.0/14400
  Memtable thresholds: 0.2953125/63/1440
  GC grace seconds: 864000
  Compaction min/max thresholds: 4/32
  Read repair chance: 1.0
  Built indexes: []
ColumnFamily: Super2 (Super)
"A column family with supercolumns, whose column and subcolumn names are
UTF8 strings"
  Columns sorted by: org.apache.cassandra.db.marshal.BytesType/
org.apache.cassandra.db.marshal.UTF8Type
  Row cache size / save period: 10000.0/0
  Key cache size / save period: 50.0/14400
  Memtable thresholds: 0.2953125/63/1440
  GC grace seconds: 864000
  Compaction min/max thresholds: 4/32
  Read repair chance: 1.0
  Built indexes: []
ColumnFamily: Super3 (Super)
"A column family with supercolumns, whose column names are Longs (8 bytes)"
  Columns sorted by: org.apache.cassandra.db.marshal.LongType/
org.apache.cassandra.db.marshal.BytesType
  Row cache size / save period: 0.0/0
  Key cache size / save period: 200000.0/14400
  Memtable thresholds: 0.2953125/63/1440
  GC grace seconds: 864000
```

```
        Compaction min/max thresholds: 4/32
        Read repair chance: 1.0
        Built indexes: []
Keyspace: system:
...(Information on the system keyspace is not included here as it's
    the same as what you have seen earlier in this section)
```

Next, create a CarDataStore keyspace and a Cars column-family within this keyspace using the script in Listing 2-1.

Available for download on Wrox.com

LISTING 2-1: Schema script for CarDataStore keyspace

```
/*schema-cardatastore.txt*/

create keyspace CarDataStore
    with replication_factor = 1
    and placement_strategy = 'org.apache.cassandra.locator.SimpleStrategy';

use CarDataStore;

create column family Cars
    with comparator = UTF8Type
    and read_repair_chance = 0.1
    and keys_cached = 100
    and gc_grace = 0
    and min_compaction_threshold = 5
    and max_compaction_threshold = 31;
```

schema-cardatastore.txt

You can run the script, illustrated in Listing 2-1, as follows:

```
PS C:\applications\apache-cassandra-0.7.4> bin/cassandra-cli -host localhost
    --file C:\workspace\nosql\examples\schema-cardatastore.txt
```

You have successfully added a new keyspace! Go back to the script and briefly review how you added a keyspace. You added a keyspace called CarDataStore. You also added an artifact called a ColumnFamily within this keystore. The name of the ColumnFamily was Cars. You will see ColumnFamily in action in a while, but think of them as tables for now, especially if you can't hold your curiosity. Within the ColumnFamily tag an attribute called CompareWith was also included. The value of CompareWith was specified as UTF8Type. The CompareWith attribute value affects how row-keys are indexed and sorted. The other tags within the keyspace definition specify the replication options. CarDataStore has a replication factor of 1, which means there is only one copy of data stored in Cassandra.

Next, add some data to the CarDataStore keyspace like so:

```
 [default@unknown] use CarDataStore;
Authenticated to keyspace: CarDataStore
[default@CarDataStore] set Cars['Prius']['make'] = 'toyota';
```

```
Value inserted.
[default@CarDataStore] set Cars['Prius']['model'] = 'prius 3';
Value inserted.
[default@CarDataStore] set Cars['Corolla']['make'] = 'toyota';
Value inserted.
[default@CarDataStore] set Cars['Corolla']['model'] = 'le';
Value inserted.
[default@CarDataStore] set Cars['fit']['make'] = 'honda';
Value inserted.
[default@CarDataStore] set Cars['fit']['model'] = 'fit sport';
Value inserted.
[default@CarDataStore] set Cars['focus']['make'] = 'ford';
Value inserted.
[default@CarDataStore] set Cars['focus']['model'] = 'sel';
Value inserted.
```

The set of commands illustrated is a way to add data to Cassandra. Using this command, a name-value pair or column value is added within a row, which in turn is defined in a ColumnFamily in a keyspace. For example, set Cars['Prius']['make'] = 'toyota', a name-value pair: 'make' = 'toyota' is added to a row, which is identified by the key 'Prius'. The row identified by 'Prius' is part of the Cars ColumnFamily. The Cars ColumnFamily is defined within the CarDataStore, which you know is a keyspace.

Once the data is added, you can query and retrieve it. To get the name-value pairs or column names and values for a row identified by Prius, use the following command: get Cars['Prius']. The output should be like so:

```
[default@CarDataStore] get Cars['Prius'];
=> (column=make, value=746f796f7461, timestamp=1301824068109000)
=> (column=model, value=70726975732033, timestamp=1301824129807000)
Returned 2 results.
```

Be careful while constructing your queries because the row-keys, column-family identifiers, and column keys are case sensitive. Therefore, passing in 'prius' instead of 'Prius' does not return any name-value tuples. Try running get Cars['prius'] via the CLI. You will receive a response that reads Returned 0 results. Also, before you query, remember to issue use CarDataStore to make CarDataStore the current keyspace.

To access just the 'make' name-value data for the 'Prius' row you could query like so:

```
[default@CarDataStore] get Cars['Prius']['make'];
=> (column=make, value=746f796f7461, timestamp=1301824068109000)
```

Cassandra data sets can support richer data models than those shown so far and querying capabilities are also more complex than those illustrated, but I will leave those topics for a later chapter. For now, I am convinced you have had your first taste.

After walking through two simple examples, one that involved a document store, MongoDB, and another that involved a column database, Apache Cassandra, you may be ready to start interfacing with these using a programming language of your choice.

WORKING WITH LANGUAGE BINDINGS

To include NoSQL solutions into the application stack, it's extremely important that robust and flexible language bindings allow access and manipulation of these stores from some of the most popular languages.

This section covers two types of interfaces between NoSQL stores and programming languages. The first illustration covers the essentials of MongoDB drivers for Java, PHP, Ruby, and Python. The second illustration covers the language agnostic and, therefore, multilanguage-supported Thrift interface for Apache Cassandra. The coverage of these topics is elementary. Later chapters build on this initial introduction to show more powerful and detailed use cases.

MongoDB's Drivers

In this section, MongoDB drivers for four different languages, Java, PHP, Ruby, and Python, are introduced in the order in which they are listed.

Mongo Java Driver

First, download the latest distribution of the MongoDB Java driver from the MongoDB github code repository at `http://github.com/mongodb`. All officially supported drivers are hosted in this code repository. The latest version of the driver is 2.5.2, so the downloaded jar file is named `mongo-2.5.2,jar`.

Once again start the local MongoDB server by running `bin/mongod` from within the MongoDB distribution. Now use a Java program to connect to this server. Look at Listing 2-2 for a sample Java program that connects to MongoDB, lists all the collections in the `prefs` database, and then lists all the documents within the `location` collection.

Available for download on Wrox.com

LISTING 2-2: Sample Java program to connect to MongoDB

```java
import java.net.UnknownHostException;
import java.util.Set;
import com.mongodb.DB;
import com.mongodb.DBCollection;
import com.mongodb.DBCursor;
import com.mongodb.Mongo;
import com.mongodb.MongoException;

public class ConnectToMongoDB {
    Mongo m = null;
    DB db;

    public void connect() {
        try {
            m = new Mongo("localhost", 27017 );
        } catch (UnknownHostException e) {
            e.printStackTrace();
        } catch (MongoException e) {
            e.printStackTrace();
```

continues

LISTING 2-2 *(continued)*

```java
        }
    }

    public void listAllCollections(String dbName) {
        if(m!=null){
            db = m.getDB(dbName);
            Set<String> collections = db.getCollectionNames();

            for (String s : collections) {
                System.out.println(s);
            }
        }
    }

    public void listLocationCollectionDocuments() {
        if(m!=null){
            db = m.getDB("prefs");
            DBCollection collection = db.getCollection("location");

            DBCursor cur = collection.find();

            while(cur.hasNext()) {
                System.out.println(cur.next());
            }
        } else {
            System.out.println("Please connect to MongoDB
and then fetch the collection");
        }
    }

    public static void main(String[] args) {
        ConnectToMongoDB connectToMongoDB = new ConnectToMongoDB();
        connectToMongoDB.connect();
        connectToMongoDB.listAllCollections("prefs");
        connectToMongoDB.listLocationCollectionDocuments();
    }
}
```

ConnectToMongoDB.java

Make sure to have the MongoDB Java driver in the classpath when you compile and run this program. On running the program, the output is as follows:

```
location
system.indexes
{ "_id" : { "$oid" : "4c97053abe67000000003857"} , "name" : "John Doe" ,
    "zip" : 10001.0}
{ "_id" : { "$oid" : "4c970541be67000000003858"} , "name" : "Lee Chang" ,
    "zip" : 94129.0}
{ "_id" : { "$oid" : "4c970548be67000000003859"} , "name" : "Jenny Gonzalez" ,
    "zip" : 33101.0}
```

```
{ "_id" : { "$oid" : "4c970555be6700000000385a"} , "name" : "Srinivas Shastri" ,
    "zip" : 1089.0}
{ "_id" : { "$oid" : "4c97a6555c760000000054d8"} , "name" : "Don Joe" ,
    "zip" : 10001.0}
{ "_id" : { "$oid" : "4c97a7ef5c760000000054da"} , "name" : "John Doe" ,
    "zip" : 94129.0}
{ "_id" : { "$oid" : "4c97add25c760000000054db"} , "name" : "Lee Chang" ,
    "zip" : 94129.0 , "streetAddress" : "37000 Graham Street"}
```

The output of the Java program tallies with what you saw with the command-line interactive JavaScript shell earlier in the chapter.

Now see how the same example works with PHP.

MongoDB PHP Driver

First, download the PHP driver from the MongoDB github code repository and configure the driver to work with your local PHP environment. Refer to the Appendix A subsection on MongoDB installation for further details.

A sample PHP program that connects to a local MongoDB server and lists the documents in the `location` collections in the `prefs` database is as follows:

Available for download on Wrox.com

```
$connection = new Mongo( "localhost:27017" );
$collection = $connection->prefs->location;
$cursor = $collection->find();
foreach ($cursor as $id => $value) {
    echo "$id: ";
    var_dump( $value );
}
```

connect_to_mongodb.php

The program is succinct but does the job! Next, you see how Ruby handles this same task.

MongoDB Ruby Driver

MongoDB has drivers for all mainstream languages and Ruby is no exception. You can obtain the driver from the MongoDB github code repository but it may be easier to simply rely on RubyGems to manage the installation. To get ready to connect to MongoDB from Ruby, get at least the `mongo` and `bson` gems. You can install the `mongo` gem as follows:

```
gem install mongo
```

The `bson` gem will be installed automatically. In addition, installing `bson_ext` may be recommended as well.

Listing 2-3 depicts a sample Ruby program that connects to the MongoDB server and lists all the documents in the `location` collection in the `prefs` database.

LISTING 2-3: Get all documents in a MongoDB collection using Ruby

```ruby
db = Mongo::Connection.new("localhost", 27017).db("prefs")
locationCollection = db.collection("location")
locationCollection.find().each { |row| puts row.inspect
```

connect_to_mongodb.rb

The next MongoDB driver discussed in this chapter is the one that helps connect Python to MongoDB.

MongoDB Python Driver

The easiest way to install the Python driver is to run `easy_install pymongo`. Once it is installed, you can invoke the Python program in Listing 2-4 to get a list of all documents in the `location` collection in the `prefs` database.

LISTING 2-4: Python program to interface with MongoDB

```python
from pymongo import Connection
connection = Connection('localhost', 27017)
db = connection.prefs
collection = db.location
for doc in collection.find():
    doc
```

connect_to_mongodb.py

At this stage, this example has been created and run in at least five different ways. It's a simple and useful example that illustrates the directly relevant concepts of establishing a connection, fetching a database, a collection, and documents within that collection.

A First Look at Thrift

Thrift is a framework for cross-language services development. It consists of a software stack and a code-generation engine to connect smoothly between multiple languages. Apache Cassandra uses the Thrift interface to provide a layer of abstraction to interact with the column data store. You can learn more about Apache Thrift at `http://incubator.apache.org/thrift/`.

The Cassandra Thrift interface definitions are available in the Apache Cassandra distribution in a file, named `cassandra.thrift`, which resides in the `interface` directory. The Thrift interface definitions vary between Cassandra versions so make sure that you get the correct version of the interface file. Also, make sure you have a compatible version of Thrift itself.

Thrift can create language bindings for a number of languages. In the case of Cassandra, you could generate interfaces for Java, C++, C#, Python, PHP, and Perl. The simplest command to generate all Thrift interfaces is:

```
thrift --gen interface/cassandra.thrift
```

Additionally, you could specify the languages as parameters to the Thrift generator program. For example, to create only the Java Thrift interface run:

```
thrift --gen java interface/cassandra.thrift
```

Once the Thrift modules are generated, you can use it in your program. Assuming you have generated the Python Thrift interfaces and modules successfully, you can connect to the CarDataStore keyspace and query for data as depicted in Listing 2-5.

LISTING 2-5: Querying CarDataStore keyspace using the Thrift interface

```python
from thrift import Thrift
from thrift.transport import TTransport
from thrift.transport import TSocket
from thrift.protocol.TBinaryProtocol import TBinaryProtocolAccelerated
from cassandra import Cassandra
from cassandra.ttypes import *
import time
import pprint

def main():

    socket = TSocket.TSocket("localhost", 9160)
    protocol = TBinaryProtocol.TBinaryProtocolAccelerated(transport)
    transport = TTransport.TBufferedTransport(socket)
    client = Cassandra.Client(protocol)
    pp = pprint.PrettyPrinter(indent=2)
    keyspace = "CarDataStore"
    column_path = ColumnPath(column_family="Cars", column="make")
    key = "1"
    try:
        transport.open()
        #Query for data
        column_parent = ColumnParent(column_family="Cars")
        slice_range = SliceRange(start="", finish="")
        predicate = SlicePredicate(slice_range=slice_range)
        result = client.get_slice(keyspace,
                                  key,
                                  column_parent,
                                  predicate,
                                  ConsistencyLevel.ONE)
        pp.pprint(result)
    except Thrift.TException, tx:
        print 'Thrift: %s' % tx.message
    finally:
        transport.close()

if __name__ == '__main__':
    main()
```

query_cardatastore_using_thrift.py

Although, Thrift is a very useful multilanguage interface, sometimes you may just chose to go with a pre-existing language API. Some of these API(s) provide the much-needed reliability and stability as they are tested and actively supported, while the products they connect to evolve rapidly. Many of these use Thrift under the hood. A number of such libraries, especially Hector, for Java; Pycassa, for Python; and Phpcassa, for PHP, exist for Cassandra.

SUMMARY

The aim of this chapter was to give a first feel of NoSQL databases by providing a hands-on walkthrough of some of the core concepts. The chapter delivered that promise and managed to cover more than simple "Hello World" printing to console.

Introductory concepts that relate to NoSQL were explained in this chapter through small and terse examples. Examples gently started with the basics and developed to a point where they helped explain the simple concepts. In all these examples, MongoDB and Apache Cassandra, two leading NoSQL options, served as the underlying product.

The chapter was logically divided into two parts: one that dealt with the core NoSQL storage concepts and the other that helped connect NoSQL stores to a few mainstream programming languages. Therefore, the initial part involved examples run via the command-line client and the later part included examples that can be run as a standalone program.

The next chapter builds on what was introduced in this chapter. More examples on interfacing with NoSQL databases and querying the available data set are explored in that chapter. Newer and different NoSQL products are also introduced there.

3

Interfacing and Interacting with NoSQL

WHAT'S IN THIS CHAPTER?

➤ How to access the popular NoSQL databases

➤ Examples of data storage in the popular NoSQL stores

➤ How to query collections in popular NoSQL stores

➤ Introduction to drivers and language bindings for popular NoSQL databases

This chapter introduces the essential ways of interacting with NoSQL data stores. The types of NoSQL stores vary and so do the ways of accessing and interacting with them. The chapter attempts to summarize a few of the most prominent of these disparate ways of accessing and querying data in NoSQL databases. By no means is the coverage exhaustive, although it is fairly comprehensive to get you started on a strong footing.

NoSQL is an evolving technology and its current pace of change is substantial. Therefore, the ways of interacting with it are evolving as NoSQL stores are used in newer contexts and interfaced from newer programming languages and technology platforms. So be prepared for continued learning and look out for possible standardization in the future.

IF NO SQL, THEN WHAT?

A big reason for the popularity of relational databases is their standardized access and query mechanism using SQL. SQL, short for structured query language, is the language you speak when talking to relational databases. It involves a simple intuitive syntax and structure that users become fluent in within a short period of time. Based on relational algebra, SQL allows users to fetch records from a single collection or join records across tables. To reinforce its simplicity, here's a walk through of a few simple examples:

➤ To fetch all data from a table that maintains the names and e-mail addresses of all the people in an organization, use `SELECT * FROM people`. The name of the table in this case is `people`.

➤ To get just a list of names of all the people from the `people` table, use `SELECT name FROM people`. The name is stored in a column called `name`.

➤ To get a subset from this list, say only those who have a Gmail account, use `SELECT * FROM people where email LIKE '%gmail.com'`.

➤ To get a list of people with a list of books they like, assuming that names of people and titles of books they like are in a separate but associated table named `books_people_like`, use `SELECT people.name, books_people_like.book_title FROM people, books_people_like WHERE people.name = books_people_like.person_name`. The table `books_people_like` has two columns: `person_name` and `title`, where `person_name` references the same set of values as the `name` column of the `people` table and `title` column stores book titles.

Although the benefits of SQL are many, it has several drawbacks as well. The drawbacks typically show up when you deal with large and spare data sets. However, in NoSQL stores there is no SQL, or more accurately there are no relational data sets. Therefore, the ways of accessing and querying data are different. In the next few sections, you learn how accessing and querying data in NoSQL databases is different from those same processes in SQL. You also learn about the similarities that exist between these processes.

I begin by exploring the essentials of storing and accessing data.

Storing and Accessing Data

In the previous chapter you had a first taste of NoSQL through a couple of elementary examples. In that chapter you indulged in some basic data storage and access using the document store MongoDB and the eventually consistent store Apache Cassandra. In this section I build on that first experience and present a more detailed view into the world of NoSQL data storage and access. To explain the different ways of data storage and access in NoSQL, I first classify them into the following types:

➤ **Document store** — MongoDB and CouchDB

➤ **Key/value store (in-memory, persistent and even ordered)** — Redis and BerkeleyDB

➤ **Column-family-based store** — HBase and Hypertable

➤ **Eventually consistent key/value store** — Apache Cassandra and Voldermot

This classification is not exhaustive. For example, it leaves out the entire set of object databases, graph databases, or XML data stores, which are excluded from this book altogether. The classification does not segregate non-relational databases into disjoint and mutually exclusive sets either. A few NoSQL stores have features that cut across the categories listed here. The classification merely sorts the non-relational stores into logical bundles by putting them within a set that best describes them.

As I discuss storage, access, and querying in NoSQL, I restrict the discussion to only a few of the categories listed and consider a small subset of the available products. I cover only the most popular ones. Learning to interface and interact with even a couple of NoSQL databases establishes a few fundamentals and common underpinning ideas in NoSQL. It will also prepare you for more advanced topics and more exhaustive coverage in the remaining chapters in this book.

Since you have been introduced to MongoDB, a document store, in the previous chapter, I will start the storage and access details with document databases.

To leverage the learn-by-example technique, I start here with a simple but interesting use case that illustrates the analysis of web server log data. The web server logs in the example follow the Combined Log Format for logging web server access and request activity. You can read more about the Apache web server Combined Log Format at `http://httpd.apache.org/docs/2.2/logs .html#combined`.

Storing Data In and Accessing Data from MongoDB

The Apache web server Combined Log Format captures the following request and response attributes for a web server:

> **IP address of the client** — This value could be the IP address of the proxy if the client requests the resource via a proxy.

> **Identity of the client** — Usually this is not a reliable piece of information and often is not recorded.

> **User name as identified during authentication** — This value is blank if no authentication is required to access the web resource.

> **Time when the request was received** — Includes date and time, along with timezone.

> **The request itself** — This can be further broken down into four different pieces: method used, resource, request parameters, and protocol.

> **Status code** — The HTTP status code.

> **Size of the object returned** — Size is bytes.

> **Referrer** — Typically, the URI or the URL that links to a web page or resource.

> **User-agent** — The client application, usually the program or device that accesses a web page or resource.

The log file itself is a text file that stores each request in a separate row. To get the data from the text file, you would need to parse it and extract the values. A simple elementary Python program to parse this log file can be quickly put together as illustrated in Listing 3-1.

LISTING 3-1: Log parser program

```python
import re
import fileinput
_lineRegex = re.compile(r'(\d+\.\d+\.\d+\.\d+) ([^ ]*) ([^ ]*)
\[([^\]]*)\] "([^"]*)" (\d+) ([^ ]*) "([^"]*)" "([^"]*)"')

class ApacheLogRecord(object):

    def __init__(self, *rgroups ):
        self.ip, self.ident, \
        self.http_user, self.time, \
        self.request_line, self.http_response_code, \
        self.http_response_size, self.referrer, self.user_agent = rgroups
        self.http_method, self.url, self.http_vers = self.request_line.split()

    def __str__(self):
        return ' '.join([self.ip, self.ident, self.time, self.request_line,
        self.http_response_code, self.http_response_size, self.referrer,
        self.user_agent])

class ApacheLogFile(object):

    def __init__(self, *filename):
        self.f = fileinput.input(filename)

    def close(self):
        self.f.close()

    def __iter__(self):
        match = _lineRegex.match
        for line in self.f:
            m = match(line)
            if m:
                try:
                    log_line = ApacheLogRecord(*m.groups())
                    yield log_line
                except GeneratorExit:
                    pass
                except Exception as e:
                    print "NON_COMPLIANT_FORMAT: ", line, "Exception: ", e
```

apache_log_parser.py

After the data is available from the parser, you can persist the data in MongoDB. Because the example log parser is written in Python, it would be easiest to use PyMongo — the Python MongoDB driver — to write the data to MongoDB. However, before I get to the specifics of using PyMongo, I recommend a slight deviation to the essentials of data storage in MongoDB.

MongoDB is a document store that can persist arbitrary collections of data as long as it can be represented using a JSON-like object hierarchy. (If you aren't familiar with JSON, read about the specification at www.json.org/. *It's a fast, lightweight, and popular data interchange format for web applications.) To present a flavor of the JSON format, a log file element extracted from the access log can be represented as follows:*

```
{
    "ApacheLogRecord": {
        "ip": "127.0.0.1",
        "ident" : "-",
        "http_user" : "frank",
        "time" : "10/Oct/2000:13:55:36 -0700",
        "request_line" : {
            "http_method" : "GET",
            "url" : "/apache_pb.gif",
            "http_vers" : "HTTP/1.0",
        },
        "http_response_code" : "200",
        "http_response_size" : "2326",
        "referrer" : "http://www.example.com/start.html",
        "user_agent" : "Mozilla/4.08 [en] (Win98; I ;Nav)",
    },
}
```

The corresponding line in the log file is as follows:

```
127.0.0.1 - frank [10/Oct/2000:13:55:36 -0700]
"GET /apache_pb.gif HTTP/1.0" 200
2326 "http://www.example.com/start.html" "Mozilla/4.08 [en]
(Win98; I ;Nav)"
```

MongoDB supports all JSON data types, namely, string, integer, boolean, double, null, array, and object. It also supports a few additional data types. These additional data types are date, object id, binary data, regular expression, and code. Mongo supports these additional data types because it supports BSON, a binary encoded serialization of JSON-like structures, and not just plain vanilla JSON. You can learn about the BSON specification at http://bsonspec.org/.

To insert the JSON-like document for the line in the log file into a collection named logdata, *you could do the following in the Mongo shell:*

```
doc = {
    "ApacheLogRecord": {
        "ip": "127.0.0.1",
        "ident" : "-",
        "http_user" : "frank",
        "time" : "10/Oct/2000:13:55:36 -0700",
        "request_line" : {
            "http_method" : "GET",
```

continues

```
continued
                        "url" : "/apache_pb.gif",
                        "http_vers" : "HTTP/1.0",
                },
                "http_response_code" : "200",
                "http_response_size" : "2326",
                "referrer" : "http://www.example.com/start.html",
                "user_agent" : "Mozilla/4.08 [en] (Win98; I ;Nav)",
        },
        };
        db.logdata.insert(doc);
```

Mongo also provides a convenience method, named save, *which updates a record if it exists in the collection and inserts it if it's not.*

In the Python example, you could save data in a dictionary (also referred to as map, hash map, or associative arrays in other languages) directly to MongoDB. This is because PyMongo — the driver — does the job of translating a dictionary to a BSON data format. To complete the example, create a utility function to publish all attributes of an object and their corresponding values as a dictionary like so:

```python
def props(obj):
    pr = {}
    for name in dir(obj):
        value = getattr(obj, name)
        if not name.startswith('__') and not inspect.ismethod(value):
            pr[name] = value
    return pr
```

apache_log_parser_mongodb.py

This function saves the `request_line` as a single element. You may prefer to save it as three separate fields: HTTP method, URL, and protocol version, as shown in Listing 3-1. You may also prefer to create a nested object hierarchy, which I touch upon a little later in this chapter during the discussion on queries.

With this function in place, storing data to MongoDB requires just a few lines of code:

```python
connection = Connection()
db = connection.mydb
collection = db.logdata
alf = ApacheLogFile(<path to access_log>)
for log_line in alf:
    collection.insert(props(log_line))
alf.close()
```

apache_log_parser_mongodb.py

Isn't that simple? Now that you have the log data stored, you can filter and analyze it.

Querying MongoDB

I used a current snapshot of my web server access log to populate a sample data set. If you don't have access to web server logs, download the file named `sample_access_log` from the code download bundle available with this book.

After you have some data persisted in a Mongo instance, you are ready to query and filter that set. In the previous chapter you learned some essential querying mechanisms using MongoDB. Let's revise some of those and explore a few additional concepts that relate to queries.

All my log data is stored in a collection named `logdata`. To list all the records in the `logdata` collection, fire up the Mongo shell (a JavaScript shell, which can be invoked with the help of the `bin/mongo` command) and query like so:

```
> var cursor = db.logdata.find()
> while (cursor.hasNext()) printjson(cursor.next());
```

This prints the data set in a nice presentable format like this:

```
{
    "_id" : ObjectId("4cb164b75a91870732000000"),
    "http_vers" : "HTTP/1.1",
    "ident" : "-",
    "http_response_code" : "200",
    "referrer" : "-",
    "url" : "/hi/tag/2009/",
    "ip" : "123.125.66.32",
    "time" : "09/Oct/2010:07:30:01 -0600",
    "http_response_size" : "13308",
    "http_method" : "GET",
    "user_agent" : "Baiduspider+(+http://www.baidu.com/search/spider.htm)",
    "http_user" : "-",
    "request_line" : "GET /hi/tag/2009/ HTTP/1.1"
}
{
    "_id" : ObjectId("4cb164b75a91870732000001"),
    "http_vers" : "HTTP/1.0",
    "ident" : "-",
    "http_response_code" : "200",
    "referrer" : "-",
    "url" : "/favicon.ico",
    "ip" : "89.132.89.62",
    "time" : "09/Oct/2010:07:30:07 -0600",
    "http_response_size" : "1136",
    "http_method" : "GET",
    "user_agent" : "Safari/6531.9 CFNetwork/454.4 Darwin/10.0.0 (i386)
(MacBook5%2C1)",
    "http_user" : "-",
    "request_line" : "GET /favicon.ico HTTP/1.0"
}
...
```

Let's dice through the query and the result set to explore a few more details of the query and response elements.

First, a cursor is declared and then all the data available in the `logdata` collection is fetched and assigned to it. Cursors or iterators are as common in relational databases as they are in MongoDB.

Look at Figure 3-1 to see how cursors work. The method `db.logdata.find()` returns all the records in the `logdata` collection, so you have the entire set to iterate over using the cursor. The previous code sample simply iterates through the elements of the cursor and prints them out. The `printjson` function prints out the elements in a nice JSON-style formatting for easy readability.

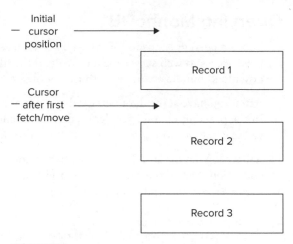

FIGURE 3-1

Although it's nice to get hold of the entire collection, oftentimes all you need is a subset of available data. Next, you see how you can filter the collection and get a smaller set to work with. In the world of SQL it's common to do the following two types of manipulations to get a subset of records:

➤   Restrict the output to only a select few columns instead of all the columns in a table.

➤   Restrict the number of rows in the table by filtering them on the basis of one or more column values.

In MongoDB, restricting the output to a few columns or attributes is not a smart strategy because each document is always returned in its entirety with all its attributes when fetched. Even then, you could choose to fetch only a few attributes for a document, although it would require you to restrict the collection. Restricting the document set to a subset of the entire collection is analogous to restricting SQL result sets to a limited set of rows. Remember the SQL WHERE clause!

I will fall back on my log file data example to illustrate ways to return a subset from a collection.

To get all log file records where `http_response_code` is 200, you can query like this:

```
db.logdata.find({ "http_response_code": "200" });
```

This query takes a query document, `{ "http_response_code": "200" }`, defining the pattern, as an argument to the `find` method.

To get all log file records where `http_response_code` is 200 and `http_vers` (protocol version) is HTTP/1.1, you can query as follows:

```
db.logdata.find({ "http_response_code":"200", "http_vers":"HTTP/1.1" })
```

A query document is passed as an argument to the `find` method again. However, the pattern now includes two attributes instead of one.

To get all log file records where the `user_agent` was a Baidu search engine spider, you can query like so:

```
db.logdata.find({ "user_agent": /baidu/i })
```

If you look at the syntax carefully, you will notice that the query document actually contains a regular expression and not an exact value. The expression `/baidu/i` matches any document that has `baidu` in the `user_agent` value. The `i` flag suggests ignoring case, so all phrases whether `baidu`, `Baidu`, `baiDU`, or `BAIDU` would be matched. To get all log file records where `user_agent` starts with Mozilla, you can query as shown:

```
db.logdata.find({ "user_agent": /^Mozilla/ })
```

The possibility of using a regular expression for a query document pattern allows for innumerable possibilities and puts a lot of power in the hands of the user. However, as the cliché goes: with power comes responsibility. Therefore, use regular expressions to get the required subset but be aware that complex regular expressions could lead to expensive and complete scans, which for large data sets could be big trouble.

For fields that hold numeric values, comparison operators like greater than, greater than or equal to, less than, and less than or equal to also work. To get all log file records where response size is greater than 1111 k, you could query like so:

```
db.logdata.find({ "http_response_size" : { $gt : 1111 }})
```

Now that you have seen a few examples of restricting results to a subset, let's cut down the number of fields to just one attribute or field: `url`. You can query the `logdata` collection to get a list of all URLs accessed by the MSN bot as shown:

```
db.logdata.find({ "user_agent":/msn/i }, { "url":true })
```

In addition, you could simply choose to restrict the number of rows returned in the last query to 10 as follows:

```
db.logdata.find({ "user_agent":/msn/i }, { "url":true }).limit(10)
```

Sometimes, all you need to know is the number of matches and not the entire documents. To find out the number of request from the MSN bot, you query the `logdata` collection like this:

```
db.logdata.find({ "user_agent":/msn/i }).count()
```

Although a lot more can be explained about the intricacies of advanced queries in MongoDB, I will leave that discussion for chapter 6, which covers advanced queries. Next, let's turn to an alternate NoSQL store, Redis, to hold some data for us.

Storing Data In and Accessing Data from Redis

Redis is a persistent key/value store. For efficiency it holds the database in memory and writes to disks in an asynchronous thread. The values it holds can be strings, lists, hashes, sets, and sorted sets. It provides a rich set of commands to manipulate its collections and insert and fetch data.

If you haven't already, install and set up Redis. Refer to Appendix A for help setting up Redis.

To explain Redis, I rely on the Redis command-line client (`redis-cli`) — and a simple use case that involves a categorized list of books.

To begin, start `redis-cli` and make sure it's working. First, go to the Redis distribution folder. Redis is distributed as source. You can extract it anywhere in the file system and compile the source. Once compiled executables are available in the distribution folder. On some operating systems, symbolic links to executables are created at locations, where executables are commonly found. On my system Redis is available within a folder named Redis-2.2.2, which corresponds to the latest release of Redis. Start the Redis server by using the `redis-server` command. To use the default configuration, run `./redis-server` from within the Redis distribution folder. Now run `redis-cli` to connect to this server. By default, the Redis server listens for connections on port 6379.

To save a key/value pair — `{ akey: "avalue" }` — simply type the following, from within the Redis distribution folder:

```
./redis-cli set akey "avalue"
```

If you see OK on the console in response to the command you just typed, then things look good. If not, go through the installation instructions and verify that the setup is correct. To confirm that `avalue` is stored for `akey`, simply get the value for `akey` like so:

```
./redis-cli get akey
```

You should see a `value` in response to this request.

UNDERSTANDING THE REDIS EXAMPLE

In this Redis example, a database stores a list of book titles. Each book is tagged using an arbitrary set of tags. For example, I add "The Omnivore's Dilemma" by "Michael Pollan" to the list and tag it with the following: "organic," "industrialization," "local," "written by a journalist," "best seller," and "insight" or add "Outliers" by "Malcolm Gladwell" and tag it with the following: "insight," "best seller," and "written by a journalist." Now I can get all the books on my list or all the books "written by a journalist" or all those that relate to "organic." I could also get a list of the books by a given author. Querying will come in the next section, but for now storing the data appropriately is the focus.

 If you install Redis using `"make install"` *after compiling from source, the* `redis-server` *and* `redis-cli` *will be added to* `/usr/local/bin` *by default. If* `/usr/local/bin` *is added to the PATH environment variable you will be able to run* `redis-server` *and* `redis-cli` *from any directory.*

Redis supports a few different data structures, namely:

➤ **Lists, or more specifically, linked lists** — Collections that maintain an indexed list of elements in a particular order. With linked lists, access to either of the end points is fast irrespective of the number of elements in the list.

➤ **Sets** — Collections that store unique elements and are unordered.

➤ **Sorted sets** — Collections that store sorted sets of elements.

➤ **Hashes** — Collections that store key/value pairs.

➤ **Strings** — Collections of characters.

For the example at hand, I chose to use a set, because order isn't important. I call my set `books`. Each book, which is a member of the set of books, has the following properties:

➤ Id

➤ Title

➤ Author

➤ Tags (a collection)

Each tag is identified with the help of the following properties:

➤ Id

➤ Name

Assuming the `redis-server` is running, open a `redis-cli` instance and input the following commands to create the first members of the set of books:

```
$ ./redis-cli incr next.books.id
(integer) 1
$ ./redis-cli sadd books:1:title "The Omnivore's Dilemma"
(integer) 1
$ ./redis-cli sadd books:1:author "Michael Pollan"
```

books_and_tags.txt

Redis offers a number of very useful commands, which are catalogued and defined at `http://redis.io/commands`. The first command in the previous code example generates a sequence number by incrementing the set member identifier to the next id. Because you have just started creating the set, the output of the increment is logically "1". The next two commands create a member of the set named `books`. The member is identified with the id value of 1, which was just generated. So far, the member itself has two properties — `title` and `author` — the values for which are strings. The `sadd` command adds a member to a set. Analogous functions exist for lists, hashes and sorted sets. The `lpush` and `rpush` commands for a list add an element to the head and the tail, respectively. The `zadd` command adds a member to a sorted set.

Next, add a bunch of tags to the member you added to the set named `books`. Here is how you do it:

Available for download on Wrox.com

```
$ ./redis-cli sadd books:1:tags 1
(integer) 1
$ ./redis-cli sadd books:1:tags 2
(integer) 1
$ ./redis-cli sadd books:1:tags 3
(integer) 1
$ ./redis-cli sadd books:1:tags 4
(integer) 1
$ ./redis-cli sadd books:1:tags 5
(integer) 1
$ ./redis-cli sadd books:1:tags 6
(integer) 1
```

books_and_tags.txt

A bunch of numeric tag identifiers have been added to the member identified by the id value of 1. The tags themselves have not been defined any more than having been assigned an id so far. It may be worthwhile to break down the constituents of `books:1:tags` a bit further and explain how the key naming systems work in Redis. Any string, except those containing whitespace and special characters, are good choices for a key in Redis. Avoid very long or short keys. Keys can be structured in a manner where a hierarchical relationship can be established and nesting of objects and their properties can be established. It is a suggested practice and convention to use a scheme like `object-type:id:field` for key names. Therefore, a key such as `books:1:tags` implies a tag collection for a member identified by the id 1 within a set named "books." Similarly, `books:1:title` means title field of a member, identified by an id value of 1, within the set of books.

After adding a bunch of tags to the first member of the set of books, you can define the tags themselves like so:

Available for download on Wrox.com

```
$ ./redis-cli sadd tag:1:name "organic"
(integer) 1
$ ./redis-cli sadd tag:2:name "industrialization"
(integer) 1
$ ./redis-cli sadd tag:3:name "local"
(integer) 1
$ ./redis-cli sadd tag:4:name "written by a journalist"
(integer) 1
$ ./redis-cli sadd tag:5:name "best seller"
(integer) 1
$ ./redis-cli sadd tag:6:name "insight"
(integer) 1
```

books_and_tags.txt

With tags defined, you establish the reciprocal relationship to associate books that have the particular tags. The first member has all six tags so you add it to each of the tags as follows:

```
$ ./redis-cli sadd tag:1:books 1
(integer) 1
$ ./redis-cli sadd tag:2:books 1
(integer) 1
$ ./redis-cli sadd tag:3:books 1
(integer) 1
$ ./redis-cli sadd tag:4:books 1
(integer) 1
$ ./redis-cli sadd tag:5:books 1
(integer) 1
$ ./redis-cli sadd tag:6:books 1
(integer) 1
```

books_and_tags.txt

After the cross-relationships are established, you would create a second member of the set like so:

```
$ ./redis-cli incr next.books.id
(integer) 2
$ ./redis-cli sadd books:2:title "Outliers"
(integer) 1
$ ./redis-cli sadd books:2:author "Malcolm Gladwell"
(integer) 1
```

books_and_tags.txt

The `incr` function is used to generate the id for the second member of the set. Functions like `incrby`, which allows increment by a defined step; `decr`, which allows you to decrement; and `decrby`, which allows you to decrement by a defined step, are also available as useful utility functions whenever sequence number generation is required. You can choose the appropriate function and define the step as required. For now `incr` does the job.

Next, you add the tags for the second member and establish the reverse relationships to the tags themselves as follows:

```
$ ./redis-cli sadd books:2:tags 6
(integer) 1
$ ./redis-cli sadd books:2:tags 5
(integer) 1
$ ./redis-cli sadd books:2:tags 4
(integer) 1
$ ./redis-cli sadd tag:4:books 2
(integer) 1
$ ./redis-cli sadd tag:5:books 2
(integer) 1
$ ./redis-cli sadd tag:6:books 2
(integer) 1
```

books_and_tags.txt

That creates the rudimentary but useful enough set of the two members. Next, you look at how to query this set.

Querying Redis

Continuing with the `redis-cli` session, you can first list the title and author of member 1, identified by the id 1, of the set of books as follows:

```
$ ./redis-cli smembers books:1:title
1. "The Omnivore\xe2\x80\x99s Dilemma"
$ ./redis-cli smembers books:1:author
1. "Michael Pollan"
```

books_and_tags.txt

The special characters in the title string represent the apostrophe that was introduced in the string value.

You can list all the tags for this book like so:

```
$ ./redis-cli smembers books:1:tags
1. "4"
2. "1"
3. "2"
4. "3"
5. "5"
6. "6"
```

books_and_tags.txt

Notice that the list of tag ids is not ordered in the same way as they were entered. This is because sets have no sense of order within their members. If you need an ordered set, use a sorted set instead of a set.

Similarly, you can list title, author, and tags of the second book, identified by the id 2, like so:

```
$ ./redis-cli smembers books:2:title
1. "Outliers"
$ ./redis-cli smembers books:2:author
1. "Malcolm Gladwell"
$ ./redis-cli smembers books:2:tags
1. "4"
2. "5"
3. "6"
```

books_and_tags.txt

Now, viewing the set from the tags standpoint you can list all books that have the tag, identified by id 1 as follows:

```
$ ./redis-cli smembers tag:1:books
"1"
```

Tag 1 was identified by the name `organic` and you can query that like so:

```
$ ./redis-cli smembers tag:1:name
"organic"
```

Some tags like tag 6, identified by the name `insight`, have been attached to both the books in the set. You can confirm that by querying the set of books that have tag 6 like so:

```
$ ./redis-cli smembers tag:6:books
1. "1"
2. "2"
```

Next, you can list the books that have both tags 1 and 6, like so:

```
$ ./redis-cli sinter tag:1:books tag:6:books
"1"
```

The `sinter` command allows you to query for the intersection of two or more sets. If the word "intersection" has befuddled you, then review the Venn diagram in Figure 3-2 to set things back to normal.

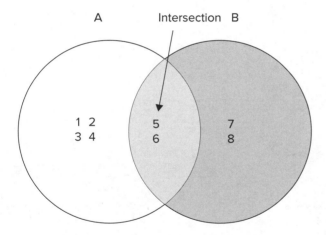

5 and 6 belong to both sets A and B

FIGURE 3-2

You know both books 1 and 2 have tags 5 and 6, so a `sinter` between the books of tags 5 and 6 should list both books. You can run the `sinter` command to confirm this. The command and output are as follows:

```
$ ./redis-cli sinter tag:5:books tag:6:books
1. "1"
2. "2"
```

Like set intersection, you can also query for set union and difference. Figures 3-3 and 3-4 demonstrate what set union and difference imply.

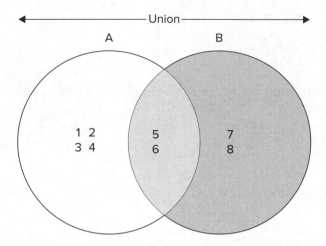

1, 2, 3, 4, 5, 6, 7, and 8 (all members in both A and B)
belong to the union of sets A and B

FIGURE 3-3

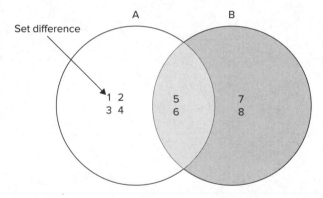

The difference A-B contains members that belong to A but not B.
Thus, A-B contains 1, 2, 3 and 4.

FIGURE 3-4

To create a union of all members that contain tags 1 and 6, you can use the following command:

```
$ ./redis-cli sunion tag:1:books tag:6:books
1. "1"
2. "2"
```

Both books 1 and 2 contain tags 5 and 6, so a difference set operation between books which have tag 5 and those that have tag 6 should be an empty set. Let's see if it's the case

```
$ ./redis-cli sdiff tag:5:books tag:6:books
(empty list or set)
```

Aren't all these commands useful for some quick queries? As mentioned earlier, Redis has a rich set of commands for string values, lists, hashes, and sorted sets as well. However, I will skip those details for now and move on to another NoSQL store. Details of each of these Redis commands are covered in context later in this book.

Storing Data In and Accessing Data from HBase

HBase could very well be considered the NoSQL flag bearer. It's an open-source implementation of the Google Bigtable, which you can read more about at `http://labs.google.com/papers/bigtable.html`. While key/value stores and non-relational alternatives like object databases have existed for a while, HBase and its associated Hadoop tools were the first piece of software to bring the relevance of large-scale Google-type NoSQL success catalysts in the hands of the masses.

HBase is not the only Google Bigtable clone. Hypertable is another one. HBase is also not the ideal tabular data store for all situations. There are eventually consistent data stores like Apache Cassandra and more that have additional features beyond those HBase provides. Before exploring where HBase is relevant and where it's not, let's first get familiar with the essentials of data store and querying in HBase. The relevance of HBase and other tabular databases is discussed later in this book.

As with the earlier two NoSQL data stores, I explain the HBase fundamentals with the help of an example and leave the more detailed architectural discussion for Chapter 4. The focus here is on data storage and access. For this section, I cook up a hypothetical example of a feed of blog posts, where you can extract and save the following pieces of information:

- ➤ Blog post title
- ➤ Blog post author
- ➤ Blog post content or body
- ➤ Blog post header multimedia (for example, an image)
- ➤ Blog post body multimedia (for example, an image, a video, or an audio file)

To store this data, I intend to create a collection named `blogposts` and save pieces of information into two categories, `post` and `multimedia`. So, a possible entry, in JSON-like format, could be as follows:

Available for download on Wrox.com

```
{
    "post" : {
        "title": "an interesting blog post",
        "author": "a blogger",
        "body": "interesting content",
    },
    "multimedia": {
        "header": header.png,
        "body": body.mpeg,
    },
}
```

blogposts.txt

or could be like so:

```
{
    "post" : {
        "title": "yet an interesting blog post",
        "author": "another blogger",
        "body": "interesting content",
    },
    "multimedia": {
        "body-image": body_image.png,
        "body-video": body_video.mpeg,
    },
}
```

blogposts.txt

Now if you look at the two sample data sets carefully you will notice that they both share the post and multimedia categories, but don't necessarily have the same set of fields. Stated another way, their columns differ. In HBase jargon it means they have the same column-families — post and multimedia — but don't have the same set of columns. Effectively, there are four columns within the multimedia column-family, namely, header, body, body-image, and body-video, and in some data points these columns have no value (null). In a traditional relational database you would have to create all four columns and set a few values to null as required. In HBase and column databases the data is stored by column and it doesn't need to store values when they are null. Thus, these are great for sparse data sets.

To create this data set and save two data points, first start an HBase instance and connect to it using the HBase shell. HBase runs in a distributed environment where it uses a special filesystem abstraction to save data across multiple machines. In this simple case, though, I run HBase in a standalone and single-instance environment. If you have downloaded and extracted the latest HBase release distribution, start the default single-instance server by running bin/start-hbase.sh.

After the server is up and running, connect to the HBase local server by starting the shell like so:

```
bin/hbase shell
```

When connected, create the HBase collection blogposts with its two column-families, post and multimedia, as follows:

```
$ bin/hbase shell
HBase Shell; enter 'help<RETURN>' for list of supported commands.
Type "exit<RETURN>" to leave the HBase Shell
Version 0.90.1, r1070708, Mon Feb 14 16:56:17 PST 2011

hbase(main):001:0> create 'blogposts', 'post', 'multimedia'
0 row(s) in 1.7880 seconds
```

Populate the two data points like so:

```
hbase(main):001:0> put 'blogposts', 'post1', 'post:title',
hbase(main):002:0* 'an interesting blog post'
```

```
0 row(s) in 0.5570 seconds


hbase(main):003:0> put 'blogposts', 'post1', 'post:author', 'a blogger'
0 row(s) in 0.0400 seconds

hbase(main):004:0> put 'blogposts', 'post1', 'post:body', 'interesting content'
0 row(s) in 0.0240 seconds

hbase(main):005:0> put 'blogposts', 'post1', 'multimedia:header', 'header.png'
0 row(s) in 0.0250 seconds

hbase(main):006:0> put 'blogposts', 'post1', 'multimedia:body', 'body.png'
0 row(s) in 0.0310 seconds

hbase(main):012:0> put 'blogposts', 'post2', 'post:title',
hbase(main):013:0* 'yet an interesting blog post'
0 row(s) in 0.0320 seconds

hbase(main):014:0> put 'blogposts', 'post2', 'post:title',
hbase(main):015:0* 'yet another blog post'
0 row(s) in 0.0350 seconds

hbase(main):016:0> put 'blogposts', 'post2', 'post:author', 'another blogger'
0 row(s) in 0.0250 seconds

hbase(main):017:0> put 'blogposts', 'post2', 'post:author', 'another blogger'
0 row(s) in 0.0290 seconds

hbase(main):018:0> put 'blogposts', 'post2', 'post:author', 'another blogger'
0 row(s) in 0.0400 seconds

hbase(main):019:0> put 'blogposts', 'post2', 'multimedia:body-image',
hbase(main):020:0* 'body_image.png'
0 row(s) in 0.0440 seconds

hbase(main):021:0> put 'blogposts', 'post2', 'post:body', 'interesting content'
0 row(s) in 0.0300 seconds

hbase(main):022:0> put 'blogposts', 'post2', 'multimedia:body-video',
hbase(main):023:0* 'body_video.mpeg'
0 row(s) in 0.0380 seconds
```

The two sample data points are given ids of post1 and post2, respectively. If you notice, I made a mistake while entering the title for post2 so I reentered it. I also reentered the same author information three items for post2. In the relational world, this would imply a data update. In HBase, though, records are immutable. Reentering data leads to creation of a newer version of the data set. This has two benefits: the atomicity conflicts for data update are avoided and an implicit built-in versioning system is available in the data store.

Now that the data is stored, you are ready to write a couple of elementary queries to retrieve it.

Querying HBase

The simplest way to query an HBase store is via its shell. If you are logged in to the shell already — meaning you have started it using `bin/hbase shell` and connected to the same local store where you just entered some data — you may be ready to query for that data.

To get all data pertaining to `post1`, simply query like so:

```
hbase(main):024:0> get 'blogposts', 'post1'
COLUMN                                      CELL
multimedia:body                             timestamp=1302059666802,
value=body.png
multimedia:header                           timestamp=1302059638880,
value=header.png
post:author                                 timestamp=1302059570361,
value=a blogger
post:body                                   timestamp=1302059604738,
value=interesting content
post:title                                  timestamp=1302059434638,
value=an interesting blog post
5 row(s) in 0.1080 seconds
```

blogposts.txt

This shows all the `post1` attributes and their values. To get all data pertaining to `post2`, simply query like so:

```
hbase(main):025:0> get 'blogposts', 'post2'
COLUMN                                      CELL
multimedia:body-image                       timestamp=1302059995926,
value=body_image.png
multimedia:body-video                       timestamp=1302060050405,
value=body_video.mpeg
post:author                                 timestamp=1302059954733,
value=another blogger
post:body                                   timestamp=1302060008837,
value=interesting content
post:title                                  timestamp=1302059851203,
value=yet another blog post
5 row(s) in 0.0760 seconds
```

blogposts.txt

To get a filtered list containing only the title column for `post1`, query like so:

```
hbase(main):026:0> get 'blogposts', 'post1', { COLUMN=>'post:title' }
COLUMN                                      CELL
post:title                                  timestamp=1302059434638,
value=an interesting blog post
1 row(s) in 0.0480 seconds
```

blogposts.txt

You may recall I reentered data for the `post2` title, so you could query for both versions like so:

```
hbase(main):027:0> get 'blogposts', 'post2', { COLUMN=>'post:title', VERSIONS=>2 }
COLUMN                                    CELL
post:title                                timestamp=1302059851203,
value=yet another blog post
post:title                                timestamp=1302059819904,
value=yet an interesting blog post
2 row(s) in 0.0440 seconds
```

blogposts.txt

By default, HBase returns only the latest version but you can always ask for multiple versions or get an explicit older version if you like.

With these simple queries working, let's move on to the last example data store, Apache Cassandra.

Storing Data In and Accessing Data from Apache Cassandra

In this section, I reuse the `blogposts` example from the previous section to show some of the fundamental features of Apache Cassandra. In the preceding chapter, you had a first feel of Apache Cassandra; now you will build on that and get familiar with more of its features.

To get started, go to the Apache Cassandra installation folder and start the server in the foreground by running the following command:

```
bin/cassandra -f
```

When the server starts up, run the `cassandra-cli` or command-line client like so:

```
bin/cassandra-cli -host localhost -port 9160
```

Now query for available keyspaces like so:

```
show keyspaces;
```

You will see the system and any additional keyspaces that you may have created. In the previous chapter, you created a sample keyspace called `CarDataStore`. For this example, create a new keyspace called `BlogPosts` with the help of the following script:

```
/*schema-blogposts.txt*/

create keyspace BlogPosts
    with replication_factor = 1
    and placement_strategy = 'org.apache.cassandra.locator.SimpleStrategy';

use BlogPosts;

create column family post
    with comparator = UTF8Type
```

```
        and read_repair_chance = 0.1
        and keys_cached = 100
        and gc_grace = 0
        and min_compaction_threshold = 5
        and max_compaction_threshold = 31;

    create column family multimedia
        with comparator = UTF8Type
        and read_repair_chance = 0.1
        and keys_cached = 100
        and gc_grace = 0
        and min_compaction_threshold = 5
        and max_compaction_threshold = 31;
```

schema-blogposts.txt

Next, add the blog post sample data points like so:

```
Cassandra> use BlogPosts;
Authenticated to keyspace: BlogPosts
cassandra> set post['post1']['title'] = 'an interesting blog post';
Value inserted.
cassandra> set post['post1']['author'] = 'a blogger';
Value inserted.
cassandra> set post['post1']['body'] = 'interesting content';
Value inserted.
cassandra> set multimedia['post1']['header'] = 'header.png';
Value inserted.
cassandra> set multimedia['post1']['body'] = 'body.mpeg';
Value inserted.
cassandra> set post['post2']['title'] = 'yet an interesting blog post';
Value inserted.
cassandra> set post['post2']['author'] = 'another blogger';
Value inserted.
cassandra> set post['post2']['body'] = 'interesting content';
Value inserted.
cassandra> set multimedia['post2']['body-image'] = 'body_image.png';
Value inserted.
cassandra> set multimedia['post2']['body-video'] = 'body_video.mpeg';
Value inserted.
```

cassandra_blogposts.txt

That's about it. The example is ready. Next you query the BlogPosts keyspace for data.

Querying Apache Cassandra

Assuming you are still logged in to the cassandra-cli session and the BlogPosts keyspace is in use, you can query for Post1 data like so:

```
get post['post1'];
=> (column=author, value=6120626c6f67676572, timestamp=1302061955309000)
=> (column=body, value=696e746572657374696e6720636f6e74656e74,
     timestamp=1302062452072000)
=> (column=title, value=616e20696e746572657374696e6720626c6f6720706f7374,
     timestamp=1302061834881000)
Returned 3 results.
```

cassandra_blogposts.txt

You could also query for a specific column like `body-video` for a post, say `post2`, within the multimedia column-family. The query and output would be as follows:

```
get multimedia['post2']['body-video'];
=> (column=body-video, value=626f64795f766964656f2e6d706567,
     timestamp=1302062623668000)
```

cassandra_blogposts.txt

LANGUAGE BINDINGS FOR NOSQL DATA STORES

Although the command-line client is a convenient way to access and query a NoSQL data store quickly, you probably want a programming language interface to work with NoSQL in a real application. As the types and flavors of NoSQL data stores vary, so do the types of programming interfaces and drivers. In general, though, there exists enough support for accessing NoSQL stores from popular high-level programming languages like Python, Ruby, Java, and PHP. In this section you look at the wonderful code generator Thrift and a few select language-specific drivers and libraries. Again, the intent is not to provide exhaustive coverage but more to establish the fundamental ways of interfacing NoSQL from your favorite programming language.

Being Agnostic with Thrift

Apache Thrift is an open-source cross-language services development framework. It's a code-generator engine to create services to interface with a variety of different programming languages. Thrift originated in Facebook and was open sourced thereafter.

Thrift itself is written in C. To build, install, use, and run Thrift follow these steps:

1. Download Thrift from `http://incubator.apache.org/thrift/download/`.
2. Extract the source distribution.
3. Build and install Thrift following the familiar configure, make, and make install routine.
4. Write a Thrift services definition. This is the most important part of Thrift. It's the underlying definition that generates code.
5. Use the Thrift compiler to generate the source for a particular language.

This gets things ready. Next, run the Thrift server and then use a Thrift client to connect to the server.

You may not need to generate Thrift clients for a NoSQL store like Apache Cassandra that supports Thrift bindings but may be able to use a language-specific client instead. The language-specific client in turn leverages Thrift. The next few sections explore language bindings for a few specific data stores.

Language Bindings for Java

Java is a ubiquitous programming language. It may have lost some of its glory but it certainly hasn't lost its popularity or pervasiveness. In this section I explain a bit about the Java drivers and libraries for MongoDB and HBase.

The makers of MongoDB officially support a Java driver. You can download and learn more about the MongoDB Java driver at www.mongodb.org/display/DOCS/Java+Language+Center. It is distributed as a single JAR file and its most recent version is 2.5.2. After you have downloaded the JAR, just add it to your application classpath and you should be good to go.

A `logdata` collection was created in a MongoDB instance earlier in this chapter. Use the Java driver to connect to that database and list out all the elements of that collection. Walk through the code in Listing 3-2 to see how it's done.

LISTING 3-2: Java program to list all elements of the logdata MongoDB collection

```java
import com.mongodb.DB;
import com.mongodb.DBCollection;
import com.mongodb.DBCursor;
import com.mongodb.Mongo;

public class JavaMongoDBClient {

    Mongo m;
    DB db;
    DBCollection coll;

    public void init() throws Exception {
        m = new Mongo( "localhost" , 27017 );
        db = m.getDB( "mydb" );
        coll = db.getCollection("logdata");
    }

    public void getLogData() {
        DBCursor cur = coll.find();

        while(cur.hasNext()) {
            System.out.println(cur.next());
        }
    }

    public static void main(String[] args) {
```

```
        try{
            JavaMongoDBClient javaMongoDBClient = new JavaMongoDBClient();
            javaMongoDBClient.init();
            javaMongoDBClient.getLogData();

        } catch(Exception e) {
            e.printStackTrace();
        }

    }

}
```

javaMongoDBClient.java

With this example, it's clear that interfacing from Java is easy and convenient. Isn't it?

Let's move on to HBase. To query the `blogposts` collection you created in HBase, first get the following JAR files and add them to your classpath:

➤   `commons-logging-1.1.1.jar`

➤   `hadoop-core-0.20-append-r1056497.jar`

➤   `hbase-0.90.1.jar`

➤   `log4j-1.2.16.jar`

To list the title and author of `post1` in the `blogposts` data store, use the program in Listing 3-3.

LISTING 3-3: Java program to connect and query HBase

Available for
download on
Wrox.com

```
import org.apache.hadoop.hbase.client.HTable;
import org.apache.hadoop.hbase.HBaseConfiguration;
import org.apache.hadoop.hbase.io.RowResult;

import java.util.HashMap;
import java.util.Map;
import java.io.IOException;

public class HBaseConnector {

public static Map retrievePost(String postId) throws IOException {
HTable table = new HTable(new HBaseConfiguration(), "blogposts");
Map post = new HashMap();

RowResult result = table.getRow(postId);

for (byte[] column : result.keySet()) {
post.put(new String(column), new String(result.get(column).getValue()));
}
return post;
```

continues

LISTING 3-3 *(continued)*

```
}

public static void main(String[] args) throws IOException {
Map blogpost = HBaseConnector.retrievePost("post1");
System.out.println(blogpost.get("post:title"));
System.out.println(blogpost.get("post:author"));
}
}
```

HBaseConnector.java

Now that you have seen a couple of Java code samples, let's move on to the next programming language: Python.

Language Bindings for Python

You have already had a taste of Python in the original illustration of the sample log data example in relation to MongoDB. Now you see another example of Python's usage. This time, Python interacts with Apache Cassandra using Pycassa.

First, get Pycassa from `http://github.com/pycassa/pycassa` and then install it within your local Python installation. Once installed import Pycassa like so:

```
import pycassa
```

Then, connect to the local Cassandra server, which you must remember to start. You connect to the server like so:

```
connection = pycassa.connect('BlogPosts')
```

Once connected, get the `post` column-family like so:

```
column_family = pycassa.ColumnFamily(connection, 'post')
```

Now you can get the data in all the columns of the column-family with the help of a call to the `get()` method as follows:

```
column_family.get()
```

You can restrict the output to only a select few columns by passing in the row key as an argument to the `get` method.

Language Bindings for Ruby

For Ruby, I will pick up the Redis client as an example. The Redis data set contains books and tags, associated with the books. First, clone the `redis-rb git` repository and build `redis-rb` as follows:

```
git clone git://github.com/ezmobius/redis-rb.git
cd redis-rb/
rake redis:install
rake dtach:install
rake redis:start &
rake install
```

Alternatively, just install Redis gem as follows:

```
sudo gem install redis
```

Once `redis-rb` is installed, open an irb (interactive ruby console) session and connect and query Redis.

First, import rubygems and Redis using the `require` command like so:

```
irb(main):001:0> require 'rubygems'
=> true
irb(main):002:0> require 'redis'
=> true
```

Next, make sure the Redis server is running and then connect to it by simply instantiating Redis like so:

```
irb(main):004:0> r = Redis.new
=> #<Redis client v2.2.0 connected to redis://127.0.0.1:6379/0 (Redis v2.2.2)>
```

Next, you can list all the tags for the first book, with id 1, in the `books` collection like so:

```
irb(main):006:0> r.smembers('books:1:tags')
=> ["3", "4", "5", "6", "1", "2"]
```

You can also list the books that have both tags 5 and 6 (refer to the example earlier in this chapter), like so:

```
irb(main):007:0> r.sinter('tag:5:books', 'tag:6:books')
=> ["1", "2"]
```

You can run many more advanced queries but for now you should be convinced that it's really easy to do so. The final example is in PHP.

Language Bindings for PHP

Like Pycassa, which provides a Python wrapper on top of Thrift, phpcassa provides a PHP wrapper on top of the Thrift bindings. You can download phpcassa from `http://github .com/hoan/phpcassa`.

With phpcassa, querying for all columns from the post column-family in the `BlogPosts` collection is just a few lines of code like so:

```php
<?php  // Copy all the files in this repository to your include directory.
$GLOBALS['THRIFT_ROOT'] = dirname(__FILE__) . '/include/thrift/';
require_once $GLOBALS['THRIFT_ROOT'].'/packages/cassandra/Cassandra.php';
require_once $GLOBALS['THRIFT_ROOT'].'/transport/TSocket.php';
require_once $GLOBALS['THRIFT_ROOT'].'/protocol/TBinaryProtocol.php';
require_once $GLOBALS['THRIFT_ROOT'].'/transport/TFramedTransport.php';
require_once $GLOBALS['THRIFT_ROOT'].'/transport/TBufferedTransport.php';
include_once(dirname(__FILE__) . '/include/phpcassa.php');
include_once(dirname(__FILE__) . '/include/uuid.php');

$posts = new CassandraCF('BlogPosts', 'post');
$posts ->get();
?>
```

phpcassa_example.php

With that small but elegant example, it is time to review what we covered and move on to learn more about the NoSQL schema possibilities.

SUMMARY

This chapter established the fundamental concepts of interacting with, accessing, and querying NoSQL stores. Four leading NoSQL stores, namely, MongoDB, Redis, HBase, and Apache Cassandra, were considered as representative examples. Interaction with these data stores was explained through simple examples, where hash-like structures or tabular data sets were stored.

Once the data was stored, ways of querying the store were explained. For the most part, initial examples used simple command-line clients. In the last few sections, language bindings and a few client libraries for Java, Python, Ruby, and PHP were explored. The coverage of these libraries was not exhaustive but it certainly was enough to not only get you started, but to do most of the basic operations. In the next chapter, you learn about the concepts and relevance of structure and metadata in NoSQL.

PART II
Learning the NoSQL Basics

Understanding the Storage Architecture

WHAT'S IN THIS CHAPTER?

➤ Introducing column-oriented database storage scheme

➤ Reviewing document store internals

➤ Peeking into key/value cache and key/value stores on disk

➤ Working with schemas that support eventual consistency of column-oriented data sets

Column-oriented databases are among the most popular types of non-relational databases. Made famous by the venerable Google engineering efforts and popularized by the growth of social networking giants like Facebook, LinkedIn, and Twitter, they could very rightly be called the flag bearers of the NoSQL revolution. Although column databases have existed in many forms in academia for the past few years, they were introduced to the developer community with the publication of the following Google research papers:

➤ **The Google File System** — http://labs.google.com/papers/gfs.html (October 2003)

➤ **MapReduce: Simplified Data Processing on Large Clusters** — http://labs.google .com/papers/mapreduce.html (December 2004)

➤ **Bigtable: A Distributed Storage System for Structured Data** — http://labs.google .com/papers/bigtable.html (November 2006)

These publications provided a view into the world of Google's search engine success and shed light on the mechanics of large-scale and big data efforts like Google Earth, Google Analytics, and Google Maps. It was established beyond a doubt that a cluster of inexpensive hardware can be leveraged to hold huge amounts data, way more than a single machine can hold, and be processed effectively and efficiently within a reasonable timeframe. Three key themes emerged:

➤ Data needs to be stored in a networked filesystem that can expand to multiple machines. Files themselves can be very large and be stored in multiple nodes, each running on a separate machine.

➤ Data needs to be stored in a structure that provides more flexibility than the traditional normalized relational database structures. The storage scheme needs to allow for effective storage of huge amounts of sparse data sets. It needs to accommodate for changing schemas without the necessity of altering the underlying tables.

➤ Data needs to be processed in a way that computations on it can be performed in isolated subsets of the data and then combined to generate the desired output. This would imply computational efficiency if algorithms run on the same locations where the data resides. It would also avoid large amounts of data transfer across the network for carrying out the computations on the humungous data set.

Building on these themes and the wisdom that Google shared, a number of open-source implementations spun off, creating a few compelling column-oriented database products. The most famous of these products that mirrors all the pieces of the Google infrastructure is Apache Hadoop. Between 2004 and 2006, Doug Cutting, creator of Lucene and Nutch, the open-source search engine software, initiated Hadoop in an attempt to solve his own scaling problems while building Nutch. Afterwards, Hadoop was bolstered with the help of Yahoo! engineers, a number of open-source contributors, and its early users, into becoming a serious production-ready platform. At the same time, the NoSQL movement was gathering momentum and a number of alternatives to Hadoop, including those that improved on the original model, emerged. Many of these alternatives did not reinvent the wheel as far as the networked filesystem or the processing methodology was concerned, but instead added features to the column data store. In the following section, I focus exclusively on the underpinning of these column-oriented databases.

 A brief history of Hadoop is documented in a presentation by Doug Cutting, available online at `http://research.yahoo.com/files/cutting.pdf`*.*

WORKING WITH COLUMN-ORIENTED DATABASES

Google's Bigtable and Apache HBase, part of Hadoop, are both column-oriented databases. So are Hypertable and Cloudata. Each of these data stores vary in a few ways but have common fundamental underpinnings. In this section, I explain the essential concepts that define them and make them what they are.

Current-generation developers are thoroughly ingrained in relational database systems. Taught in colleges, used on the job, and perpetually being talked and read about, the fundamental Relational Database Management System (RDBMS) concepts like entities and their relationships have become inseparable from the concept of a database. Therefore, I will start explaining column-oriented databases from the RDBMS viewpoint. This would make everyone comfortable and at home. Subsequently, I present the same story from an alternative viewpoint of maps, which are key/value pairs.

Using Tables and Columns in Relational Databases

In an RDBMS, attributes of an entity are stored in table columns. Columns are defined upfront and values are stored in all columns for all elements or rows in the table. See Figure 4-1 to reinforce what you probably already know well.

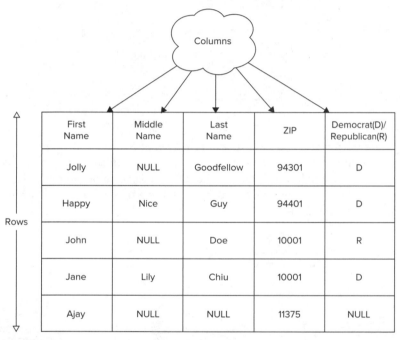

First Name	Middle Name	Last Name	ZIP	Democrat(D)/ Republican(R)
Jolly	NULL	Goodfellow	94301	D
Happy	Nice	Guy	94401	D
John	NULL	Doe	10001	R
Jane	Lily	Chiu	10001	D
Ajay	NULL	NULL	11375	NULL

FIGURE 4-1

This elementary example has five columns. When you store this table in an RDBMS, you define the data type for each column. For example, you would set the column that stores the first name to VARCHAR, or variable character type, and ZIP to integer (in the United States all ZIP codes are integers). You can have some cells, intersections of rows and columns, with nonexistent values (that is, NULL). For example, Jolly Goodfellow has no middle name and so the middle name column value for this person is NULL.

Typically, an RDBMS table has a few columns, sometimes tens of them. The table itself would hold at most a few thousand records. In special cases, millions of rows could potentially be held in a relational table but keeping such large amounts of data may bring the data access to a halt, unless special considerations like denormalization are applied.

As you begin to use your table to store and access data, you may need to alter it to hold a few additional attributes. Such attributes could be street address and food preferences. As newer records are stored, with values for these newer attributes, you may have null values for these attributes in the existing records. Also, as you keep greater variety of attributes the likelihood of sparse data sets — sets with null in many cells — becomes increasingly real. At some point, your table may look like the one in Figure 4-2.

First Name	Middle Name	Last Name	Street Address	ZIP	D/R	Veg/ Non-Veg

FIGURE 4-2

Now, consider that this data is evolving and you have to store each version of the cell value as it evolves. Think of it like a three-dimensional Excel spreadsheet, where the third dimension is time. Then the values as they evolve through time could be thought of as cell values in multiple spreadsheets put one behind the other in chronological order. Browse Figure 4-3 to wrap your head around the 3-D Excel spreadsheet abstraction.

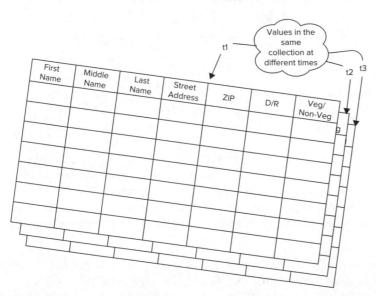

FIGURE 4-3

Although the example is extremely simple, you may have sensed that altering the table as data evolves, storing a lot of sparse cells, and working through value versions can get complex. Or more accurately, complex if dealt with the help of RDBMS! You have most likely experienced some of this in your own application.

Contrasting Column Databases with RDBMS

Next, column databases are introduced to model and store the same example. Because the example has been presented using RDBMS so far, understanding column databases in contrast to RDBMS clearly highlights its key features.

First and foremost, a column-oriented database imposes minimal need for upfront schema definition and can easily accommodate newer columns as the data evolves. In a typical column-oriented store, you predefine a column-family and not a column. A column-family is a set of columns grouped together into a bundle. Columns in a column-family are logically related to each other, although this not a requirement. Column-family members are physically stored together and typically a user benefits by clubbing together columns with similar access characteristics into the same family. Few if any theoretical limitations exist on the number of column-families you can define, but keeping them to a minimum can help keep the schema malleable. In the example at hand, defining three column-families, specifically name, location, and preferences, could be enough.

In a column database, a column-family is analogous to a column in an RDBMS. Both are typically defined before data is stored in tables and are fairly static in nature. Columns in RDBMS define the type of data they can store. Column-families have no such limitation; they can contain any number of columns, which can store any type of data, as far as they can be persisted as an array of bytes.

Each row of a column-oriented database table stores data values in only those columns for which it has valid values. Null values are not stored at all. At this stage, you may benefit from seeing Figure 4-4, where the current example is morphed to fit a column store model.

	name	location	preferences
	first name=>"...", last name=>"..."	zip=>"..."	d/r=>"...", veg/non-veg=>"..."

FIGURE 4-4

Apart from being friendly storage containers for sparse and malleable data sets, column databases also store multiple versions of each cell. Therefore, continuously evolving data in the current example would get stored in a column database as shown in Figure 4-5.

On physical stores, data isn't stored as a single table but is stored by column-families. Column databases are designed to scale and can easily accommodate millions of columns and billions of rows. Therefore, a single table often spans multiple machines. A row-key uniquely identifies a row in a column database. Rows are ordered and split into bundles, containing contiguous values, as data grows. Figure 4-6 is a closer depiction of how data is stored physically.

	time	name	location	preferences
	t9	first name=>"...", last name=>"..."	zip=>"..."	d/r=>"...", veg/non-veg=>"..."
	t8			
	t7			
	t5			

FIGURE 4-5

row-key	time	name
	t9	
	t8	
	t7	
	t5	

row-key	time	location
	t9	
	t8	

row-key	time	preferences
	t9	
	t7	

FIGURE 4-6

A typical column database is deployed in a cluster, although you can run it in a single node for development and experimental purposes. Each column database has its own idiosyncratic network topology and deployment architecture, but learning about any one of them in depth should provide a typical scenario.

 The HBase architecture is explained in a section titled, "HBase Distributed Storage Architecture," later in this chapter. In that section you learn more about a typical deployment layout.

Column Databases as Nested Maps of Key/Value Pairs

Although thinking of column databases as tables with special properties is easy to understand, it creates confusion. Often terms like columns and tables immediately conjure ideas of relational databases and lead you to planning the schema as such. This can be detrimental and often causes developers to relapse into using column databases like relational stores. That is certainly one design pitfall everyone needs to avoid. Always remember that using the right tool for the job is more important than the tool itself. If RDBMS is what you need, then just use it. However, if you are using a column database to scale out your huge data store, then work with it without any RDBMS baggage.

Oftentimes, it's easier to think of column databases as a set of nested maps. Maps or hash maps, which are also referred to as associative arrays, are pairs of keys and their corresponding values. Keys need to be unique to avoid collision and values can often be any array of bytes. Some maps can hold only string keys and values but most column databases don't have such a restriction.

It's not surprising that Google Bigtable, the original inspiration for current-generation column databases, is officially defined as a sparse, distributed, persistent, multidimensional, and sorted map.

 "Bigtable: A Distributed Storage System for Structured Data," Fay Chang, et al. OSDI 2006, `http://labs.google.com/papers/bigtable-osdi06.pdf` *in section 2, titled Data Model, defines Bigtable like so:*

"A Bigtable is a sparse, distributed, persistent multi-dimensional sorted map. The map is indexed by a row-key, column key, and a timestamp; each value in the map is an un-interpreted array of bytes."

Viewing the running example as a multidimensional nested map, you could create the first two levels of keys in JSON-like representation, like so:

```
{
  "row_key_1" : {
    "name" : {
    ...
    },
```

```
      "location" : {
      ...
      },
      "preferences" : {
      ...
      }
    },
    "row_key_2" : {
      "name" : {
      ...
      },
      "location" : {
      ...
      },
      "preferences" : {
      ...
      }
    },
    "row_key_3" : {
    ...
  }
```

The first-level key is the row-key that uniquely identifies a record in a column database. The second-level key is the column-family identifier. Three column-families — name, location, and preferences — were defined earlier. Those three appear as second-level keys. Going by the pattern, you may have guessed that the third-level key is the column identifier. Each row may have a different set of columns within a column-family, so the keys at level three may vary between any two data points in the multidimensional map. Adding the third level, the map is like so:

```
{
  "row_key_1" : {
    "name" : {
      "first_name" : "Jolly",
      "last_name" : "Goodfellow"
      }

      }
    },
    "location" : {
      "zip": "94301"
    },
    "preferences" : {
      "d/r" : "D"
    }
  },
  "row_key_2" : {
    "name" : {
      "first_name" : "Very",
      "middle_name" : "Happy",
      "last_name" : "Guy"
    },
    "location" : {
      "zip" : "10001"
```

```
    },
    "preferences" : {
      "v/nv": "V"
    }
  },
  ...
}
```

Finally, adding the version element to it, the third level can be expanded to include timestamped versions. To show this, the example uses arbitrary integers to represent timestamp-driven versions and concocts a tale that Jolly Goodfellow declared his democratic inclinations at time 1 and changed his political affiliation to the Republicans at time 5. The map for this row then appears like so:

```
{
  "row_key_1" : {
    "name" : {
      "first_name" : {
        1 : "Jolly"
      },
      "last_name" : {
        1 : "Goodfellow"
      }
    },
    "location" : {
      "zip": {
        1 : "94301"
      }
    },
    "preferences" : {
      "d/r" : {
        1 : "D",
        5 : "R"
      }
    }
  },
  ...
}
```

That limns a map-oriented picture of a column-oriented database. If the example isn't detailed enough for you, consider reading Jim Wilson's write-up titled, "Understanding HBase and Bigtable," accessible online at http://jimbojw.com/wiki/index.php?title=Understanding_Hbase_and_BigTable.

Laying out the Webtable

No discussion of column databases is complete without the quintessential example of a so-called Webtable that stores copies of crawled web pages. Such a table stores the contents of a web page in addition to attributes that relate to the page. Such attributes can be an anchor that references the page or the mime types that relate to the content. Google first introduced this example in its research paper on Bigtable. A Webtable uses a reversed web page URL as the row-key for a web page. Therefore, a URL `www.example.com` implies a row-key `com.example.www`. The row-key forms the premise of order for rows of data in a column-oriented database. Therefore, rows that relate to two subdomains of example.com, like `www.example.com` and `news.example.com`, are stored close to each other when reversed URL is used as a row-key. This makes querying for all content relating to a domain easier.

Typically, contents, anchors, and mime serve as column-families, which leads to a conceptual model that resembles the column-based table shown Figure 4-7.

row-key	time	contents	anchor	mime
com.cnn.www	t9		cnnsi.com	
	t8		my.look.ca	
	t6	"<html>..."	my.look.ca	"text/html"
	t5	"<html>..."		
	t3	"<html>..."		

FIGURE 4-7

Many popular open-source implementations of Bigtable include the Webtable as an example in their documentation. The HBase architecture wiki entry, at `http://wiki.apache.org/hadoop/Hbase/HbaseArchitecture`, talks about Webtable and so does the Hypertable data model documentation at `http://code.google.com/p/hypertable/wiki/ArchitecturalOverview#Data_Model`.

Now that you have a conceptual overview of column databases, it's time to peek under the hood of a prescribed HBase deployment and storage model. The distributed HBase deployment model is typical of many column-oriented databases and serves as a good starting point for understanding web scale database architecture.

HBASE DISTRIBUTED STORAGE ARCHITECTURE

A robust HBase architecture involves a few more parts than HBase alone. At the very least, an underlying distributed, centralized service for configuration and synchronization is involved. Figure 4-8 depicts an overview of the architecture.

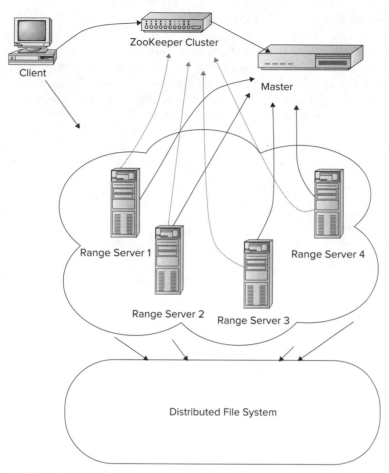

FIGURE 4-8

HBase deployment adheres to a master-worker pattern. Therefore, there is usually a master and a set of workers, commonly known as range servers. When HBase starts, the master allocates a set of ranges to a range server. Each range stores an ordered set of rows, where each row is identified by a unique row-key. As the number of rows stored in a range grows in size beyond a configured threshold, the range is split into two and rows are divided between the two new ranges.

Like most column-databases, HBase stores columns in a column-family together. Therefore, each region maintains a separate store for each column-family in every table. Each store in turn maps to a physical file that is stored in the underlying distributed filesystem. For each store, HBase abstracts access to the underlying filesystem with the help of a thin wrapper that acts as the intermediary between the store and the underlying physical file.

Each region has an in-memory store, or cache, and a write-ahead-log (WAL). To quote Wikipedia, `http://en.wikipedia.org/wiki/Write-ahead_logging`, "write-ahead logging (WAL) is a family of techniques for providing atomicity and durability (two of the ACID properties) in database systems." WAL is a common technique used across a variety of database systems, including the popular relational database systems like PostgreSQL and MySQL. In HBase a client program could decide to turn WAL on or switch it off. Switching it off would boost performance but reduce reliability and recovery, in case of failure. When data is written to a region, it's first written to the write-ahead-log, if enabled. Soon afterwards, it's written to the region's in-memory store. If the in-memory store is full, data is flushed to disk and persisted in the underlying distributed storage. See Figure 4-9, which recaps the core aspects of a region server and a region.

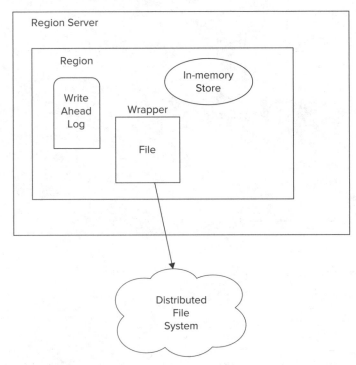

FIGURE 4-9

If a distributed filesystem like the Hadoop distributed filesystem (HDFS) is used, then a master-worker pattern extends to the underlying storage scheme as well. In HDFS, a namenode and a set of datanodes form a structure analogous to the configuration of master and range servers that column databases like HBase follow. Thus, in such a situation each physical storage file for an HBase column-family store ends up residing in an HDFS datanode. HBase leverages a filesystem API to avoid strong coupling with HDFS and so this API acts as the intermediary for conversations between an HBase store and a corresponding HDFS file. The API allows HBase to work seamlessly with other types of filesystems as well. For example, HBase could be used with CloudStore, formerly known as Kosmos FileSystem (KFS), instead of HDFS.

 Read more about CloudStore, formerly known as Kosmos FileSystem (KFS), at `http://kosmosfs.sourceforge.net/`.

In addition to having the distributed filesystem for storage, an HBase cluster also leverages an external configuration and coordination utility. In the seminal paper on Bigtable, Google named this configuration program Chubby. Hadoop, being a Google infrastructure clone, created an exact counterpart and called it ZooKeeper. Hypertable calls the similar infrastructure piece Hyperspace. A ZooKeeper cluster typically front-ends an HBase cluster for new clients and manages configuration.

To access HBase the first time, a client accesses two catalogs via ZooKeeper. These catalogs are named -ROOT- and .META. The catalogs maintain state and location information for all the regions. -ROOT- keeps information of all .META. tables and a .META. file keeps records for a user-space table, that is, the table that holds the data. When a client wants to access a specific row it first asks ZooKeeper for the -ROOT- catalog. The -ROOT- catalog locates the .META. catalog relevant for the row, which in turn provides all the region details for accessing the specific row. Using this information the row is accessed. The three-step process of accessing a row is not repeated the next time the client asks for the row data. Column databases rely heavily on caching all relevant information, from this three-step lookup process. This means clients directly contact the region servers the next time they need the row data. The long loop of lookups is repeated only if the region information in the cache is stale or the region is disabled and inaccessible.

Each region is often identified by the smallest row-key it stores, so looking up a row is usually as easy as verifying that the specific row-key is greater than or equal to the region identifier.

So far, the essential conceptual and physical models of column database storage have been introduced. The behind-the-scenes mechanics of data write and read into these stores have also been exposed. Advanced features and detailed nuances of column databases will be picked up again in the later chapters, but for now I shift focus to document stores.

DOCUMENT STORE INTERNALS

The previous couple of chapters have offered a user's view into a popular document store MongoDB. Now take the next step to peel the onion's skin.

MongoDB is a document store, where documents are grouped together into collections. Collections can be conceptually thought of as relational tables. However, collections don't impose the strict schema constraints that relational tables do. Arbitrary documents could be grouped together in a single collection. Documents in a collection should be similar, though, to facilitate effective indexing. Collections can be segregated using namespaces but down in the guts the representation isn't hierarchical.

Each document is stored in BSON format. BSON is a binary-encoded representation of a JSON-type document format where the structure is close to a nested set of key/value pairs. BSON is a superset of JSON and supports additional types like regular expression, binary data, and date. Each document has a unique identifier, which MongoDB can generate, if it is not explicitly specified when the data is inserted into a collection, like when auto-generated object ids are, as depicted in Figure 4-10.

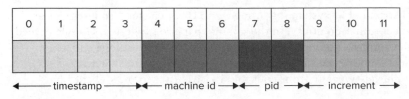

FIGURE 4-10

MongoDB drivers and clients serialize and de-serialize to and from BSON as they access BSON-encoded data. The MongoDB server, on the other hand, understands the BSON format and doesn't need the additional overhead of serialization. The binary representations are read in the same format as they are transferred across the wire. This provides a great performance boost.

IS BSON LIKE PROTOCOL BUFFERS?

Protocol buffers, sometimes also referred to as protobuf, is Google's way of encoding structured data for efficient transmission. Google uses it for all its internal Remote Procedure Calls (RPCs) and exchange formats. Protobuf is a structured format like XML but it's much lighter, faster, and more efficient. Protobuf is a language- and platform-neutral specification and encoding mechanism, which can be used with a variety of languages. Read more about protobuf at `http://code.google.com/p/protobuf/`.

BSON is similar to protobuf in that it is also a language- and platform-neutral encoding mechanism and format for data exchange and file format. However, BSON is more schema-less as compared to protobuf. Though less structure makes it more flexible, it also takes away some of the performance benefits of a defined schema. Although BSON exists in conjunction with MongoDB there is nothing stopping you from using the format outside of MongoDB. The BSON serialization features in MongoDB drivers can be leveraged outside of their primary role of interacting with a MongoDB server. Read more about BSON at `http://bsonspec.org/`.

High performance is an important philosophy that pervades much of MongoDB design. One such choice is demonstrated in the use of memory-mapped files for storage.

Storing Data in Memory-Mapped Files

A memory-mapped file is a segment of virtual memory that is assigned byte-for-byte to a file or a file-like resource that can be referenced through a file descriptor. This implies that applications can interact with such files as if they were parts of the primary memory. This obviously improves I/O performance as compared to usual disk read and write. Accessing and manipulating memory is much faster than making system calls. In addition, in many operating systems, like Linux, memory region mapped to a file is part of the buffer of disk-backed pages in RAM. This transparent buffer is commonly called page cache. It is implemented in the operating system's kernel.

MongoDB's strategy of using memory-mapped files for storage is a clever one but it has its ramifications. First, memory-mapped files imply that there is no separation between the operating system cache and the database cache. This means there is no cache redundancy either. Second, caching is controlled by the operating system, because virtual memory mapping does not work the same on all operating systems. This means cache-management policies that govern what is kept in cache and what is discarded also varies from one operating system to the other. Third, MongoDB can expand its database cache to use all available memory without any additional configuration. This means you could enhance MongoDB performance by throwing in a larger RAM and allocating a larger virtual memory.

Memory mapping also introduces a few limitations. For example, MongoDB's implementation restricts data size to a maximum of 2 GB on 32-bit systems. These restrictions don't apply to MongoDB running on 64-bit machines.

Database size isn't the only size limitation, though. Additional limitations govern the size of each document and the number of collections a MongoDB server can hold. A document can be no larger than 8 MiB, which obviously means using MongoDB to store large blobs is not appropriate. If storing large documents is absolutely necessary, then leverage the GridFS to store documents larger than 8 MiB. Furthermore, there is a limit on the number of namespaces that can be assigned in a database instance. The default number of namespaces supported is 24,000. Each collection and each index uses up a namespace. This means, by default, two indexes per collection would allow a maximum of 8,000 collections per database. Usually, such a large number is enough. However, if you need to, you can raise the namespace size beyond 24,000.

Increasing the namespace size has implications and limitations as well. Each collection namespace uses up a few kilobytes. In MongoDB, an index is implemented as a B-tree. Each B-tree page is 8 kB. Therefore, adding additional namespaces, whether for collections or indexes, implies adding a few kB for each additional instance. Namespaces for a MongoDB database named mydb are maintained in a file named `mydb.ns`. An `.ns` file like `mydb.ns` can grow up to a maximum size of 2 GB.

Because size limitations can restrict unbounded database growth, it's important to understand a few more behavioral patterns of collections and indexes.

Guidelines for Using Collections and Indexes in MongoDB

Although there is no formula to determine the optimal number of collections in a database, it's advisable to stay away from putting a lot of disparate data into a single collection. Mixing an eclectic bunch together creates complexities for indexes. A good rule of thumb is to ask yourself whether you often need to query across the varied data set. If your answer is yes you should keep the data together, otherwise portioning it into separate collections is more efficient.

Sometimes, a collection may grow indefinitely and threaten to hit the 2 GB database size limit. Then it may be worthwhile to use capped collections. Capped collections in MongoDB are like a stack that has a predefined size. When a capped collection hits its limit, old data records are deleted. Old records are identified on the basis of the Least Recently Used (LRU) algorithm. Document fetching in capped collection follows a Last-In-First-Out (LIFO) strategy.

Read more about the Least Recently Used (LRU) caching algorithm at
`http://en.wikipedia.org/wiki/Cache_algorithms#Least_Recently_Used`.

Its `_id` field indexes every MongoDB collection. Additionally, indexes can be defined on any other attributes of the document. When queried, documents in a collection are returned in natural order of their `_id` in the collection. Only capped collections use a LIFO-based order, that is, insertion order. Cursors return applicable data in batches, each restricted by a maximum size of 8 MiB. Updates to records are in-place.

MongoDB offers enhanced performance but it does so at the expense of reliability.

MongoDB Reliability and Durability

First and foremost, MongoDB does not always respect atomicity and does not define transactional integrity or isolation levels during concurrent operations. So it's possible for processes to step on each other's toes while updating a collection. Only a certain class of operations, called modifier operations, offers atomic consistency.

MongoDB defines a few modifier operations for atomic updates:

➤   `$inc` — *Increments the value of a given field*

➤   `$set` — *Sets the value for a field*

➤   `$unset` — *Deletes the field*

➤   `$push` — *Appends value to a field*

➤   `$pushAll` — *Appends each value in an array to a field*

➤   `$addToSet` — *Adds value to an array if it isn't there already*

➤   `$pop` — *Removes the last element in an array*

➤   `$pull` — *Removes all occurrences of values from a field*

➤   `$pullAll` — *Removes all occurrences of each value in an array from a field*

➤   `$rename` — *Renames a field*

The lack of isolation levels also sometimes leads to phantom reads. Cursors don't automatically get refreshed if the underlying data is modified.

By default, MongoDB flushes to disk once every minute. That's when the data inserts and updates are recorded on disk. Any failure between two synchronizations can lead to inconsistency. You can increase the sync frequency or force a flush to disk but all of that comes at the expense of some performance.

To avoid complete loss during a system failure, it's advisable to set up replication. Two MongoDB instances can be set up in a master-slave arrangement to replicate and keep the data in synch. Replication is an asynchronous process so changes aren't propagated as soon as they occur. However, it's better to have data replicated than not have any alternative at all. In the current versions of MongoDB, replica pairs of master and slave have been replaced with replica sets, where three replicas are in a set. One of the three assumes the role of master and the other two act as slaves. Replica sets allow automatic recovery and automatic failover.

Whereas replication is viewed more as a failover and disaster recovery plan, sharding could be leveraged for horizontal scaling.

Horizontal Scaling

One common reason for using MongoDB is its schema-less collections and the other is its inherent capacity to perform well and scale. In more recent versions, MongoDB supports auto-sharding for scaling horizontally with ease.

The fundamental concept of sharding is fairly similar to the idea of the column database's master-worker pattern where data is distributed across multiple range servers. MongoDB allows ordered collections to be saved across multiple machines. Each machine that saves part of the collection is then a shard. Shards are replicated to allow failover. So, a large collection could be split into four shards and each shard in turn may be replicated three times. This would create 12 units of a MongoDB server. The two additional copies of each shard serve as failover units.

Shards are at the collection level and not at the database level. Thus, one collection in a database may reside on a single node, whereas another in the same database may be sharded out to multiple nodes.

Each shard stores contiguous sets of the ordered documents. Such bundles are called chunks in MongoDB jargon. Each chunk is identified by three attributes, namely the first document key (min key), the last document key (max key), and the collection.

A collection can be sharded based on any valid shard key pattern. Any document field of a collection or a combination of two or more document fields in a collection can be used as the basis of a shard key. Shard keys also contain an order direction property in addition to the field to define a shard key. The order direction can be 1, meaning ascending or –1, meaning descending. It's important to choose the shard keys prudently and make sure those keys can partition the data in an evenly balanced manner.

All definitions about the shards and the chunks they maintain are kept in metadata catalogs in a config server. Like the shards themselves, config servers are also replicated to support failover.

Client processes reach out to a MongoDB cluster via a mongos process. A mongos process does not have a persistent state and pulls state from the config servers. There can be one or more mongos processes for a MongoDB cluster. Mongos processes have the responsibility of routing queries appropriately and combining results where required. A query to a MongoDB cluster can be targeted or can be global. All queries that can leverage the shard key on which the data is ordered typically are targeted queries and those that can't leverage the index are global. Targeted queries are more efficient than global queries. Think of global queries as those involving full collection scans.

Figure 4-11 depicts a sharding architecture topology for MongoDB.

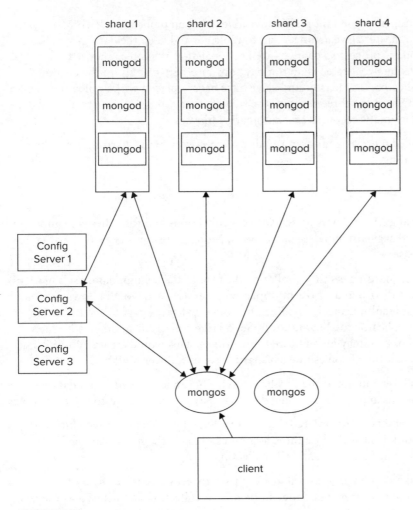

FIGURE 4-11

Next, I survey the storage schemes and nuances of a key/value store.

UNDERSTANDING KEY/VALUE STORES IN MEMCACHED AND REDIS

Though all key/value stores are not the same, they do have many things in common. For example, they all store data as maps. In this section I walk through the internals of Memcached and Redis to show what a robust key/value store is made up of.

Under the Hood of Memcached

Memcached, which you can download from `http://memcached.org`, is a distributed high-performance object-caching system. It's extremely popular and used by a number of high-traffic venues like Facebook, Twitter, Wikipedia, and YouTube. Memcached is extremely simple and has a bare minimum set of features. For example, there is no support for backup, failover, or recovery. It has a simple API and can be used with almost any web-programming language. The primary objective of using Memcached in an application stack is often to reduce database load. See Figure 4-12 to understand a possible configuration for Memcached in a typical web application.

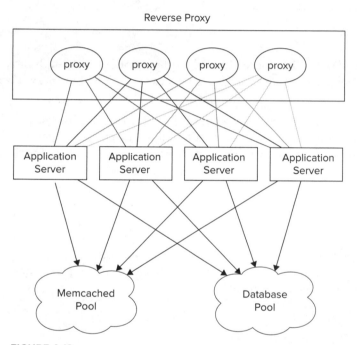

FIGURE 4-12

The heart of Memcached is a slab allocator. Memcached stores its values in a slab. A slab itself is composed of pages, which in turn are made up of chunks or buckets. The smallest size a slab can be is 1 kB and slab sizes grow at a power of 1.25. Therefore, slab sizes can be 1 kB (1.25 power 0), 1.25 kB (1.25 power 1), 1.5625 kB (1.25 power 2), and so on. Memcached can store data values up to a maximum of 1 MB in size. Values are stored and referenced by a key. A key can be up to 250 bytes in size. Each object is stored in a closest sized chunk or bucket. This means an object 1.4 kB in size would be stored in a chuck that is 1.5625 kB in size. This leads to wasted space, especially when objects are barely larger than the next smaller chunk size. By default, Memcached uses up all available memory and is limited only by the underlying architecture. Figure 4-13 illustrates some of the fundamental Memcached characteristics.

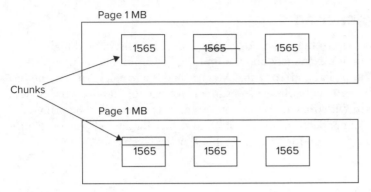

FIGURE 4-13

LRU algorithms govern the eviction of old cache objects. LRU algorithms work on a per-slab class basis. Fragmentation may occur as objects are stored and cleaned up. Reallocation of memory solves part of this problem.

Memcached is an object cache that doesn't organize data elements in collections, like lists, sets, sorted sets, or maps. Redis, on the other hand, provides support for all these rich data structures. Redis is similar to Memcached in approach but more robust. You have set up and interacted with Redis in the last couple of chapters.

Next, the innards of Redis are briefly explored.

Redis Internals

Everything in Redis is ultimately represented as a string. Even collections like lists, sets, sorted sets, and maps are composed of strings. Redis defines a special structure, which it calls simple dynamic string or SDS. This structure consists of three parts, namely:

➤ **buff** — A character array that stores the string

➤ **len** — A long type that stores the length of the buff array

➤ **free** — Number of additional bytes available for use

Although you may think of storing len separately as an overhead, because it can be easily calculated based on the buff array, it allows for string length lookup in fixed time.

Redis keeps its data set in the primary memory, persisting it to disk as required. Unlike MongoDB, it does not use memory-mapped files for that purpose. Instead, Redis implements its own virtual memory subsystem. When a value is swapped to disk, a pointer to that disk page is stored with the key. Read more about the virtual memory technical specification at `http://code.google .com/p/redis/wiki/VirtualMemorySpecification`.

In addition to the virtual memory manager, Redis also includes an event library that helps coordinate the non-blocking socket operations.

Figure 4-14 depicts an overview of the Redis architecture.

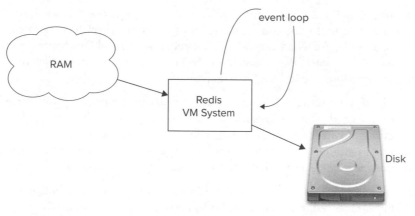

FIGURE 4-14

WHY DOESN'T REDIS RELY ON OPERATING SYSTEM VIRTUAL MEMORY SWAPPING?

Redis doesn't rely on operating system swapping because:

➤ Redis objects don't map one-to-one with swap pages. Swap pages are 4,096 bytes long and Redis objects could span more than one page. Similarly, more than one Redis object could be in a single swap page. Therefore, even when a small percentage of the Redis objects are accessed, it's possible a large number of swap pages are touched. Operating system swapping keeps track of swap page access. Therefore, even if a byte in a swap page is accessed it is left out by the swapping system.

➤ Unlike MongoDB, Redis data format when in RAM and in disk are not similar. Data on disk is compressed way more as compared to its RAM counterpart. Therefore, using custom swapping involves less disk I/O.

Salvatore Sanfillipo, the creator of Redis, talks about the Redis virtual memory system in his blog post titled, "Redis Virtual Memory: the story and the code," at `http://antirez.com/post/redis-virtual-memory-story.html`.

Next and last of all, attention is diverted back to column-oriented databases. However, this time it's a special class of column-oriented databases, those that are eventually consistent.

EVENTUALLY CONSISTENT NON-RELATIONAL DATABASES

Whereas Google's Bigtable serves as the inspiration for column databases, Amazon's Dynamo acts as the prototype for an eventually consistent store. The ideas behind Amazon Dynamo were presented in 2007 at the Symposium on Operating Systems Principles and were made available to the public via a technical paper, which is available online at `www.allthingsdistributed.com/files/amazon-dynamo-sosp2007.pdf`. In due course, the ideas of Dynamo where incorporated into open-source implementations like Apache Cassandra, Voldemort, Riak, and Dynomite. In this section the fundamental tenets of an eventually consistent key/value store are discussed. Specifics of any of the open-source implementations are left for later chapters.

Amazon Dynamo powers a lot of the internal Amazon services that drive its massive e-commerce system. This system has a few essential requirements like high availability and fault tolerance. However, data sets are structured such that query by primary keys is enough for most cases. Relational references and joins are not required. Dynamo is built on the ideas of consistent hashing, object versioning, gossip-based membership protocol, merkle trees, and hinted handoff.

Dynamo supports simple get-and-put-based interface to the data store. Put requests include data related to object version, which are stored in the context. Dynamo is built to incrementally scale as the data grows. Thus, it relies on consistent hashing for effective partitioning.

Consistent Hashing

Consistent hashing forms an important principle for distributed hash tables. In consistent hashing, addition or removal of a slot does not significantly change the mapping of keys to the slots. To appreciate this hashing scheme, let's first look at an elementary hashing scheme and understand the problems that show up as slots are added or removed.

A very rudimentary key allocation strategy among a set of nodes could involve the use of modulo function. So, 50 keys can be distributed among 7 nodes like so: key with value 85 goes to node 1 because 85 modulo 7 is 1 and key with value 18 goes to node 4 because 18 modulo 7 is 4, and so on for others. This strategy works well until the number of nodes changes, that is, newer ones get added or existing ones get removed. When the number of nodes changes, the modulo function applied to the existing keys produces a different output and leads to rearrangement of the keys among the nodes. This isn't that effective and that's when consistent hashing comes to the rescue.

In consistent hashing, the rearrangement of keys is not majorly affected when nodes are added or removed. A good way to explain consistent hashing is to draw out a circle and mark the nodes on it as shown in Figure 4-15.

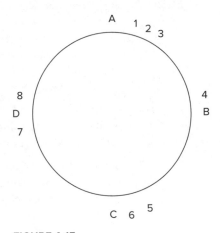

FIGURE 4-15

Now the keys themselves are assigned to the nodes that they are closest to. Which means in Figure 4-15, 1, 2, 3 get assigned to node A, 4 gets assigned to B, 5 and 6 get assigned to C, and 7 and 8 to D. In order to set up such a scheme, you may create a large hash space, say all the SHA1 keys up to a very large number, and map that onto a circle. Starting from 0 and going clockwise, you would map all values to a maximum, at which point you would restart at 0. The nodes would also be hashed and mapped on the same scheme.

Now say node A is removed and instead node E gets added at a new position as shown in Figure 4-16, then minimum rearrangement occurs. 1 goes to E and 2 and 3 get allocated to B but nothing else gets affected.

Whereas consistent hashing provides effective partitioning, object versioning helps keep the data consistent.

Object Versioning

In a large distributed and highly scalable system, ACID transactions impose a huge overhead. So Dynamo proposes object versioning and vector clocks for keeping consistency. Let's try to understand how a vector clock works with the help of an example.

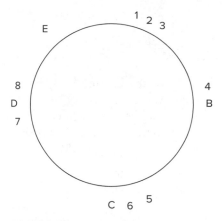

FIGURE 4-16

Let's consider that four hackers, Joe, Hillary, Eric, and Ajay, decide to meet to talk about vector clocks. Joe suggests they all meet up in Palo Alto. Then later, Hillary and Eric meet at work and decide that Mountain View may be the best place for the meeting. The same day, Eric and Ajay message each other and conclude that meeting at Los Altos may be the best idea. When the day of the meeting arrives, Joe e-mails everyone with a meet-up reminder and the venue address in Palo Alto. Hillary responds that the venue was changed to Mountain View and Ajay says it's Los Altos. Both claim that Eric knows of the decision. Now Eric is contacted to resolve the issue. At this stage you can create vector clocks to resolve the conflict.

A vector clock can be created for each of the three values for the venue, Palo Alto, Mountain View, and Los Altos, as follows:

```
Venue: Palo Alto
Vector Clock: Joe (ver 1)

Venue: Mountain View
Vector Clock: Joe (ver 1), Hillary (ver 1), Eric (ver 1)

Venue: Los Altos
Vector Clock: Joe (ver 1), Ajay (ver 1), Eric (ver 1)
```

The vector clocks for Mountain View and Los Altos include Joe's original choice because everyone was aware of it. The vector clock for Mountain View is based on Hillary's response, and the vector clock for Los Altos is based on Ajay's response. The Mountain View and Los Altos vector clocks are out of sync, because they don't descend from each other. A vector clock needs to have versions greater than or equal to all values in another vector clock to descend from it.

Finally, Joe gets hold of Eric on the phone and asks him to resolve the confusion. Eric realizes the problem and quickly decides that meeting in Mountain View is probably the best idea. Now Joe draws out the updated vector clocks as follows:

```
Venue: Palo Alto
Vector Clock: Joe (ver 1)

Venue: Mountain View
```

```
Vector Clock: Joe (ver 1), Hillary (ver 1), Ajay (ver 0), Eric (ver 2)

Venue: Los Altos
Vector Clock: Joe (ver 1), Hillary (ver 0), Ajay (ver 1), Eric (ver 1)
```

Version 0 is created for Hillary and Ajay in the vector clocks for the venues they had not suggested but are now aware of. Now, vector clocks descend from each other and Mountain View is the venue for the meet up. From the example, you would have observed that vector clocks not only help determine the order of the events but also help resolve any inconsistencies by identifying the root causes for those problems.

Apart from object versioning, Dynamo uses gossip-based membership for the nodes and uses hinted handoff for consistency.

Gossip-Based Membership and Hinted Handoff

A gossip protocol is a style of communication protocol inspired by the form of gossip or rumor in social networks and offices. A gossip communication protocol involves periodic, pair wise, inter-process interactions. Reliability is usually low and peer selection is often random.

In hinted handoff, instead of a full quorum during message write for durability, a relaxed quorum is allowed. Write is performed on the healthy nodes and hints are recorded to let the failed node know when it's up again.

SUMMARY

This chapter was a brief introduction to the basic principles of NoSQL databases. The essentials of data models, storage schemes, and configuration in some of the popular NoSQL stores were explained. Typical parts of column-oriented databases were presented and examples from HBase were used to illustrate some of the common underlying themes. Then the internals of both document databases and key/value stores were covered. Finally, eventually consistent databases were introduced.

5

Performing CRUD Operations

WHAT'S IN THIS CHAPTER?

➤ Describing create, read, update, and delete operations as they relate to data sets in a NoSQL database

➤ Explaining and illustrating the emphasis on create over update

➤ Exploring the atomicity and integrity of updates

➤ Explaining the ways of persisting related data

The set of essential operations — create, read, update, and delete, often popularly known as CRUD — are the fundamental ways of interacting with any data. So it's important to see how these operations apply to the world of NoSQL. As you know, NoSQL isn't a single product or technology, but an umbrella term for a category of databases; therefore, the implication of CRUD operations varies from one NoSQL product to the other. However, there is one predominant characteristic they all share: in NoSQL stores, the create and read operations are more important than the update and delete operations, so much so that sometimes those are the only operations. In the next few sections you learn what this implies. As the land of NoSQL is explored from the standpoint of the CRUD operations, it will be divided into subsets of column-oriented, document-centric, and key-value maps to keep the illustration within logical and related units.

The first pillar of CRUD is the create operation.

CREATING RECORDS

The record-creation operation hardly needs a definition. When you need a new record to be saved for the first time, you create a new entry. This means there should be a way to identify a record easily and find out if it already exists. If it does, you probably want to update the record and not re-create it.

In relational databases, records are stored within a table, where a key, called the primary key, identifies each record uniquely. When you need to check if a record already exists, you retrieve the primary key of the record in question and see if the key exists in the table. What if the record has no value for a primary key, but the values it holds for each of the columns or fields in the table match exactly to the corresponding values of an existing record? This is where things get tricky.

Relational databases uphold the normalization principles introduced by E.F. Codd, a proponent of the relational model. E.F. Codd and Raymond F. Boyce put together a Boyce-Codd Normal Form (BCNF) in 1974 that is often taken as the minimum expected level to keep a database schema normalized. Informally stated, a normalized schema tries to reduce the modification anomalies in record sets by storing data only once and creating references to associated data where necessary. You can read more about database normalization at `http://en.wikipedia.org/wiki/Database_normalization` and at `http://databases.about.com/od/specificproducts/a/normalization.htm`.

In a normalized schema, two records with identical values are the same record. So there is an implicit compare-by-value, which is codified in a single column — the primary key — in a relational model. In the world of programming languages, especially object-oriented languages, this notion of identity is often replaced by the compare-by-reference semantics, where a unique record set, existing as an object, is identified uniquely by the memory space it addresses. Because NoSQL encompasses databases that resemble both traditional tabular structures and object stores, the identity semantics vary from value-based to reference-based. In all cases, though, the notion of a unique primary key is important and helps identify a record.

Although a majority of databases allow you to choose an arbitrary string or an array of bytes for a unique record key, they often prescribe a few rules to make sure such a key is unique and meaningful. In some databases, you are assisted with utility functions to generate primary keys.

THE UNIQUE PRIMARY KEY

You have already seen the default MongoDB BSON object id (summarized in Figure 4-10 in the previous chapter) that proposes a 12-byte structure for a key, with the following as its constituents:

➤ The first four bytes represent the timestamp

➤ The next three bytes represent the machine id

➤ The following two bytes encode the process id

➤ The last three bytes are the increment or the sequence counter

You have also seen the HBase row-key that is usually an array of bytes that requires only that the characters have a string representation. HBase row-keys are often 64-bytes long, but that is not a restriction — although larger keys take up more memory. Rows in HBase are byte-ordered by their row-keys so it is useful to define the row-key as a logical unit pertinent to your application.

Now that you understand the record identifier, the following sections cover creating records in a few NoSQL databases. In the previous few chapters, MongoDB, HBase, and Redis were used as examples for document-centric, column-oriented, and key/value maps, respectively. In this section, these three databases are leveraged again.

Creating Records in a Document-Centric Database

A typical example used in many relational database examples is that of a simplified retail system, which creates and manages order records. Each person's purchase at this fictitious store is an order. An order consists of a bunch of line items. Each order line item includes a product (an item) and number of units of that product purchased. A line item also has a price attribute, which is calculated by multiplying the unit price of the product by the number of units purchased. Each order table has an associated product table that stores the product description and a few other attributes about the product. Figure 5-1 depicts order, product, and their relationship table in a traditional entity-relationship diagram.

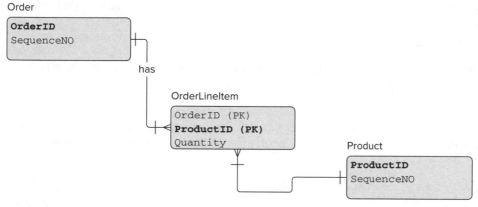

FIGURE 5-1

To store this same data in MongoDB, a document store, you would de-normalize the structure and store each order line item detail with the order record itself. As a specific case, consider an order of four coffees: one latte, one cappuccino, and two regular. This coffee order would be stored in MongoDB as a graph of nested JSON-like documents as follows:

```
{
    order_date: new Date(),
    "line_items": [
        {
            item : {
                name: "latte",
                unit_price: 4.00
            },
            quantity: 1
        },
        {
            item: {
```

```
            name: "cappuccino",
            unit_price: 4.25
        },
        quantity: 1
    },
    {
        item: {
            name: "regular",
            unit_price: 2.00
        },
        quantity: 2
    }
  ]
}
```

coffee_order.txt

Open a command-line window, change to the root of the MongoDB folder, and start the MongoDB server as follows:

```
bin/mongod --dbpath ~/data/db
```

Now, in a separate command window, start a command-line client to interact with the server:

```
bin/mongo
```

Use the command-line client to store the coffee order in the `orders` collection, within the `mydb` database. A partial listing of the command input and response on the console is as follows:

```
> t = {
...     order_date: new Date(),
...     "line_items": [ ...
...     ]
... };
{
    "order_date" : "Sat Oct 30 2010 22:30:12 GMT-0700 (PDT)",
    "line_items" : [
        {
            "item" : {
                "name" : "latte",
                "unit_price" : 4
            },
            "quantity" : 1
        },
        {
            "item" : {
                "name" : "cappuccino",
                "unit_price" : 4.25
            },
            "quantity" : 1
        },
        {
```

```
            "item" : {
                "name" : "regular",
                "unit_price" : 2
            },
            "quantity" : 2
        }
    ]
}

> db.orders.save(t);
> db.orders.find();
{ "_id" : ObjectId("4cccff35d3c7ab3d1941b103"), "order_date" : "Sat Oct 30 2010
22:30:12 GMT-0700 (PDT)", "line_items" : [
    ...
] }
```

coffee_order.txt

Although storing the entire nested document collection is advised, sometimes it's necessary to store the nested objects separately. When nested documents are stored separately, it's your responsibility to join the record sets together. There is no notion of a database join in MongoDB so you must either manually implement the join operation by using the object id on the client side or leverage the concept of DBRef.

> *In MongoDB DBRef is a formal specification for creating references between documents. A DBRef includes a collection name as well as an object id. Read more about MongoDB DBRef at* www.mongodb.org/display/DOCS/Database+ References#DatabaseReferences-DBRef.

You can restructure this example in a way that doesn't store the unit price data for a product in the nested document but keeps it separately in another collection, which stores information on products. In the new format, the item name serves as the key to link between the two collections.

Therefore, the restructured orders data is stored in a collection called orders2 as follows:

```
> t2 = {
...         order_date: new Date(),
...         "line_items": [
...             {
...                 "item_name":"latte",
...                 "quantity":1
...             },
...             {
...                 "item_name":"cappuccino",
...                 "quantity":1
...             },
...             {
...                 "item_name":"regular",
```

```
  ...                  "quantity":2
  ...            }
  ...       ]
  ... };
  {
      "order_date" : "Sat Oct 30 2010 23:03:31 GMT-0700 (PDT)",
      "line_items" : [
             {
                 "item_name" : "latte",
                 "quantity" : 1
             },
             {
                 "item_name" : "cappuccino",
                 "quantity" : 1
             },
             {
                 "item_name" : "regular",
                 "quantity" : 2
             }
      ]
  }
  > db.orders2.save(t2);
```

coffee_order.txt

To verify that the data is stored correctly, you can return the contents of the orders2 collection as
follows:

```
> db.orders2.find();
{ "_id" : ObjectId("4ccd06e8d3c7ab3d1941b104"), "order_date" : "Sat Oct 30 2010
  23:03:31 GMT-0700 (PDT)", "line_items" : [
      {
          "item_name" : "latte",
          "quantity" : 1
      },
  ...
  ] }
```

coffee_order.txt

Next, save the product data, wherein item name and unit price are stored, as follows:

```
> p1 = {
  ...      "_id": "latte",
  ...      "unit_price":4
  ... };
{ "_id" : "latte", "unit_price" : 4 }
> db.products.save(p1);
```

coffee_order.txt

Again, you can verify the record in the `products` collection with the help of the `find` method:

```
> db.products.find();
{ "_id" : "latte", "unit_price" : 4 }
```

coffee_order.txt

Now, you could manually link the two collections and retrieve related data sets like this:

```
> order1 = db.orders2.findOne();
{
    "_id" : ObjectId("4ccd06e8d3c7ab3d1941b104"),
    "order_date" : "Sat Oct 30 2010 23:03:31 GMT-0700 (PDT)",
    "line_items" : [
        {
            "item_name" : "latte",
            "quantity" : 1
        },
        {
            "item_name" : "cappuccino",
            "quantity" : 1
        },
        {
            "item_name" : "regular",
            "quantity" : 2
        }
    ]
}
> db.products.findOne( { _id: order1.line_items[0].item_name } );
{ "_id" : "latte", "unit_price" : 4 }
```

coffee_order.txt

Alternatively, part of this manual process can be automated with the help of `DBRef`, which is a more formal specification for relating two document collections in MongoDB. To illustrate `DBRef`, you rehash the orders example and establish the relationship by first defining the products and then setting up a `DBRef` to products from within the `orders` collection.

Add `latte`, `cappuccino`, and `regular`, with their respective unit prices, to the `product2` collection as follows:

```
> p4 = {"name":"latte", "unit_price":4};
{ "name" : "latte", "unit_price" : 4 }
> p5 = {
...     "name": "cappuccino",
...     "unit_price":4.25
... };
{ "_id" : "cappuccino", "unit_price" : 4.25 }
> p6 = {
...     "name": "regular",
...     "unit_price":2
```

```
... };
{ "_id" : "regular", "unit_price" : 2 }
> db.products2.save(p4);
> db.products2.save(p5);
> db.products2.save(p6);
```

coffee_order.txt

Verify that all the three products are in the collection:

Available for
download on
Wrox.com

```
> db.products.find();
{ "_id" : ObjectId("4ccd1209d3c7ab3d1941b105"), "name" : "latte",
  "unit_price" : 4 }
{ "_id" : ObjectId("4ccd1373d3c7ab3d1941b106"), "name" : "cappuccino",
  "unit_price" : 4.25 }
{ "_id" : ObjectId("4ccd1377d3c7ab3d1941b107"), "name" : "regular",
  "unit_price" : 2 }
```

coffee_order.txt

Next, define a new `orders` collection, called `orders3`, and use `DBRef` to establish the relationship between `orders3` and `products`. The `orders3` collection can be defined as follows:

Available for
download on
Wrox.com

```
t3 = {
...     order_date: new Date(),
...     "line_items": [
...         {
...             "item_name": new DBRef('products2', p4._id),
...             "quantity:1
...         },
...         {
...             "item_name": new DBRef('products2', p5._id),
...             "quantity":1
...         },
...         {
...             "item_name": new DBRef('products2', p6._id),
...             "quantity":2
...         }
...     ]
... };

db.orders3.save(t3);
```

coffee_order.txt

The MongoDB creation process is fairly simple and as you saw, some aspects of the relationship can also be formally established using `DBRef`. Next, the create operation is viewed in the context of column-oriented databases.

Using the Create Operation in Column-Oriented Databases

Unlike MongoDB databases, column-oriented databases don't define any concept of relational references. Like all NoSQL products, they avoid joins between collections. So there is no concept of foreign keys or constraints across multiple collections. Column databases store their collections in a de-normalized fashion, almost resembling a data warehouse fact table that keeps large amounts of transactional de-normalized records. Data is stored in such a way that a row-key uniquely identifies each record and that all columns within a column-family are stored together.

Column-oriented databases, in particular HBase, also have a time dimension to save data. Therefore, a create or data insert operation is important but the notion of update is effectively nonexistent. Let's view these aspects of HBase through an example. Say you had to create and maintain a large catalog of different types of products, where the amounts of information on the type, category, characteristics, price, and source of the product could vary widely. Then you may want to create a table with type, characteristics, and source as three column-families. Individual attributes or fields (also referred to as columns) would then fall within one of these column-families. To create this collection or table of products in HBase, first start the HBase server and then connect to it using the HBase shell. To start the HBase server, open up a command-line window or terminal and change it to the HBase installation directory. Then start the HBase server in local standalone mode as follows:

```
bin/start-hbase.sh
```

Open another command-line window and connect to the HBase server using the HBase shell:

```
bin/hbase shell
```

Next, create the products table:

```
hbase(main):001:0> create 'products', 'type', 'characteristics', 'source'
0 row(s) in 1.1570 seconds
```

products_hbase.txt

Once the table is created, you can save data in it. HBase uses the put keyword to denote a data-creation operation. The word "put" connotes a hash map-like operation for data insertion and because HBase under the hood is like a nested hash map, it's probably more appropriate than the create keyword.

To create a record with the following fields:

➤ type:category = "coffee beans"

➤ type:name = "arabica"

➤ type:genus = "Coffea"

➤ characteristics: cultivation_method = "organic"

➤ characteristics: acidity = "low"

➤ source: country = "yemen"

➤ source: terrain = "mountainous"

you can put it into the products table like so:

```
hbase(main):001:0> put 'products', 'product1', 'type:category', 'coffee beans'
0 row(s) in 0.0710 seconds
hbase(main):002:0> put 'products', 'product1', 'type:name', 'arabica'
0 row(s) in 0.0020 seconds
hbase(main):003:0> put 'products', 'product1', 'type:genus', 'Coffea'
0 row(s) in 0.0050 seconds
hbase(main):004:0> put 'products', 'product1',
   'characteristics: cultivation_method', 'organic'
0 row(s) in 0.0060 seconds
hbase(main):005:0> put 'products', 'product1', 'characteristics: acidity', 'low'
0 row(s) in 0.0030 seconds
hbase(main):006:0> put 'products', 'product1', 'source: country', 'yemen'
0 row(s) in 0.0050 seconds
hbase(main):007:0> put 'products', 'product1', 'source: terrain', 'mountainous'
0 row(s) in 0.0050 seconds
hbase(main):008:0>
```

products_hbase.txt

Now you can query for the same record to make sure it's in the data store. To get the record do the following:

```
hbase(main):008:0> get 'products', 'product1'
COLUMN                      CELL
characteristics: acidity    timestamp=1288555025970, value=lo
characteristics: cultivatio timestamp=1288554998029, value=organic
n_method
source: country             timestamp=1288555050543, value=yemen
source: terrain             timestamp=1288555088136, value=mountainous
type:category               timestamp=1288554892522, value=coffee beans
type:genus                  timestamp=1288554961942, value=Coffea
type:name                   timestamp=1288554934169, value=Arabica
7 row(s) in 0.0190 seconds
```

products_hbase.txt

What if you put in a value for "type:category" a second time stored as "beans" instead of its original value of "coffee beans" as follows?

```
hbase(main):009:0> put 'products', 'product1', 'type:category', 'beans'
0 row(s) in 0.0050 seconds
```

products_hbase.txt

Now, if you get the record again, the output is as follows:

```
hbase(main):010:0> get 'products', 'product1'
COLUMN                        CELL
characteristics: acidity      timestamp=1288555025970, value=low
characteristics: cultivatio   timestamp=1288554998029, value=organic
n_method
source: country               timestamp=1288555050543, value=yemen
source: terrain               timestamp=1288555088136, value=mountainous
type:category                 timestamp=1288555272656, value=beans
type:genus                    timestamp=1288554961942, value=Coffea
type:name                     timestamp=1288554934169, value=Arabica
7 row(s) in 0.0370 seconds
```

products_hbase.txt

You may notice that the value for type:category is now beans instead of coffee beans. In reality, both values are still stored as different versions of the same field value and only the latest one of these is returned by default. To look at the last four versions of the type:category field, run the following command:

```
hbase(main):011:0> get 'products', 'product1', { COLUMN => 'type:category',
   VERSIONS => 4 }
COLUMN                        CELL
type:category                 timestamp=1288555272656, value=beans
type:category                 timestamp=1288554892522, value=coffee beans
```

There are only two versions so far, so those are returned.

Now, what if the data is very structured, limited, and relational in nature? It's possible HBase isn't the right solution at all then.

HBase flattens the data structure, only creating a hierarchy between a column-family and its constituent columns. In addition, it also stores each cell's data along a time dimension, so you need to flatten nested data sets when such data is stored in HBase.

Consider the retail order system. In HBase, the retail order data could be stored in a couple of ways:

➤ Flatten all the data sets and store all fields of an order, including all product data, in a single row.

➤ For each order, maintain all order line items within a single row. Save the product information in a separate table and save a reference to the product row-key with the order line item information.

Going with the first option of flattening the order data, you could end up making the following choices:

➤ Create one column-family for regular line items and create another one for additional types of line items like discount or rebate.

➤ Within a regular line item column-family, you could have columns for item or product name, item or product description, quantity, and price. If you flatten everything, remember to have a different key for each line item or else they will end up getting stored together as versions of the same key/value pair. For example, call the product name column `product_name_1` instead of calling all of them `product_name`.

The next example uses Redis to illustrate creating data in a key/value map.

Using the Create Operation in Key/Value Maps

Redis is a simple, yet powerful, data structure server that lets you store values as a simple key/value pair or as a member of a collection. Each key/value pair can be a standalone map of strings or reside in a collection. A collection could be any of the following types: list, set, sorted set, or hash. A standalone key/value string pair is like a variable that can take string values.

You can create a Redis string key/value map like so:

```
./redis-cli set akey avalue
```

You can confirm that the value is created successfully with the help of the `get` command as follows:

```
./redis-cli get akey
```

The response, as expected, is `avalue`. The `set` method is the same as the `create` or the `put` method. If you invoke the `set` method again but this time set `anothervalue` for the key, `akey`, the original value is replaced with the new one. Try out the following:

```
./redis-cli set akey anothervalue
./redis-cli get akey
```

The response, as expected, would be the new value: `anothervalue`.

The familiar `set` and `get` commands for a string can't be used for Redis collections, though. For example, using `lpush` and `rpush` creates and populates a list. A nonexistent list can be created along with its first member as follows:

```
./redis-cli lpush list_of_books 'MongoDB: The Definitive Guide'
```

books_list_redis.txt

You can use the range operation to verify and see the first few members of the list — `list_of_books` — like so:

```
./redis-cli lrange list_of_books  0 -1
1. "MongoDB: The Definitive Guide"
```

books_list_redis.txt

The range operation uses the index of the first element, 0, and the index of the last element, -1, to get all elements in the list.

In Redis, when you query a nonexistent list, it returns an empty list and doesn't throw an exception. You run a range query for a nonexistent list — `mylist` — like so:

```
./redis-cli lrange mylist 0 -1
```

Redis returns a message: `empty list or set`. You can use `lpush` much as you use `rpush` to add a member to `mylist` like so:

```
./redis-cli rpush mylist 'a member'
```

Now, of course `mylist` isn't empty and repeating a range query reveals the presence of `a member`.

Members can be added to a list, either on the left or on the right, and can be popped from either direction as well. This allows you to leverage lists as queues or stacks.

For a set data structure, a member can be added using the SADD operation. Therefore, you can add `'a set member'` to `aset` like so:

```
./redis-cli sadd aset 'a set member'
```

The command-line program would respond with an integral value of 1 confirming that it's added to the set. When you rerun the same SADD command, the member is not added again. You may recall that a set, by definition, holds a value only once and so once present it doesn't make sense to add it again. You will also notice that the program responds with a 0, which indicates that nothing was added. Like sets, sorted sets store a member only once but they also have a sense of order like a list. You can easily add `'a sset member'` to a sorted set, called `azset`, like so:

```
./redis-cli zadd azset 1 'a sset member'
```

The value 1 is the position or score of the sorted set member. You can add another member, `'sset member 2'`, to this sorted set as follows:

```
./redis-cli zadd azset 4 'sset member 2'
```

You could verify that the values are stored by running a range operation, similar to the one you used for a list. The sorted set range command is called `zrange` and you can ask for a range containing the first five values as follows:

```
./redis-cli zrange azset 0 4
1. "a sset member"
2. "sset member 2"
```

What happens when you now add a value at position or score 3 and what happens when you try and add another value to position or score 4, which already has a value?

Adding a value to `azset` at score 3 like so:

```
./redis-cli zadd azset 3 'member 3'
```

and running the `zrange` query like so:

```
./redis-cli zrange azset 0 4
```

reveals:

1. "a sset member"
2. "member 3"
3. "sset member 2"

Adding a value at position or score 3 again, like so:

```
./redis-cli zadd azset 3 'member 3 again'
```

and running the `zrange` query like so:

```
./redis-cli zrange azset 0 4
```

reveals that the members have been re-positioned to accommodate the new member, like so:

1. "a sset member"
2. "member 3"
3. "member 3 again"
4. "sset member 2"

Therefore, adding a new member to a sorted set does not replace existing values but instead re-orders the members as required.

Redis also defines the concept of a hash, in which members could be added like so:

```
./redis-cli hset bank account1 2350
./redis-cli hset bank account2 4300
```

You can verify the presence of the member using the `hget`, or its variant `hgetall`, command:

```
./redis-cli hgetall bank
```

To store a complicated nested hash, you could create a hierarchical hash key like so:

```
./redis-cli hset product:fruits apple 1.35
./redis-cli hset product:fruits banana 2.20
```

Once data is stored in any of the NoSQL data stores, you need to access and retrieve it. After all, the entire idea of saving data is to retrieve it and use it later.

ACCESSING DATA

You have already seen some of the ways to access data. In an attempt to verify whether records were created, some of the simplest `get` commands have already been explored. Some of the earlier chapters also demonstrated a few standard query mechanisms.

Next, a few advanced data access methods, syntax, and semantics are explored.

Accessing Documents from MongoDB

MongoDB allows for document queries using syntax and semantics that closely resemble SQL. Ironic as it may be, the similarity to SQL in a NoSQL world makes querying for documents easy and powerful in MongoDB.

You are familiar with the query documents from the previous chapters, so you can dive right in to accessing a few nested MongoDB documents. Once again, you use the orders collection in the database mydb, which was created earlier in this chapter.

Start the MongoDB server and connect to it using the mongo JavaScript shell. Change to the mydb database with the use mydb command. First, get all the documents in the orders collection like so:

```
db.orders.find()
```

Now, start filtering the collection. Get all the orders after October 25, 2010, that is, with order_date greater than October 25, 2010. Start by creating a date object. In the JavaScript shell it would be:

```
var refdate = new Date(2010, 9, 25);
```

JavaScript dates have months starting at 0 instead of 1, so the number 9 represents October. In Python the same variable creation could be like so:

```
from datetime import datetime
refdate = datetime(2010, 10, 25)
```

and in Ruby it would be like so:

```
require 'date'
refdate = Date.new(2010, 10, 25)
```

Then, pass refdate in a comparator that compares the order_date field values against refdate. The query is as follows:

```
db.orders.find({"order_date": {$gt: refdate}});
```

MongoDB supports a rich variety of comparators, including less than, greater than, less than or equal to, greater than or equal to, equal to, and not equal to. In addition, it supports set inclusion and exclusion logic operators like contained in and not contained in a given set.

The data set is a nested document so it can be beneficial to query on the basis of a value of a nested property. In Mongo, doing that is easy. Traversing through the tree using dot notation could access any nested field. To get all documents from the orders collection where line item name is latte, you write the following query:

```
db.orders.find({ "line_items.item.name" : "latte" })
```

The dot notation works whether there are single nested values or a list of them as was the case in the `orders` collection.

MongoDB expression matching supports regular expressions. Regular expressions can be used in nested documents the same way they are used with top-level fields.

In relational databases, indexes are the smart way of making queries faster. In general, the way that works is simple. Indexes provide an efficient lookup mechanism based on a B-tree-like structure that avoids complete table scans. Because less data is searched through to find the relevant records, the queries are faster and more efficient.

MongoDB supports the notion of indexes to speed up queries. By default, all collections are indexed on the basis of the `_id` value. In addition to this default index, MongoDB allows you to create secondary indexes. Secondary indexes can be created at the top field level or at the nested field levels. For example, you could create an index on the quantity value of a line item as follows:

```
db.orders.ensureIndex({ "line_items.quantity" : 1 });
```

Now, querying for all documents where quantity of a line item is 2 can be fairly fast. Try running the following query:

```
db.orders.find({ "line_items.quantity" : 2 });
```

Indexes are stored separate from the table and you may recall from an earlier chapter that they use up a namespace.

MongoDB data access seems fairly simple, rich, and robust. However, this isn't the case for all NoSQL stores, especially not for column-oriented databases.

Accessing Data from HBase

The easiest and most efficient query to run on HBase is one that is based on the row-key. Row-keys in HBase are ordered and ranges of these contiguous row-keys are stored together. Therefore, looking up a row-key typically means finding the highest order range that has the starting row-key smaller than or equal to the given row-key.

This means that designing the row-key correctly for an application is extremely important. It's a good idea to relate the row-key semantically to the data contained in the table. In the Google Bigtable research paper, row-keys are made up of inverted domain names so all content related to a specific domain is grouped together. Going by these guidelines, it would be a good idea to model the `orders` table with row-keys that are a combination of the item or product name, the order date, and possibly category. Depending on how the data is to be most often accessed, the combination sequence of these three fields could vary. So, if orders will be most often accessed in chronological order, you may want to create row-keys like so:

```
<date> + <timestamp> + <category> + <product>
```

However, if orders would most often be accessed by the category and product names, then create a row-key like so:

```
<category> + <product> + <date> + <timestamp>
```

Although row-keys are important and provide an efficient lookup mechanism for huge amounts of data, there is little built in to support secondary indexes. Any query that doesn't leverage the row-key leads to table scans, which are both expensive and slow.

Third-party tools like Lucene, the search engine framework, have the ability to help create secondary indexes on HBase tables. Next, you review querying the data structure server, Redis.

Querying Redis

Querying Redis is as elegant and easy as inserting records into it is. Earlier you learned that you could get the value of a specific string by using the get command like so:

```
./redis-cli get akey
```

or get a range of list values like so:

```
./redis-cli lrange list_of_books 0 4
```

Similarly, you could get members of a set like so:

```
./redis-cli smembers asset
```

or members of a sorted set like so:

```
./redis-cli zrevrange azset  0 4
```

You also saw that set operations like intersection, union, and difference can also be carried out quite easily using the SINTER, SUNION, and SDIFF commands, respectively.

When you move over from the relational world to the world of NoSQL, it isn't the data creation or querying that you hear about but it's the data updates and transactional integrity around it that people talk about the most.

Next, you explore how updating and modifying data is managed in NoSQL databases.

UPDATING AND DELETING DATA

The relational world is deeply rooted in ACID semantics for database integrity and upholds different levels of isolation for data update and modification. NoSQL, on the contrary, does not give extreme importance to ACID transactions and in some cases completely ignores it.

To set the context, you first need to understand what ACID means. ACID is an acronym that stands for atomicity, consistency, isolation, and durability. Informally stated, atomicity means a transaction either happens in totality or rolls back. Consistency means each modification to the database takes it from one consistent state to the other. Inconsistent and unresolved states do not exist. Isolation provides the assurance that some other process cannot modify a piece of data when an operation in progress is using it. Durability implies all committed data can be recovered from any sort of a system failure.

As in the other sections, I go over the different types of NoSQL databases one at a time, starting with MongoDB.

Updating and Modifying Data in MongoDB, HBase, and Redis

Unlike relational databases, the concept of locking doesn't exist in NoSQL stores. This is a choice by design, not coincidence. Databases like MongoDB are meant to be sharded and scalable. In such a situation, locking across distributed shards can be complex and make the process of data updates very slow.

However, despite the lack of locking, a few tips and tricks could help you in updating data in an atomic manner. First of all, update an entire document and not just a few fields of a document. Preferably use the atomic methods to update the document. Available atomic methods are as follows:

- ➤ `$set` — Set a value
- ➤ `$inc` — Increment a particular value by a given amount
- ➤ `$push` — Append a value to an array
- ➤ `$pushAll` — Append several values to an array
- ➤ `$pull` — Remove a value from an existing array
- ➤ `$pullAll` — Remove several value(s) from an existing array

For example, `{ $set : { "order_date" : new Date(2010, 10, 01) } }` updates the `order_date` in the `orders` collection in an atomic manner.

An alternative strategy to using atomic operations is to use the update if current principle. Essentially this involves three steps:

1. Fetch the object.
2. Modify the object locally.
3. Send an update request that says "update the object to this new value if it still matches its old value."

The document or row-level locking and atomicity also applies to HBase.

HBase supports a row-level read-write lock. This means rows are locked when any column in that row is being modified, updated, or created. In HBase terms the distinction between create and update is not clear. Both operations perform similar logic. If the value is not present, it's inserted or else updated.

Therefore, row-level locking is a great idea, unless a lock is acquired on an empty row and then it's unavailable until it times out.

Redis has a limited concept of a transaction and an operation can be performed within the confines of such a transaction. Redis MULTI command initiates a transactional unit. Calling EXEC after a MULTI executes all the commands and calling DISCARD rolls back the operations. A simple example of atomic increment of two keys: key1 and key2 could be as follows:

```
> MULTI
OK
> INCR key1
QUEUED
> INCR key2
QUEUED
> EXEC
1) (integer) 1
2) (integer) 1
```

Limited Atomicity and Transactional Integrity

Though the specifics of minimal atomic support vary from one database to the other, many of these have quite a few similar characteristics. In this subsection, I cover some of the more pervasive ideas around CAP Theorem and eventual consistency.

CAP Theorem states that two of the following three can be maximized at one time:

➤ **Consistency** — Each client has the same view of the data

➤ **Availability** — Each client can always read and write

➤ **Partition tolerance** — System works well across distributed physical networks

More details on CAP Theorem and its impact on NoSQL are explained in Chapter 9.

One more topic that comes up often is the concept of eventual consistency. This term is sometimes confusing and often not properly understood.

Eventual consistency is a consistency model used in the domain of parallel programming and distributed programming. Eventual consistency could be interpreted in two ways, as follows:

➤ Given a sufficiently long period of time, over which no updates are sent, one can expect that all updates will, eventually, propagate through the system and all the replicas will be consistent.

➤ In the presence of continuing updates, an accepted update eventually either reaches a replica or the replica retires from service.

Eventual consistency implies Basically Available, Soft state, Eventual consistency (BASE), as opposed to ACID, which I covered earlier.

SUMMARY

This chapter introduced the essential create, read, update, and delete operations in the context of NoSQL databases. The chapter explored the essential operations in light of three kinds of NoSQL stores, namely, document stores, column-oriented databases, and key/value hash maps. MongoDB represents the document stores, HBase represents the column stores, and Redis represents the key/value hash maps.

During the discussion it became clear that for all the data stores, data creation or insertion is more important than updates. In some cases, updates are limited. Toward the end of the chapter, the topic of updates, transactional integrity, and consistency were also explained.

Querying NoSQL Stores

SQL is possibly the simplest yet most powerful domain-specific language created so far. It is easy to learn because it has a limited vocabulary, unambiguous grammar, and a simple syntax. It is terse and limited in scope but it does precisely what it's meant to do. It enables you to manipulate structured data sets like a ninja. You can easily filter, sort, dice, and slice the data sets. Based on relations, you can join data sets and create intersections and unions. You can summarize data sets and manipulate them to group by a specific attribute or filter them on the basis of their grouping criteria. There is one limitation, though: SQL is based on relational algebra, which works well with relational databases only. As is evident from its name, there is no SQL with NoSQL.

The absence of SQL does not mean that you need to stop querying data sets. After all, any data is stored to be possibly retrieved and manipulated later. NoSQL stores have their own ways of accessing and manipulating data and you have already seen some of that.

NoSQL should really have been NonRel, implying non-relational. Although the creators and proponents of the so-called NoSQL databases were moved away from relational databases because of the structural relational constraints it imposed and the ACID transactions that it upheld, especially as these became impediments to scaling and dealing with large data sets, they weren't necessarily opposed to SQL. In fact, some still crave SQL in the world of NoSQL and as a result have created query languages that in syntax and style resemble the same old SQL. Old habits die hard, and why shouldn't they if they are the virtuous ones!

In this chapter, you learn many tips and tricks for querying NoSQL stores. As in the previous chapters, you learn the tips and tricks in the context of multiple products and varying technologies, all grouped under the large umbrella of NoSQL. The lesson starts with querying data sets stored in MongoDB and then moves on to cover HBase and Redis.

SIMILARITIES BETWEEN SQL AND MONGODB QUERY FEATURES

Although MongoDB is a document database and has little resemblance to a relational database, the MongoDB query language feels a lot like SQL. You have already seen some initial examples, so I presume I don't need to convince you about its SQL-like query features.

To understand the MongoDB query language capabilities and see how it performs, start by loading a data set into a MongoDB database. So far, the data sets used in this book have been small and limited because the focus has been more on introducing MongoDB's core features and less on its applicability to real-life situations. For this chapter, though, I introduce a data set that is slightly more substantial than used in this book so far. I load up the MovieLens data set of millions of movie-rating records.

> **MOVIELENS**
>
> The GroupLens research lab in the Department of Computer Science and Engineering at the University of Minnesota conducts research in a number of disciplines:
>
> ➤ Recommender systems
>
> ➤ Online communities
>
> ➤ Mobile and ubiquitous technologies
>
> ➤ Digital libraries
>
> ➤ Local geographic information systems
>
> The MovieLens data set is a part of the available GroupLens data sets. The MovieLens data set contains user ratings for movies. It is a structured data set and is available in three different download bundles, containing 100,000, 1 million, and 10 million records, respectively. You can download the MovieLens data set from `grouplens.org/node/73`.

First, go to `grouplens.org/node/73` and download the data set that has 1 million movie-rating records. Download bundles are available in `tar.gz` (tarred and zipped) and `.zip` archive formats. Download the format that is best for your platform. After you get the bundle, extract the contents of the archive file to a folder in your filesystem. On extracting the 1 million ratings data set, you should have the following three files:

- ➤ `movies.dat`

- ➤ `ratings.dat`

- ➤ `users.dat`

The `movies.dat` data file contains data on the movies themselves. This file contains 3,952 records, and each line in that file contains one record. The record is saved in the following format:

```
<MovieID>::<Title>::<Genres>
```

The `MovieId` is a simple integral sequence of numbers. The movie title is a string, which includes the year the movie was released, specified in brackets appended to its name. The movie titles are the same as those in IMDB (`www.imdb.com`). Each movie may be classified under multiple genres, which are specified in a pipe-delimited format. A sample line from the file is like so:

```
1::Toy Story (1995)::Animation|Children's|Comedy
```

The `ratings.dat` file contains the ratings of the 3,952 movies by more than 6,000 users. The ratings file has more than 1 million records. Each line is a different record that contains data in the following format:

```
UserID::MovieID::Rating::Timestamp
```

`UserID` and `MovieID` identify and establish a relationship with the user and the movie, respectively. The rating is a measure on a 5-point (5-star) scale. `Timestamp` captures the time when the ratings were recorded.

The `users.dat` file contains data on the users who rated the movies. The information on more than 6,000 users is recorded in the following format:

```
UserID::Gender::Age::Occupation::Zip-code
```

Loading the MovieLens Data

For simplicity, upload the data into three MongoDB collections: `movies`, `ratings`, and `users`, each mapping to a `.dat` data file. The mongoimport utility, `www.mongodb.org/display/DOCS/ Import+Export+Tools`, is suited to extracting the data from the `.dat` files and loading it into the MongoDB document store but that's not an option here. The MovieLens data is delimited by the double-colon (`::`) character and mongoimport recognizes only JSON, comma-separated, and tab-delimited formats.

So, I fall back on a programming language and an associated MongoDB driver to help parse a text file and load the data set into a MongoDB collection. For the purpose of brevity I chose Ruby. Alternatively, you could use Python (which is also brief and elegant), Java, PHP, C, or any of the other supported languages.

A small bit of code, as shown in Listing 6-1, easily extracts and loads the data from the `users`, `movies`, and `ratings` data files to respective MongoDB collections. This code uses simple file-reading and string-splitting features, along with the MongoDB driver to carry out the task. It's not the most elegant code. It doesn't take care of exceptions or work fast with extremely large files, but it works for the purpose at hand.

LISTING 6-1: movielens_dataloader.rb

```ruby
require 'rubygems' #can skip this line in Ruby 1.9
require 'mongo'

field_map = {
    "users" => %w(_id gender age occupation zip_code),
    "movies" => %w(_id title genres),
    "ratings" => %w(user_id movie_id rating timestamp)
}

db = Mongo::Connection.new.db("mydb")
collection_map = {
    "users" => db.collection("users"),
    "movies" => db.collection("movies"),
    "ratings" => db.collection("ratings")
}

unless ARGV.length == 1
    puts "Usage: movielens_dataloader data_filename"
    exit(0)
end

class Array
  def to_h(key_definition)
    result_hash = Hash.new()

    counter = 0
    key_definition.each do |definition|
      if not self[counter] == nil then
          if self[counter].is_a? Array or self[counter].is_a? Integer then
              result_hash[definition] = self[counter]
          else
              result_hash[definition] = self[counter].strip
          end
      else
        # Insert the key definition with an empty value.
        # Because we probably still want the hash to contain the key.
        result_hash[definition] = ""
      end
      # For some reason counter.next didn't work here....
      counter = counter + 1
    end

    return result_hash
  end
end

if File.exists?(ARGV[0])
    file = File.open(ARGV[0], 'r')
    data_set = ARGV[0].chomp.split(".")[0]
```

```
    file.each { |line|
        field_names = field_map[data_set]
        field_values = line.split("::").map { |item|
            if item.to_i.to_s == item
                item = item.to_i
            else
                item
            end
        }
        puts "field_values: #{field_values}"
        #last_field_value = line.split("::").last
        last_field_value = field_values.last
        puts "last_field_value: #{last_field_value}"
        if last_field_value.split("|").length > 1
            field_values.pop
            field_values.push(last_field_value.split().join('\n').split("|"))
        end
        field_values_doc = field_values.to_h(field_names)
        collection_map[data_set].insert(field_values_doc)
    }
    puts "inserted #{collection_map[data_set].count()} records into the
#{collection_map[data_set].to_s} collection"
end
```

movielens_dataloader.rb

When the data is loaded, you are ready to run a few queries to slice and dice it. Queries can be run from the JavaScript shell or from any of the supported languages. For this example, I run most queries using the JavaScript shell and a select few using a couple of different programming languages and their respective drivers. The only purpose of including programming language examples is to demonstrate that most, if not all, of what's possible via the JavaScript shell is available through the different language drivers.

To commence with querying the MongoDB collections, start up the MongoDB server and connect to it using the Mongo shell. The necessary programs are accessible from the bin folder of your MongoDB installation. Having started MongoDB a couple of times in the past few chapters, you are hopefully well versed with starting and stopping these programs by now.

On your Mongo JavaScript shell, first get a count of all the values in the ratings collection as follows:

```
db.ratings.count();
```

In response, you should see 1000209. A million plus ratings were uploaded so this looks right.

Next, get a sample set of the ratings data with the help of the following command:

```
db.ratings.find();
```

On the shell you don't need an explicit cursor to print out the values from a collection. The shell restricts the number of rows to a maximum of 20 at a time. To iterate over more data, simply type **it** (short for iterate) on your shell. In response to the it command, you should see 20 more records and a label saying "has more," if more records exist beyond the ones you have already browsed on your shell.

The ratings data, for example, `{ "_id" : ObjectId("4cdcf1ea5a918708b0000001"), "user_id" : 1, "movie_id" : 1193, "rating" : 5, "timestamp" : "978300760" }`, makes little intuitive sense about the movie it relates to because it's linked to the movie id and not its name. You can get around this problem by answering the following questions:

➤ How can I get all the ratings data for a given movie?

➤ How do I get the movie information for a given rating?

➤ How do I put together a list all the movies with the ratings data grouped by the movies they relate to?

In relational databases, these types of relationships are traversed using joins. In MongoDB, this relational data is explicitly co-related outside the scope of the server. MongoDB defines the concept of a DBRef to establish a relationship between two fields of two separate collections, but that feature has a few limitations and doesn't provide the same power as explicit id-based linking does. I won't cover DBRef in this section but I included a few examples of DBRef in the previous chapters and will revisit it in future chapters as well.

To get all the ratings data for a given movie, you filter the data set using the movie id as the criteria. For example, to view all ratings for the famous Academy Award-winning movie *Titanic*, you need to first find its id and then use that to filter the ratings collection. If you aren't sure what the exact title string for "Titanic" is like but you are confident the word *titanic* appears in it, you can try an approximate, and not an exact, match with the title strings in the `movies` collection. In an RDBMS, to find the movie id under such circumstances, you are likely to rely on the `like` expression in a SQL `where` clause to get a list of all possible candidates. In MongoDB, there is no `like` expression but there is a more powerful feature available, which is the ability to define a pattern using regular expressions. So to get a list of all records in the `movies` collection that have *Titanic* or *titanic* in their title, you can query like so:

```
db.movies.find({ title: /titanic/i});
```

This query returns the following set of documents:

```
{ "_id" : 1721, "title" : "Titanic (1997)", "genres" : [ "Drama", "Romance" ] }
{ "_id" : 2157, "title" : "Chambermaid on the Titanic, The (1998)", "genres" :
"Romance" }
{ "_id" : 3403, "title" : "Raise the Titanic (1980)", "genres" : [ "Drama",
"Thriller" ] }
{ "_id" : 3404, "title" : "Titanic (1953)", "genres" : [ "Action", "Drama" ] }
```

The title field in the MovieLens data set includes the year the movie was released. Within the title field, the release year is included in parentheses. So, if you remembered or happen to know that *Titanic* was released in the year 1997, you can write a more tuned query expression as follows:

```
db.movies.find({ title: /titanic.*\(1997\).*/i});
```

This returns just one document:

```
{ "_id" : 1721, "title" : "Titanic (1997)", "genres" : [ "Drama", "Romance" ] }
```

The expression essentially looks for all title strings that have Titanic, titanic, TitaniC, or TiTAnic in it. In short, it ignores case. In addition, it looks for the string (1997). It also states that there may be 0 or more characters between titanic and (1997) and after (1997). The support for regular expressions is a powerful feature and it is always worthwhile to gain mastery over them.

The range of values for the `movie_id` field of the ratings collection is defined by the `_id` of the movies collection. So to get all ratings for the movie *Titanic*, which has an id of 1721, you could query like so:

```
db.ratings.find({ movie_id: 1721 });
```

To find out the number of available ratings for *Titanic*, you can count them as follows:

```
db.ratings.find({ movie_id: 1721 }).count();
```

The response to the count is 1546. The ratings are on a 5-point scale. To get a list and count of only the 5-star ratings for the movie *Titanic* you can further filter the record set like so:

```
db.ratings.find({ movie_id: 1721, rating: 5 });
db.ratings.find({ movie_id: 1721, rating: 5 }).count();
```

DATA-TYPE SENSITIVITY IN QUERY DOCUMENTS

MongoDB query documents are data-type sensitive. That is, `{ movie_id: "1721" }` and `{ movie_id: 1721 }` are not the same, the first one matches a string and the second one considers the value as a number. When specifying documents, be sure to use the correct data type. To illustrate further, the `movie_id` is stored as a number (integer) in the `ratings` and the `movies` collections, so querying for a string match doesn't return correct results. Therefore, the response to `db.ratings` `.find({ movie_id: 1721 });` returns up to a total of 1,546 documents, but the response to `db.ratings.find({ movie_id: "1721" });` returns none.

If you browse Listing 6-1 carefully, you will notice the following line:

```
field_values = line.split("::").map { |item|
        if item.to_i.to_s == item
            item = item.to_i
        else
            item
        end
    }
```

This bit of code checks to see if the split string holds an integer value and saves it as an integer, if that's the case. Making this little extra effort to save numerical values as numbers has its benefits. Indexing and querying on numerical records is usually faster and more efficient than on character-based (string) records.

Next, you may want to get some statistics of all the ratings for *Titanic*. To find out the distinct set of ratings by users (from the possible set of integers between 1 and 5, both inclusive), you could query as follows:

```
db.runCommand({ distinct: 'ratings', key: 'rating', query: { movie_id: 1721} });
```

Ratings for *Titanic* include all possible cases between 1 and 5 (both inclusive) so the response is like so:

```
{ "values" : [ 1, 2, 3, 4, 5 ], "ok" : 1 }
```

`runCommand` takes the following arguments:

➤ Collection name for the field labeled `distinct`

➤ Field name for `key`, whose distinct values would be listed

➤ Query to optionally filter the collection

`runCommand` is slightly different in pattern than the query style you have seen so far because the collection is filtered before the distinct values are searched for. Distinct values for all ratings in the collection can be listed in a way that you have seen so far, as follows:

```
db.ratings.distinct("rating");
```

You know from the distinct values that *Titanic* has all possible ratings from 1 to 5. To see how these ratings break down by each rating value on the 5-point scale, you could group the counts like so:

```
db.ratings.group(
... { key: { rating:true },
...   initial: { count:0 },
...   cond: { movie_id:1721 },
...   reduce: function(obj, prev) { prev.count++; }
... }
... );
```

The output of this grouping query is an array as follows:

```
[
    {
        "rating" : 4,
        "count" : 500
    },
    {
        "rating" : 1,
        "count" : 100
    },
    {
        "rating" : 5,
        "count" : 389
    },
    {
        "rating" : 3,
        "count" : 381
```

```
    },
    {
        "rating" : 2,
        "count" : 176
    }
]
```

This group by function is quite handy for single MongoDB instances but doesn't work in sharded deployments. Use MongoDB's MapReduce facility to run grouping functions in a sharded MongoDB setup. A MapReduce version of the grouping function is included right after the group operation is explained.

The group operation takes an object as an input. This group operation object includes the following fields:

➤ **key** — The document field to group by. The preceding example has only one field: rating. Additional group by fields can be included in a comma-separated list and assigned as the value of the key field. A possible configuration could be – key: { fieldA: true, fieldB: true}.

➤ **initial** — Initial value of the aggregation statistic. In the previous example the initial count is set to 0.

➤ **cond** — The query document to filter the collection.

➤ **reduce** — The aggregation function.

➤ **keyf (optional)** — An alternative derived key if the desired key is not an existing document field.

➤ **finalize (optional)** — A function that can run on every item that the reduce function iterates through. This could be used to modify existing items.

Theoretically, the example could easily be morphed into a case where ratings for each movie are grouped by the rating points by simply using the following group operation:

```
db.ratings.group(
... { key: { movie_id:true, rating:true },
...    initial: { count:0 },
...    reduce: function(obj, prev) { prev.count++; }
... }
... );
```

In real cases, though, this wouldn't work for the ratings collection of 1 million items. You would be greeted instead with the following error message:

```
Fri Nov 12 14:27:03 uncaught exception: group command failed: {
    "errmsg" : "exception: group() can't handle more than 10000 unique keys",
    "code" : 10043,
    "ok" : 0
}
```

The result is returned as a single BSON object and therefore the collection over which the group operation is applied should not have more than 10,000 keys. This limitation can also be overcome with the MapReduce facility.

In the following section you explore MongoDB's MapReduce facility and run a few aggregation functions on the entire ratings data set.

MapReduce in MongoDB

MapReduce is a patented software framework from Google that supports distributed computing on a large distributed cluster of computers. You can read about Google's MapReduce in a research paper titled "MapReduce: Simplified Data Processing on Large Clusters" available online at `http://labs.google.com/papers/mapreduce.html`.

Google's MapReduce framework has inspired many clones and distributed computing frameworks in the open-source community. MongoDB's is one of those. Google's and MongoDB's MapReduce features are also inspired by similar constructs in the world of functional programming. In functional programming, a map function is one that applies to each member of a collection and a reduce function or a fold function is one that runs an aggregation function across the collection.

 MongoDB's MapReduce features are not a clone of the Google's MapReduce infrastructure. Hadoop's MapReduce is an open-source implementation of Google's distributed computing ideas and includes infrastructure for both column databases (HBase) and MapReduce-based computing.

Understanding MapReduce can sometimes be intimidating, but once you understand its structure and flow, it's a powerful tool that helps you carry out large computations across distributed collections of data. So, starting out with a few simple examples and then graduating to more complex ones is a good way to smooth the learning curve and achieve mastery of the topic.

The simplest aggregation example could be a count of each type of an item in a collection. To use MapReduce, you need to define a `map` function and a `reduce` function and then run the `map` and `reduce` functions against a collection. A `map` function applies a function to every member of the collection and emits a key/value pair for each member as an outcome of this process. The key/ value output of a `map` function is consumed by the `reduce` function. The `reduce` function runs an aggregation function across all key/value pairs and generates an output in turn.

The `map` function to count the number of female (F) and male (M) respondents in the `users` collection is as follows:

```
> var map = function() {
... emit({ gender:this.gender }, { count:1 });
... };
```

movielens_queries.txt

This `map` function emits a key/value pair for each item in the collection that has a `gender` property. It counts 1 for each such occurrence.

The `reduce` function for counting the number of total occurrences of male and female types among all users is as follows:

```
> var reduce = function(key, values) {
... var count = 0;
... values.forEach(function(v) {
... count += v['count'];
... });
...
... return { count:count };
... };
```

movielens_queries.txt

A `reduce` function takes a key/value pair emitted by the `map` function. In this particular `reduce` function, each value in the key/value pair is passed through a function that counts the number of occurrences of a particular type. The line `count += v['count']` could also be written as `count += v.count` because of JavaScript's ability to access object members and their values as a hash data structure.

Finally, running this `map` and `reduce` function pair against the `users` collection leads to an output of the total count of female and male members in the `users` collection. The `mapReduce` run and `result` extraction commands are as follows:

```
> var ratings_respondents_by_gender = db.users.mapReduce(map, reduce);
> ratings_respondents_by_gender
{
    "result" : "tmp.mr.mapreduce_1290399924_2",
    "timeMillis" : 538,
    "counts" : {
        "input" : 6040,
        "emit" : 6040,
        "output" : 2
    },
    "ok" : 1,
}
> db[ratings_respondents_by_gender.result].find();
{ "_id" : { "gender" : "F" }, "value" : { "count" : 1709 } }
{ "_id" : { "gender" : "M" }, "value" : { "count" : 4331 } }
```

movielens_queries.txt

To verify the output, filter the `users` collection for gender values `"F"` and `"M"` and count the number of documents in each filtered sub-collection. The commands for filtering and counting the `users` collection for gender values `"F"` and `"M"` is like so:

```
> db.users.find({ "gender":"F" }).count();
1709
> db.users.find({ "gender":"M" }).count();
4331
```

movielens_queries.txt

Next, you can modify the `map` function slightly and run the `map` and `reduce` functions against the `ratings` collection to count the number of each type of rating (1, 2, 3, 4 or 5) for each movie. In other words, you are counting the collection grouped by rating value for each movie. Here are the complete `map` and `reduce` function definitions run against the `ratings` collection:

```
> var map = function() {
... emit({ movie_id:this.movie_id, rating:this.rating }, { count:1 });
... };
> var reduce = function(key, values) {
... var count = 0;
... values.forEach(function(v) {
... count += v['count'];
... });
...
... return { count: count };
... };
> var group_by_movies_by_rating = db.ratings.mapReduce(map, reduce);
> db[group_by_movies_by_rating.result].find();
```

movielens_queries.txt

To get a count of each type of rating for the movie *Titanic*, identified by `movie_id 1721`, you simply filter the MapReduce output using nested property access method like so:

```
> db[group_by_movies_by_rating.result].find({ "_id.movie_id":1721 });
{ "_id" : { "movie_id" : 1721, "rating" : 1 }, "value" : { "count" : 100 } }
{ "_id" : { "movie_id" : 1721, "rating" : 2 }, "value" : { "count" : 176 } }
{ "_id" : { "movie_id" : 1721, "rating" : 3 }, "value" : { "count" : 381 } }
{ "_id" : { "movie_id" : 1721, "rating" : 4 }, "value" : { "count" : 500 } }
{ "_id" : { "movie_id" : 1721, "rating" : 5 }, "value" : { "count" : 389 } }
```

movielens_queries.txt

In the two examples of MapReduce so far, the `reduce` function is identical but the `map` function is different. In each case a count of 1 is established for a different emitted key/value pair. In one a key/value pair is emitted for each document that has a gender property, whereas in the other a key/value pair is emitted for each document identified by the combination of a movie id and a rating id.

Next, you could calculate the average rating for each movie in the `ratings` collection as follows:

```
> var map = function() {
... emit({ movie_id:this.movie_id }, { rating:this.rating, count:1 });
... };

> var reduce = function(key, values) {
... var sum = 0;
... var count = 0;
... values.forEach(function(v) {
... sum += v['rating'];
... count += v['count'];
... });
```

```
...
... return { average:(sum/count) };
... };
> var average_rating_per_movie = db.ratings.mapReduce(map, reduce);
> db[average_rating_per_movie.result].find();
```

movielens_queries.txt

MapReduce allows you to write many types of sophisticated aggregation algorithms, some of which were presented in this section. A few others are introduced later in the book.

By now you have had a chance to understand many ways of querying MongoDB collections. Next, you get a chance to familiarize yourself with querying tabular databases. HBase is used to illustrate the querying mechanism.

ACCESSING DATA FROM COLUMN-ORIENTED DATABASES LIKE HBASE

Before you get into querying an HBase data store, you need to store some data in it. As with MongoDB, you have already had a first taste of storing and accessing data in HBase and its underlying filesystem, which often defaults to Hadoop Distributed FileSystem (HDFS). You are also aware of HBase and Hadoop basics. This section builds on that basic familiarity. As a working example, historical daily stock market data from NYSE since the 1970s until February 2010 is loaded into an HBase instance. This loaded data set is accessed using an HBase-style querying mechanism. The historical market data is collated from original sources by Infochimp.org and can be accessed at `www.infochimps.com/datasets/nyse-daily-1970-2010-open-close-high-low-and-volume`.

The Historical Daily Market Data

The zipped-up download of the entire data set is substantial at 199 MB but very small by HDFS and HBase standards. The HBase and Hadoop infrastructures are capable of and often used for dealing with petabytes of data that span multiple physical machines. I chose an easily manageable data set for the example as I intentionally want to avoid getting distracted by the immensity of preparing and loading up a large data set for now. This chapter is about the query methods in NoSQL stores and the focus in this section is on column-oriented databases. Understanding data access in smaller data sets is more manageable and the concepts apply equally well to larger amounts of data.

The data fields are partitioned logically into three different types:

➤ Combination of exchange, stock symbol, and date served as the unique id

➤ The open, high, low, close, and adjusted close are a measure of price

➤ The daily volume

The row-key can be created using a combination of the exchange, stock symbol, and date. So NYSE,AA,2008-02-27 could be structured as `NYSEAA20080227` to be a row-key for the data. All price-related information can be stored in a column-family named `price` and volume data can be stored in a column-family named `volume`.

The table itself is named `historical_daily_stock_price`. To get the row data for NYSE, AA, 2008-02-27, you can query as follows:

```
get 'historical_daily_stock_price', 'NYSEAA20080227'
```

You can get the open price as follows:

```
get 'historical_daily_stock_price', 'NYSEAA20080227', 'price:open'
```

You could also use a programming language to query for the data. A sample Java program to get the open and high price data could be as follows:

```java
import org.apache.hadoop.hbase.client.HTable;
import org.apache.hadoop.hbase.HBaseConfiguration;
import org.apache.hadoop.hbase.io.RowResult;

import java.util.HashMap;
import java.util.Map;
import java.io.IOException;

public class HBaseConnector {

public static Map retrievePriceData(String rowKey) throws IOException {
HTable table = new HTable(new HBaseConfiguration(),
 "historical_daily_stock_price");
Map stockData = new HashMap();

RowResult result = table.getRow(rowKey);

for (byte[] column : result.keySet()) {
    stockData.put(new String(column), new
String(result.get(column).getValue()));
}

return stockData;
}

public static void main(String[] args) throws IOException {
    Map stock_data = HBaseConnector.retrievePriceData("NYSEAA20080227");
    System.out.println(stock_data.get("price:open"));
    System.out.println(stock_data.get("price:high"));
}

}
```

HBaseConnector.java

HBase includes very few advanced querying techniques beyond what is illustrated, but its capability to index and query can be extended with the help of Lucene and Hive. Details of using Hive with HBase is illustrated in Chapter 12.

QUERYING REDIS DATA STORES

As in the case of MongoDB and HBase you have had a chance to interact with Redis in the earlier chapters. In the past few chapters you learned the essentials of data storage and access with Redis. In this section, the subject of querying data is explored a bit further. In line with the other illustrations in this chapter so far, a sample data set is first loaded into a Redis instance.

For the purpose of demonstration, the NYC Data Mine public raw data on parking spaces available online at www.nyc.gov/data is used. The data download is available in a comma-separated text file format. The download file is named parking_facilities.csv. See Listing 6-2 for a simple Python program that parses this CSV data set and loads it into a local Redis store. Remember to start your local Redis server before you run the Python script to load up the data. Running the Redis-server program, available in the Redis installation directory, starts a Redis server instance, which by default listens for client connections on port 6379.

LISTING 6-2: Python program to extract NYC parking facilities data

```python
import csv
import redis

f = open("parking_facilities.csv", "r")
parking_facilities = csv.DictReader(f, delimiter=',')
r = redis.Redis(host='localhost', port=6379, db=0)

def add_parking_facility(license_number,
        facility_type,
        entity_name,
        camis_trade_name,
        address_bldg,
        address_street_name,
        address_location,
        address_city,
        address_state,
        address_zip_code,
        telephone_number,
        number_of_spaces):
    if r.sadd("parking_facilities_set", license_number):
        r.hset("parking_facility:%s" % license_number, "facility_type",
facility_type)
        r.hset("parking_facility:%s" % license_number, "entity_name",
entity_name)
        r.hset("parking_facility:%s" % license_number, "camis_trade_name",
camis_trade_name)
        r.hset("parking_facility:%s" % license_number, "address_bldg",
address_bldg)
        r.hset("parking_facility:%s" % license_number, "address_street_name",
address_street_name)
        r.hset("parking_facility:%s" % license_number, "address_location",
address_location)
        r.hset("parking_facility:%s" % license_number, "address_city",
```

continues

LISTING 6-2 *(continued)*

```
address_city)
        r.hset("parking_facility:%s" % license_number, "address_state",
address_state)
        r.hset("parking_facility:%s" % license_number, "address_zip_code",
address_zip_code)
        r.hset("parking_facility:%s" % license_number, "telephone_number",
telephone_number)
        r.hset("parking_facility:%s" % license_number, "number_of_spaces",
number_of_spaces)
        return True
    else:
        return False


if __name__ == "__main__":
    for parking_facility_hash in parking_facilities:
        add_parking_facility(parking_facility_hash['License Number'],
            parking_facility_hash['Facility Type'],
            parking_facility_hash['Entity Name'],
            parking_facility_hash['Camis Trade Name'],
            parking_facility_hash['Address Bldg'],
            parking_facility_hash['Address Street Name'],
            parking_facility_hash['Address Location'],
            parking_facility_hash['Address City'],
            parking_facility_hash['Address State'],
            parking_facility_hash['Address Zip Code'],
            parking_facility_hash['Telephone Number'],
            parking_facility_hash['Number of Spaces'])
        print "added parking_facility with %s" % parking_facility_hash['License
Number']
```

nyc_parking_data_loader.py

The Python program loops through a list of extracted hash records and saves the values to a Redis instance. Each hash record is keyed using the license number. All license numbers themselves are saved in a set named `parking_facilities_set`.

To get a list of all license numbers in the set named `parking_facilities_list`, connect via another program or simply the command-line client and use the following command:

```
SMEMBERS parking_facilities_set
```

All 1,912 license numbers in the set would be printed out. You can run `wc -l  paking_facilities.csv` to verify if this number is correct. Each line in the CSV corresponds to a parking facility so the two numbers should reconcile.

For each parking facility the attributes are stored in a hash, which is identified by the key of the form `parking_facility:<license_number>`. Thus, to see all keys in the hash associated with license number 1105006 you can use the following command:

```
HKEYS parking_facility:1105006
```

The response is as follows:

```
 1. "facility_type"
 2. "entity_name"
 3. "camis_trade_name"
 4. "address_bldg"
 5. "address_street_name"
 6. "address_location"
 7. "address_city"
 8. "address_state"
 9. "address_zip_code"
10. "telephone_number"
11. "number_of_spaces"
```

The license number 1105006 was first on the list returned by the SMEMBERS `parking_facilities_set` command. However, sets are not ordered, so rerunning this command may not result in the same license number on top. If you need the list of members to appear in a certain order, use the sorted sets instead of the set. All you may need to do to use a sorted set is to replace the line `if r.sadd("parking_facilities_set", license_number):` with the following:

```
if r.zadd("parking_facilities_set", license_number):
```

Now, you can query for specific values in the hash, say facility type, as follows:

```
HGET parking_facility:1105006 facility_type
```

The response is `"Parking Lot"`. You can also print out all values using the HVALS command as follows:

```
HVALS parking_facility:1105006
```

The response is:

```
 1. "Parking Lot"
 2. "CENTRAL PARKING SYSTEM OF NEW YORK, INC"
 3. ""
 4. "41-61"
 5. "KISSENA BOULEVARD"
 6. ""
 7. "QUEENS"
 8. "NY"
 9. "11355"
10. "2126296602"
11. "808"
```

Of course, it would be much nicer if you could print out all the keys and the corresponding values in a hash. You can do that using the HGETALL command as follows:

```
HGETALL parking_facility:1105006
```

The response is as follows:

```
1.  "facility_type"
2.  "Parking Lot"
3.  "entity_name"
4.  "CENTRAL PARKING SYSTEM OF NEW YORK, INC"
5.  "camis_trade_name"
6.  ""
7.  "address_bldg"
8.  "41-61"
9.  "address_street_name"
10. "KISSENA BOULEVARD"
11. "address_location"
12. ""
13. "address_city"
14. "QUEENS"
15. "address_state"
16. "NY"
17. "address_zip_code"
18. "11355"
19. "telephone_number"
20. "2126296602"
21. "number_of_spaces"
22. "808"
```

Sometimes, you may not need all the key/value pairs but just want to print out the values for a specific set of fields. For example, you may want to print out only the address_city and the address_zip_code as follows:

```
HMGET parking_facility:1105006 address_city address_zip_code
```

The response is:

```
1.  "QUEENS"
2.  "11355"
```

You could similarly set values for a set of fields using the HMSET command. To get a count of the number of keys, you can use the HLEN command as follows:

```
HLEN parking_facility:1105006
```

The response is 11. If you wanted to check if address_city was one of these, you can use the HEXISTS command to verify if it exists as a key. The command is used as follows:

```
HEXISTS parking_facility:1105006 address_city
```

The response is 1 if the field exists and 0 if it doesn't.

Going back to the set `parking_facilities_set`, you may just want to count the number of members instead of listing them all using the SCARD command as follows:

```
SCARD parking_facilities_set
```

As expected, the response is 1912. You could verify if a specific member exists in the set using the SISMEMBER command. To verify if 1005006 is a member of the set, you could use the following command:

```
SISMEMBER parking_facilities_set 1105006
```

Integral values of 0 and 1 are returned to depict false and true for this query that verifies if a member exists in a set.

SUMMARY

This chapter illustrated a few query mechanisms that are more advanced than those you have seen so far. Querying was explained using examples. MongoDB querying details were explained using a sample movies rating data set. The HBase example was illustrated using historical stock market data and the Redis querying capabilities were demonstrated using sample NYC government data.

The coverage of the querying capabilities is not exhaustive and doesn't cover all types of use cases. The use cases illustrated in this chapter are just some of the innumerable possibilities. However, walking through the example should get you familiar with the style and mechanics of querying NoSQL data stores.

7

Modifying Data Stores and Managing Evolution

WHAT'S IN THIS CHAPTER?

➤ Managing data schema in document databases, column-oriented stores, and key/value databases

➤ Maintaining data stores as the attributes of a data set evolves

➤ Importing and exporting data

Over time, data evolves and changes; sometimes drastically and other times at a slower pace and in less radical ways. In addition, data often outlives a single application. Probably designed and structured with a specific use case in mind, data often gets consumed in ways never thought of originally.

The world of relational databases, however, doesn't normally pay much heed to the evolution of data. It does provide ways to alter schema definitions and data types but presumes that, for the most part, the metadata remains static. It also assumes uniformity of structure is common across most types of data sets and believes in getting the schema right up front. Relational databases focus on effective storage of structured and dense data sets where normalization of data records is important.

Although the debate in this chapter isn't whether RDBMS can adapt to change, it's worth noting that modifying schemas and data types and merging data from two versions of a schema in an RDBMS is generally complex and involves many workarounds. For example, something as benign as adding a new column to an existing table (that has some data) could pose serious issues, especially if the new column needs to have unique values. Workarounds exist for such problems but they aren't elegant or seamless solutions. In contrast, many NoSQL databases promote a schema-less data store where evolution is easy and natural.

As in the previous chapters, the topic of database modification and evolution is explored in the context of the three popular types of NoSQL products, namely:

➤ Document databases

➤ Column databases

➤ Key/value stores

CHANGING DOCUMENT DATABASES

Document databases are schema-less in form, allowing self-contained documents to be stored as a record or item in a collection. Being less rigid about a formal schema or form, document databases by definition accommodate variations and modifications to the average form. In fact, a document database doesn't prevent you from storing a completely disparate set of documents in a single collection, although such a collection may not be logically very useful.

CouchDB, now part of Couchbase, and MongoDB, the two leading open-source document databases, are extremely flexible about storing documents with different sets of properties in the same collection. For example, you could easily store the following two documents together:

```
{ name => "John Doe", organization => "Great Co", email => "john.doe@example.com" }
{ name => "Wei Chin", company => "Work Well", phone => "123-456-7890" }
```

Start up CouchDB and actually store these two documents in a database named `contacts`.

A MongoDB server can host multiple databases, where each database can have multiple collections. In contrast, a CouchDB server can host multiple databases but has no notion of a collection.

You can use the command-line utility, Futon, or an external program to interface with CouchDB and store the documents.

CouchDB offers a REST API to carry out all the tasks, including creating and managing databases and documents and even triggering replication. Please install CouchDB before you proceed any further. There is no better way to learn than to try out the examples and test the concepts yourself. Read Appendix A if you need help setting it up. Appendix A has installation and setup instructions for all NoSQL products covered in this book.

Look at the screenshot in Figure 7-1 to see a list of the two documents in the `contacts` database, as viewed in Futon. The list shows only the id, CouchDB-generated UUIDs, and the version number of the documents.

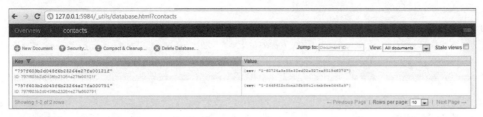

FIGURE 7-1

Expanding out the information for Wei Chin shows the complete document with all its fields, as depicted in Figure 7-2.

FIGURE 7-2

The navigation arrows at the bottom right in Figure 7-2 allow you to navigate through the document versions. This may seem out of place in many databases and remind you of version control software or document management systems, but it is an inherent and important feature in CouchDB. An update to a CouchDB document under the hood translates to the addition of a new version of the document. Therefore, if you update the name from "Wei Chin" to "Wei Lee Chin" the current updated version of the document (in JSON format) would be as follows:

```
{
    "_id": "797f603b2d043f6b23264e27fa00121f",
    "_rev": "2-949a21d63459638cbd392e6b3a27989d",
    "name": "Wei Lee Chin",
    "company": "Work Well",
    "phone": "123-456-7890"
}
```

couchdb_example.txt

Apart from an updated value for the name field, you should see a difference in value of the _rev property. The _rev field holds the revision number for the document. The original revision number of the document was 1-63726a5e55e33ed02a927ca8518df073. After the update the revision number is 2-949a21d63459638cbd392e6b3a27989d. Revision numbers in CouchDB are of the form *N-<hash value>*, where N depicts the number of times the document has been updated and the hash value is the MD5 hash of the transport representation of the document. N is 1 when the document is created.

MD5 is a one-way hash algorithm that takes any length of data and produces a 128-bit fingerprint or message digest. Read about MD5 at www.ietf.org/rfc/ rfc1321.txt.

CouchDB uses MultiVersion Concurrency Control (MVCC) to facilitate concurrent access to the database. Using MVCC enables CouchDB to avoid locking mechanisms to assure write fidelity. Every document is versioned, and document versions help reconcile conflicts. Before a document is updated, it is verified if the current version (before update) is the same as the version at the time the document was read for update. If the versions don't match, it suggests a possible conflict, due to an update by another independent process between the read and the subsequent update. When documents are updated, newer versions of entire documents are saved instead of updates on existing documents. A side effect of this process is that you enjoy a performance boost because appending to contiguous memory is faster than updating in place. Because version or revision numbers are central concepts in CouchDB, you see multiple versions.

However, multiple versions of documents, by default, aren't persisted forever. The purpose of versioning is to avoid conflicts and provide concurrency. Compaction and replication prunes old versions and at any given moment only the presence of the latest version is guaranteed. This means by default you cannot use the _rev field to query or access old versions of a document. In a single node scenario you may be tempted to switch compaction off and retain the versions. However, the strategy fails as soon as you set up a cluster because only the latest version gets replicated.

If you do need to keep versions and query older versions of a document, you would need to do it programmatically. The CouchDB founders have a simple but effective solution to the problem. Read it online at http://blog.couchone.com/post/632718824/simple-document-versioning-with-couchdb. The solution is rather straightforward. It suggests that you do the following:

➤ Extract a string representation of the current version of the document when it is accessed.

➤ Before an update, encode the string representation using Base64 encoding and then save the binary representation as an attachment to the document. Use the current version number (before update) as the name of the attachment.

This means if a document itself is accessed as follows:

```
http://127.0.0.1:5984/contacts/797f603b2d043f6b23264e27fa00121f
```

Then version 2, which is available with the document as an attachment, can be accessed as follows:

```
http://127.0.0.1:5984/contacts/797f603b2d043f6b23264e27fa00121f/2-949a21d63459
638cbd392e6b3a27989d
```

This way of managing versions is simple and useful for most cases. More sophisticated version management systems could be built by saving the document versions as per the use case.

Futon manages document versions using the technique illustrated. This technique is implemented in the jQuery JavaScript client library for CouchDB. The jQuery client library is available at `http://svn.apache.org/viewvc?revision=948262&view=revision`.

So while versioning in CouchDB is an interesting feature, the document store malleability and flexibility is a more generic feature, which is also found in other schema-less NoSQL databases.

Schema-less Flexibility

It's evident from the previous example that CouchDB is fully capable of storing two documents with different sets of fields in a single database. This has many advantages, especially in situations such as these:

➤ Sparse data sets can be stored effectively because fields that are null needn't be stored at all.

➤ As documents evolve, adding additional fields is trivial.

In the preceding example, `"John Doe"` has an e-mail address, whereas "`Wei Chin`" doesn't have one. It's not a problem; they can still be in the same database. In the future if "`Wei Chin`" gets an e-mail address, say `wei.chin@example.com`, an additional field can be added to the document without any overhead. Similarly, fields can be deleted and values for fields can be modified.

Apart from fields themselves being added and removed, there aren't any strong rules about the data types a field can hold either. So a field that stores a string value can also hold an integer. It can even have an array type as a value. This means that you don't have to worry about strong typing. On the flip side, though, it implies your application needs to make sure that the data is validated and semantically the values are consistent.

So far, the fundamentals of schema-less flexibility have been explained in the context of CouchDB. To demonstrate a few other aspects of this flexibility, you use MongoDB next. First, create a MongoDB collection named `contacts` and add the two documents to the collection. You can do this by starting up MongoDB and executing the following commands in order as follows:

```
use mydb
db.contacts.insert({ name:"John Doe", organization:"Great Co",
  email:"john.doe@example.com" });
db.contacts.insert({ name:"Wei Chin", company:"Work Well", phone:"123-456-7890"
  });
```

mongodb_example.txt

Next, confirm that the collection was created and the two documents are in it. You can verify by simply listing the documents as follows:

```
db.contacts.find();
```

mongodb_example.txt

The result of this query should be as follows:

```
{ "_id" : ObjectId("4d2bbad6febd3e2b32bed964"), "name" : "John Doe",
"organization" : "Great Co", "email" : "john.doe@example.com" }
{ "_id" : ObjectId("4d2bbb43febd3e2b32bed965"), "name" : "Wei Chin", "company" :
"Work Well", "phone" : "123-456-7890" }
```

The _id values may be different because these are the MongoDB-generated values on my system and will certainly vary from one instance to the other. Now, you could add an additional field, email, to the document that relates to "Wei Chin" as follows:

```
var doc = db.contacts.findOne({ _id:ObjectId("4d2bbb43febd3e2b32bed965") });
doc.email = "wei.chin@example.com";
db.contacts.save(doc);
```

mongodb_example.txt

I use the _id to get hold of the document and then simply assign a value to the email field and save the document. To verify that the new field is now added, simply get the documents from the contacts collection again as follows:

```
db.contacts.find();
```

mongodb_example.txt

The response should be as follows:

```
{ "_id" : ObjectId("4d2bbad6febd3e2b32bed964"), "name" : "John Doe",
"organization" : "Great Co", "email" : "john.doe@example.com" }
{ "_id" : ObjectId("4d2bbb43febd3e2b32bed965"), "name" : "Wei Chin", "company":
"Work Well", "phone" : "123-456-7890", "email" : "wei.chin@example.com" }
```

Unlike CouchDB, MongoDB doesn't maintain document versions and an update modifies the document in place.

Now, say you had another collection named contacts2, which had some more contact documents and you needed to merge the two collections, contacts and contacts2, into one. How would you do that?

Unfortunately, there is no magic button or command that merges collections at the moment but it's not terribly difficult to write a quick script in a language of your choice to merge two collections. A few considerations in designing a merge script could be:

➤ A switch with possible values of overwrite, update, or copy could decide how two documents with the same _id in two different collections need to be merged. Two documents cannot have the same _id value in a single collection. Overwrite would imply the document in the second collection overwrites the corresponding document in the first collection. Update and copy would define alternate merge strategies.

➤ Merge on the basis of a field other than the _id.

A ruby script to merge two MongoDB collections is available via a project named mongo-tools, available online at `https://github.com/tshanky/mongo-tools`.

Exporting and Importing Data from and into MongoDB

Exporting data out and importing data into a database is an important and often-used step in backing up, restoring, and merging databases. MongoDB provides a few useful utilities to assist you in this regard.

mongoimport

If you have the data to import in a single file and it is either in JSON format or is text data in comma- or tab-separated format, the `mongoimport` utility can help you import the data into a MongoDB collection. The utility has a few options that you can learn about by simply executing the command without any options. Running `bin/mongoimport` with no options produces the following output:

```
connected to: 127.0.0.1
no collection specified!
options:
  --help                    produce help message
  -v [ --verbose ]          be more verbose (include multiple times for more
                            verbosity e.g. -vvvvv)
  -h [ --host ] arg         mongo host to connect to ("left,right" for pairs)
  --port arg                server port. Can also use --host hostname:port
  -d [ --db ] arg           database to use
  -c [ --collection ] arg   collection to use (some commands)
  -u [ --username ] arg     username
  -p [ --password ] arg     password
  --ipv6                    enable IPv6 support (disabled by default)
  --dbpath arg              directly access mongod database files in the given
                            path, instead of connecting to a mongod  server -
                            needs to lock the data directory, so cannot be used
                            if a mongod is currently accessing the same path
  --directoryperdb          if dbpath specified, each db is in a separate
                            directory
  -f [ --fields ] arg       comma separated list of field names e.g. -f name,age
  --fieldFile arg           file with fields names - 1 per line
  --ignoreBlanks            if given, empty fields in csv and tsv will be ignored
  --type arg                type of file to import.  default: json (json,csv,tsv)
  --file arg                file to import from; if not specified stdin is used
  --drop                    drop collection first
  --headerline              CSV,TSV only - use first line as headers
  --upsert                  insert or update objects that already exist
  --upsertFields arg        comma-separated fields for the query part of the
                            upsert. You should make sure this is indexed
  --stopOnError             stop importing at first error rather than continuing
  --jsonArray               load a json array, not one item per line. Currently
                            limited to 4MB.
```

Although useful, this utility hits the limits as soon as you start importing data that is a little more complicated than comma-separated or tab-separated values (or the JSON format). You may recall the Ruby script that was used in Chapter 6 to load the MovieLens data into MongoDB collections. You couldn't use mongoimport for that task.

mongoexport

The exact opposite of loading data into a MongoDB collection is to export data out of a collection. If JSON or CSV format is what you need, you can use this tool to export the data out of a collection. To explore the options, again simply run the mongoexport command without any collections specified. You will be prompted with a message stating all the options as follows:

```
connected to: 127.0.0.1
no collection specified!
options:
  --help                    produce help message
  -v [ --verbose ]          be more verbose (include multiple times for more
                            verbosity e.g. -vvvvv)
  -h [ --host ] arg         mongo host to connect to ("left,right" for pairs)
  --port arg                server port. Can also use --host hostname:port
  -d [ --db ] arg           database to use
  -c [ --collection ] arg   collection to use (some commands)
  -u [ --username ] arg     username
  -p [ --password ] arg     password
  --ipv6                    enable IPv6 support (disabled by default)
  --dbpath arg              directly access mongod database files in the given
                            path, instead of connecting to a mongod  server -
                            needs to lock the data directory, so cannot be used
                            if a mongod is currently accessing the same path
  --directoryperdb          if dbpath specified, each db is in a separate
                            directory
  -f [ --fields ] arg       comma separated list of field names e.g. -f name,age
  --fieldFile arg           file with fields names - 1 per line
  -q [ --query ] arg        query filter, as a JSON string
  --csv                     export to csv instead of json
  -o [ --out ] arg          output file; if not specified, stdout is used
  --jsonArray               output to a json array rather than one object per
                            line
```

mongodump

The mongoimport and mongoexport utilities help import into and export from a single collection and deal with human-readable data formats. If the purpose is simply to take a hot backup, you could rely on mongodump to dump a complete database copy in a binary format. To explore the mongodump options, run the mongodump commands with –help as the argument. The output would be as follows:

 Running mongodump *with no options dumps the relevant MongoDB database so don't run it the way you have run* mongoimport *and* mongoexport *to explore the options.*

```
options:
  --help                      produce help message
  -v [ --verbose ]            be more verbose (include multiple times for more
                              verbosity e.g. -vvvvv)
  -h [ --host ] arg           mongo host to connect to ("left,right" for pairs)
  --port arg                  server port. Can also use --host hostname:port
  -d [ --db ] arg             database to use
  -c [ --collection ] arg     collection to use (some commands)
  -u [ --username ] arg       username
  -p [ --password ] arg       password
  --ipv6                      enable IPv6 support (disabled by default)
  --dbpath arg                directly access mongod database files in the given
                              path, instead of connecting to a mongod  server -
                              needs to lock the data directory, so cannot be used
                              if a mongod is currently accessing the same path
  --directoryperdb            if dbpath specified, each db is in a separate
                              directory
  -o [ --out ] arg (=dump)    output directory
  -q [ --query ] arg          json query
```

With good coverage about document database flexibility and a survey of some of the maintenance tools, you may now be ready to move on to column databases.

SCHEMA EVOLUTION IN COLUMN-ORIENTED DATABASES

HBase is not completely schema-less. There is a loosely defined schema, especially in terms of the column-family definitions. A column-family is a fairly static definition that partitions the more dynamic and flexible column definitions into logical bundles. For the purpose of explanation, I reuse and extend an example that you saw when you first started out with HBase in Chapter 3. It's about a set of blogposts. If you would like to get the details, review the section on HBase in Chapter 3.

The elements of that collection are like so:

```
{
    "post" : {
        "title": "an interesting blog post",
        "author": "a blogger",
        "body": "interesting content",
    },
    "multimedia": {
        "header": header.png,
        "body": body.mpeg,
    },
}
```

or

```
{
    "post" : {
        "title": "yet an interesting blog post",
        "author": "another blogger",
        "body": "interesting content",
```

```
        },
        "multimedia": {
            "body-image": body_image.png,
            "body-video": body_video.mpeg,
        },
    }
```

blogposts.txt

You can start HBase using `bin/start-hbase.sh` and connect via the shell using `bin/hbase shell`. Then, you can run the following commands in sequence to create the tables and populate some sample data:

```
create 'blogposts', 'post', 'multimedia'
put 'blogposts', 'post1', 'post:title', 'an interesting blog post'
put 'blogposts', 'post1', 'post:author', 'a blogger'
put 'blogposts', 'post1', 'post:body', 'interesting content'
put 'blogposts', 'post1', 'multimedia:header', 'header.png'
put 'blogposts', 'post1', 'multimedia:body', 'body.mpeg'
put 'blogposts', 'post2', 'post:title', 'yet an interesting blog post'
put 'blogposts', 'post2', 'post:title', 'yet another interesting blog post'
put 'blogposts', 'post2', 'post:author', 'another blogger'
put 'blogposts', 'post2', 'post:body', 'interesting content'
put 'blogposts', 'post2', 'multimedia:body-image', 'body_image.png'
put 'blogposts', 'post2', 'multimedia:body-video', 'body_video.mpeg'
```

blogposts.txt

Once the database is ready you could run a simple `get` query like so:

```
get 'blogposts', 'post1'
```

blogposts.txt

The output would be something like this:

```
COLUMN                      CELL
 multimedia:body            timestamp=1294717543345, value=body.mpeg
 multimedia:header          timestamp=1294717521136, value=header.png
 post:author               timestamp=1294717483381, value=a blogger
 post:body                 timestamp=1294717502262, value=interesting content

 post:title                timestamp=1294717467992, value=an interesting blog
 post
5 row(s) in 0.0140 seconds
```

Now that the data set is ready, I recap a few more fundamental aspects of HBase and show you how HBase evolves as the data schema changes.

First, all data updates in HBase are overwrites with newer versions of the record and not in-place updates of existing records. You have seen analogous behavior in CouchDB. By default, HBase is configured to keep the last three versions but you could configure to store more than three versions for each. The number of versions is set at a per column-family level. You can specify the number of versions when you define a column-family. In the HBase shell you could create a table named `'mytable'` and define a column-family named `'afamily'` with the configuration to keep 15 past versions as follows:

```
create 'mytable', { NAME => 'afamily', VERSIONS => 15 }
```

The VERSIONS property takes an integer value and so the maximum value it can take is `Integer .MAX_VALUE`. Although you can define a large value for the number of versions to keep, using this data it is not easy to retrieve and query the value because there is no built-in index based on versions. Also, versions have a timestamp but querying across this time series for the data set is not a feature that is easy or efficient to implement.

Although the configuration was done using a command-line utility, you could also achieve the same programmatically. The maximum versions property needs to be passed as an argument to the `HColumnDescriptor` constructor.

Columns in HBase don't need to be defined up front so they provide a flexible way of managing evolving schemas. Column-families, on the other hand, are more static. However, columns can't be renamed or assigned easily from one column-family to the other. Making such changes requires creation of the new columns, migration of data from the existing columns to the new column, and then potentially deletion of the old columns.

Though HBase allows creation of column-families from the shell or through programmatic options, Cassandra has traditionally been far more rigid. The definition of column-families in older versions of Cassandra needed a database restart. The current version of Cassandra is more flexible and allows for configuration changes at runtime.

HBASE DATA IMPORT AND EXPORT

The data in a table, say `'blogposts'`, can be exported out to the local filesystem or exported to HDFS.

You can export the data to the local filesystem as follows:

```
bin/hbase org.apache.hadoop.hbase.mapreduce.Driver export blogposts
  path/to/local/filesystem
```

You can export the same data to HDFS as follows:

```
bin/hbase org.apache.hadoop.hbase.mapreduce.Driver export blogposts
  hdfs://namenode/path/to/hdfs
```

Like export, you can also import the data into an HBase table. You could import the data from the local filesystem or from HDFS. Analogous to export, import from the local filesystem is as follows:

```
bin/hbase org.apache.hadoop.hbase.mapreduce.Driver import blogposts
  path/to/local/filesystem
```

Importing from HDFS is similar. You could import the data like so:

```
bin/hbase org.apache.hadoop.hbase.mapreduce.Driver import blogposts
  hdfs://namenode/path/to/hdfs
```

DATA EVOLUTION IN KEY/VALUE STORES

Key/value stores usually support fairly limited data sets and either hold string or object values. Some, like Redis, allow a few sophisticated data structures. Some key/value stores, like Memcached and Membase, store time-sensitive data, purging everything that is old as per the configuration.

Redis has collection structures like hashes, sets, lists, and such but it has little if any metadata facility. To Redis, everything is a hash or a collection of hashes. It is totally agnostic to what the key is and what it means.

Key/value databases don't hold documents, data structures or objects and so have little sense of a schema beyond the key/value pair itself. Therefore, the notion of schema evolution isn't that relevant to key/value databases.

Somewhat similar to renaming a field name would be renaming a key. If a key exists you can easily rename it as follows:

```
RENAME old_key_name new_key_name
```

Redis persists all the data it holds by flushing it out to disks. In order to back up a Redis database, you could simply copy the Redis DB file and configure another instance to use it. Alternatively, you could issue a BGSAVE to run and save the database job asynchronously.

SUMMARY

NoSQL databases support schema-less structures and thus accommodate flexible and continuing evolution. Though not explicitly observed, this is one of the key NoSQL features. The notion of no strict schema allows document databases to focus on storing real-world-centric data as such and not force fitting them into the normalized relational model.

In column databases, the lack of strict schema allows for easy maintenance and growth of sparse data. In key/value-based stores, the notion of a schema is limited.

Indexing and Ordering Data Sets

WHAT'S IN THIS CHAPTER?

➤ Creating indexes that help enhance query performance

➤ Creating and maintaining indexes in document databases and column-family databases

➤ Ordering NoSQL data sets

➤ Making effective design choices to create optimal indexes and ordering patterns

You have already learned the essentials of querying NoSQL databases. In this chapter, you take the next step to ensure that your queries are fast and efficient. In relational databases, a common way to optimize query performance is to leverage database indexes. Similar concepts apply to the world of NoSQL as well.

Indexes exist to increase data access performance. In theory, they are similar in behavior to the index in a book. When you need to search for a term or a word in a book, you have two options, namely:

➤ Scan the entire book page by page to search for the term or word.

➤ Look up the index at the end to find the pages where the term or word can be found and then browse to those specific pages.

Between these two options it's a no-brainer to look up the index as opposed to a page-by-page scan to find the term. It makes the job easy and saves time.

In an analogous manner you have two choices when accessing a record in a database:

➤ Look through the entire collection or data set item by item.

➤ Leverage the index to get to the relevant data quickly.

Obviously, again the index lookup is a preferred choice. Although the book index and database index are analogous, stretching the similarity too far can cause confusion. Book indexes are on free text and so the number of words or terms indexed is restricted to an important subset of the entire possible set. On the other hand, database indexes apply to all data sets in a collection. Indexes are created on an item identifier or a specific property.

ESSENTIAL CONCEPTS BEHIND A DATABASE INDEX

There is no single universal formula for creating an index but most useful methods hinge on a few common ideas. The building blocks of these common ideas reside in hash functions and B-tree and B+-tree data structures. In this section you peruse these ideas to understand the underlying theory.

A hash function is a well-defined mathematical function to convert a large, and often variable-sized and complex, data value to a single integer or a set of bytes. The output of a hash function is known by various names, including hash code, hash value, hash sum, and checksum. A hash code is often used as the key for an associative array, also called a hash map. Hash functions come in handy when you are mapping complex database property values to hash codes for index creation.

A tree data structure distributes a set of values in a tree-like structure. Values are structured in a hierarchical manner with links or pointers between certain nodes in the tree. A binary tree is a tree that has at most two child nodes: one on the left and other on the right. A node can be a parent, in which case it has at most two nodes, or it can be a leaf, in which case it's the last node in the chain. At the base of a tree structure is a root node. See Figure 8-1 to understand a binary tree data structure.

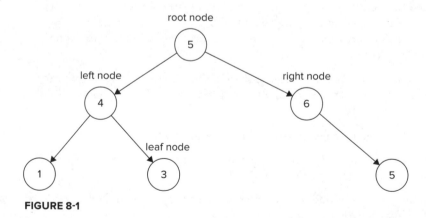

FIGURE 8-1

A B-tree is a generalization of a binary tree. It allows more than two child nodes for a parent node. A B-tree keeps the data sorted and therefore allows for efficient search and data access. A B+-tree is a special variant of a B-tree. In a B+-tree, all records are stored in the leaves and leaves are sequentially linked. A B+-tree is the most common tree structure used to store a database index.

If you are itching to learn more about the details of B-trees and B+-trees, read through the following content, available online:

➤ `http://en.wikipedia.org/wiki/B-tree`

➤ `www.semaphorecorp.com/btp/algo.html`

➤ `http://en.wikipedia.org/wiki/B%2B_tree`

Alternatively, for a more structured tutorial consider reading Cormen, Leiserson, Rivest, and Stein's *Introduction to Algorithms, ISBN 0-262-03384-4.*

Though the essential building blocks are the same, indexes are created and applied differently in different NoSQL products. In the subsequent sections in this chapter, indexes in MongoDB, CouchDB, and Apache Cassandra are explained. Effective data sorting is also covered as a part of the exposition on indexes, because the two are closely related.

INDEXING AND ORDERING IN MONGODB

MongoDB provides a wide range of rich options around indexing collections to enhance query performance. By default, it creates an index on the `_id` property for all collections it contains.

Indexing is best explained in the context of examples. I start out with the MongoDB movie-ratings collection, introduced in Chapter 6. If you don't have the movie-ratings collection in your MongoDB instance, follow along with the example in Chapter 6 to set up and load the collection. Once it is set up you should have three collections, namely, `movies`, `ratings`, and `users`, at your disposal.

To understand the significance and impact of an index you also need to have a few tools to measure query performance with and without an index. In MongoDB, measuring query performance is facilitated by built-in tools that explain query plans and identify slow-running queries.

A query plan describes what the database server has to do to run a given query. To get started, run the explain plan utility before you delve deeper into its output and what it conveys. To get all the items in the `ratings` collection, you can query like so:

```
db.ratings.find();
```

movielens_indexes.txt

To run explain plan for this query you can run this query:

```
db.ratings.find().explain();
```

movielens_indexes.txt

The output of the explain plan would be something like this:

```
{
    "cursor" : "BasicCursor",
    "nscanned" : 1000209,
```

```
        "nscannedObjects" : 1000209,
        "n" : 1000209,
        "millis" : 1549,
        "indexBounds" : {

        }
    }
```

The output says it took 1,549 milliseconds to return 1,000,209 (more than 1 million) documents. In returning these 1,000,209 documents, 1,000,209 items were examined. It also states that `BasicCursor` was used.

As is evident, the output of the explain function is a document as well. Its properties, as shown in the previous example, are as follows:

➤ **cursor** — The cursor used to return the result sets of the query. A cursor can be of two types: basic cursor and B-tree cursor. Basic cursor implies table scan and B-tree cursor means an index was used.

➤ **nscanned** — Number of entries scanned. When using an index, it would correspond to the number of index entries.

➤ **nscannedObjects** — Number of documents scanned.

➤ **n** — The number of documents returned.

➤ **millis** — The time, in milliseconds, taken to run the query.

➤ **indexBounds** — Represents the minimum and maximum index keys within which the query was matched. This field is relevant only when an index is used.

The next example queries for a subset of the ratings. The `ratings` collection consists of rankings (on a scale of 1 to 5) for a set of movies by a set of users. To filter the `ratings` collection, restrict it to a subset that relates to a particular movie. The `ratings` collection has only movie IDs, so to correlate IDs to names you need to look up the value in the `movies` collection. I use the original *Toy Story* (that is, *Toy Story 1*) movie as an example. You can choose to pick up another one!

To get the document that relates to *Toy Story* you can leverage a good old regular expression. You know of these query-filtering techniques from Chapter 6. If you feel unsure, don't hesitate to refer to that chapter to review the concepts. All documents relating to *Toy Story* in the `movies` collection can be queried like so:

```
db.movies.find({title: /Toy Story/i});
```

movielens_indexes.txt

The output should be as follows:

```
{ "_id" : 1, "title" : "Toy Story (1995)", "genres" : [ "Animation",
"Children's", "Comedy" ] }
{ "_id" : 3114, "title" : "Toy Story 2 (1999)", "genres" : [ "Animation",
"Children's", "Comedy" ] }
```

I guess *Toy Story 3* wasn't released when these ratings were compiled. That's why you don't see that in the list. Next, take the movie ID for `"Toy Story"`, which happens to be 1, and use that to find all the relevant ratings from all the users. Before you do that, though, run the explain plan function to view how the database ran the regular expression query to find `Toy Story` in the `movies` collection. You can run the explain plan like so:

```
db.movies.find({title: /Toy Story/i}).explain();
```

The output should be as follows:

```
{
    "cursor" : "BasicCursor",
    "nscanned" : 3883,
    "nscannedObjects" : 3883,
    "n" : 2,
    "millis" : 6,
    "indexBounds" : {

    }
}
```

Run a count, using `db.movies.count();`, on the `movies` collection to verify the number of documents and you will observe that it matches with the `nscanned` and `nscannedObjects` value of the query explanation. This means the regular expression query led to a table scan, which isn't efficient. The number of documents was limited to 3,883 so the query still ran fast enough and took only 6 milliseconds. In a short bit you will see how you could leverage indexes to make this query more efficient, but for now return to the `ratings` collection to get a subset that relates to *Toy Story*.

To list all ratings that relate to `Toy Story` (more accurately Toy Story (1995)) you can query as follows:

```
db.ratings.find({movie_id: 1});
```

To see the query plan for the previous query run explain as follows:

```
db.ratings.find({movie_id: 1}).explain();
```

The output should be as follows:

```
{
    "cursor" : "BasicCursor",
    "nscanned" : 1000209,
    "nscannedObjects" : 1000209,
    "n" : 2077,
    "millis" : 484,
    "indexBounds" : {

    }
}
```

At this stage it's evident that the query is not running optimally because the `nscanned` and `nscannedObjects` count reads 1,000,209, which is all the documents in the collection. This is a good point to introduce indexes and optimize things.

CREATING AND USING INDEXES IN MONGODB

The `ensureIndex` keyword does most of the index creation magic in MongoDB. The last query filtered the `ratings` collection based on the `movie_id` so creating an index on that property should transform the lookup from table scan to B-tree index traversal. First, verify if the theory does hold good.

Create the index by running the following command:

Available for download on Wrox.com

```
db.ratings.ensureIndex({ movie_id:1 });
```

movielens_indexes.txt

This creates an index on `movie_id` and sorts the keys in the index in an ascending order. To create an index with keys sorted in descending order use the following:

Available for download on Wrox.com

```
db.ratings.ensureIndex({ movie_id:-1 });
```

movielens_indexes.txt

Then rerun the earlier query as follows:

Available for download on Wrox.com

```
db.ratings.find({movie_id: 1});
```

movielens_indexes.txt

Verify the query plan after that as follows:

```
db.ratings.find({movie_id: 1}).explain();
```

The output should be:

```
{
    "cursor" : "BtreeCursor movie_id_1",
    "nscanned" : 2077,
    "nscannedObjects" : 2077,
    "n" : 2077,
    "millis" : 2,
    "indexBounds" : {
        "movie_id" : [
            [
                1,
                1
            ]
        ]
    }
}
```

At first glance, it's clear that the number of items (and documents) looked up have reduced from 1,000,209 (the total number of documents in the collection) to 2,077 (the number of documents that match the filter criteria). This is a huge performance boost. In algorithmic speak, the document search has been reduced from a linearly scalable time to constant time. Therefore, the total time to run the query is reduced from 484 ms to 2 ms, which is over a 99-percent reduction in the time taken to run the query.

From the query plan cursor value, it's clear that the index movie_id_1 was used. You can try to create an index with keys sorted in a descending order and rerun the query and the query plan. However, before you run the query, analyze the list of indexes in the ratings collection and find how you could force a particular index.

Getting a list, or more accurately an array, of all indexes is easy. You can query as follows:

```
db.ratings.getIndexes();
```

There are two indexes on movie_id with ascending and descending order and the default _id, so the list of indexes should have these three. The output of getIndexes is as follows:

```
[
    {
        "name" : "_id_",
```

```
            "ns" : "mydb.ratings",
            "key" : {
                "_id" : 1
            }
    },
    {
            "_id" : ObjectId("4d02ef30e63c3e677005636f"),
            "ns" : "mydb.ratings",
            "key" : {
                "movie_id" : -1
            },
            "name" : "movie_id_-1"
    },
    {
            "_id" : ObjectId("4d032faee63c3e6770056370"),
            "ns" : "mydb.ratings",
            "key" : {
                "movie_id" : 1
            },
            "name" : "movie_id_1"
    }
]
```

You have already created an index on `movie_id` using a descending order sort using the
following command:

```
db.ratings.ensureIndex({ movie_id:-1 });
```

movielens_indexes.txt

If required, you could force a query to use a particular index using the `hint` method. To force
the descending order index on `movie_id` to get ratings related to "Toy Story (1995)" you can query
as follows:

```
db.ratings.find({ movie_id:1 }).hint({ movie_id:-1 });
```

movielens_indexes.txt

Soon after running this query, you can verify the query plan to see which index was used and how
it performed. A query plan for the last query using the descending order index on `movie_id` can be
accessed as follows:

```
db.ratings.find({ movie_id:1 }).hint({ movie_id:-1 }).explain();
```

movielens_indexes.txt

The output of the query explain plan is as follows:

```
{
    "cursor" : "BtreeCursor movie_id_-1",
    "nscanned" : 2077,
    "nscannedObjects" : 2077,
    "n" : 2077,
    "millis" : 17,
    "indexBounds" : {
        "movie_id" : [
            [
                1,
                1
            ]
        ]
    }
}
```

The explain plan output confirms that the descending order index on movie_id, identified by movie_id_-1, was used. It also shows that like the ascending order index, the descending order index accessed only 2,077 items.

There is one peculiarity in the output, though. Although an index was used and only a select few documents were scanned it took 17 ms to return the result set. This is much less than the 484 ms used for the table scan but is substantially more than the 2 ms the ascending order index took to return the result set. This is possibly because in this case, the movie_id is 1 and is at the beginning of the ascending order list and the results were cached from a previous query. Ascending order indexes do not deterministically outperform descending order indexes when accessing documents in the beginning of the list. Likewise, descending order indexes do not deterministically outperform ascending order indexes when accessing documents at the end of the list. In most cases, especially for items somewhere near the middle, both index types perform equally well. To test this performance claim you can use both of the indexes to search for ratings for a movie, whose movie_id is at the other end.

The movie_id field (or property) of the ratings collection corresponds to the _id field of the movies collection. The _id field (and of course the movie_id field) has integer values so finding the movie_id at the top of the descending order sort is the same as finding the maximum value for the _id field in the movies collection. One way to find the maximum value of _id in the movies collection is to sort it in descending order as follows:

```
db.movies.find().sort({ _id:-1 });
```

movielens_indexes.txt

The JavaScript console returns only 20 documents at a time so it's easy to find the maximum value, which is 3,952, at a quick glance. If you are running this query using a language API or any other mechanism you may want to limit the number of items in the result. Because only one item is required, you could simply run the query like so:

```
db.movies.find().sort({ _id:-1 }).limit(1);
```

movielens_indexes.txt

 If you are wondering why the `limit` *method and not the* `findOne` *method was used to return the top item in the list sorted in descending order, you may benefit from knowing that sort doesn't work with* `findOne`. *This is because* `findOne` *can return only a single document and the concept of sorting a single document has no meaning. On the other hand, the* `limit` *method restricts only the final output to a subset of the total result set.*

The `movie_id` 3952 corresponds to Contender, The (2000). To get ratings for the movie *The Contender*, you could use either the ascending or the descending ordered index on `movie_id`. Because the objective here is to analyze how both of these indexes perform for an item that satisfies boundary conditions, you can use both of them one after the other. In both cases you can also run the query plans. The query and query plan commands for the ascending order `movie_id` index are as follows:

```
db.ratings.find({ movie_id:3952 }).hint({ movie_id:1 });
db.ratings.find({ movie_id:3952 }).hint({ movie_id:1 }).explain();
```

movielens_indexes.txt

The output of the query plan is like so:

```
{
    "cursor" : "BtreeCursor movie_id_1",
    "nscanned" : 388,
    "nscannedObjects" : 388,
    "n" : 388,
    "millis" : 2,
    "indexBounds" : {
        "movie_id" : [
            [
                3952,
                3952
            ]
        ]
    }
}
```

The query and query plan commands for the descending order `movie_id` index is as follows:

```
db.ratings.find({ movie_id:3952 }).hint({ movie_id:-1 });
db.ratings.find({ movie_id:3952 }).hint({ movie_id:-1 }).explain();
{
    "cursor" : "BtreeCursor movie_id_-1",
    "nscanned" : 388,
    "nscannedObjects" : 388,
    "n" : 388,
    "millis" : 0,
    "indexBounds" : {
        "movie_id" : [
            [
                3952,
                3952
            ]
        ]
    }
}
```

movielens_indexes.txt

From multiple runs of these queries it seems the theory that values at the extremes don't always benefit from indexes that start out at the corresponding end seems to be true. However, you need to bear in mind that query plan output is not idempotent. Every run could produce a unique output. For example, values could be cached and so may never hit the underlying data structures on a rerun. Also, for smaller data sets, as is the case with the `movies` collection, the difference is negligible and often the extraneous overheads like I/O lag substantially affect response time. In general, though, and especially for large data sets, a sort order that favors the item queried should be used.

Sometimes, after numerous modifications to a collection it may be worthwhile to rebuild indexes. To rebuild all indexes for the `ratings` collection you can run this command:

```
db.ratings.reIndex();
```

movielens_indexes.txt

You can alternatively use the `runCommand` to reindex:

```
db.runCommand({ reIndex:'ratings' });
```

movielens_indexes.txt

Rebuilding indexes is not required in most cases unless the size of the collection has changed in a considerable way or the index seems to be occupying an unusually large amount of disk space.

Sometimes, you may want to drop and create new indexes instead of rebuilding the ones that exist. Indexes can be dropped with the `dropIndex` command:

```
db.ratings.dropIndex({ movie_id:-1 });
```

movielens_indexes.txt

This command drops the descending order `movie_id` index. You can also drop all indexes if need be. All indexes (except the one of the `_id` field) can be dropped as follows:

```
db.ratings.dropIndexes();
```

movielens_indexes.txt

Compound and Embedded Keys

So far, you have created indexes on only a single field or property. It's also possible to create compound indexes that involve multiple fields. For example, you may choose to create an index on `movie_id` and ratings fields together. The command to create such an index is:

```
db.ratings.ensureIndex({ movie_id:1, rating:-1 });
```

movielens_indexes.txt

This creates a compound index on `movie_id` (ascending order sorted) and `rating` (descending order sorted). You can create three more indexes out of the four total possible compound indexes involving `movie_id` and `rating`. The four possibilities arise due to possible ascending and descending order sorts of the two keys. The order of the sort can have an impact on queries that involve sorting and range queries so keep the order in mind when you define the compound indexes for your collection.

A compound index involving `movie_id` and `rating` can be used to query for documents that are matched on both these keys and the first key (that is, `movie_id`) alone. When using this index to filter documents on the basis of `movie_id` alone, the behavior is similar to a single field index on `movie_id`.

Compound keys are not restricted to two keys. You can include as many keys as you like. A compound index for `movie_id`, `rating`, and `user_id` can be created like so:

```
db.ratings.ensureIndex({ movie_id:1, rating:-1, user_id:1 });
```

movielens_indexes.txt

This index can be used to query for any of these following combinations:

➤   movie_id, rating, and user_id

➤   movie_id and rating

➤   movie_id

Compound indexes can also include nested (or embedded) fields. Before you see how compound indexes involve nested fields, I cover how to create a single index involving a nested field. To illustrate, a collection of people (named people2) is used. An element of the people2 collection is as follows:

I already have a collection called people *so I named a second one* people2. *You can choose to call it something else if you prefer.*

```
{
    "_id" : ObjectId("4d0688c6851e434340b173b7"),
    "name" : "joe",
    "age" : 27,
    "address" : {
        "city" : "palo alto",
        "state" : "ca",
        "zip" : "94303",
        "country" : "us"
    }
}
```

You can create an index on the zip field of the address field as follows:

```
db.people2.ensureIndex({ "address.zip":1 });
```

movielens_indexes.txt

Next, you can create a compound index for the name and address.zip fields:

```
db.people2.ensureIndex({ name:1, "address.zip":1 });
```

movielens_indexes.txt

You can also choose the entire sub-document as the key of an index so you can create a single index for the address field:

```
db.people2.ensureIndex({ address:1 });
```

movielens_indexes.txt

This indexes the entire document and not just the `zip` field of the document. Such an index can be used if an entire document is passed as a query document to get a subset of the collection.

A MongoDB collection field can also contain an array instead of a document. You can index such fields as well. Now consider another example of an `orders` collection to illustrate how array properties can be indexed. An element of the `orders` collection is as follows:

```
{
    "_id" : ObjectId("4cccff35d3c7ab3d1941b103"),
    "order_date" : "Sat Oct 30 2010 22:30:12 GMT-0700 (PDT)",
    "line_items" : [
        {
            "item" : {
                "name" : "latte",
                "unit_price" : 4
            },
            "quantity" : 1
        },
        {
            "item" : {
                "name" : "cappuccino",
                "unit_price" : 4.25
            },
            "quantity" : 1
        },
        {
            "item" : {
                "name" : "regular",
                "unit_price" : 2
            },
            "quantity" : 2
        }
    ]
}
```

You could index with `line_items`:

```
db.orders.ensureIndex({ line_items:1 });
```

movielens_indexes.txt

When an indexed field contains an array, each element of the array is added to the index.

In addition, you could index by the `item` property of the `line_items` array:

```
db.orders.ensureIndex({ "line_items.item":1 });
```

movielens_indexes.txt

You could go one level further and index it by the `name` property of the item document contained in the `line_items` array as follows:

```
db.orders.ensureIndex({ "line_items.item.name":1 });
```

movielens_indexes.txt

So, you could query by this nested name field as follows:

```
db.orders.find({ "line_items.item.name":"latte" });
```

movielens_indexes.txt

Run the query plan to confirm that the cursor value used for the query is `BtreeCursor line_items .item.name_1`, which as you know indicates the use of the nested index.

Creating Unique and Sparse Indexes

By now you must be convinced that MongoDB provides a wide array of options to index documents and provide for efficient query performance. In addition to enhancing the query performance, indexes can also serve the purpose of imposing constraints.

You could create a sparse index by explicitly specifying it as follows:

```
db.ratings.ensureIndex({ movie_id:1 }, { sparse:true });
```

movielens_indexes.txt

A sparse index implies that those documents that have a missing indexed field are completely ignored and left out of the index. This may sometimes be desirable but you need to be aware that a sparse index may not reference all the documents in the collection.

MongoDB also provides a facility for creating unique indexes. You could create a unique index on the title field of the `movies` collection as follows:

```
db.movies.ensureIndex({ title:1 }, { unique:true });
```

movielens_indexes.txt

Two items in the `movies` collection don't have the same title but if it were the case, a unique index would not be created unless you explicitly specified that all duplicates after the first entry be dropped. Such explicit specification can be done as follows:

```
db.movies.ensureIndex({ title:1 }, { unique:true, dropDups : true });
```

movielens_indexes.txt

If a collection contains documents with a missing value for the indexed field a null value will be inserted in place of the missing value. Unlike the sparse index, the document will not be skipped. Also, if two documents are missing from the indexed field, only the first one is saved; the rest would be ignored in the collection.

Keyword-based Search and Multikeys

So far, a lot has been said about indexes in MongoDB. All the essential concepts have been covered and most of the nuances illustrated. To wrap up this section and move onto another document database, namely CouchDB, I present one last example and that is about the regular expression-based search in a text field. Earlier in this chapter, the search for the movie ID corresponding to `Toy Story` prompted the following query:

```
db.movies.find({title: /Toy Story/i});
```

A query plan was also run and it showed that all 3,883 documents were scanned to get the response back in 6 ms. The collection of movies is small so a table scan wasn't that expensive. However, running this same query on a large collection could have been much slower.

To enhance the query performance you could simply create an index like so:

```
db.movies.ensureIndex({ title:1 });
```

In some cases, though, creating a traditional index may not be enough, especially when you don't want to rely on regular expressions and need to do a full text search. You have already seen that a field that contains an array of values can be indexed. In such instances, MongoDB creates multikeys: one for each unique value in the array. For example, you could save a set of blogposts in a collection, named `blogposts`, where each element could be as follows:

```
{
    "_id" : ObjectId("4d06bf4c851e434340b173c3"),
    "title" : "NoSQL Sessions at Silicon Valley Cloud Computing Meetup in January
2011",
    "creation_date" : "2010-12-06",
    "tags" : [
        "amazon dynamo",
        "big data",
        "cassandra",
        "cloud",
        "couchdb",
        "google bigtable",
```

```
            "hbase",
            "memcached",
            "mongodb",
            "nosql",
            "redis",
            "web scale"
        ]
    }
```

Now, you could easily create a multikey index on the `tags` field as follows:

```
db.blogposts.ensureIndex({ tags:1 });
```

So far it's like any other index but next you could search by any one of the tag values like so:

```
db.blogposts.find({ tags:"nosql" });
```

This feature can be used to build out a complete keyword-based search. As with tags, you would need to save the keywords in an array that could be saved as a value of a field. The extraction of the keywords itself is not done automatically by MongoDB. You need to build that part of the system yourself.

Maintaining a large array and querying through numerous documents that each hold a large array could impose a performance drag on the database. To identify and preemptively correct some of the slow queries you can leverage the MongoDB database profiler. In fact, you can use the profiler to log all the operations.

The profiler lets you define three levels:

➤ 0 — Profiler is off

➤ 1 — Slow operations (greater than 100 ms) are logged

➤ 2 — All operations are logged

To log all operations you can set the profiler level to 2 like so:

```
db.setProfilingLevel(2);
```

The profiler logs themselves are available as a MongoDB collection, which you can view using a query as follows:

```
db.system.profile.find();
```

If you have been following along until now, you have theoretically learned almost everything there is to learn about indexes and sorting in MongoDB. Next, you use the available tools to tune the query to optimal performance as you access data from your collections.

INDEXING AND ORDERING IN COUCHDB

You have seen the RESTful query mechanisms in CouchDB. Now, you delve a bit into how the values are indexed to make queries efficient. Unlike MongoDB, the indexing features in CouchDB are automatic and triggered for all changed data sets when they are read first after the change. To understand this further, step back a bit to review the essential mechanics of data access in CouchDB. CouchDB follows the MapReduce style data manipulation.

The map function that emits key/value pairs based on the collection data leads to view results. When such views are accessed for the first time a B-tree index is built out of this data. On subsequent querying the data is returned from the B-tree and the underlying data is untouched. This means queries beyond the very first one leverage the B-tree index.

The B-tree Index in CouchDB

A B-tree index scales well for large amounts of data. Despite huge data growth, the height of a B-tree remains in single digits and allows for fast data retrieval. In CouchDB, the B-tree implementation has specialized features like MultiVersion Concurrency Control and append-only design.

MultiVersion Concurrency Control (MVCC) implies that multiple reads and writes can occur in parallel without the need for exclusive locking. The simplest parallel of this is distributed software version control like GitHub. All writes are sequenced and reads are not impacted by writes. CouchDB has a `_rev` property that holds the most current revision value. Like optimistic locking, writes and reads are coordinated based on the `_rev` value.

Therefore, each version is the latest one at the time a client starts reading the data. As documents are modified or deleted the index in the view results are updated.

 The couchdb-lucene project (`https://github.com/rnewson/couchdb-lucene`) provides full text search capability using Lucene, the open-source search engine, and CouchDB.

INDEXING IN APACHE CASSANDRA

Column-oriented databases like HBase and Hypertable have a default row-key-based order and index. Indexes on column values, which are often called secondary indexes, are typically not available out-of-box in these databases. HBase has some minimal support for secondary indexes. Hypertable intends to support secondary index by the time of its version 1.0 release, which will be available later this year.

Apache Cassandra is a hybrid between a column-oriented database and a pure key/value data store. It incorporates ideas from Google Bigtable and Amazon Dynamo. Like column-oriented databases, Cassandra supports row-key-based order and index by default. In addition, Cassandra also supports secondary indexes.

Secondary indexes support in Cassandra is explained using a simple example. You may recall a Cassandra database example with `CarDataStore` keyspace and the `Cars` column-family from Chapter 2. The same example is revisited for explaining support for secondary indexes.

To follow along, start the Cassandra server using the `cassandra` program in the `bin` directory of the Cassandra distribution. Then connect to Cassandra using the CLI as follows:

```
PS C:\applications\apache-cassandra-0.7.4> .\bin\cassandra-cli -host localhost
Starting Cassandra Client
Connected to: "Test Cluster" on localhost/9160
Welcome to cassandra CLI.

Type 'help;' or '?' for help. Type 'quit;' or 'exit;' to quit.
```

The `CarDataStore` should already be in the local database if you followed along with the examples in Chapter 2. If not, then please revisit Chapter 2 and set up the keyspace and column-family as required. When your setup is complete, make `CarDataStore` the current keyspace as follows:

```
[default@unknown] use CarDataStore;
Authenticated to keyspace: CarDataStore
```

Use the following command to verify that the data you added earlier exists in your local Cassandra data store:

```
[default@CarDataStore] get Cars['Prius'];
=> (column=make, value=746f796f7461, timestamp=1301824068109000)
=> (column=model, value=70726975732033, timestamp=1301824129807000)
Returned 2 results.
```

The `Cars` column-family has two columns: `make` and `model`. To make querying by values in the `make` column more efficient, create a secondary index on the values in that column. Since the column already exists, modify the definition to include an index. You can update the column-family and column definition as follows:

```
[default@CarDataStore] update column family Cars with comparator=UTF8Type
...        and column_metadata=[{column_name: make, validation_class: UTF8Type,
 index_type: KEYS},
...        {column_name: model, validation_class: UTF8Type}];
9f03d6cb-7923-11e0-aa26-e700f669bcfc
Waiting for schema agreement...
... schemas agree across the cluster
```

cassandra_secondary_index.txt

The `update` command created an index on the column `make`. The type of index created is of type `KEYS`. Cassandra defines a `KEYS` type index, which resembles a simple hash of key/value pairs.

Now, query for all values that have a `make` value of `toyota`. Use the familiar SQL-like syntax as follows:

```
[default@CarDataStore] get Cars where make = 'toyota';
-------------------
RowKey: Prius
=> (column=make, value=toyota, timestamp=1301824068109000)
=> (column=model, value=prius 3, timestamp=1301824129807000)
-------------------
```

```
RowKey: Corolla
=> (column=make, value=toyota, timestamp=1301824154174000)
=> (column=model, value=le, timestamp=1301824173253000)

2 Rows Returned.
```

cassandra_secondary_index.txt

Try another query, but this time filter the `Cars` data by `model` value of `prius 3` as follows:

Available for
download on
Wrox.com

```
[default@CarDataStore] get Cars where model = 'prius 3';
No indexed columns present in index clause with operator EQ
```

cassandra_secondary_index.txt

The query that filters by `make` works smoothly but the one that filters by `model` fails. This is because there is an index on `make` but not on `model`. Try another query where you combine both `make` and `model` as follows:

Available for
download on
Wrox.com

```
[default@CarDataStore] get Cars where model = 'prius 3' and make = 'toyota';
------------------
RowKey: Prius
=> (column=make, value=toyota, timestamp=1301824068109000)
=> (column=model, value=prius 3, timestamp=1301824129807000)

1 Row Returned.
```

cassandra_secondary_index.txt

The index works again because at least one of the filter criteria has an indexed set of values.

The example at hand doesn't have any numerical values in its columns so showing a greater-than or less-than filter is not possible. However, if you did want to leverage a filter for such an inequality comparator-based query then you are going to be out of luck. Currently, the KEYS index does not have the capability to perform range queries. Range queries via indexes may be supported in the future if Cassandra includes a B-tree, or a similar index type. The rudimentary KEYS index isn't sufficient for range queries.

SUMMARY

In this chapter you delved into the details of indexing documents and their fields in MongoDB. You also had a chance to learn about the automatic view indexing in CouchDB. The one prominent theme that emerged was that both databases support indexes and that these indexes aren't drastically different from the indexes you see in relational databases.

You also learned about special features like how arrays in MongoDB are indexed as multikeys and how CouchDB provisions for automatic indexing of all documents that have changed since the last read.

In addition to indexes in document databases you also learned about indexing capabilities in Apache Cassandra, a popular column-family database.

Managing Transactions and Data Integrity

WHAT'S IN THIS CHAPTER?

➤ Understanding essentials of ACID transactions

➤ Applying transactional guarantee in distributed systems

➤ Understanding Brewer's CAP Theorem

➤ Exploring transactional support in NoSQL products

The best way to understand transactions and data integrity in the world of NoSQL is to first review these same concepts in the context of the familiar RDBMS environment. Once the fundamental transactional notions and vocabulary are established and a couple of use cases are illustrated, it gets easier to conceive how the transactional concepts are challenged in large-scale distributed environments; places where NoSQL shines.

Not all NoSQL products share a similar view of transactions and data integrity. So once the broad and generalized expectations of transactional integrity in large-scale distributed systems is explained, it's pertinent to show how it's implemented in specific products and that is exactly how this chapter approaches the topic.

So to get started, you need to begin with ACID.

RDBMS AND ACID

ACID, which stands for Atomicity, Consistency, Isolation, and Durability, has become the gold standard to define the highest level of transactional integrity in database systems. As the acronym suggests it implies the following:

➤ **Atomicity** — Either a transactional operation fully succeeds or completely fails. Nothing that is inconsistent between the two states is acceptable. The canonical example that illustrates this property is transferring funds from one account, say A, to another, say B. If $100 needs to be transferred from A to B, $100 needs to be debited from (taken out of) A and credited to (deposited into) B. This could logically mean the operation involves two steps: debit from A and credit to B. Atomicity implies that if for some reason, debit from A occurs successfully and then the operation fails, the entire operation is rolled back and the operation is not left in an inconsistent state (where the money has been debited from A but not credited to B).

➤ **Consistency** — Consistency implies that data is never persisted if it violates a predefined constraint or rule. For example, if a particular field states that it should hold only integer values, then a float value is not accepted or is rounded to the nearest integer and then saved. Consistency is often confused with atomicity. Also, its implication in the context of RDBMS often relates to unique constraints, data type validations, and referential integrity. In a larger application scenario, consistency could include more complex rules imposed on the data but in such cases the task of maintaining consistency is mostly left to the application.

➤ **Isolation** — Isolation gets relevant where data is accessed concurrently. If two independent processes or threads manipulate the same data set, it's possible that they could step on each other's toes. Depending on the requirement, the two processes or threads could be isolated from each other. As an example, consider two processes, X and Y, modifying the value of a field V, which holds an initial value V0. Say X reads the value V0 and wants to update the value to V1 but before it completes the update Y reads the value V0 and updates it to V2. Now when X wants to write the value V1 it finds that the original value has been updated. In an uncontrolled situation, X would overwrite the new value that Y has written, which may not be desirable. Look at Figure 9-1 to view the stated use case pictorially. Isolation assures that such discrepancies are avoided. The different levels and strategies of isolation are explained later in a following section.

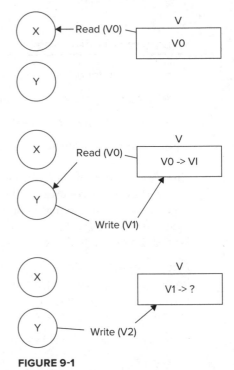

FIGURE 9-1

➤ **Durability** — Durability implies that once a transactional operation is confirmed, it is assured. The case where durability is questioned is when a client program has received confirmation that a transactional operation has succeeded but then a system failure prevents the data from being persisted to the store. An RDBMS often maintains a transaction log. A transaction is confirmed only after it's written to the transaction log. If a system fails between the confirmation and the data persistence, the transaction log is synchronized with the persistent store to bring it to a consistent state.

The ACID guarantee is well recognized and expected in RDBMSs. Often, application frameworks and languages that work with RDBMS attempt to extend the ACID promise to the entire application. This works fine in cases where the entire stack, that is, the database and the application, resides on a single server or node but it starts getting stretched the moment the stack constituents are distributed out to multiple nodes.

Isolation Levels and Isolation Strategies

A strict isolation level directly impacts concurrency. Therefore, to allow concurrent processing the isolation requirements are often relaxed. The ISO/ANSI SQL standard defines four isolation levels that provide varying and incremental levels of isolation. The four levels are as follows:

➤ Read Uncommitted

➤ Read Committed

➤ Repeatable Read

➤ Serializable

In addition, no isolation or complete chaos could be considered a fifth level of isolation. Isolation levels can be clearly explained using examples so I will resort to using one here as well. Consider a simple collection (or table in the RDBMS world) of data as shown in Table 9-1.

TABLE 9-1: Sample Data for Understanding Isolation Levels

ID	NAME	OCCUPATION	LOCATION (CITY)
1	James Joyce	Author	New York
2	Hari Krishna	Developer	San Francisco
3	Eric Chen	Entrepreneur	Boston

Now, say two independent transactions, Transaction 1 and Transaction 2, manipulate this data set concurrently. The sequence is as follows:

1. Transaction 1 reads all the three data points in the set.

2. Transaction 2 then reads the data point with id 2 and updates the Location (City) property of that data item from "San Francisco" to "San Jose." However, it does not commit the change.

3. Transaction 1 re-reads all the three data points in the set.

4. Transaction 2 rolls back the update carried out in step 2.

Depending on the isolation level the result will be different. If the isolation level is set to Read Uncommitted, Transaction 1 sees the updated but uncommitted change by Transaction 2 (from step 2) in step 3. As in step 4, such uncommitted changes can be rolled back, and therefore, such reads are appropriately called *dirty reads*. If the isolation level is a bit stricter and set to the next level — Read Committed — Transaction 1 doesn't see the uncommitted changes when it re-reads the data in step 3.

Now, consider interchanging steps 3 and 4 and a situation where Transaction 2 commits the update. The new sequence of steps is as follows:

1. Transaction 1 reads all the three data points in the set.

2. Transaction 2 then reads the data point with id 2 and updates the Location (City) property of that data item from "San Francisco" to "San Jose." However, it does not commit the change yet.

3. Transaction 2 commits the update carried out in step 2.

4. Transaction 1 re-reads all the three data points in the set.

The Read Uncommitted isolation level isn't affected by the change in steps. It's the level that allows dirty reads, so obviously committed updates are read without any trouble. Read Committed behaves differently though. Now, because changes have been committed in step 3, Transaction 1 reads the updated data in step 4. The reads from step 1 and step 4 are not the same so it's a case of no-repeatable reads.

As the isolation level is upped to Repeatable Read, the reads in step 1 and step 4 are identical. That is, Transaction 1 is isolated from the committed updates from Transaction 2 while they are both concurrently in process. Although a repeatable read is guaranteed at this level, insertion and deletion of pertinent records could occur. This could lead to inclusion and exclusion of data items in subsequent reads and is often referred to as a *phantom read*. To walk through a case of phantom read consider a new sequence of steps as follows:

1. Transaction 1 runs a range query asking for all data items with id between 1 and 5 (both inclusive). Because there are three data points originally in the collection and all meet the criteria, all three are returned.

2. Transaction 2 then inserts a new data item with the following values: {Id = 4, Name = 'Jane Watson', Occupation = 'Chef', Location (City) = 'Atlanta'}.

3. Transaction 2 commits the data inserted in step 2.

4. Transaction 1 re-runs the range query as in step 1.

Now, with isolation set to the Repeatable Read level, the data set returned to Transaction 1 in step 1 and step 4 are not same. Step 4 sees the data item with id 4 in addition to the original three data points. To avoid phantom reads you need to involve range locks for reads and resort to using the highest level of isolation, Serializable. The term *serializable* connotes a sequential processing or serial ordering of transactions but that is not always the case. It does block other concurrent transactions when one of them is working on the data range, though. In some databases, snapshot isolation is used to achieve serializable isolation. Such databases provide a transaction with a snapshot when they start and allow commits only if nothing has changed since the snapshot.

Use of higher isolation levels enhances the possibility of starvation and deadlocks. Starvation occurs when one transaction locks out resources from others to use and deadlock occurs when two concurrent transactions wait on each other to finish and free up a resource.

With the concepts of ACID transactions and isolation levels reviewed, you are ready to start exploring how these ideas play out in highly distributed systems.

DISTRIBUTED ACID SYSTEMS

To understand fully whether or not ACID expectations apply to distributed systems you need to first explore the properties of distributed systems and see how they get impacted by the ACID promise.

Distributed systems come in varying shapes, sizes, and forms but they all have a few typical characteristics and are exposed to similar complications. As distributed systems get larger and more spread out, the complications get more challenging. Added to that, if the system needs to be highly available the challenges only get multiplied. To start out, consider an elementary situation as illustrated in Figure 9-2.

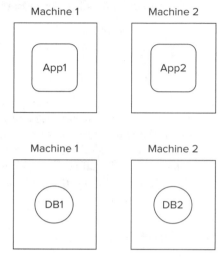

Even in this simple situation with two applications, each connected to a database and all four parts running on a separate machine, the challenges of providing the ACID guarantee is not trivial. In distributed systems, the ACID principles are applied using the concept laid down by the open XA consortium, which specifies the need for a transaction manager or coordinator to manage transactions distributed across multiple transactional resources. Even with a central coordinator, implementing isolation across multiple databases is extremely difficult. This is because

FIGURE 9-2

different databases provide isolation guarantees differently. A few techniques like two-phase locking (and its variant Strong Strict Two-Phase Locking or SS2PL) and two-phase commit help ameliorate the situation a bit. However, these techniques lead to blocking operations and keep parts of the system from being available during the states when the transaction is in process and data moves from one consistent state to another. In long-running transactions, XA-based distributed transactions don't work, as keeping resources blocked for a long time is not practical. Alternative strategies like compensating operations help implement transactional fidelity in long-running distributed transactions.

Two-phase locking (2PL) is a style of locking in distributed transactions where locks are only acquired (and not released) in the first phase and locks are only released (and not acquired) in the second phase.

SS2PL is a special case of a technique called commitment ordering. Read more about commitment ordering in a research paper by: Yoav Raz (1992): "The Principle of Commitment Ordering, or Guaranteeing Serializability in a Heterogeneous Environment of Multiple Autonomous Resource Managers Using Atomic Commitment" (www.vldb.org/conf/1992/P292.PDF), Proceedings of the Eighteenth International Conference on Very Large Data Bases (VLDB), pp. 292-312, Vancouver, Canada, August 1992, ISBN 1-55860-151-1 (also DEC-TR 841, Digital Equipment Corporation, November 1990).

Two-phase commit (2PC) is a technique where the transaction coordinator verifies with all involved transactional objects in the first phase and actually sends a commit request to all in the second. This typically avoids partial failures as commitment conflicts are identified in the first phase.

The challenges of resource unavailability in long-running transactions also appear in high-availability scenarios. The problem takes center stage especially when there is less tolerance for resource unavailability and outage.

A congruent and logical way of assessing the problems involved in assuring ACID-like guarantees in distributed systems is to understand how the following three factors get impacted in such systems:

➤ Consistency

➤ Availability

➤ Partition Tolerance

Consistency, Availability, and Partition Tolerance (CAP) are the three pillars of Brewer's Theorem that underlies much of the recent generation of thinking around transactional integrity in large and scalable distributed systems. Succinctly put, Brewer's Theorem states that in systems that are distributed or scaled out it's impossible to achieve all three (Consistency, Availability, and Partition Tolerance) at the same time. You must make trade-offs and sacrifice at least one in favor of the other two. However, before the trade-offs are discussed, it's important to explore some more on what these three factors mean and imply.

Consistency

Consistency is not a very well-defined term but in the context of CAP it alludes to atomicity and isolation. Consistency means consistent reads and writes so that concurrent operations see the same valid and consistent data state, which at minimum means no stale data.

In ACID, consistency means that data that does not satisfy predefined constraints is not persisted. That's not the same as the consistency in CAP.

Brewer's Theorem was conjectured by Eric Brewer and presented by him (www.cs.berkeley.edu/~brewer/cs262b-2004/PODC-keynote.pdf) as a keynote address at the ACM Symposium on the Principles of Distributed Computing (PODC) in 2000. Brewer's ideas on CAP developed as a part of his work at UC Berkeley and at Inktomi. In 2002, Seth Gilbert and Nancy Lynch proved Brewer's conjecture and hence it's now referred to as Brewer's Theorem (and sometimes as Brewer's CAP Theorem). In Gilbert and Lynch's proof, consistency is considered as atomicity. Gilbert and Lynch's proof is available as a published paper titled "Brewer's Conjecture and the Feasibility of Consistent, Available, Partition-Tolerant Web Services" and can be accessed online at http://theory.lcs.mit.edu/tds/papers/Gilbert/Brewer6.ps.

In a single-node situation, consistency can be achieved using the database ACID semantics but things get complicated as the system is scaled out and distributed.

Availability

Availability means the system is available to serve at the time when it's needed. As a corollary, a system that is busy, uncommunicative, or unresponsive when accessed is not available. Some, especially those who try to refute the CAP Theorem and its importance, argue that a system with minor delays or minimal hold-up is still an available system. Nevertheless, in terms of CAP the definition is not ambiguous; if a system is not available to serve a request at the very moment it's needed, it's not available.

That said, many applications could compromise on availability and that is a possible trade-off choice they can make.

Partition Tolerance

Parallel processing and scaling out are proven methods and are being adopted as the model for scalability and higher performance as opposed to scaling up and building massive super computers. The past few years have shown that building giant monolithic computational contraptions is expensive and impractical in most cases. Adding a number of commodity hardware units in a cluster and making them work together is a more cost-, algorithm-, and resource-effective and efficient solution. The emergence of cloud computing is a testimony to this fact.

Read the note titled "Vertical Scaling Challenges and Fallacies of Distributed Computing" to understand some of trade-offs associated with the two alternative scaling strategies.

Because scaling out is the chosen path, partitioning and occasional faults in a cluster are a given. The third pillar of CAP rests on partition tolerance or fault-tolerance. In other words, partition tolerance measures the ability of a system to continue to service in the event a few of its cluster members become unavailable.

VERTICAL SCALING CHALLENGES AND FALLACIES OF DISTRIBUTED COMPUTING

The traditional choice has been in favor of consistency and so system architects have in the past shied away from scaling out and gone in favor of scaling up. Scaling up or vertical scaling involves larger and more powerful machines. Involving larger and more powerful machines works in many cases but is often characterized by the following:

➤ **Vendor lock-in** — Not everyone makes large and powerful machines and those who do often rely on proprietary technologies for delivering the power and efficiency that you desire. This means there is a possibility of vendor lock-in. Vendor lock-in in itself is not bad, at least not as much as it is often projected. Many applications over the years have successfully been built and run on proprietary technology. Nevertheless, it does restrict your choices and is less flexible than its open counterparts.

➤ **Higher costs** — Powerful machines usually cost a lot more than the price of commodity hardware.

➤ **Data growth perimeter** — Powerful and large machines work well until the data grows to fill it. At that point, there is no choice but to move to a yet larger machine or to scale out. The largest of machines has a limit to the amount of data it can hold and the amount of processing it can carry out successfully. (In real life a team of people is better than a superhero!)

continues

continued

➤ **Proactive provisioning** — Many applications have no idea of the final large scale when they start out. When scaling vertically in your scaling strategy, you need to budget for large scale upfront. It's extremely difficult and complex to assess and plan scalability requirements because the growth in usage, data, and transactions is often impossible to predict.

Given the challenges associated with vertical scaling, horizontal scaling has, for the past few years, become the scaling strategy of choice. Horizontal scaling implies systems are distributed across multiple machines or nodes. Each of these nodes can be some sort of a commodity machine that is cost effective. Anything distributed across multiple nodes is subject to fallacies of distributed computing, which is a list of assumptions in the context of distributed systems that developers take for granted but often does not hold true. The fallacies are as follows:

➤ The network is reliable.

➤ Latency is zero.

➤ Bandwidth is infinite.

➤ The network is secure.

➤ Topology doesn't change.

➤ There is one administrator.

➤ Transport cost is zero.

➤ The network is homogeneous.

The fallacies of distributed computing is attributed to Sun Microsystems (now part of Oracle). Peter Deutsch created the original seven on the list. Bill Joy, Tom Lyon, and James Gosling also contributed to the list. Read more about the fallacies at `http://blogs.oracle.com/jag/resource/Fallacies.html`.

UPHOLDING CAP

Achieving consistency, availability, and partition tolerance at all times in a large distributed system is not possible and Brewer's Theorem already states that. You can and should read Gilbert and Lynch's proof to delve deeper into how and why Brewer is correct. However, for a quick and intuitive illustration, I explain the central ideas using a simple example, which is shown in a set of two figures: Figures 9-3 and 9-4.

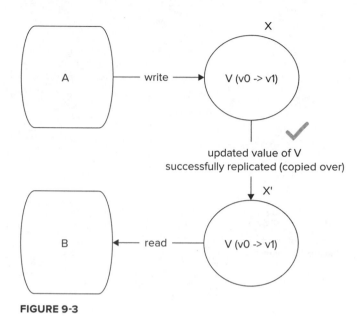

FIGURE 9-3

Figures 9-3 and 9-4 show two nodes of a clustered system where processes A and B access data from X and X', respectively. X and X' are replicated data stores (or structures) and hold copies of the same data set. A writes to X and B reads from X'. X and X' synchronize between each other. V is an entity or object stored in X and X'. V has an original value v0. Figure 9-3 shows a success use case where A writes v1 to V (updating its value from v0), v1 gets synchronized over from X to X', and then B reads v1 as the value of V from X'. Figure 9-4, on the other hand, shows a failure use case where A writes v1 to V and B reads the value of V, but the synchronizing between X and X' fails and therefore the value read by B is not consistent with the most recent value of V. B still reads v0 whereas the latest updated value is v1.

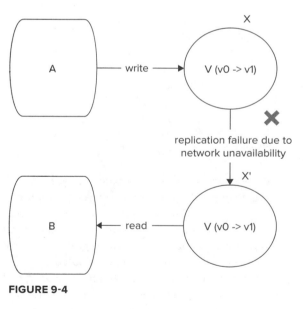

FIGURE 9-4

If you are to ensure that B always reads the correct value, you need to make sure that you synchronously copy the updated value v1 from X to X'. In other words, the two operations — (1) A updates the value of V in X from v0 to v1 and (2) The updated value of V (that is, v1) is copied over from X to X' — would need to be in a single transaction. Such a setting is depicted in Figure 9-5. This setup would guarantee atomicity in this distributed transaction but would impact latency and availability. If a failure case as illustrated in Figure 9-4 arises, resources will be blocked until the network heals and the updated value replication between X and X' is complete.

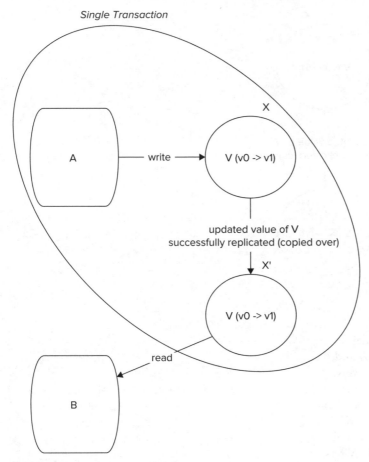

FIGURE 9-5

If the process of data replication between X and X' is asynchronous, there is no way of knowing the exact time when it occurs. If one doesn't know when an event exactly occurs there is obviously no way of guaranteeing if the event has occurred or not unless one seeks explicit consensus or confirmation. If you need to wait for a consensus or confirmation, the impact on latency and availability of the asynchronous operation is not very different from that of the synchronous operation. So one way or the other where systems are distributed and faults can occur, the trade-off among data consistency, system availability, and partition tolerance needs to be understood and choices need to be made where two of these are favored over the third, and therefore, the third is compromised.

The choices could be as follows:

➤ **Option 1** — Availability is compromised but consistency and partition tolerance are preferred over it.

➤ **Option 2** — The system has little or no partition tolerance. Consistency and availability are preferred.

➤ **Option 3** — Consistency is compromised but systems are always available and can work when parts of it are partitioned.

Traditional transactional RDBMS chooses option 1 under circumstances of horizontal scaling. In such cases, the availability is affected by many factors, including the following:

➤ Delays due to network lag

➤ Communication bottlenecks

➤ Resource starvation

➤ Hardware failure leading to partitioning

Compromising on Availability

In extreme cases, when nodes fail the system may become completely unavailable until it's healed and the system is restored to a consistent state. Although unavailability seems terribly detrimental to business continuity, sometimes that's the only choice at hand. You can have either a consistent data state or the transaction fails. This is typical of money- and time-sensitive transactions where compensating transactions in failure cases is completely unacceptable or bears a very high cost. The quintessential example of money transfer between two accounts is often quoted as an example for such a use case. In real life, though, banks sometimes have relaxed alternatives for such extreme cases as well and you will learn about them a little later when I discuss weak consistency.

In many situations, systems — including those based on RDBMS — provide for backup and quick replication and recovery from failure. This means the system may still be unavailable but for a very short time. In a majority of cases, minor unavailability is not catastrophic and is a viable choice.

Compromising on Partition Tolerance

In some cases, it's better not to accommodate partition tolerance. A little while back I stated that in horizontally scaled systems, node failure is a given and the chances of failure increase as the number of nodes increases. How then can partition intolerance be an option? Many people confuse partition tolerance with fault tolerance but the two are not one and the same. A system that does not service partitions that gets isolated from the network but allows for recovery by re-provisioning other nodes almost instantaneously is fault tolerant but not partition tolerant.

Google's Bigtable is a good example of a data store that is highly available and provides for strong consistency but compromises on partition tolerance. The system is fault tolerant and easily survives a node failure but it's not partition tolerant. More appropriately, under a fault condition it identifies primary and secondary parts of a partition and tries to resolve the problem by establishing a quorum.

To understand this a bit further, it may be worthwhile to review what you learned earlier about Bigtable (and its clones like HBase) in Chapter 4. Reading the section titled "HBase Distributed Storage Architecture" from Chapter 4 would be most pertinent.

Bigtable and its clones use a master-worker pattern where column-family data is stored together in a region server. Region servers are dynamically configured and managed by a master. In Google's Bigtable, data is persisted to the underlying Google FileSystem (GFS) and the entire infrastructure is coordinated by Chubby, which uses a quorum algorithm like Paxos to assure consistency. In the case of HBase, Hadoop Distributed FileSystem (HDFS) carries out the same function as GFS and ZooKeeper replaces Chubby. ZooKeeper uses a quorum algorithm to recover from a failed node.

On failure, ZooKeeper determines which is the primary partition and which one is the secondary. Based on these inferences, ZooKeeper directs all read and write operations to the primary partition and makes the secondary one a read-only partition until this problem is resolved.

In addition, Bigtable and HBase (and its underlying filesystems, GFS and HDFS, respectively) store three copies of every data set. This assures consistency by consensus when one out of the three copies fails or is out of synch. Having less than three copies does not assure consensus.

Compromising on Consistency

In some situations, availability cannot be compromised and the system is so distributed that partition tolerance is required. In such cases, it may be possible to compromise strong consistency. The counterpart of strong consistency is weak consistency, so all such cases where consistency is compromised could be clubbed in this bundle. Weak consistency, is a spectrum so this could include cases of no consistency and eventual consistency. Inconsistent data is probably not a choice for any serious system that allows any form of data updates but eventual consistency could be an option. Eventual consistency again isn't a well-defined term but alludes to the fact that after an update all nodes in the cluster see the same state eventually. If the eventuality can be defined within certain limits, then the eventual consistency model could work.

For example, a shopping cart could allow orders even if it's not able to confirm with the inventory system about availability. In a possible limit case, the product ordered may be out of stock. In such a case, the order could be taken as a back order and filled when the inventory is restocked. In another example, a bank could allow a customer to withdraw up to an overdraft amount even if it's unable to confirm the available balance so that in the worst situation if the money isn't sufficient the transaction could still be valid and the overdraft facility could be used.

To understand eventual consistency, one may try to illustrate a situation in terms of the following three criteria:

➤   **R** — Number of nodes that are read from.

➤   **W** — Number of nodes that are written to.

➤   **N** — Total number of nodes in the cluster.

Different combinations of these three parameters can have different impacts on overall consistency. Keeping $R < N$ and $W < N$ allows for higher availability. Following are some common situations worth reviewing:

➤   **$R + W > N$** — In such situations, a consistent state can easily be established, because there is an overlap between some read and write nodes. An extreme case when $R = N$ and $W = N$ (that is, $R + W = 2N$) the system is absolutely consistent and can provide an ACID guarantee.

➤   **$R = 1$, $W = N$** — When a system has more reads than writes, it makes sense to balance the read load out to all nodes of the cluster. When $R = 1$, each node acts independent of any other node as far as a read operation is concerned. A $W = N$ write configuration means all nodes are written to for an update. In cases of a node failure the entire system then becomes unavailable for writes.

> ➤ **R = N, W = 1** — When writing to one node is enough, the chance of data inconsistency can be quite high. However, in an R = N scenario, a read is only possible when all nodes in the cluster are available.

> ➤ **R = W = ceiling ((N + 1)/2)** — Such a situation provides an effective quorum to provide eventual consistency.

Eric Brewer and his followers coined the term BASE to denote the case of eventual consistency. BASE, which stands for Basically Available Soft-state Eventually consistent, is obviously contrived and was coined to counter ACID. However, ACID and BASE are not opposites but really depict different points in the consistency spectrum.

Eventual consistency can manifest in many forms and can be implemented in many different ways. A possible strategy could involve messaging-oriented systems and another could involve a quorum-based consensus. In a messaging-oriented system you could propagate an update using a message queue. In the simplest of cases, updates could be ordered using unique sequential ids. Chapter 4 explains some of the fundamentals of Amazon Dynamo and its eventual consistency model. You may want to review that part of the chapter.

In the following sections, I explain how consistency applies to a few different popular NoSQL products. This isn't an exhaustive coverage but a select survey of a couple of them. The essentials of the consistency model in Google's Bigtable and HBase has already been covered so I will skip those. In this section, consistency in a few others, namely document databases and eventually consistent flag bearers like Cassandra, will be explored.

CONSISTENCY IMPLEMENTATIONS IN A FEW NOSQL PRODUCTS

In this section, consistency in distributed document databases, namely MongoDB and CouchDB, is explained first.

Distributed Consistency in MongoDB

MongoDB does not prescribe a specific consistency model but defaults in favor of strong consistency. In some cases, MongoDB can be and is configured for eventual consistency.

In the default case of an auto-sharded replication-enabled cluster, there is a master in every shard. The consistency model of such a deployment is strong. In some other cases, though, you could deploy MongoDB for greater availability and partition tolerance. One such case could be one master, which is the node for all writes, and multiple slaves for read. In the event a slave is detached from the cluster but still servicing a client, it could potentially offer stale data. On partition healing the slave would receive all updates and provide for eventual consistency.

Eventual Consistency in CouchDB

CouchDB's eventual consistency model relies on two important properties:

> ➤ Multiversion Concurrency Control (MVCC)
> ➤ Replication

Every document in CouchDB is versioned and all updates to a document are tagged with a unique revision number. CouchDB is a highly available and distributed system that relaxes consistency in favor of availability.

At the time of a read operation, a client (A) accesses a versioned document with a current revision number. For sake of specificity let's assume the document is named D and its current version or revision number is v1. As client A is busy reading and possibly contemplating updating the document, client B accesses the same document D and also learns that its latest version is v1. B in an independent thread or process that manipulates D. Next, client B is ready to update the document before A returns. It updates D and increments its version or revision number to v2. When client A subsequently returns with an update to document D, it realizes that the document has been updated since the snapshot it accessed at the time of read.

This creates a conflicting situation at commit time. Luckily, version or revision numbers are available to possibly resolve the conflict. See Figure 9-6 for a pictorial representation of the conflicting update use case just illustrated.

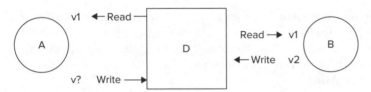

FIGURE 9-6

Such conflicts can often be resolved by client A re-reading D before it's ready for committing a new update. On re-read, if A discovers the snapshot version it's working with (in this case v1) is stale, it can possibly re-apply the updates on the newest read and then commit the changes. Such methods of conflict resolution are commonly seen in version control software. Many current version control software products like Git and Mercurial have adopted MVCC to manage data fidelity and avoid commit conflicts.

CouchDB stores are scalable distributed databases so while MVCC resolves the conflict resolution scenarios in a single instance it doesn't necessarily solve the issue of keeping all copies of the database current and up to date. This is where replication takes over. Replication is a common and well-established method for synchronizing any two data storage units. In its simplest form the file synchronization program `rsync` achieves the same for filesystem units like a folder or a directory.

Data in all nodes of a CouchDB cluster eventually becomes consistent with the help of the process of replication. The replication in CouchDB is both incremental and fault-tolerant. Therefore, only changes (or delta updates) are propagated at the time of replication and the process recovers gracefully if it fails, while the changes are being transmitted. CouchDB replication is state aware and on failure, it picks up where it stopped last. Therefore, redundant restarts are avoided and the inherent tendency of network failure or node unavailability is considered as a part of the design.

CouchDB's eventual consistency model is both effective and efficient. CouchDB clusters are typically master-master nodes so each node can independently service requests and therefore enhance both availability and responsiveness.

Having surveyed the document databases, let's move on to cover a few things about the eventual consistency model in Apache Cassandra.

Eventual Consistency in Apache Cassandra

Apache Cassandra aims to be like Google Bigtable and Amazon Dynamo. From a viewpoint of the CAP Theorem, this means Cassandra provisions for two trade-off choices:

➤ **Favor consistency and availability** — The Bigtable model, which you were exposed to earlier in this chapter.

➤ **Favor availability and partition-tolerance** — The Dynamo model, which you also learned about earlier in this chapter.

Cassandra achieves this by leaving the final consistency configuration in the hands of the developer. As a developer, your choices are as follows:

➤ Set R + W > N and achieve consistency, where R, W, and N being number of read replica nodes, number of write replicas, and total number of nodes, respectively.

➤ Achieve a Quorum by setting R = W = ceiling ((N+1)/2). This is the case of eventual consistency.

You can also set a write consistency all situation where W = N, but such a configuration can be tricky because failure can render the entire application unavailable.

Finally, I will quickly look at the consistency model in Membase.

Consistency in Membase

Membase is a Memcached protocol compatible distributed key/value store that provides for high availability and strong consistency but does not favor partition tolerance. Membase is immediately consistent. In cases of partitioning you could replicate Membase stores from master to slave replicas using an external tool but this isn't a feature of the system.

Also, Membase, like Memcached, is adept at keeping a time-sensitive cache. In a strong and immediate consistency model, purging data beyond defined time intervals is easily and reliably supported. Supporting inconsistency windows for time-sensitive data can put forth its own challenges.

With the essentials of transaction management in NoSQL covered and a few products surveyed it may be appropriate to summarize and wrap the chapter up.

SUMMARY

Although succinct, this chapter is possibly one of the most important chapters in the book. This chapter clearly explained the notions of ACID and its possible alternative, BASE. It explained Brewer's CAP Theorem and tried to relate its significance to distributed systems, which are increasingly becoming the norm in popular and widely used systems.

Consistency and its varying forms, strong and weak, were analyzed and eventual consistency was proposed as a viable alternative for higher availability under cases of partitioning.

Strong consistency advocates have often declined to consider NoSQL databases seriously due to its relaxed consistency configurations. Though consistency is an important requirement in many transactional systems, the strong-or-nothing approach has created a lot of fear, uncertainty, and doubt among users. Hopefully, this chapter laid out the choices explicitly for you to understand.

Last but not the least, although the chapter explained eventual consistency, it didn't necessarily recommend it as a consistency model. Eventual consistency has its place and should be used where it safely provides high availability under partition conditions. However, you must bear in mind that eventual consistency is fraught with potential trouble. It's neither trivial nor elementary to design and architect applications effortlessly to work under the eventual consistency model. If transactional integrity is important and the lack of it can severely disrupt normal operations, you should adopt eventual consistency only with extreme caution, fully realizing the pros and cons of your choice.

PART III
Gaining Proficiency with NoSQL

10

Using NoSQL in the Cloud

WHAT'S IN THIS CHAPTER?

➤ Exploring ready-to-use NoSQL databases in the cloud

➤ Leveraging Google AppEngine and its scalable data store

➤ Using Amazon SimpleDB

Most current-generation popular applications, like Google and Amazon, have achieved high availability and the ability to concurrently service millions of users by scaling out horizontally among multiple machines, spread across multiple data centers. Success stories of large-scale web applications like those from Google and Amazon have proven that in horizontally scaled environments, NoSQL solutions tend to shine over their relational counterparts. Horizontally scaled environments available on-demand and provisioned as required have been christened as the "cloud." If scalability and availability is your priority, NoSQL in the cloud is possibly the ideal setup.

> In some situations, both relational and non-relational stores have been used in combination. It would be inaccurate to say that only NoSQL works in horizontally scaled environments. A lot depends on the required scale, the underlying data structure, and the transactional integrity expectations in the application.

Many cloud service providers exist and multiple NoSQL products are available. In many cases, like Amazon EC2 (Elastic Compute Cloud), you have the choice to install any NoSQL product you want to use. Appendix A covers instructions on how you could successfully install some of the popular NoSQL product clusters on EC2. Notwithstanding the freedom of choice, a few cloud service providers make your life easier by providing you with a fully installed, set up, and configured database infrastructure, ready for you to use. This chapter covers such fully ready NoSQL options in the cloud.

RELATIONAL DATABASES IN THE CLOUD

A number of relational database options are offered in the cloud. Prominent among these are:

➤   Microsoft's SQL data services on the Windows Azure platform (`microsoft.com/windowsazure/`)

➤   Amazon Relational Database Service (RDS), which hosts clusters of MySQL instances (`http://aws.amazon.com/rds/`)

Alternatively, many Amazon Machine Image (AMI) options for Oracle, PostgresSQL, MySQL, and others allow you to set up your own database clusters in the EC2 environment. A few RDBMS vendors like Oracle and Greenplum have begun to offer solutions for private cloud environments as an appliance. Although possibly scalable, there is open debate as to whether a private cloud is a cloud at all.

This chapter walks through the details of two NoSQL options in the cloud: Google's Bigtable data store and Amazon SimpleDB. It includes a passing reference to a few other emerging database options on tap: CouchOne, MongoHQ, and Riak on Joyent's Smart machines.

Google revolutionized the cloud computing landscape by launching a services-ready, easy-to-use infrastructure. However, Google wasn't the first to launch cloud offerings. Amazon EC2 was already an established player in the market when Google first announced its service. Google's model was so convenient, though, that its cloud platform, the Google App Engine (GAE), has seen widespread and rapid adoption in a short time frame. The app engine isn't without its share of limitations. Its sandboxed environment and lack of support for long-running processes are among a few of its aspects that are much disliked.

This chapter starts with GAE's Bigtable-based data store. Using illustrations and examples, the chapters presents the data store's capabilities and its recommended usage patterns.

GOOGLE APP ENGINE DATA STORE

The Google App Engine (GAE) provides a sandboxed deployment environment for applications, which are written using either the Python programming language or a language that can run on a Java Virtual Machine (JVM). Google provides developers with a set of rich APIs and an SDK to build applications for the app engine.

To explain the data store features and the available APIs for data modeling, I first cover all that relates to the Python SDK for the app engine. Subsequently, I extend the discussion to include the features that are above and beyond the common concepts and relate specifically to the Java SDK for the same underlying facility.

GAE Python SDK: Installation, Setup, and Getting Started

To get started you need to install Python and the GAE Python SDK. You can download Python from `python.org` and the GAE Python SDK is available online at `http://code.google.com/appengine/downloads.html#Google_App_Engine_SDK_for_Python`. Detailed installation instructions are beyond the scope of this chapter but installation of both Python and GAE Python SDK on all supported environments is fairly easy and straightforward. If you still run into trouble while setting up your environment, just Google for a solution to your problem and like most developers you won't be disappointed.

Although this chapter exclusively focuses on the GAE data store, you will benefit from understanding the essentials of application development on the app engine. For the Python SDK, spend a little while reading through the tutorial titled "Getting Started: Python," which is available online at `http://code.google.com/appengine/docs/python/gettingstarted/`. Applications built on GAE are web applications. The getting started tutorial explains the following:

➤   The essentials of how Python web applications are built on the GAE.

➤   How requests are handled and responses served.

➤   How URL(s) are mapped to handlers.

➤   How dynamic and static content are included.

➤   How data is modeled and persisted in the underlying data store.

➤   How templates can be used to decouple view and logic elements.

➤   How services, like authentication, mail, task queues, and Memcache can be leveraged.

➤   How applications, once built, can be locally run in a development web server.

➤   How applications can be deployed to the production environment.

The tutorial is terse and to the point and you can quickly get up to speed with the basics by reading it. If you have limited or no experience with developing web applications using Python, you should go through some basic Python web development lessons before you continue with this chapter. If you are conversant with Python web development, you may still consider quickly reading through the getting started tutorial to make sure you understand which of your familiar tools and methods are available and where is it that you may need to use an alternative strategy.

 If you are a complete newcomer who has no experience of programming in Python, consider learning the language basics by reading Mark Pilgrim's wonderful book, Dive into Python, *available online at* `diveintopython.org`.

The next few sections get deeper into data modeling and create, read, update, and delete (CRUD) operations for application data in the GAE data store. For the purposes of context and specificity, concepts are explained via a sample application instead of abstract ideas.

Task Manager: A Sample Application

Consider a simple task management application in which a user can define a task, track its status, and check it as done once completed. To define a task, the user needs to give it a name and a description. Tags can be added to categorize it and start, and expected due dates could be specified. Once completed, the end date can be recorded. Tasks belong to a user and in the first version of the application they are not shared with anyone other than the owner.

To model a task, it would be helpful to list the properties, specify the data type for each property, state whether it's required or optional, and mention whether it is single or multiple valued. Table 10-1 lists a task's properties and its characteristics.

TABLE 10-1: Properties of a Task

PROPERTY NAME	DATA TYPE	REQUIRED	SINGLE OR MULTIPLE VALUED
Name	String	Yes	Single
Description	String	No	Single
start_date	Date	Yes	Single
due_date	Date	No	Single
end_date	Date	No	Single
Tags	array (list collection)	No	Multiple

The GAE Python SDK provides a data modeling API that enables a developer to create a Python class to represent a task. The simplest form of such a model class for tasks can be as follows:

Available for
download on
Wrox.com

```
import datetime
from google.appengine.ext import db

class Task(db.Model):
    name = db.StringProperty()
    description = db.StringProperty()
    start_date = db.DateProperty()
    due_date = db.DateProperty()
    end_date = db.DateProperty()
    tags = db.StringListProperty()
```

taskmanager GAE project

If you have programmed in a web framework like Django (djangoproject.com/) or used an ORM like SQLAlchemy, a popular database toolkit for Python (sqlalchemy.org/), you have certainly seen similar data modeling APIs. The GAE Python data modeling API adheres to syntax and semantics that a Python web developer is familiar with.

 ORM, or Object-Relational Mapping, provides a bridge between the object-oriented programming and the relational database worlds.

In Table 10-1, name and start_date are specified as required fields but they haven't been incorporated into the model yet. Here, the Task class is modified to specify constraints:

Available for download on Wrox.com

```python
import datetime
from google.appengine.ext import db

class Task(db.Model):
    name = db.StringProperty(required=True)
    description = db.StringProperty()
    start_date = db.DateProperty(required=True)
    due_date = db.DateProperty()
    end_date = db.DateProperty()
    tags = db.StringListProperty()
```

taskmanager GAE project

 A number of validation options are available. For example, required=True *makes a property value mandatory. The argument* choices=set(["choice1", "choice2", "choice3", "choice4"]) *restricts the value to members of the defined set. Custom validation logic defined in a function can be passed as a value to the* validator *argument of a particular property class.*

GAE uses Google's Bigtable as the data store. Bigtable is a sorted, ordered, distributed sparse column-family-oriented map, which imposes little restrictions on the number or types of columns in a column-family or the data type of the values stored in these columns. Also, Bigtable allows sparse data sets to be saved effectively, thereby allowing two rows in a table to have completely different sets of columns. It also permits different value types for the same columns. In other words, in a single data store, two entities of the same kind (for example, Task) can have different sets of properties or two entities of the same kind can have a property (identified by the same name) that can contain different types of data.

The data modeling API provides a level of structure on top of the more accommodating Bigtable. The data modeling API provides an application-level restriction on the property data types, its values sets, and the relationship among them. In the simple example that depicts a "Task" entity, a Python class named Task defines the data model.

The GAE data store can be thought of as an object store where each entity is an object. That means data store entities or members could be instances of a Python class, like `Task`. The class name, `Task`, translates to an entity kind. A key uniquely identifies an entity among all entities in the data store. A key is a combined identifier that includes:

➤ Inheritance path

➤ Entity kind

➤ Entity ID or entity key name

Hypothetically, that means if an entity of the `BaseTask` kind is a parent of a `Task` entity, then the inheritance path for the `Task` entity includes references to the parent entity of the `BaseTask` kind. `Task` itself becomes the entity kind. A specific entity of the kind, `Task`, has an ID, which can be thought of as the primary key. An ID can be either of the following:

➤ Application provided value, named `key_name`, which is a string

➤ System-generated (i.e., GAE data store) unique numeric ID

So, you could create and save an entity as follows:

```
task = Task(name = "Design task manager app",
            description = "Design the task management application.
Create the initial blueprint and the app architecture.",
            start_date = datetime.datetime.now().date())
task.put()
```

taskmanager GAE project

This creates a task instance. The instance was created by passing values for `name`, `description`, and `start_date` to the constructor. Alternatively, you could create an instance and then assign values to the properties of that instance. You need to pass in values to the constructor for all required properties at instantiation time. Values to the non-mandatory properties can be assigned using either of the methods: via the constructor or via property assignments.

In the preceding example, no value was passed in for the `key_name` property so the data store created a unique numeric ID for the entity. You can query for the key like so:

```
my_entity_key = task.key()
```

The output is a numeric value appended to the kind, which in this case is `Task`. Alternatively, you could create a key for an entity and pass that in at creation time. Say you wanted to use `task1` as the key for an entity of the `Task` kind, you could instantiate a task entity like so:

```
another_task = Task(key_name = "task1",
        name = "Yet another task",
        description = "Yet another task is, as the name says, yet another task.",
        start_date = datetime.datetime(2011, 2, 1, 12, 0, 0).date())
```

Now, querying for the key using `another_task.key()` returns `Task: task1`, which includes the `key_name` you assigned at the time of creation.

In the example where I created `another_task`, I assigned the `start_date` value as 2011/02/01. This was an arbitrary date I picked just to demonstrate that it could be any valid date value. The standard Python `datetime.datetime` module is used to create date values in the correct format. The `datetime.datetime` module, by default, creates and reads dates using the UTC time zone. You can choose to set the time zone and other attributes using the module's capabilities. This is all standard Python and you can manipulate dates the Python way that you may be accustomed to.

Next, I revisit the model class and explain a few features that were originally only alluded to in the code sample. I will also modify the model class to depict a few additional capabilities.

Essentials of Data Modeling for GAE in Python

Although a first rudimentary model class example has already been presented, a slightly more formal and detailed explanation will be useful. As I explain the details, I will build on what I have already covered. Look again at the `Task` model class:

Available for download on Wrox.com

```
class Task(db.Model):
    name = db.StringProperty(required=True)
    description = db.StringProperty()
    start_date = db.DateProperty(required=True)
    due_date = db.DateProperty()
    end_date = db.DateProperty()
    tags = db.StringListProperty()
```

taskmanager GAE project

The first thing to note is that the `Task` model class extends the `db.Model` class. The `Model` class (in the `google.appengine.ext.db` module) is one of the three built-in model classes provided in the data modeling API. The other two classes are named `Expando` and `PolyModel`. The `Model` class is the most rigid and formal of the three model classes. A `Model` defines a structured data model, with a well-defined set of properties, where the data types for each of the properties is stated at design time. In some ways, defining a `Model` class or inheriting from it is analogous to defining a traditional database schema.

The `Task` class, which is a `Model` type, defines six properties. Each of the six properties have a well-defined type, where the type is defined using a subclass of the `Property` class. The Python wrapper (SDK and API) defines and supports a set of property data types. A corresponding set of classes helps define properties in a data model. A `Property` class defines a data type for the property's value. It also defines how values are validated and stored in the data store. For example, the `StringProperty` class represents all Python `str` or `unicode` value types that are up to 500 characters in length. `DateProperty`, which is a subtype of a `DateTimeProperty`, represents just the date part of a date and time value. `StringListProperty` represents a list of string values.

You can get a list of all supported value types in a subsection in the online documentation for the GAE Python API. The subsection is titled "Properties and Values." You can access the document online at `http://code.google.com/appengine/docs/python/datastore/entities.html#Properties_and_Value_Types`. You can access the list of corresponding types and property classes at `http://code.google.com/appengine/docs/python/datastore/typesandpropertyclasses.html`. The most common of the supported types and corresponding classes are summarized in Table 10-2.

TABLE 10-2: Property Types and Corresponding Classes in GAE Python API

VALUE TYPE	PROPERTY CLASS	SORT ORDER	ADDITIONAL NOTES	GAE API DEFINE DATA TYPE
str, Unicode	StringProperty	Unicode	< 500 characters. str treated as ASCII for sorting.	No
db.Text	TextProperty	not orderable	long string (>500 characters).	Yes
db.ByteString	ByteStringProperty	byte order	< 500 bytes. Db.ByteString extends str and represents unencoded string of bytes.	Yes
db.Blob	BlobProperty	not orderable	Byte strings up to 1 MB.	Yes
Bool	BooleanProperty	False < True		No
int, long (64 bit)	IntegerProperty	Numeric		No
Float	FloatProperty	Numeric	If float and int together then int < float, which means 5 < 4.5.	No
datetime .datetime	DateTimeProperty, DateProperty, TimeProperty	chronological		No
List of supported value types	ListProperty, StringListProperty	If ASC, by least element / If DESC, by greatest element		No
Null			Python 'None'.	No

 A value of 'No' in this column implies that the data type isn't defined in the GAE Python API but is defined in the Python language and its standard libraries.

In addition to the common data types listed in Table 10-2, additional types are supported to define an entity key and to model Google accounts and typical communication identities that involve e-mail, instant messaging, postal address, and phone number. Classes are also defined to model a geographical point, a tag or a rating value. A data store key is modeled using the `Key` class in the `google.appengine.ext.db` module. The additional supported types are as follows:

➤ **Google accounts** — `users.User`

➤ **Email** — `db.Email`

➤ **IM** — `db.IM` (Instant Messaging ID)

➤ **Postal address** — `db.PostalAddress`

➤ **Phone number** — `db.PhoneNumber`

➤ **Category** — `db.Category`

➤ **Link** — `db.Link`

➤ **Rating** — `db.Rating`

➤ **Geographical point** — `db.GeoPt`

While the `Model` class with the help of supported types allows you to precisely define a desired data schema, sometimes flexibility in the model is important. You may also recall that the underlying data store imposes no restrictions either in terms of a schema or data types. In other words, you are allowed to add properties as required and the set of properties could vary between two entities of the same kind. Also, two entities may choose to store a different data type for the same property. In order to model such dynamic and flexible schemas, the GAE Python API defines a model class named `Expando`.

> *Google App Engine also offers a Blobstore, distinct from the data store. The Blobstore service allows you to store objects that are too large for the data store. A blob in the Blobstore is identified by a blobstore.BlobKey. BlobKey(s) can be sorted on byte order.*

Expando

Properties can be of two types:

➤ Fixed properties

➤ Dynamic properties

Properties defined as attributes of a model class are fixed properties. Properties added as attributes to a model instance are dynamic properties.

> *A model instance, and not a class, persists as an entity.*

An instance of a model class that inherits from the `Expando` model class can have both fixed and dynamic properties. This allows two model instances, which are persisted as entities, to have different data types for the same attribute. It also makes it possible that one instance adds an attribute (say, `new_attribute`) and the other does not add this attribute at all. Instances can include a new attribute but leave it unset. I refactored the `Task` model class to inherit from `Expando`. A code snippet for the new `Task` class and its instances is as follows:

```python
import datetime
from google.appengine.ext import db

class Task(db.Expando):
    name = db.StringProperty(required=True)
    description = db.StringProperty()
    start_date = db.DateProperty(required=True)
    due_date = db.DateProperty()
    end_date = db.DateProperty()
    tags = db.StringListProperty()

t1 = Task(name="task1", start_date=datetime.datetime.now().date())
t1.description = "this is task 1"
t1.tags = ["important", "sample"]
t1.collaborator = "John Doe"

t2 = Task(name="task2", start_date=datetime.datetime.now().date())
t2.description = "this is task 2"
t2.tags = ["important", "sample"]
t2.resources = ["resource1", "resource2"]
```

taskmanager GAE project

The example is self-explanatory and demonstrates the power of the flexible `Expando` model. Flexibility comes at some cost, though. The dynamic properties are not validated like their fixed counterparts. The modeling API provides another model class variant that allows you to define polymorphic behavior.

PolyModel

The `PolyModel` class (in the `google.appengine.ext.db.polymodel` module) allows you to define an inheritance hierarchy among a set of model classes. Once a hierarchical structure is established via class inheritance, you can query for a class type and get qualifying entities of both the class and its subclasses in the result set. To illustrate, I modified the `Task` class one more time. I refactored the `Task` class to extend the `PolyModel` class. Then I created two subclasses of the `Task` class. The subclasses are `IndividualTask` and `TeamTask`, which represent tasks for individual owners and groups, respectively. The sample code is as follows:

```python
from google.appengine.ext import db
from google.appengine.ext.db import polymodel

class Task(polymodel.PolyModel):
    name = db.StringProperty(required=True)
```

```
    description = db.StringProperty()
    start_date = db.DateProperty(required=True)
    due_date = db.DateProperty()
    end_date = db.DateProperty()
    tags = db.StringListProperty()

class IndividualTask(Task):
    owner = db.StringProperty()

class TeamTask(Task):
    team_name = db.StringProperty()
    collaborators = db.StringListProperty()
```

taskmanager GAE project

Now if I query for `Task` entities, I will get `IndividualTask` entities and `TeamTask` entities in addition to `Task` entities in my result set. You will understand this better once you understand the query mechanisms available in the app engine. Next, I cover queries and indexes.

Queries and Indexes

The app engine provides a SQL-like query language called GQL. Although not as fully capable as SQL, GQL closely mirrors the syntax and semantics that we are all used to in the world of SQL. GQL queries on entities and their properties. Entities manifest as objects in the GAE Python and the Java SDK. Therefore, GQL is quite similar to object-oriented query languages that are used to query, filter, and get model instances and their properties. Java Persistence Query Language (JPQL), `http://download.oracle.com/javaee/5/tutorial/doc/bnbtg.html`, is an example of a popular object-oriented query language.

To retrieve five `Task` entities with `start_date` of January 1, 2011 and print their names you could query like so:

Available for
download on
Wrox.com

```
q = db.GqlQuery("SELECT * FROM Task" +
                "WHERE start_date = :1", datetime.datetime(2011, 1, 1, 12, 0,
0).date())
results = q.fetch(5)
for task in results:
    print "Task name: %s" % (task.name)
```

taskmanager GAE project

Alternatively, you could get the same result by querying using the `Query` interface like so:

Available for
download on
Wrox.com

```
q = Task.all()
q.filter("start_date =", datetime.datetime(2011, 1, 1, 12, 0, 0).date())
results = q.fetch(5)
for task in results:
    print "Task name: %s" % (task.name)
```

taskmanager GAE project

The first option uses the `GqlQuery` interface and the second variant uses the `Query` interface. In each case, a filter criterion is specified to narrow the result set down to only those entities whose `start_date` property matches a specified date. This is similar to passing in a conditional value via a SQL `where` clause. In the previous example, 12 noon of January 1, 2011 is used as the parameter. The time part could be any other relevant value like 10 a.m. or 8 p.m. and the effective parameter would remain the same. Only the date part of the parameter is used.

The app engine allows a fairly rich set of filter criteria, which I explain in a following subsection.

The result in the preceding example is obtained using the `fetch` method. The `fetch` method takes a `limit` argument to restrict the result set. Optionally, an `offset` argument can also be passed to the `fetch` method. Therefore, calling `fetch(limit=5, offset=10)` instead of `fetch(5)` in the example returns the 11th to the 15th record instead of the first 5 records. That brings us to the notion of order and an obvious question could be: "What is the order of the entities in the result set?" Because no explicit order criterion was specified, the order of the result set is not deterministic and thus could change from one query run to the other. To assure a specific order you could add that to the query. For example, you could order the result set by `name` as follows:

```
q = db.GqlQuery("SELECT * FROM Task" +
        "WHERE start_date = :1" +
        "ORDER BY name", datetime.datetime(2011, 1, 1, 12, 0, 0).date())
```

taskmanager GAE project

You may recall that Bigtable stores rows in a sorted and ordered manner. Therefore, seeking a specific row does not involve a random read. Instead, the row-key can easily be used to identify the region server that hosts the row and the row data (or entity) can be read sequentially. When a property of an entity is used to filter the complete collection, a corresponding index that keeps the rows in the desired sorted order is looked up. A query that accesses `Task` entities by filtering them on the basis of the `start_date` property and then ordering them on the basis of `name` property uses an index where the data is kept in a pre-sorted order, first by `start_date` and then by `name`. In fact, every valid query is served with the help of an underlying index. To put it another way, no query can run if there is no corresponding index for it. Some queries that look different may leverage the same index. The app engine creates a few implicit indexes, especially for those that involve filtering on equality operators on property values, keys, or ancestors. For queries that involve filtering on the basis of multiple properties or involve inequality comparators or have multiple orders by properties, you need to necessarily and explicitly define an index. The development server helps in identifying required indexes and creates one when a corresponding query is run. Indexes are explicitly defined in a configuration file named `index.yaml`.

Next, a survey of the supported filter operators is illustrated.

Allowed Filters and Result Ordering

The app engine allows you to use the following operators on property values:

- ➤ =

- ➤ >

- ➤ >=

➤   <

➤   <=

➤   !

➤   IN

To match an inequality filter the index is scanned to find the first matching row, from where on all consecutive rows are returned until a row is not matched. Remember, all rows are ordered in the index by that property! You can define multiple inequality filters on a single property but you are not allowed to have multiple inequality filters on different properties in the same query. Multiple inequality filters on a single property are split into multiple queries where the result sets are merged before returned. So a query as follows:

```
SELECT * FROM Task WHERE start_date >= :a_specified_date
                   AND start_date <= :another_specified_date
```

is run in two parts, where one part matches all rows where `start_date` is greater than or equal to a specified date and another matches all rows where `start_date` is less than or equal to another start date. Finally, the results from both queries are merged.

When ordering queries that involve inequality filters it is required that you first order by the property on which the inequality filter operator is applied. You can include other properties in the ordering only after the property on which the inequality filter is applied.

Multiple equality filter operators on different properties can be used in the same query that uses an inequality filter operator on a property. However, again when it comes to defining an ORDER BY criteria for this query, remember to order the result first by the property that defines the inequality property.

The data store allows properties to contain a list of values. It also allows two entities to have different data types for the same property. The IN operator works on values that contain a list. The IN operator evaluates membership. An entity is returned in the result if even one element in the list matches the filter. For example, `a_prop = [1, 2]` will match both `a_prop =1` and `a_prop = 2`. However, `a_prop = [1, 2]` will not match if the query specifies `a_prop > 1` and `a_prop < 2` because although one element matches either condition, none matches both. When it comes to multi-valued properties, the ones that contain a list of values, each property in the list is added to the index. This, apart from the stated matching behavior, also imposes a few side effects when it comes to ordering. A multi-valued property is ordered by the smallest value in ascending order and by the largest value in descending order. So a multi-valued property that contains [1, 3, 5, 7] is treated as 1 when ascending order is applied and the same property value is treated as 7 when a descending order is applied. Thus, when it comes to order [1, 3, 5, 7] is both smaller and greater than [2, 3, 4, 5, 6].

Two entities can contain different data types for the same property and some entities may not even have that property. Entities that don't define a property are skipped when a query filters on the basis of that property. If you would like that entity to be included in the result, then at least set a null (or None in Python) value for the property in the particular entity. Queries match only those entities that contain the same data type as that specified by the query filter. So, a query that matches on a string value will only look for matches with those entities that have a string type for the same property. Mixing of data types in a single property also creates a few side effects when it comes to ordering. There is a hierarchy in ordering between data types. For example, integers are ordered before floats. Therefore, ordering by a property that, for example, contains both integer and float values can be tricky because 5 < 4.5.

I mentioned earlier that every query needs an index. A query and its explicitly defined index could be like so:

```
q = db.GqlQuery("SELECT * FROM Task" +
                "WHERE start_date >= :1" +
                "tags IN :2" +
                "ORDER BY start_date",
    datetime.datetime(2011, 1, 1, 12, 0, 0).date(), ["Important", "Sample"])
```

taskmanager GAE project

```
indexes:
- kind: Task
  properties:
  - name: start_date
  - name: tags
```

index.yaml in taskmanager GAE project

In the example so far, a query result has been obtained with the help of the `fetch` method. The `fetch` method allows you to get a set of records in a single call. The number of result records returned is defined by the limit. If you just want a single entity you can use the `get` method to retrieve the entity at the top of the order. If all you want to know is the number of entities in the result, then simply use the `count` method. The `count` method returns with a count of all entities in the result unless it times out. The app engine is suited for fast responses that can scale easily. Any response that takes more than 30 seconds times out.

If you need to traverse through the entire result set, you need use the `Query` interface as an iterable object. An example could be as follows:

```
q = db.GqlQuery("SELECT * FROM Task" +
                "WHERE start_date = :1" +
                "ORDER BY name", datetime.datetime(2011, 1, 1, 12, 0, 0).date())
for task in q:
    print "Task name: %s" % (task.name)
```

taskmanager GAE project

The iterable object allows you to access the result set in small chunks until you receive all the results. Although an iterable object allows you to traverse the entire set it is doesn't let you go back later and fetch incrementally since the last fetch. For such an incremental fetch the cursor is a suitable feature.

After a fetch, you can get a cursor using the query object's `cursor` method. A cursor is a base64-encoded data pointer that allows you to fetch additional results incrementally. The second query to fetch incremental results should be identical to the first one as far as the filters, sort order, and ancestors are concerned. Before executing the query, you need to pass the cursor to the query object's `with_cursor` method. Cursors remain unaffected by any changes to the data that is already fetched. Any updates or inserts in the range prior to the current cursor are overlooked.

To facilitate consistent data state, the app engine supports atomic transactions for all entity and entity group-level updates. Transactional integrity means either the operation succeeds or it's rolled back. All writes to the data store (that is, create, update, and delete operations) in the context of a single entity are atomic.

An entity, its ancestors, and its children form an entity group. A function manipulating entities in an entity group can be enclosed within a transactional boundary. A function can explicitly run as a transactional unit if it is passed along with its arguments to the `db.run_in_transaction` method. An example is depicted in Listing 10-1.

LISTING 10-1: taskmanager GAE project

Available for download on Wrox.com

```
import datetime
from google.appengine.ext import db

class Task(db.Model):
  name = db.StringProperty(required=True)
  description = db.StringProperty()
  start_date = db.DateProperty(required=True)
  due_date = db.DateProperty()
  end_date = db.DateProperty()
  tags = db.StringListProperty()
  status = db.StringProperty(choices=('in progress', 'complete', 'not started'))

def update_as_complete(key, status):
  obj = db.get(key)
  if status == 'complete':
    obj.status = 'complete'
    obj.end_date = datetime.datetime.now().day()

  obj.put()

q = db.GqlQuery("SELECT * FROM Task" +
                "WHERE name = :1", "task1")
completed_task = q.get()

db.run_in_transaction(update_as_complete, completed_task.key(), "complete")
```

jtaskmanager GAE project

The app engine does not lock any rows. Optimist locking and reconciling on the basis of the last updated time resolves any conflicts. Transactions across operations that span two or more root entities are not supported.

Having explored most of the essential features of the app engine and the Python SDK for the app engine, let's cover some of the idioms in the Java app engine SDK next.

Tersely Exploring the Java App Engine SDK

To get started, read the introductory tutorial, available online at `http://code.google.com/ appengine/docs/java/gettingstarted/`. Programs written in Java to run on the app engine are web applications that leverage the standard Java specification like Java Servlets. The app engine run time hosts a Java application server. The container itself is a customized implementation of the Webtide Jetty application server.

The fundamentals of the app engine remain the same whether they are accessed from Python or Java so repeating what has already been described would be futile. Therefore, this section jumps right in to show a few bits about accessing the data store using the Java standards like JDO and JPA.

The DataNucleus (`www.datanucleus.org/`) open-source app engine plug-in bridges the gap between the Java standard persistence frameworks (in particular JDO and JPA) and the Google Bigtable-based data store.

To set up and configure JDO read the online documentation at `http://code.google.com/ appengine/docs/java/datastore/jdo/`. For JPA configuration look at `http://code.google .com/appengine/docs/java/datastore/jpa/`.

The `Task` class from the Python example can be created as a JDO-aware plain old Java object (POJO) like so:

```java
package taskmanager;

import com.google.appengine.api.datastore.Key;
import java.util.Date;
import javax.jdo.annotations.IdGeneratorStrategy;
import javax.jdo.annotations.PersistenceCapable;
import javax.jdo.annotations.Persistent;
import javax.jdo.annotations.PrimaryKey;

@PersistenceCapable
public class Task {
    @PrimaryKey
    @Persistent(valueStrategy = IdGeneratorStrategy.IDENTITY)
    private Key key;

    @Persistent
    private String name;

    @Persistent
    private String description;

    @Persistent
    private Date startDate;

    @Persistent
    private String status;

    public Greeting(String name, String description, Date startDate,
String status) {
        this.name = name;
        this.description = description;
```

```
            this.startDate = startDate;
            this.status = status;
        }

        public Key getKey() {
            return key;
        }

        public User getName() {
            return name;
        }

        public String getDescription() {
            return description;
        }

        public Date getStartDate() {
            return startDate;
        }

        public String getStatus() {
            return status;
        }

        public void setName(String name) {
            this.name = name;
        }

        public void setDescription(String description) {
            this.description = description;
        }

        public void setStartDate(Date startDate) {
            this.startDate = startDate;
        }

        public void setStatus(String status) {
            this.status = status;
        }
    }
```

jtaskmanager GAE project

A JDO `PersistenceManager` class takes care of persisting the entity just defined to the data store. You need to get a `PersistenceManager` instance from the `PersistenceManagerFactory` like so:

```
package taskmanager;

import javax.jdo.JDOHelper;
import javax.jdo.PersistenceManagerFactory;

public final class PMF {
    private static final PersistenceManagerFactory pmfInstance =
```

```
              JDOHelper.getPersistenceManagerFactory("transactions-optional");

    private PMF() {}

    public static PersistenceManagerFactory get() {
        return pmfInstance;
    }
}
```

jtaskmanager GAE project

Finally, you can save an object as follows:

```
String name = "task1";
String description = "a task";
Date startDate = new Date();
String status = "task created";

Task task = new Task(name, description, startDate, status);
PersistenceManager pm = PMF.get().getPersistenceManager();
try {
    pm.makePersistent(task);
    } finally {
    pm.close();
    }
```

jtaskmanager GAE project

Then you can query for all tasks using the JDO Query Language (JDOQL), which is similar to GQL, like so:

```
PersistenceManager pm = PMF.get().getPersistenceManager();
String query = "select from " + Task.class.getName();
List<Task> tasks = (List<Task>) pm.newQuery(query).execute();
```

jtaskmanager GAE project

The use of JDO and JPA (which is not illustrated in this chapter) bridge the gap between the typical object-centric application development and a scalable ordered and sorted column-family store like GAE's data store. They help developers leverage the app engine's scalable environment without the necessity to learn a completely new database technology. However, one must keep in mind that the JDO and JPA that apply to the app engine are just a subset of the overall specification.

All that was explained about the queries, their behavior, and their limitations remains the same, whether used with the Python or the Java SDK. Also, indexes and transactional capabilities and concepts remain the same.

Next, I explore Amazon SimpleDB.

AMAZON SIMPLEDB

In the preceding section you saw how GAE's data store provided a fully managed database for use. The complexity and burden of managing a large and scalable database was completely abstracted from you. You did not have to worry about database administration, database index management, or performance tuning. As far as the data store goes, all you had to do was concentrate on your application and its data logic.

Amazon SimpleDB is a ready-to-run database alternative to the app engine data store. It's elastic and is a fully managed database in the cloud. The two data stores — app engine data store and SimpleDB — are quite different in their API as well as the internal fabric but both provide you a highly scalable and grow-as-you-use model to a data store.

 Amazon EC2 database AMI(s) allow you to spin your own favorite database (Oracle, MySQL, PostgreSQL, DB2 or any other) in the AWS cloud but the onus of managing it is yours.

Getting Started with SimpleDB

Amazon SimpleDB is offered as a part of the Amazon Web Services (AWS) offerings. Getting started is as simple as setting up a SimpleDB account at `http://aws.amazon.com/sdb`. You need two sets of credentials: an access key and a secret key to access AWS. These credentials can be obtained from the account details section, accessible once you have logged in to your `http://aws.amazon.com/` page. Details on AWS registration and access are not covered in this chapter or elsewhere in this book. However, following the instructions on the AWS home page, `http://aws.amazon.com/`, should get you easily set up.

SimpleDB is a very simple database by design. It imposes a few restrictions and provides a very simple API to interact with your data. The highest level of abstraction in SimpleDB is an account. Think of it as a database instance in a traditional RDBMS setup. Better still, think of it as a Microsoft Excel document with a number of different worksheets.

Each account can have one or more domains and each domain is a collection of items. By default, a SimpleDB domain (a collection) can hold up to 10 GB of data and you can have up to 100 domains per account. That's not the ceiling, though, it's only the default. You can contact AWS to provision higher capabilities if your configuration needs it. Even at default levels, you can set up a 1 TB data set. That's not all that small! Also, a clever combination of SimpleDB and Amazon Simple Storage Service (S3) could help you optimize your storage. Keep all large objects in S3 and keep all smaller objects and the metadata for the large objects in SimpleDB. That should do the trick.

Within a domain you can persist items. Items can be of any type as long as they can be defined using attribute-value pairs. Therefore, each item is a collection of attribute-value pairs. Two items in the same domain are not required to have the same set of attribute-value pairs. In fact, in an extreme case, you can choose to keep two items in a domain even if the two don't have a single attribute in common. This sort of an extreme case may have little practical use but from SimpleDB's standpoint it's all acceptable.

Earlier in the book you saw document databases had similar characteristics. CouchDB and MongoDB provided similar freedom and capabilities. SimpleDB can be thought of as a document database in the cloud, expandable on demand. It would be both easy and appropriate to store data on SimpleDB that is in the following log file data format (from Chapter 3):

```
{
    "ApacheLogRecord": {
        "ip": "127.0.0.1",
        "ident" : "-",
        "http_user" : "frank",
        "time" : "10/Oct/2000:13:55:36 -0700",
        "request_line" : {
            "http_method" : "GET",
            "url" : "/apache_pb.gif",
            "http_vers" : "HTTP/1.0",
        },
        "http_response_code" : "200",
        "http_response_size" : "2326",
        "referrer" : "http://www.example.com/start.html",
        "user_agent" : "Mozilla/4.08 [en] (Win98; I ;Nav)",
    },
}
```

This example is a JSON document. Each key/value pair of JSON elements will correspond to an attribute-value pair in SimpleDB.

 The JSON format in the example above is used simply to illustrate key/value pairs. SimpleDB is not natively capable of understanding JSON formats or querying JSON documents. You will need to parse a JSON document and extract the key/value pairs before you can store it in SimpleDB.

Like most AWS options, SimpleDB offers a simple API to manipulate your domain, its items, and the attribute-value pairs of an item. The API follows both REST- and SOAP-style idioms and is available as a web service. The client makes a request to carry out a specific operation, such as create a domain, insert an item, or update an attribute-value pair. The SimpleDB server completes the operations, unless there is an error, and responds with a success code and response data. The response data is an HTTP response packet, which has headers, storing metadata, and some payload, which is in XML format.

Next, I quickly list the available commands in the SimpleDB API. I start by listing commands that help manipulate a domain.

Commands for managing SimpleDB domains:

➤ `CreateDomain` — Create a domain to store your items.

➤ `DeleteDomain` — Delete an existing domain.

➤ `ListDomains` — List all the domains within your account.

➤ `DomainMetadata` — Get information on a domain, its items, and the items' attribute-value pairs. Information like domain creation date, number of items in the domain, and the size of attribute-value pairs can be obtained.

Once you create a domain, you can use the `PutAttributes` method to insert or update an item. Remember that an item is a collection of attribute-value pairs. Inserting an item implies creating the set of attribute-value pairs that logically forms an item. Updating an item implies retrieving a particular item and then updating the value for one or more attributes of the item. `BatchPutAttributes` is also available to carry out multiple `put` operations in a single call.

`DeleteAttributes` allows you to delete an item, an attribute-value pair, or just an attribute-value from your domain. `BatchDeleteAttributes` allows multiple `delete` operations in a single call.

You can get the attribute-value pairs of a single item by using the `GetAttributes` operation. Alternatively, you can use the `SELECT` operations to query and filter items in your domain. SimpleDB supports a rich set of features to filter a data set in a domain. The syntax and semantics are similar to that offered by SQL. SimpleDB automatically creates and manages indexes to make querying efficient.

Although SimpleDB's query mechanism feels a bit like SQL, you should not confuse SimpleDB for an RDBMS. It's not a relational store and does not support complex transactions or referential foreign key-based constraints as relational databases do.

SIMPLEDB REGIONS

Currently, AWS offers SimpleDB in four different regions: U.S. East, U.S. West, Europe, and Asia. You need to choose a region before you create a domain. Choose a region close to your users to reduce latency and improve performance. Two domains in different regions could have the same name but they are different and completely isolated from each other. They do not share any data between them.

The four available regions (with their physical locations) are as follows:

➤ **sdb.amazonaws.com** — U.S. East (Northern Virginia)

➤ **sdb.us-west-1.amazonaws.com** — U.S. West (Northern California)

➤ **sdb.eu-west-1.amazonaws.com** — Europe (Ireland)

➤ **sdb.ap-southeast** — Asia (Singapore)

Next, I illustrate a few ways to access and use SimpleDB.

Using the REST API

The easiest way to use SimpleDB is to use its REST API. Although SimpleDB's REST API isn't thoroughly RESTful from a purist's standpoint, it provides a simple HTTP-based request-response model. Read Subbu Allamaraju's post titled, "A RESTful version of Amazon SimpleDB" at `www.subbu.org/weblogs/main/2007/12/a_restful_versi.html`, to understand why the SimpleDB REST API isn't truly RESTful. The easiest way to test this API is to run the operations using a command-line client. I will use a Perl-based command-line client in this subsection. The name of this command-line client is amazon-simpledb-cli. You can download a copy of this client from its project page, accessible online at `http://code.google.com/p/amazon-simpledb-cli/`. The amazon-simpledb-cli program depends on the Amazon-provided Perl modules for AWS. The Perl modules for AWS are available for download at `http://aws.amazon.com/code/1136`.

 A SOAP API is also available for Amazon SimpleDB. I don't cover the SOAP API in this book but you can learn more about the SOAP API in the online developer documentation at `http://aws.amazon.com/documentation/simpledb/`.

To install amazon-simpledb-cli, first make sure you have Perl installed on your machine. If you are a POSIX system user (which includes various flavors of Linux, BSD, and Mac OSX) you will likely have Perl preinstalled on your machine. If not, you need to get a copy of the Perl compiler and interpreter and get it up and running first. Instructions for installing Perl are beyond the scope of this book, but start at `perl.org` if you need help.

To get started, first make sure to get (or update) the following Perl modules:

➤ `Getopt::Long`

➤ `Pod::Usage`

➤ `Digest::SHA1`

➤ `Digest::HMAC`

➤ `XML::Simple`

➤ `Bundle::LWP`

➤ `Crypt::SSLeay`

You can install `Getopt::Long` like so:

```
perl -MCPAN -e 'install Getopt:Long'
```

You can install the other required Perl modules in the same manner. Just make sure to replace `Getpot::Long` with the name of the specific module. On some systems and for some modules you may need to run the commands as root. Once the required modules are installed and updated you can install the downloaded AWS Perl module as follows:

1. First, unzip the downloaded distribution as follows: `unzip AmazonSimpleDB-*-perl-library.zip`

2. Then get the Perl sitelib like so: `sitelib=$(perl -MConfig -le 'print $Config{sitelib}')`

3. Finally, copy the Amazon module to the `sitelib` as follows: `sudo scp -r AmazonSimpleDB-*-perl-library/src/Amazon $sitelib`

After the AWS Perl module is installed, get the `amazon-simpledb-cli` script like so:

```
sudo curl -Lo /usr/local/bin/simpledb http://simpledb-cli.notlong.com
```

and set the script permissions to allow everyone to execute the script as follows:

```
sudo chmod +x /usr/local/bin/simpledb
```

The program is now all ready to be used. Next, make sure to locate the AWS credentials — the AWS access key and the AWS access secret key, which are available from your account page — and have them handy to test the `amazon-simpledb-cli` script (installed as `simpledb` in the `/usr/local/bin` folder) you just installed.

To use the `simpledb` script you need to pass in the access key and the secret access key to the `aws-access-key-id` and `aws-secret-access-key` command-line arguments, respectively. Alternatively, you can set default access key and secret access key values using the `$AWS_ACCESS_KEY_ID` and `$AWS_SECRET_ACCESS_KEY` environment variables.

You can create a domain as follows:

```
simpledb create-domain domain1
```

You can add items to this domain as follows:

```
simpledb put domain1 item1 key1=valueA key2=value2 anotherKey=someValue
simpledb put domain1 item2 key1=valueB key2=value2 differentKey=aValue
```

Then you can edit `item1` and add another attribute-value pair to it as follows:

```
simpledb put domain1 item1 yetAnotherKey=anotherValue
```

You can replace an attribute-value pair with a newer one as follows:

```
simpledb put-replace domain1 item1 key1=value1 newKey1=newValue1
```

You can delete an attribute or just the value of an attribute. Examples could be:

```
simpledb delete mydomain item1 anotherKey
simpledb delete mydomain item2 key2=value2
```

At the account level you can list all domains like so:

```
simpledb list-domains
```

You can list all item names in a domain like so:

```
simpledb select 'select itemName() from domain1'
```

Or choose to filter the list of items using a SQL-like syntax and list all matching items and its attributes as follows:

```
simpledb select 'select * from domain1 where key1="valueA"'
```

If you would like to list all attributes on a specific item, say `item1`, then you could use `simpledb` like so:

```
simpledb get domain1 item1
```

If you would like to restrict the output to only a specified set of attributes, you can pass in the attribute names to the last command as follows:

```
simpledb get mydomain item1 newKey1 key2
```

If you don't need a domain any more and want to remove a domain and all its constituents, you can run a `simpledb` command like so:

```
simpledb delete-domain domain1
```

AUTHENTICATING REQUESTS

Every request to SimpleDB needs to be authenticated. A client passes in the following with the request:

➤   AWS access key

➤   An HMAC-SHA1 signature generated on the basis of the AWS secret access key and the request

➤   Timestamp

AWS accesses the secret access key on the basis of the passed-in AWS access key and then generates an HMAC-SHA1 signature using the secret access key and the passed-in request. If the HMAC-SHA1 signature passed in by the client matches the one generated by the server, the request is served with an appropriate response; otherwise an authentication error is thrown.

A passed-in timestamp acts as an additional level of security. Requests with timestamps older than 15 minutes are considered too stale to be served.

The command stated previously gives a flavor of what's possible with `amazon-simpledb-cli`. It also hints to the simple data querying and management commands available in Amazon SimpleDB.

For the sake of completeness I will also illustrate a little about the underlying request and response when the REST API is used. A call like:

```
simpledb put domain1 item1 key1=valueA key2=value2 anotherKey=someValue
```

is translated to:

```
https://sdb.amazonaws.com/
?Action=PutAttributes
&DomainName=domain1
&ItemName=item1
&Attribute.1.Name=key1
&Attribute.1.Value=valueA
&Attribute.2.Name=key2
&Attribute.2.Value=value2
&Attribute.3.Name=anotherKey
&Attribute.3.Value=someValue
&AWSAccessKeyId=[valid access key id]
&SignatureVersion=2
&SignatureMethod=HmacSHA256
&Timestamp=2011-01-29T15%3A03%3A05-07%3A00
&Version=2009-04-15
&Signature=[valid signature]
```

The response to this is an XML document, whose format is as follows:

```
<PutAttributesResponse>
  <ResponseMetadata>
    <RequestId></RequestId>
    <BoxUsage></BoxUsage>
  </ResponseMetadata>
</PutAttributesResponse>
```

The Amazon SimpleDB XSD is available online at `http://sdb.amazonaws.com/doc/` `2009-04-15/AmazonSimpleDB.xsd`. Details of the response XML schema are defined in this document.

Having illustrated many of SimpleDB's features, I will cover a few libraries to access SimpleDB from Java, Python, and Ruby.

Accessing SimpleDB Using Java

AWS provides a comprehensive and well-supported SDK for Java developers to write applications to interact with AWS. The AWS SDK for Java is available online at `http://aws.amazon.com/` `sdkforjava/`. To get started, read the introductory tutorial on the SDK at `http://aws.amazon` `.com/articles/3586`. The SDK supports a range of AWS including the SimpleDB. The download bundle includes a few samples to get you started. An elementary example that shows its usage is included in Listing 10-2.

LISTING 10-2: A simple Java program that interacts with SimpleDB using the AWS SDK

```java
import java.util.ArrayList;
import java.util.List;
import com.amazonaws.AmazonClientException;
import com.amazonaws.AmazonServiceException;
import com.amazonaws.auth.PropertiesCredentials;
import com.amazonaws.services.simpledb.AmazonSimpleDB;
import com.amazonaws.services.simpledb.AmazonSimpleDBClient;
import com.amazonaws.services.simpledb.model.Attribute;
import com.amazonaws.services.simpledb.model.BatchPutAttributesRequest;
import com.amazonaws.services.simpledb.model.CreateDomainRequest;
import com.amazonaws.services.simpledb.model.Item;
import com.amazonaws.services.simpledb.model.ReplaceableAttribute;
import com.amazonaws.services.simpledb.model.ReplaceableItem;

public class SimpleDBExample {

    public static void main(String[] args) throws Exception {
        AmazonSimpleDB sdb = new AmazonSimpleDBClient(new PropertiesCredentials(
SimpleDBExample.class.getResourceAsStream("aws_credentials.properties")));

        try {
            String aDomain = "domain1";
            sdb.createDomain(new CreateDomainRequest(aDomain));

            // Put data into a domain
            sdb.batchPutAttributes(new BatchPutAttributesRequest(myDomain,
createSampleData()));
        } catch (AmazonServiceException ase) {
            System.out.println("Error Message:    " + ase.getMessage());
            System.out.println("HTTP Status Code: " + ase.getStatusCode());
            System.out.println("AWS Error Code:   " + ase.getErrorCode());
            System.out.println("Error Type:       " + ase.getErrorType());
            System.out.println("Request ID:       " + ase.getRequestId());
        } catch (AmazonClientException ace) {
            System.out.println("Error Message: " + ace.getMessage());
        }
    }

    private static List<ReplaceableItem> createSampleData() {
        List<ReplaceableItem> myData = new ArrayList<ReplaceableItem>();

        sampleData.add(new ReplaceableItem("item1").withAttributes(
                new ReplaceableAttribute("key1", "valueA", true),
                new ReplaceableAttribute("key2", "value2", true),
                new ReplaceableAttribute("anotherKey", "someValue", true)
                );

        sampleData.add(new ReplaceableItem("item2").withAttributes(
                new ReplaceableAttribute("key1", "valueB", true),
                new ReplaceableAttribute("key2", "value2", true),
                new ReplaceableAttribute("differentKey", "aValue", true)
                );
```

```
        return myData;
    }
}
```

SimpleDBExample.java

The example in Listing 11-2 assumes that you specify the AWS credentials in a file named `aws_credentials.properties`. The contents of `aws_credentials.properties` are as follows:

```
accessKey =
secretKey =
```

The example so far demonstrates the usage of the API from a standalone Java program. If the program were more complex than a simple standalone program, you are likely to leverage standard Java idioms including the Java Persistence API (JPA). A few open-source options exist for using JPA to persist to SimpleDB. SimpleJPA is one such project. SimpleJPA covers a subset of JPA, relevant in the context of SimpleDB.

Using SimpleDB with Ruby and Python

Rails is the choice web development in the Ruby community. If you would like to use SimpleDB with your Rails application, you wouldn't be able to simply plug SimpleDB in place of your relational database like MySQL without any external help. However, SimpleRecord can solve much of your problem. SimpleRecord implemented via an open-source project by the same name is available at `https://github.com/appoxy/simple_record/`. SimpleRecord is an ActiveRecord replacement for Rails applications that would like to use Amazon SimpleDB as their persistent store.

Using SimpleRecord is easy. Installing SimpleRecord is a single-line effort:

```
gem install simple_record
```

The assumption is that you have Ruby, RubyGems, and Rails already installed and set up. The simplest example could be as follows:

```
require 'simple_record'
 class MyModel < SimpleRecord::Base
    has_strings :key1
    has_ints :key2
 end
```

As always is the case with AWS, configure the AWS credentials so that you are ready to persist your model to SimpleDB. You can configure AWS credentials like so:

```
AWS_ACCESS_KEY_ID='<aws_access_key_id>'
 AWS_SECRET_ACCESS_KEY='<aws_secret_access_key>'
 SimpleRecord.establish_connection(AWS_ACCESS_KEY_ID,AWS_SECRET_ACCESS_KEY)
```

Finally, you could store a model instance as follows:

```
m_instance = MyModel.new
m_instance.key1 = "valueA"
m_instance.key2 = value1
m_instance.save
```

You can retrieve model instances by finding by id as follows:

```
m_instance_2 = MyModel.find(id)
```

Alternatively, you can find for all instances that match a filter like so:

```
all_instances = MyModel?.find(:all, ["key1=?", "valueA"],
:order=>"key2", :limit=>10)
```

That should give you a hint of how you could leverage SimpleDB with your Rails application. Other alternative libraries are available, including one from Amazon that provides a Ruby language interface to connect to Amazon's services. You can explore the Ruby library for SimpleDB by downloading it from `http://aws.amazon.com/code/Amazon-SimpleDB/3324`.

Next, and last of all, I cover AWS SimpleDB interaction from Python. Boto, available online at `http://code.google.com/p/boto/`, is the most popular choice for connecting to SimpleDB from Python. To get started, download the latest source of boto from its Github mirror as follows:

```
git clone https://github.com/boto/boto.git
```

Then change into the cloned repository directory and run `python install setup.py` to install boto. Once installed, fire up a Python interactive session and you can easily create a new domain and add items to it as follows:

```
import boto
sdb = boto.connect_sdb('<your aws access key>', '<your aws secret key'>)
domain = sdb.create_domain('domain2')
item = domain.new_item('item1')
item['key1'] = 'value1'
item['key2'] = 'value2'
item.save()
```

Beyond this, the SimpleDB commands and ways of interactions remain consistent with what you have seen in the other cases.

SUMMARY

This chapter covered the two popular and scalable database services in the cloud, illustrating their behavior characteristics and peculiarities. It also showed how libraries, specifications, and frameworks in various languages can be used in conjunction with the NoSQL stores.

Google's app engine data store and Amazon SimpleDB are revolutionizing the database landscape, making everyone rethink their current efforts around managing database complexity in their applications. Not only is it tempting for many to achieve scalable architectures on the shoulders of the giants, but it is also practical and prudent from a cost and flexibility standpoint.

Though Google's and Amazon's offerings are the most well known and robust in their category, multiple options for database in the cloud are beginning to now emerge. For example, a host of cloud-based elastic database hosts for CouchDB and MongoDB now exist. The makers of CouchDB have launched one, named CouchOne (www.couchone.com). Similarly, MongoHQ is a scalable MongoDB host. Document databases are not the only ones with hosted scalable options. Eventually consistent key/value database creator Basho is offering ready-to-use Riak 3 and 5 node clusters in association with Joyent. We are likely to see more alternatives emerge in future.

As cloud computing continues to grow in adoption, we are likely to see a lot of database services in the cloud. Many, if not most, of these databases in the cloud will leverage NoSQL products. This is likely to provide many developers the opportunity to use NoSQL and to start thinking of a database as a persistence service.

11

Scalable Parallel Processing with MapReduce

WHAT'S IN THIS CHAPTER?

- ➤ Understanding the challenges of scalable parallel processing
- ➤ Leveraging MapReduce for large scale parallel processing
- ➤ Exploring the concepts and nuances of the MapReduce computational model
- ➤ Getting hands-on MapReduce experience using MongoDB, CouchDB, and HBase
- ➤ Introducing Mahout, a MapReduce-based machine learning infrastructure

Manipulating large amounts of data requires tools and methods that can run operations in parallel with as few as possible points of intersection among them. Fewer points of intersection lead to fewer potential conflicts and less management. Such parallel processing tools also need to keep data transfer to a minimum. I/O and bandwidth can often become bottlenecks that impede fast and efficient processing. With large amounts of data the I/O bottlenecks can be amplified and can potentially slow down a system to a point where it becomes impractical to use it. Therefore, for large-scale computations, keeping data local to a computation is of immense importance. Given these considerations, manipulating large data sets spread out across multiple machines is neither trivial nor easy.

Over the years, many methods have been developed to compute large data sets. Initially, innovation was focused around building super computers. Super computers are meant to be super-powerful machines with greater-than-normal processing capabilities. These machines work well for specific and complicated algorithms that are compute intensive but are far from being good general-purpose solutions. They are expensive to build and maintain and out of reach for most organizations.

Grid computing emerged as a possible solution for a problem that super computers didn't solve. The idea behind a computational grid is to distribute work among a set of nodes and thereby reduce the computational time that a single large machine takes to complete the same task. In grid computing, the focus is on compute-intensive tasks where data passing between nodes is managed using Message Passing Interface (MPI) or one of its variants. This topology works well where the extra CPU cycles get the job done faster. However, this same topology becomes inefficient if a large amount data needs to be passed among the nodes. Large data transfer among nodes faces I/O and bandwidth limitations and can often be bound by these restrictions. In addition, the onus of managing the data-sharing logic and recovery from failed states is completely on the developer.

Public computing projects like SETI@Home (`http://setiathome.berkeley.edu/`) and Folding@ Home (`http://folding.stanford.edu/`) extend the idea of grid computing to individuals donating "spare" CPU cycles for compute-intensive tasks. These projects run on idle CPU time of hundreds of thousands, sometimes millions, of individual machines, donated by volunteers. These individual machines go on and off the Internet and provide a large compute cluster despite their individual unreliability. By combining idle CPUs, the overall infrastructure tends to work like, and often smarter than, a single super computer.

Despite the availability of varied solutions for effective distributed computing, none listed so far keep data locally in a compute grid to minimize bandwidth blockages. Few follow a policy of sharing little or nothing among the participating nodes. Inspired by functional programming notions that adhere to ideas of little interdependence among parallel processes, or threads, and committed to keeping data and computation together, is MapReduce. Developed for distributed computing and patented by Google, MapReduce has become one of the most popular ways of processing large volumes of data efficiently and reliably. MapReduce offers a simple and fault-tolerant model for effective computation on large data spread across a horizontal cluster of commodity nodes. This chapter explains MapReduce and explores the many possible computations on big data using this programming model.

MapReduce is explicitly stated as MapReduce, a camel-cased version used and popularized by Google. However, the coverage here is more generic and not restricted by Google's definition.

The idea of MapReduce is published in a research paper, which is accessible online at `http://labs.google.com/papers/mapreduce.html` (Dean, Jeffrey & Ghemawat, Sanjay (2004), "MapReduce: Simplified Data Processing on Large Clusters").

UNDERSTANDING MAPREDUCE

Chapter 6 introduced MapReduce as a way to group data on MongoDB clusters. Therefore, MapReduce isn't a complete stranger to you. However, to explain the nuances and idioms of MapReduce, I reintroduce the concept using a few illustrated examples.

I start out by using MapReduce to run a few queries that involve aggregate functions like `sum`, `maximum`, `minimum`, and `average`. The publicly available NYSE daily market data for the period between 1970 and 2010 is used for the example. Because the data is aggregated on a daily basis, only one data point represents a single trading day for a stock. Therefore, the data set is not large. Certainly not large enough to be classified big data. The example focuses on the essential mechanics of MapReduce so the size doesn't really matter. I use two document databases, MongoDB and CouchDB, in this example. The concept of MapReduce is not specific to these products and applies to a large variety of NoSQL products including sorted, ordered column-family stores, and distributed key/value maps. I start with document databases because they require the least amount of effort around installation and setup and are easy to test in local standalone mode. MapReduce with Hadoop and HBase is included later in this chapter.

To get started, download the zipped archive files for the daily NYSE market data from 1970 to 2010 from `http://infochimps.com/datasets/daily-1970-2010-open-close-hi-low-and-volume-nyse-exchange`. Extract the zip file to a local folder. The unzipped NYSE data set contains a number of files. Among these are two types of files: daily market data files and dividend data files. For the sake of simplicity, I upload only the daily market data files into a database collection. This means the only files you need from the set are those whose names start with `NYSE_daily_prices_` and include a number or a letter at the end. All such files that have a number appended to the end contain only header information and so can be skipped.

The database and collection in MongoDB are named `mydb` and `nyse`, respectively. The database in CouchDB is named `nyse`. The data is available in comma-separated values (`.csv`) format, so I leverage the mongoimport utility to import this data set into a MongoDB collection. Later in this chapter, I use a Python script to load the same `.csv` files into CouchDB.

The mongoimport utility and its output, when uploading `NYSE_daily_prices_A.csv`, are as follows:

```
~/Applications/mongodb/bin/mongoimport --type csv --db mydb --collection nyse --
headerline NYSE_daily_prices_A.csv
connected to: 127.0.0.1
    4981480/40990992 12%
        89700 29900/second
    10357231/40990992 25%
        185900 30983/second
    15484231/40990992 37%
        278000 30888/second
    20647430/40990992 50%
        370100 30841/second
    25727124/40990992 62%
        462300 30820/second
    30439300/40990992 74%
        546600 30366/second
    35669019/40990992 87%
        639600 30457/second
    40652285/40990992 99%
        729100 30379/second
imported 735027 objects
```

Other daily price data files are uploaded in a similar fashion. To avoid sequential and tedious upload of 36 different files you could consider automating the task using a shell script as included in Listing 11-1.

LISTING 11-1: infochimps_nyse_data_loader.sh

```bash
#!/bin/bash
FILES=./infochimps_dataset_4778_download_16677/NYSE/NYSE_daily_prices_*.csv
for f in $FILES
do
  echo "Processing $f file..."
  # set MONGODB_HOME environment variable to point to the MongoDB installation
folder.
  ls -l $f
  $MONGODB_HOME/bin/mongoimport --type csv --db mydb --collection nyse --
headerline $f
Done
```

infochimps_nyse_data_loader.sh

Once the data is uploaded, you can verify the format by querying for a single document as follows:

```
> db.nyse.findOne();
{
        "_id" : ObjectId("4d519529e883c3755b5f7760"),
        "exchange" : "NYSE",
        "stock_symbol" : "FDI",
        "date" : "1997-02-28",
        "stock_price_open" : 11.11,
        "stock_price_high" : 11.11,
        "stock_price_low" : 11.01,
        "stock_price_close" : 11.01,
        "stock_volume" : 4200,
        "stock_price_adj_close" : 4.54
}
```

Next, MapReduce can be used to manipulate the collection. Let the first of the tasks be to find the highest stock price for each stock over the entire data that spans the period between 1970 and 2010.

MapReduce has two parts: a map function and a reduce function. The two functions are applied to data sequentially, though the underlying system frequently runs computations in parallel. *Map* takes in a key/value pair and emits another key/value pair. *Reduce* takes the output of the map phase and manipulates the key/value pairs to derive the final result. A map function is applied on each item in a collection. Collections can be large and distributed across multiple physical machines. A map function runs on each subset of a collection local to a distributed node. The map operation on one node is completely independent of a similar operation on another node. This clear isolation provides effective parallel processing and allows you to rerun a map function on a subset in cases of failure.

After a map function has run on the entire collection, values are emitted and provided as input to the reduce phase. The MapReduce framework takes care of collecting and sorting the output from the multiple nodes and making it available from one phase to the other.

The reduce function takes in the key/value pairs that come out of a map phase and manipulate it further to come to the final result. The reduce phase could involve aggregating values on the basis of a common key. Reduce, like map, runs on each node of a distributed large cluster. Values from reduce operations on different nodes are combined to get the final result. Reduce operations on individual nodes run independent of other nodes, except of course the values could be finally combined.

Key/value pairs could pass multiple times through the map and reduce phases. This allows for aggregating and manipulating data that has already been grouped and aggregated before. This is frequently done when it may be desirable to have several different sets of summary data for a given data set.

Finding the Highest Stock Price for Each Stock

Getting back to the first task of finding the highest price for each stock in the period between 1970 and 2010, an appropriate map function could be as follows:

```
var map = function() {
    emit(this.stock_symbol, { stock_price_high: this.stock_price_high });
};
```

manipulate_nyse_market_data.txt

This function will be applied on every document in the collection. For each document, it picks up the stock_symbol as the key and emits the stock_symbol with the stock_price_high for that document as the key/value pair. Pictorially it would be as shown in Figure 11-1.

```
                     Key : "FDI",
            Value: {"stock_price_high" : 11.11}


                          map


{
    "_id" : objectID
{"4d519529e883c3755b5f7760"),
      "exchange":"NYSE",
      "stock_symbol":"FDI",
      "date":"1997-02-28",
      "stock_price_open":11.11,
      "stock_price_high":11.11,
      "stock_price_low":11.01,
      "stock_price_close":11.01,
      "stock_volume":4200,
      "stock_price_adj_close":4.54
}
```

FIGURE 11-1

The key/value pair extracted in the map phase is the input for the reduce phase. In MongoDB, a reduce function is defined as a JavaScript function as follows:

> *MongoDB supports only JavaScript as the language to define map and reduce functions.*

```
var reduce = function(key, values) {
  var highest_price = 0.0;
  values.forEach(function(doc) {
    if( typeof doc.stock_price_high != "undefined") {
      print("doc.stock_price_high" + doc.stock_price_high);
      if (parseFloat(doc.stock_price_high) > highest_price) { highest_price =
parseFloat(doc.stock_price_high); print("highest_price" + highest_price); }
    }
  });
  return { highest_stock_price: highest_price };
};
```

manipulate_nyse_market_data.txt

The reduce function receives two arguments: a key and an array of values. In the context of the current example, a stock with symbol `"FDI"` will have a number of different key/value pairs from the map phase. Some of these would be as follows:

```
(key : "FDI", { "stock_price_high" : 11.11 })
(key : "FDI", { "stock_price_high" : 11.18 })
(key : "FDI", { "stock_price_high" : 11.08 })
(key : "FDI", { "stock_price_high" : 10.99 })
(key : "FDI", { "stock_price_high" : 10.89 })
```

Running a simple count as follows: `db.nyse.find({stock_symbol: "FDI"}).count();`, reveals that there are 5,596 records. Therefore, there must be as many key/value pairs emitted from the map phase. Some of the values for these records may be undefined, so there may not be exactly 5,596 results emitted by the map phase.

The reduce function receives the values like so:

```
reduce('FDI', [{stock_price_high: 11.11}, {stock_price_high: 11.18},
{stock_price_high: 11.08}, {stock_price_high: 10.99}, ...]);
```

Now if you revisit the reduce function, you will notice that the passed-in array of values for each key is iterated over and a closure is called on the array elements. The closure, or inner function, carries out a simple comparison, determining the highest price for the set of values that are bound together by a common key.

The output of the reduce phase is a set of key/value pairs containing the symbol and the highest price value, respectively. There is exactly one key/value pair per stock symbol. MongoDB allows for an optional finalize function to pass the output of a reduce function and summarize it further.

Next, you set up the same data in CouchDB and carry out a few additional types of aggregation functions using MapReduce.

Uploading Historical NYSE Market Data into CouchDB

To start with, you need a script to parse the .csv files, convert .csv records to JSON documents, and then upload it to a CouchDB server. A simple sequential Python script easily gets the job done. However, being sequential in nature it crawls when trying to upload over 9 million documents. In most practical situations, you probably want a more robust parallel script to add data to a CouchDB database. For maximum efficiency, you may also want to leverage CouchDB's bulk upload API to upload a few thousand documents at a time.

The core function of the script is encapsulated in a function named upload_nyse_market_data, which is as follows:

Available for
download on
Wrox.com

```
def upload_nyse_market_data():
    couch_server = Couch('localhost', '5984')
    print "\nCreate database 'nyse_db':"
    couch_server.createDb('nyse_db')

    for file in os.listdir(PATH):
        if fnmatch.fnmatch(file, 'NYSE_daily_prices_*.csv'):
            print "opening file: " + file
            f = open(PATH+file, 'r' )
            reader = csv.DictReader( f )
            print "beginning to save json documents converted from csv data in
" + file for row in reader:
                json_doc = json.dumps(row)
                couch_server.saveDoc('nyse_db', json_doc)
                print "available json documents converted from csv data in
" + file + " saved"
            print "closing " + file
            f.close()
```

upload_nyse_market_data_couchdb.py

This function parses each .csv file, whose name matches a pattern as follows: 'NYSE_daily_prices_*.csv'. The Python script leverages the csv.DicReader to parse the .csv files and extract header information with ease. Then it uses the JSON module to dump a parsed record as a JSON document. The function uses a class named Couch to connect to a CouchDB server, create and delete databases, and put and delete documents. The Couch class is a simple wrapper for the CouchDB REST API and draws much inspiration from a sample wrapper illustrated in the CouchDB wiki at http://wiki.apache.org/couchdb/Getting_started_with_Python.

After the data is uploaded, you are ready to use MapReduce to run a few aggregation functions on the data. I first re-run the last query, used with MongoDB, to find the highest price for each stock for the entire period between 1970 and 2010. Right afterwards, I run another query to find the lowest price per year for each stock for the period between 1970 and 2010. As opposed to the first query, where the highest price for a stock was determined for the entire period, this second query aggregates data on two levels: year and stock.

In CouchDB, MapReduce queries that help manipulate and filter a database of documents create a view. Views are primary tools for querying and reporting on CouchDB documents. There are two types of views: permanent and temporary. I use permanent views to illustrate the examples in this section. Permanent views generate underlying data indexes that make it fast after the initial index buildup and are recommended in every production environment. Temporary views are good for ad-hoc prototyping. A view is defined within a design document. Design documents are special types of CouchDB documents that run application code. CouchDB supports the notion of multiple view servers to allow application code to be in different programming languages. This means you could write MapReduce operations for CouchDB using JavaScript, Erlang, Java, or any other supported language. I use JavaScript examples in this section to illustrate CouchDB's MapReduce-based querying features.

A design document listed immediately after this paragraph contains three views for the following:

> Listing of all documents

> Finding the highest price for each stock for the entire period between 1970 and 2010

> Finding the lowest price per stock per year

The design document itself is as follows:

```
{
  "_id":"_design/marketdata",
  "language": "javascript",
  "views": {
    "all": {
      "map": "function(doc) { emit(null, doc) }"
    },
    "highest_price_per_stock": {
      "map": "function(doc) { emit(doc.stock_symbol, doc.stock_price_high) }",
      "reduce": "function(key, values) {
        highest_price = 0.0;
        for(var i=0; i<values.length; i++) {
          if( (typeof values[i] != 'undefined') && (parseFloat(values[i]) >
highest_price) ) {
            highest_price = parseFloat(values[i]);
          }
        }
        return highest_price;
      }"
    },
    "lowest_price_per_stock_per_year": {
      "map": "function(doc) { emit([doc.stock_symbol, doc.date.substr(0,4)],
doc.stock_price_low) }",
      "reduce": "function(key, values) {
        lowest_price = parseFloat(values[0]);
        for(var i=0; i<values.length; i++) {
          if( (typeof values[i] != 'undefined') && (parseFloat(values[i]) <
lowest_price) ) {
            lowest_price = parseFloat(values[i]);
          }
        }
```

```
        return lowest_price;
      }"
    }
  }
}
```

mydesign.json

This design document is saved in a file named `mydesign.json`. The document can be uploaded to the `nyse_db` database as follows:

```
curl -X PUT http://127.0.0.1:5984/nyse_db/_design/marketdata -d @mydesign.json
```

CouchDB's REST-style interaction and adherence to JSON makes editing and uploading design documents no different from managing database documents. In response to the design document upload using the HTTP PUT method you should see a response as follows:

```
{"ok":true,"id":"_design/marketdata","rev":"1-9cce1dac6ab04845dd01802188491459"}
```

The specific content of the response will vary but if you see errors you know that there is some problem with either your design document or the upload operation.

CouchDB's web-based administration console, Futon, can be used to quickly review a design document and invoke the views to trigger the MapReduce jobs. The first MapReduce run is likely to be slow for a large data set because CouchDB is building an index for the documents based on the map function. Subsequent runs will use the index and execute much faster. Futon also provides a phased view of your map and subsequent reduce jobs and can be quite useful to understand how the data is aggregated.

In the previous example, the logic for the aggregation is quite simple and needs no explanation. However, a few aspects of the design document and the views are worth noting. First, the `"language"` property in the design document specifies the view server that should process this document. The application code uses JavaScript so the value for the `"language"` property is explicitly stated as such. If no property is stated, the value defaults to JavaScript. Do not forget to specify Erlang or Java, if that's what you are using instead of JavaScript. Second, all view code that leverages MapReduce is contained as values of the `"views"` property. Third, keys for MapReduce key/value pairs don't need to be strings only. They can be of any valid JSON type. The view that calculates the lowest price per year per stock simplifies the calculation by emitting an array of stock and year, extracted from the date property in a document, as the key. Fourth, permanent views index documents by the keys emitted in the map phase. That means if you emit a key that is an array of stock symbol and year, documents are indexed using these two properties in the given order.

You can access the view and trigger a MapReduce run. View access being RESTful can be invoked using the browser via the Futon console, via a command-line client such as curl or by any other mechanism that supports REST-based interaction.

Now that you have seen a couple of examples of MapReduce in the context of two document databases, MongoDB and CouchDB, I cover sorted ordered column-family stores.

MAPREDUCE WITH HBASE

Next, you upload the NYSE data set into an HBase instance. This time, use MapReduce itself to parse the .csv files and populate the data into HBase. Such "chained" usage of MapReduce is quite popular and serves well to parse large files. Once the data is uploaded to HBase you can use MapReduce a second time to run a few aggregate queries. Two examples of MapReduce have already been illustrated and this third one should reinforce the concept of MapReduce and demonstrate its suitability for multiple situations.

To use MapReduce with HBase you can use Java as the programming language of choice. It's not the only option though. You could write MapReduce jobs in Python, Ruby, or PHP and have HBase as the source and/or sink for the job. In this example, I create four program elements that need to work together:

➤ A mapper class that emits key/value pairs.

➤ A reducer class that takes the values emitted from mapper and manipulates it to create aggregations. In the data upload example, the mapper only inserts the data into an HBase table.

➤ A driver class that puts the mapper class and the reducer class together.

➤ A class that triggers the job in its main method.

You can also combine all these four elements into a single class. The mapper and reducer can become static inner classes in that case. For this example, though, you create four separate classes, one each for the four elements just mentioned.

I assume Hadoop and HBase are already installed and configured. Please add the following .jar files to your Java classpath to make the following example compile and run:

➤ hadoop-0.20.2-ant.jar

➤ hadoop-0.20.2-core.jar

➤ hadoop-0.20.2-tools.jar

➤ hbase-0.20.6.jar

The hadoop jar files are available in the Hadoop distribution and the hbase jar file comes with HBase.

The mapper is like so:

```
package com.treasuryofideas.hbasemr;
import java.io.BufferedReader;
import java.io.FileReader;
import java.io.IOException;

import org.apache.hadoop.io.LongWritable;
import org.apache.hadoop.io.MapWritable;
import org.apache.hadoop.io.Text;
import org.apache.hadoop.mapreduce.Mapper;

public class NyseMarketDataMapper extends
```

```
    Mapper<LongWritable, Text, Text, MapWritable> {

  public void map(LongWritable key, MapWritable value, Context context)
      throws IOException, InterruptedException {

    final Text EXCHANGE = new Text("exchange");
    final Text STOCK_SYMBOL = new Text("stockSymbol");
    final Text DATE = new Text("date");
    final Text STOCK_PRICE_OPEN = new Text("stockPriceOpen");
    final Text STOCK_PRICE_HIGH = new Text("stockPriceHigh");
    final Text STOCK_PRICE_LOW = new Text("stockPriceLow");
    final Text STOCK_PRICE_CLOSE = new Text("stockPriceClose");
    final Text STOCK_VOLUME = new Text("stockVolume");
    final Text STOCK_PRICE_ADJ_CLOSE = new Text("stockPriceAdjClose");

    try
    {
      //sample market data csv file
      String strFile = "data/NYSE_daily_prices_A.csv";

      //create BufferedReader to read csv file
      BufferedReader br = new BufferedReader( new FileReader(strFile));
      String strLine = "";
      int lineNumber = 0;

      //read comma separated file line by line
      while( (strLine = br.readLine()) != null)
      {
        lineNumber++;
              if(lineNumber > 1) {
                 String[] data_values = strLine.split(",");
                 MapWritable marketData = new MapWritable();
                 marketData.put(EXCHANGE, new Text(data_values[0]));
                 marketData.put(STOCK_SYMBOL, new Text(data_values[1]));
                 marketData.put(DATE, new Text(data_values[2]));
                 marketData.put(STOCK_PRICE_OPEN, new Text(data_values[3]));
                 marketData.put(STOCK_PRICE_HIGH, new Text(data_values[4]));
                 marketData.put(STOCK_PRICE_LOW, new Text(data_values[5]));
                 marketData.put(STOCK_PRICE_CLOSE, new Text(data_values[6]));
                 marketData.put(STOCK_VOLUME, new Text(data_values[7]));
                 marketData.put(STOCK_PRICE_ADJ_CLOSE, new Text(data_values[8]));

                 context.write(new Text(String.format("%s-%s", data_values[1],
data_values[2])), marketData);

              }
      }


    }
    catch(Exception e)
    {
      System.errout.println("Exception while reading csv file or process
```

```
interrupted: " + e);
    }

    }
}
```

NyseMarketDataMapper.java

The preceding code is rudimentary and focuses only on demonstrating the key features of a map function. The mapper class extends `org.apache.hadoop.mapreduce.Mapper` and implements the `map` method. The `map` method takes key, value, and a context object as the input parameters. In the `emit` method, you will notice that I create a complex key by joining the stock symbol and date together.

The `.csv` parsing logic itself is simple and may need to be modified to support conditions where commas appear within each data item. For the current data set, though, it works just fine.

The second part is a reducer class with a `reduce` method. The `reduce` method simply uploads data into HBase tables. The code for the reducer can be as follows:

Available for
download on
Wrox.com

```
public class NyseMarketDataReducer extends TableReducer<Text, MapWritable,
ImmutableBytesWritable> {
        public void reduce(Text arg0, Iterable arg1, Context context) {
        //Since the complex key made up of stock symbol and date is unique
                //one value comes for a key.
    Map marketData = null;
    for (MapWritable value : arg1) {
        marketData = value;
        break;
    }

    ImmutableBytesWritable key = new ImmutableBytesWritable(Bytes
            .toBytes(arg0.toString()));
    Put put = new Put(Bytes.toBytes(arg0.toString()));
    put.add(Bytes.toBytes("mdata"), Bytes.toBytes("daily"), Bytes
            .toBytes((ByteBuffer) marketData));
    try {
        context.write(key, put);
    } catch (IOException e) {
        // TODO Auto-generated catch block
    } catch (InterruptedException e) {
        // TODO Auto-generated catch block
    }
    }

    }
```

NyseMarketDataReducer.java

The `map` function and the `reduce` function are tied together in a driver class as follows:

```java
public class NyseMarketDataDriver extends Configured implements Tool {
    @Override
    public int run(String[] arg0) throws Exception {
        HBaseConfiguration conf = new HBaseConfiguration();
        Job job = new Job(conf, "NYSE Market Data Sample Application");
        job.setJarByClass(NyseMarketDataSampleApplication.class);
        job.setInputFormatClass(TextInputFormat.class);
        job.setMapperClass(NyseMarketDataMapper.class);
        job.setReducerClass(NyseMarketDataReducer.class);
        job.setMapOutputKeyClass(Text.class);
        job.setMapOutputValueClass(Text.class);

        FileInputFormat.addInputPath(job, new Path(
                "hdfs://localhost/path/to/NYSE_daily_prices_A.csv"));
        TableMapReduceUtil.initTableReducerJob("nysemarketdata",
                NyseMarketDataReducer.class, job);
        boolean jobSucceeded = job.waitForCompletion(true);
        if (jobSucceeded) {
            return 0;
        } else {
            return -1;
        }
    }

}
```

NyseMarketDataDriver.java

Finally, the driver needs to be triggered as follows:

```java
package com.treasuryofideas.hbasemr;
import org.apache.hadoop.conf.Configuration;
import org.apache.hadoop.util.ToolRunner;

public class NyseMarketDataSampleApplication {
    public static void main(String[] args) throws Exception {
        int m_rc = 0;
        m_rc = ToolRunner.run(new Configuration(),
new NyseMarketDataDriver(), args);
        System.exit(m_rc);
    }

}
```

NyseMarketDataSampleApplication.java

That wraps up a simple case of MapReduce with HBase. Next, you see additional use cases, which are a bit more advanced and complex than a simple HBase write.

MAPREDUCE POSSIBILITIES AND APACHE MAHOUT

MapReduce can be used to solve a number of problems. Google, Yahoo!, Facebook, and many other organizations are using MapReduce for a diverse range of use cases including distributed sort, web link graph traversal, log file statistics, document clustering, and machine learning. In addition, the variety of use cases where MapReduce is commonly applied continues to grow.

An open-source project, Apache Mahout, aims to build a complete set of scalable machine learning and data mining libraries by leveraging MapReduce within the Hadoop infrastructure. I introduce that project and cover a couple of examples from the project in this section. The motivation for covering Mahout is to jump-start your quest to explore MapReduce further. I am hoping the inspiration will help you apply MapReduce effectively for your specific and unique use case.

To get started, go to `mahout.apache.org` and download the latest release or the source distribution. The project is continuously evolving and rapidly adding features, so it makes sense to grab the source distribution to build it. The only tools you need, apart from the JDK, are an SVN client to download the source and Maven version 3.0.2 or higher, to build and install it.

Get the source as follows:

```
svn co http://svn.apache.org/repos/asf/mahout/trunk
```

Then change into the downloaded "trunk" source directory and run the following commands to compile and install Apache Mahout:

```
mvn compile
mvn install
```

You may also want to get hold of the Mahout examples as follows:

```
cd examples
mvn compile
```

Mahout comes with a taste-web recommender example application. You can change to the taste-web directory and run the `mvn` package to get the application compiled and running.

Although Mahout is a new project it contains implementations for clustering, categorization, collaborative filtering, and evolutionary programming. Explaining what these machine learning topics mean is beyond the scope of this book but I will walk through an elementary example to show Mahout in use.

Mahout includes a recommendation engine library, named Taste. This library can be used to quickly build systems that can have user-based and item-based recommendations. The system uses collaborative filtering.

Taste has five main parts, namely:

➤ **DataModel** — Model abstraction for storing Users, Items, and Preferences.

➤ **UserSimilarity** — Interface to define the similarity between two users.

➤ **ItemSimilarity** — Interface to define the similarity between two items.

➤ **Recommender** — Interface that recommendation provider implements.

➤ **UserNeighborhood** — Recommendation systems use the neighborhood for user similarity for coming up with recommendations. This interface defines the user neighborhood.

You can build a recommendation system that leverages Hadoop to run the batch computation on large data sets and allow for highly scalable machine learning systems.

Let's consider ratings by users for a set of items is in a simple file, named `ratings.csv`. Each line of this file has `user_id`, `item_id`, `ratings`. This is quite similar to what you saw in the MovieLens data set earlier in this book. Mahout has a rich set of model classes to map this data set. You can use the `FileDataModel` as follows:

```
FileDataModel dataModel = new FileDataModel(new File(ratings.csv));
```

Next, you need to identify a measure of distance to see how similar two different user ratings are. The Euclidean distance is the simplest such measure and the Pearson correlation is perhaps a good normalized measure that works in many cases. To use the Pearson correlation you can configure a corresponding similarity class as follows:

```
UserSimilarity userSimilarity = new PearsonCorrelationSimilarity(dataModel);
```

Next you need to define a user neighborhood and a recommender and combine them all to generate recommendations. The code could be as follows:

```
//Get a neighborhood of users
UserNeighborhood neighborhood =
        new NearestNUserNeighborhood(neighborhoodSize, userSimilarity, dataModel);
//Create the recommender
Recommender recommender =
        new GenericUserBasedRecommender(dataModel, neighborhood, userSimilarity);
User user = dataModel.getUser(userId);
System.out.println("User: " + user);
//Print out the users own preferences first
TasteUtils.printPreferences(user, handler.map);
//Get the top 5 recommendations
List<RecommendedItem> recommendations =
        recommender.recommend(userId, 5);
TasteUtils.printRecs(recommendations, handler.map);
```

'Taste' example

This is all that is required to get a simple recommendation system up and running.

The previous example did not explicitly use MapReduce and instead worked with the semantics of a collaborative filtering-based recommendation system. Mahout uses MapReduce to get the job done and leverage the Hadoop infrastructure to compute recommendation scores in large distributed data sets, but most of the underlying infrastructures are abstracted out for you.

The chapter demonstrates a set of MapReduce cases and shows how complications of very large data sets can be carried out with elegance. No low-level API manipulation is necessary and no worries about resource deadlocks or starvation occur. In addition, keeping data and compute together reduces the effect of I/O and bandwidth limitations.

SUMMARY

MapReduce is a powerful way to process a lot of information in a fast and efficient manner. Google has used it for a lot of its heavy lifting. Google has also been gracious enough to share the underlying ideas with the research and the developer community. In addition to that, the Hadoop team has built out a very robust and scalable open-source infrastructure to leverage the processing model. Other NoSQL projects and vendors have also adopted MapReduce.

MapReduce is replacing SQL in all highly scalable and distributed models that work with immense amounts of data. Its performance and "shared nothing" model proves to be a big winner over the traditional SQL model.

Writing MapReduce programs is also relatively easy because the infrastructure handles the complexity and lets a developer focus on chains of MapReduce jobs and the application of them to processing large amounts of data. Frequently, common MapReduce jobs can be handled with a common infrastructure such as CouchDB built-in reducers or projects such as Apache Mahout. However, sometimes defining keys and working through the reduce logic could need careful attention.

12

Analyzing Big Data with Hive

WHAT'S IN THIS CHAPTER?

➤ Introducing Apache Hive, a data warehousing infrastructure built on top of Hadoop

➤ Learning Hive with the help of examples

➤ Exploring Hive commands syntax and semantics

➤ Using Hive to query the MovieLens data set

Solutions to big data-centric problems involve relaxed schemas, column-family-centric storage, distributed filesystems, replication, and sometimes eventual consistency. The focus of these solutions is managing large, spare, denormalized data volumes, which is typically over a few terabytes in size. Often, when you are working with these big data stores you have specific, predefined ways of analyzing and accessing the data. Therefore, ad-hoc querying and rich query expressions aren't a high priority and usually are not a part of the currently available solutions. In addition, many of these big data solutions involve products that are rather new and still rapidly evolving. These products haven't matured to a point where they have been tested across a wide range of use cases and are far from being feature-complete. That said, they are good at what they are designed to do: manage big data.

In contrast to the new emerging big data solutions, the world of RDBMS has a repertoire of robust and mature tools for administering and querying data. The most prominent and important of these is SQL. It's a powerful and convenient way to query data: to slice, dice, aggregate, and relate data points within a set. Therefore, as ironic as it may sound, the biggest missing piece in NoSQL is something like SQL.

In wake of the need to have SQL-like syntax and semantics and the ease of higher-level abstractions, Hive and Pig come to the rescue. Apache Hive is a data-warehousing infrastructure built on top of Hadoop, and Apache Pig is a higher-level language for analyzing large amounts of data. This chapter illustrates Hive and Pig and shows how you could leverage these tools to analyze large data sets.

 Google App Engine (GAE) provides a SQL-like querying facility by offering GQL.

HIVE BASICS

Before you start learning Hive, you need to install and set it up. Hive leverages a working Hadoop installation so install Hadoop first, if you haven't already. Hadoop can be downloaded from `hadoop.apache.org` (read Appendix A if you need help with installing Hadoop). Currently, Hive works well with Java 1.6 and Hadoop 0.20.2 so make sure to get the right versions for these pieces of software. Hive works without problems on Mac OS X and any of the Linux variants. You may be able to run Hive using Cygwin on Windows but I do not cover any of that in this chapter. If you are on Windows and do not have access to a Mac OS X or Linux environment, consider using a virtual machine with VMware Player to get introduced to Hive. Please read Appendix A to find out how to access and install a virtual machine for experimentation.

Installing Hive is easy. Just carry out the following steps:

1. Download a stable release version of Hive. You can download hive-0.6.0 on Mac OS X using `curl -O http://mirror.candidhosting.com/pub/apache//hive/hive-0.6.0/ hive-0.6.0.tar.gz`. On Linux and its variants use `wget` instead of `curl`.

2. Extract the distribution, available as a compressed archive. On Mac OS X and Linux, extract as follows: `tar zxvf hive-0.6.0.tar.gz`.

3. Set up the `HIVE_HOME` environment variable to point to the Hive installation directory.

4. Add `$HIVE_HOME/bin` to the `PATH` environment variable so that Hive executables are accessible from outside their home directory.

5. Start Hadoop daemons by running `bin/start-all.sh` from within the `$HADOOP_HOME` directory. This should start HDFS namenode, secondary namenode, and datanode. It should also start the MapReduce job tracker and task tracker. Use the `jps` command to verify that these five processes are running.

6. Create `/tmp` and `/user/hive/warehouse` folders on HDFS as follows:

   ```
   bin/hadoop fs -mkdir /tmp
   bin/hadoop fs -mkdir /user/hive/warehouse
   ```

   The `/user/hive/warehouse` is the hive metastore warehouse directory.

7. Set write permission to the group on `/tmp` and `/user/hive/warehouse` folders created in HDFS. Permissions can be modified using the `chmod` command as follows:

   ```
   bin/hadoop fs -chmod g+w /tmp
   bin/hadoop fs -chmod g+w /user/hive/warehouse
   ```

If you followed through all the preceding steps, you are all set to use your Hadoop cluster for Hive. Fire up the Hive command-line interface (CLI) by running `bin/hive` in the `$HIVE_HOME` directory. Working with the Hive CLI will give you sense of déjà vu, because the semantics and syntax are quite similar to what you may have experienced with a command-line client connecting to an RDBMS.

 In my pseudo-distributed local installation, `bin/start-all.sh` *spawns five Java processes for the HDFS and MapReduce daemons.*

Start out by listing the existing tables as follows:

Available for download on Wrox.com

```
SHOW TABLES;
```

hive_examples.txt

No tables have been created yet, so you will be greeted with an `empty OK` and a metric showing the time it took the query to run. As with most database CLI(s), the time taken metric is printed out for all queries. It's a good first indicator of whether a query is running efficiently.

HIVE IS NOT FOR REAL-TIME QUERYING

Hive provides an elegant SQL-like query framework on top of Hadoop. Hadoop is a scalable infrastructure that can manipulate very large and distributed data sets. Therefore, Hive provides a powerful abstraction for querying and manipulating large data sets. It leverages HDFS and MapReduce.

However, Hive is not a real-time query system. It is best used as a batch-oriented tool. Hive's dependency on the underlying Hadoop infrastructure and the MapReduce framework causes substantial overheads around job submission and scheduling. This means Hive query responses usually have high latency. As you go through the examples and try out Hive using the CLI you will notice that time taken to execute a query, even with small data sets, is in seconds and at times in minutes. This is in sharp contrast to the time taken for similar queries in RDBMS. There is no query caching in Hive so even repeat queries require as much time as the first one.

As data sets become bigger the Hive overhead is often dwarfed by the large-scale efficiencies of Hadoop. Much like a traditional RDBMS may fall back to table scans if a query is likely to touch every row, with extremely large data sets and for batch processing Hive's performance is optimal.

Next, create a table like so:

```
CREATE TABLE books (isbn INT, title STRING);
```

hive_examples.txt

This creates a table of books, with two columns: `isbn` and `title`. The column data types are integer and string, respectively. To list the books table's schema, query as follows:

```
hive> DESCRIBE books;
OK
Isbn    int
Title   string
Time taken: 0.263 seconds
```

hive_examples.txt

Create another table named `users` as follows:

```
CREATE TABLE users (id INT, name STRING) PARTITIONED BY (vcol STRING);
```

hive_examples.txt

The `users` table has three columns: `id`, `name`, and `vcol`. You can confirm this running the `DESCRIBE` table query as follows:

```
hive> DESCRIBE users;
OK
Id      int
Name    string
Vcol    string
Time taken: 0.12 seconds
```

hive_examples.txt

The column `vcol` is a virtual column. It's a partition column derived from the partition in which the data is stored and not from the data set itself. A single table can be partitioned into multiple logical parts. Each logical part can be identified by a specific value for the virtual column that identifies the partition.

Now run the `SHOW TABLES` command to list your tables like so:

```
hive> SHOW TABLES;
OK
books
users
Time taken: 0.087 seconds
```

hive_examples.txt

A `books` table stores data about books. The `isbn` and `title` columns in the `books` table identify and describe a book, but having only these two properties is rather minimalistic. Adding an `author` column and possibly a `category` column to the `books` table seems like a good idea. In the RDBMS world such manipulations are done using the `ALTER TABLE` command. Not surprisingly, Hive has a similar syntax. You can modify the `books` table and add columns as follows:

```
ALTER TABLE books ADD COLUMNS (author STRING, category STRING);
```

hive_examples.txt

Reconfirm that the `books` table has a modified schema like so:

```
hive> DESCRIBE books;
OK
Isbn    int
Title   string
Author  string
Category        string
Time taken: 0.112 seconds
```

hive_examples.txt

Next, you may want to modify the `author` column of the `books` table to accommodate cases where a book is written by multiple authors. In such a case, an array of strings better represents the data than a single string does. When you make this modification you may also want to attach a comment to the column suggesting that the column holds multi-valued data. You can accomplish all of this as follows:

```
ALTER TABLE books CHANGE author author ARRAY<STRING> COMMENT "multi-valued";
```

hive_examples.txt

Rerunning `DESCRIBE TABLE` for `books`, after the `author` column modification, produces the following output:

```
hive> DESCRIBE books;
OK
Isbn    int
Title   string
Author array<string>     multi-valued
Category        string
Time taken: 0.109 seconds
```

hive_examples.txt

The `ALTER TABLE` command allows you to change the properties of a table's columns using the following syntax:

```
ALTER TABLE table_name CHANGE [COLUMN]
old_column_name new_column_name column_type
```

```
[COMMENT column_comment]
[FIRST|AFTER column_name]
```

The argument of the `ALTER TABLE` for a column change needs to appear in the exact order as shown. The arguments in square brackets (`[]`) are optional but everything else needs to be included in the correct sequence for the command to work. As a side effect, this means you need to state the same column name in succession twice when you don't intend to rename it but intend to change only its properties. Look at the `author` column in the previous example to see how this impacts the command. Hive supports primitive and complex data types. Complex types can be modeled in Hive using maps, arrays, or a struct. In the example just illustrated, the column is modified to hold an `ARRAY` of values. The `ARRAY` needs an additional type definition for its elements. Elements of an `ARRAY` type cannot contain data of two different types. In the case of the `author` column, the `ARRAY` contains only `STRING` type.

Next, you may want to store information on publications like short stories, magazines, and others in addition to books and so you may consider renaming the table to `published_contents` instead. You could do that as follows:

```
ALTER TABLE books RENAME TO published_contents;
```

hive_examples.txt

Running `DESCRIBE TABLE` on `published_contents` produces the following output:

```
hive> DESCRIBE published_contents;
OK
isbn    int
title   string
author  array<string>    multi-valued
category    string
Time taken: 0.136 seconds
```

hive_examples.txt

Obviously, running `DESCRIBE TABLE` on `books` now returns an error:

```
hive> DESCRIBE books;
FAILED: Execution Error, return code 1 from org.apache.hadoop.hive.ql.exec.DDLTask
```

hive_examples.txt

Next, I walk through a more complete example to illustrate Hive's querying capabilities. Because the `published_contents` and `users` tables may not be needed in the rest of this chapter, I could drop those tables as follows:

```
DROP TABLE published_contents;
DROP TABLE users;
```

BACK TO MOVIE RATINGS

In Chapter 6, you learned about querying NoSQL stores. In that chapter, I leveraged a freely available movie ratings data set to illustrate the query mechanisms available in NoSQL stores, especially in MongoDB. Let's revisit that data set and use Hive to manipulate it. You may benefit from reviewing the MovieLens example in Chapter 6 before you move forward.

You can download the movie lens data set that contains 1 million ratings with the following command:

```
curl -O http://www.grouplens.org/system/files/million-ml-data.tar__0.gz
```

Extract the tarball and you should get the following files:

➤   README

➤   movies.dat

➤   ratings.dat

➤   users.dat

The `ratings.dat` file contains rating data where each line contains one rating data point. Each data point in the ratings file is structured in the following format: *UserID::MovieID::Rating:: Timestamp*.

> *The ratings, movie, and users data in the movie lens data set is separated by* `::`*. I had trouble getting the Hive loader to correctly parse and load the data using this delimiter. So, I chose to replace* `::` *with* # *throughout the file. I simply opened the file in vi and replaced all occurrences of* `::`*, the delimiter, with* # *using the following command:*
>
> > `:%s/::/#/g`
>
> *Once the delimiter was modified I saved the results to new files, each with* `.hash_delimited` *appended to their old names. Therefore, I had three new files:*
>
> ➤   `ratings.dat.hash_delimited`
>
> ➤   `movied.dat.hash_delimited`
>
> ➤   `users.dat.hash_delimited`
>
> *I used the new files as the source data. The original* `.dat` *files were left as is.*

Load the data into a Hive table that follows the same schema as in the downloaded ratings data file. That means first create a Hive table with the same schema:

```
hive> CREATE TABLE ratings(
    > userid INT,
    > movieid INT,
```

```
    > rating INT,
    > tstamp STRING)
    > ROW FORMAT DELIMITED
    > FIELDS TERMINATED BY '#'

    > STORED AS TEXTFILE;
OK
Time taken: 0.169 seconds
```

hive_movielens.txt

Hive includes utilities to load data sets from flat files using the LOAD DATA command. The source could be the local filesystem or an HDFS volume. The command signature is like so:

```
LOAD DATA LOCAL INPATH <'path/to/flat/file'> OVERWRITE INTO TABLE <table name>;
```

No validation is performed at load time. Therefore, it's a developer's responsibility to ensure that the flat file data format and the table schema match. The syntax allows you to specify the source as the local filesystem or HDFS. Essentially, specifying LOCAL after LOAD DATA tells the command that the source is on the local filesystem. Not including LOCAL means that the data is in HDFS. When the flat file is in HDFS, the data is copied only into the Hive HDFS namespace. The operation is an HDFS file move operation and so it is much faster than a data load operation from the local filesystem. The data loading command also enables you to overwrite data into an existing table or append to it. The presence and absence of OVERWRITE in the command suggests overwrite and append, respectively.

The movie lens data is downloaded to the local filesystem. A slightly modified copy of the data is prepared by replacing the delimiter :: with #. The prepared data set is loaded into the Hive HDFS namespace. The command for data loading is as follows:

```
hive> LOAD DATA LOCAL INPATH '/path/to/ratings.dat.hash_delimited'
    > OVERWRITE INTO TABLE ratings;
Copying data from file:/path/to/ratings.dat.hash_delimited
Loading data to table ratings
OK
Time taken: 0.803 seconds
```

hive_movielens.txt

The movie lens ratings data that was just loaded into a Hive table contains over a million records. You could verify that using the familiar SELECT COUNT idiom as follows:

```
hive> SELECT COUNT(*) FROM ratings;
Total MapReduce jobs = 1
Launching Job 1 out of 1
Number of reduce tasks determined at compile time: 1
In order to change the average load for a reducer (in bytes):
  set hive.exec.reducers.bytes.per.reducer=<number>
In order to limit the maximum number of reducers:
  set hive.exec.reducers.max=<number>
```

```
In order to set a constant number of reducers:
  set mapred.reduce.tasks=<number>
Starting Job = job_201102211022_0012, Tracking URL =
http://localhost:50030/jobdetails.jsp?jobid=job_201102211022_0012
Kill Command = /Users/tshanky/Applications/hadoop/bin/../bin/hadoop job  -
Dmapred.job.tracker=localhost:9001 -kill job_201102211022_0012
2011-02-21 15:36:50,627 Stage-1 map = 0%,  reduce = 0%
2011-02-21 15:36:56,819 Stage-1 map = 100%,  reduce = 0%
2011-02-21 15:37:01,921 Stage-1 map = 100%,  reduce = 100%
Ended Job = job_201102211022_0012
OK
1000209
Time taken: 21.355 seconds
```

hive_movielens.txt

The output confirms that more than a million ratings records are in the table. The query mechanism confirms that the old ways of counting in SQL work in Hive. In the counting example, I liberally included the entire console output with the SELECT COUNT command to bring to your attention a couple of important notes, which are as follows:

➤   Hive operations translate to MapReduce jobs.

➤   The latency of Hive operation responses is relatively high. It took 21.355 seconds to run a count. An immediate re-run does no better. It again takes about the same time, because no query caching mechanisms are in place.

Hive is capable of an exhaustive set of filter and aggregation queries. You can filter data sets using the WHERE clause. Results can be grouped using the GROUP BY command. Distinct values can be listed with the help of the DISTINCT parameter and two tables can be combined using the JOIN operation. In addition, you could write custom scripts to manipulate data and pass that on to your map and reduce functions.

To learn more about Hive's capabilities and its powerful query mechanisms, let's also load the movies and users data sets from the movie lens data set into corresponding tables. This would provide a good sample set to explore Hive features by trying them out against this data set. Each row in the movies data set is in the following format: *MovieID::Title::Genres*. *MovieID* is an integer and *Title* is a string. *Genres* is also a string. The *Genres* string contains multiple values in a pipe-delimited format. In the first pass, you create a movies table as follows:

   As with the ratings data, the original delimiter in movies.dat *is changed from* :: *to* #.

Available for download on Wrox.com

```
hive> CREATE TABLE movies(
    > movieid INT,
    > title STRING,
    > genres STRING)
    > ROW FORMAT DELIMITED
```

```
    > FIELDS TERMINATED BY '#'
    > STORED AS TEXTFILE;
OK
Time taken: 0.075 seconds
```

Load the flat file data into the `movies` table as follows:

```
hive> LOAD DATA LOCAL INPATH '/path/to/movies.dat.hash_delimited'
    > OVERWRITE INTO TABLE movies;
```

The `genres` string data contains multiple values. For example, a record could be as follows: `Animation|Children's|Comedy`. Therefore, storing this data as an `ARRAY` is probably a better idea than storing it as a `STRING`. Storing as `ARRAY` allows you to include these values in query parameters more easily than if they are part of a string. Splitting and storing the genres record as a collection can easily be achieved by using Hive's ability to take delimiter parameters for collections and map keys. The modified Hive `CREATE TABLE` and `LOAD DATA` commands are as follows:

Available for download on Wrox.com

```
hive> CREATE TABLE movies_2(
    > movieid INT,
    > title STRING,
    > genres ARRAY<STRING>)
    > ROW FORMAT DELIMITED
    > FIELDS TERMINATED BY '#'
    > COLLECTION ITEMS TERMINATED BY '|'
    > STORED AS TEXTFILE;
OK
Time taken: 0.037 seconds
hive> LOAD DATA LOCAL INPATH '/path/to/movies.dat.hash_delimited'
    > OVERWRITE INTO TABLE movies_2;
Copying data from file:/path/to/movies.dat.hash_delimited
Loading data to table movies_2
OK
Time taken: 0.121 seconds
```

After the data is loaded, print out a few records using `SELECT` and limit the result set to five records using `LIMIT` as follows:

```
hive> SELECT * FROM movies_2 LIMIT 5;
OK
1       Toy Story (1995)        ["Animation","Children's","Comedy"]
2       Jumanji (1995)          ["Adventure","Children's","Fantasy"]
3       Grumpier Old Men (1995)     ["Comedy","Romance"]
4       Waiting to Exhale (1995)    ["Comedy","Drama"]
5       Father of the Bride Part II (1995)      ["Comedy"]
Time taken: 0.103 seconds
```

The third data set in the movie lens data bundle is `users.dat`. A row in the users data set is of the following format: *UserID::Gender::Age::Occupation::Zip-code*. A sample row is as follows:

```
1::F::1::10::48067
```

The values for the gender, age, and occupation properties belong to a discrete domain of possible values. Gender can be male or female, denoted by M and F, respectively. Age is represented as a step function with the value representing the lowest value in the range. All ages are rounded to the closest year and ranges are exclusive. The occupation property value is a discrete numeric value that maps to a specific string value. The occupation property can have 20 possible values as follows:

- 0: `other or not specified`
- 1: `academic/educator`
- 2: `artist`
- 3: `clerical/admin`
- 4: `college/grad student`
- 5: `customer service`
- 6: `doctor/health care`
- 7: `executive/managerial`
- 8: `farmer`
- 9: `homemaker`
- 10: `K-12 student`
- 11: `lawyer`
- 12: `programmer`
- 13: `retired`
- 14: `sales/marketing`
- 15: `scientist`
- 16: `self-employed`
- 17: `technician/engineer`
- 18: `tradesman/craftsman`
- 19: `unemployed`
- 20: `writer`

You may benefit from storing the occupation strings instead of the numeric values because it becomes easier for someone browsing through the data set to understand the data points. To manipulate the data as required, you can leverage an external script in association with the data load operations. Hive enables pluggability of external functions with `map` and `reduce` functions.

The concept of plugging external scripts with `map` and `reduce` functions, involved while copying data from one Hive table to another Hive table, is summarized in Figure 12-1.

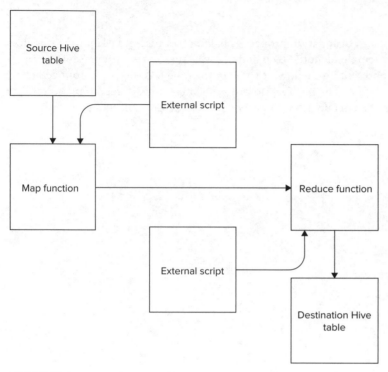

FIGURE 12-1

To see an external script in action, especially one that replaces occupation numbers with its string counterparts in the `users` table, you must first create the `users` table and load data into it. You can create the `users` table as follows:

Available for download on Wrox.com

```
hive> CREATE TABLE users(
    > userid INT,
    > gender STRING,
    > age INT,
    > occupation INT,
    > zipcode STRING)
    > ROW FORMAT DELIMITED
    > FIELDS TERMINATED BY '#'
    > STORED AS TEXTFILE;
```

hive_movielens.txt

and load users data into this table as follows:

```
hive> LOAD DATA LOCAL INPATH '/path/to/users.dat.hash_delimited'
    > OVERWRITE INTO TABLE users;
```

Next, create a second `users` table, `users_2`, and load data from the `users` table into this second table. During loading, leverage an external script, `occupation_mapper.py`, to map occupation integer values to their corresponding string values and load the string values into `users_2`. The code for this data transformation is as follows:

```
hive> CREATE TABLE users_2(
    > userid INT,
    > gender STRING,
    > age INT,
    > occupation STRING,
    > zipcode STRING)
    > ROW FORMAT DELIMITED
    > FIELDS TERMINATED BY '#'
    > STORED AS TEXTFILE;
OK
Time taken: 0.359 seconds
hive> add FILE
/Users/tshanky/workspace/hadoop_workspace/hive_workspace/occupation_mapper.py;
hive> INSERT OVERWRITE TABLE users_2
    > SELECT
    > TRANSFORM (userid, gender, age, occupation, zipcode)
    > USING 'python occupation_mapper.py'
    > AS (userid, gender, age, occupation_str, zipcode)
    > FROM users;
```

hive_movielens.txt

The `occupation_mapper.py` script is as follows:

```
occupation_dict = { 0:  "other or not specified",
    1:   "academic/educator",
    2:   "artist",
    3:   "clerical/admin",
    4:   "college/grad student",
    5:   "customer service",
    6:   "doctor/health care",
    7:   "executive/managerial",
    8:   "farmer",
    9:   "homemaker",
    10:  "K-12 student",
    11:  "lawyer",
    12:  "programmer",
    13:  "retired",
    14:  "sales/marketing",
    15:  "scientist",
    16:  "self-employed",
    17:  "technician/engineer",
    18:  "tradesman/craftsman",
    19:  "unemployed",
    20:  "writer"
    }
```

```
for line in sys.stdin:
  line = line.strip()
  userid, gender, age, occupation, zipcode = line.split('#')
  occupation_str = occupation_map[occupation]
  print '#'.join([userid, gender, age, occupation_str, zipcode])
```

occupation_mapper.py

The transformation script is fairly self-explanatory. Each value from the `users` table is transformed using the Python script to replace occupation integer values with the corresponding string values by looking it up in the `occupation_dict` dictionary.

When the data is loaded and ready you can use Hive to run your good old SQL queries.

GOOD OLD SQL

SQL has many good features but the ability to filter data using the `WHERE` clause is probably the most used and appreciated of them all. In this section you see how Hive matches up on its ability to support the `WHERE` clause.

First, get a set of any five movies from the `movies` table. You could use the `LIMIT` function to get only five records as follows:

```
SELECT * FROM movies LIMIT 5;
```

hive_movielens.txt

For me the five records were:

```
1     Toy Story (1995)       Animation|Children's|Comedy
2     Jumanji (1995)         Adventure|Children's|Fantasy
3     Grumpier Old Men (1995)        Comedy|Romance
4     Waiting to Exhale (1995)       Comedy|Drama
5     Father of the Bride Part II (1995)       Comedy
```

To list all ratings that relate to Toy Story (1995) with a movie ID of 1 use a Hive QL, the Hive query language, and query as follows:

```
hive> SELECT * FROM ratings
    > WHERE movieid = 1;
```

hive_movielens.txt

Movie IDs are numbers so to get a count of ratings for all movies with an ID lower than 10, you could use a Hive QL as follows:

```
hive> SELECT COUNT(*) FROM ratings
    > WHERE movieid < 10;
```

hive_movielens.txt

The output after a MapReduce job run is 5,290.

To find out how many users rated Toy Story (1995) as a good movie and gave it 5 out of 5 on the rating scale, you can query as follows:

```
hive> SELECT COUNT(*) FROM ratings
    > WHERE movieid = 1 and rating = 5;
```

hive_movielens.txt

This shows a case in which more than one condition is used in the WHERE clause. You could use DISTINCT in SELECT clauses to get only unique values. The default behavior is to return duplicates.

There is no LIKE operation with SELECT to allow approximate matches with the records. However, a SELECT clause allows regular expressions to be used in conjunction with column names and WHERE clause values. To select all movies that have a title that starts with the word Toy, you can query as follows:

```
hive> SELECT title FROM movies
    > WHERE title = `^Toy+`;
```

hive_movielens.txt

Notice that the regular expression is specified within backquotes. The regular expression follows the Java regular expression syntax. The regular expression facility can also be used for projection where only specific columns from a result can be returned. For example, you could return only those columns that end with the character's ID as follows:

```
hive> SELECT `*+(id)` FROM ratings
    > WHERE movieid = 1;
```

hive_movieslens.txt

The MovieLens ratings table has rating values for movies. A rating is a numerical value that can be anything between 1 and 5. If you want to get a count of the different ratings for Toy Story (1995), with movieid = 1, you can query using GROUP BY as follows:

```
hive> SELECT ratings.rating, COUNT(ratings.rating)
    > FROM ratings
    > WHERE movieid = 1
    > GROUP BY ratings.rating;
```

hive_movieslens.txt

The output is as follows:

```
1    16
2    61
3    345
```

```
4       835
5       820
Time taken: 24.908 seconds
```

You can include multiple aggregation functions, like count, sum, and average, in a single query as long as they all operate on the same column. You are not allowed to run aggregation functions on multiple columns in the same query.

To run aggregation at the map level, you could set `hive.map.aggr` to `true` and run a count query as follows:

```
set hive.map.aggr=true;
SELECT COUNT(*) FROM ratings;
```

Hive QL also supports ordering of result sets in ascending and descending order using the `ORDER BY` clause. To get all records from the `movies` tables ordered by `movieid` in descending order, you can query as follows:

```
hive> SELECT * FROM movies
    > ORDER BY movieid DESC;
```

hive_movielens.txt

Hive has another ordering facility. It's `SORT BY`, which is similar to `ORDER BY` in that it orders records in ascending or descending order. However, unlike `ORDER BY`, `SORT BY` applies ordering on a per-reducer basis. This means the final result set may be partially ordered. All records managed by the same reducer will be ordered but records across reducers will not be ordered.

Hive allows partitioning of data sets on the basis of a virtual column. You can distribute partitioned data to separate reducers by using the `DISTRIBUTE BY` method. Data distributed to different reducers can be sorted on a per-reducer basis. Shorthand for `DISTRIBUTE BY` and `ORDER BY` together is `CLUSTER BY`.

Hive QL's SQL-like syntax and semantics is very inviting for developers who are familiar with RDBMS and SQL and want to explore the world of large data processing with Hadoop using familiar tools. SQL developers who start exploring Hive soon start craving their power tool: the SQL join. Hive doesn't disappoint even in this facility. Hive QL supports joins.

JOIN(S) IN HIVE QL

Hive supports equality joins, outer joins, and left semi-joins. To get a list of movie ratings with movie titles you can obtain the result set by joining the `ratings` and the `movies` tables. You can query as follows:

```
hive> SELECT ratings.userid, ratings.rating, ratings.tstamp, movies.title
    > FROM ratings JOIN movies
    > ON (ratings.movieid = movies.movieid)
    > LIMIT 5;
```

The output is as follows:

```
376    4    980620359    Toy Story (1995)
1207   4    974845574    Toy Story (1995)
28     3    978985309    Toy Story (1995)
193    4    1025569964   Toy Story (1995)
1055   5    974953210    Toy Story (1995)
Time taken: 48.933 seconds
```

Joins are not restricted to two tables only. You can join more than two tables. To get a list of all movie ratings with movie title and user gender — the gender of the person who rated the movies — you can join the `ratings`, `movies`, and `users` tables. The query is as follows:

```
hive> SELECT ratings.userid, ratings.rating, ratings.tstamp, movies.title,
 users.gender
    > FROM ratings JOIN movies ON (ratings.movieid = movies.movieid)
    > JOIN users ON (ratings.userid = users.userid)
    > LIMIT 5;
```

The output is as follows:

```
1   3   978300760   Wallace & Gromit: The Best of Aardman Animation (1996)   F
1   5   978824195   Schindler's List (1993)   F
1   3   978301968   My Fair Lady (1964)   F
1   4   978301398   Fargo (1996)   F
1   4   978824268   Aladdin (1992)   F
Time taken: 84.785 seconds
```

The data was implicitly ordered so you receive all the values for females first. If you wanted to get only records for male users, you would modify the query with an additional WHERE clause as follows:

```
hive> SELECT ratings.userid, ratings.rating, ratings.tstamp, movies.title,
users.gender
    > FROM ratings JOIN movies ON (ratings.movieid = movies.movieid)
    > JOIN users ON (ratings.userid = users.userid)
    > WHERE users.gender = 'M'
    > LIMIT 5;
```

The output this time is as follows:

```
2   5   978298625   Doctor Zhivago (1965)   M
2   3   978299046   Children of a Lesser God (1986)   M
2   4   978299200   Kramer Vs. Kramer (1979)   M
2   4   978299861   Enemy of the State (1998)   M
2   5   978298813   Driving Miss Daisy (1989)   M
Time taken: 80.769 seconds
```

Hive supports more SQL-like features including UNION and sub-queries. For example, you could combine two result sets using the UNION operation as follows:

```
select_statement UNION ALL select_statement UNION ALL select_statement ...
```

You can query and filter the union of SELECT statements further. A possible simple SELECT could be as follows:

```
SELECT *
FROM (
  select_statement
  UNION ALL
  select_statement
) unionResult
```

Hive also supports sub-queries in FROM clauses. A possible example query to get a list of all users who have rated more than fifteen movies as the very best, with rating value 5, is as follows:

```
hive> SELECT user_id, rating_count
    > FROM (SELECT ratings.userid as user_id, COUNT(ratings.rating) as
rating_count
    > FROM ratings
    > WHERE ratings.rating = 5
    > GROUP BY ratings.userid ) top_raters
    > WHERE rating_count > 15;
```

There is more to Hive and its query language than what has been illustrated so far. However, this may be a good logical point to wrap up. The chapter so far has established that Hive QL is like SQL and fills the gap that RDBMS developers feel as soon as they start with NoSQL stores. Hive provides the right abstraction to make big data processing accessible to a larger number of developers.

Before I conclude the chapter, though, a couple of more aspects need to be covered for completeness. First, a short deviation into explain plans provides a way of peeking into the MapReduce behind a query. Second, a small example is included to show a case for data partitioning.

Explain Plan

Most RDBMSs include a facility for explaining a query's processing details. They usually detail aspects like index usage, data points accessed, and time taken for each. The Hadoop infrastructure is a batch processing system that leverages MapReduce for distributed large-scale processing. Hive builds on top of Hadoop and leverages MapReduce. An explain plan in Hive reveals the MapReduce behind a query.

A simple example could be as follows:

```
hive> EXPLAIN SELECT COUNT(*) FROM ratings
    > WHERE movieid = 1 and rating = 5;
OK
ABSTRACT SYNTAX TREE:
  (TOK_QUERY (TOK_FROM (TOK_TABREF ratings))
(TOK_INSERT (TOK_DESTINATION (TOK_DIR TOK_TMP_FILE))
(TOK_SELECT (TOK_SELEXPR (TOK_FUNCTIONSTAR COUNT)))
(TOK_WHERE (and (= (TOK_TABLE_OR_COL movieid) 1)
(= (TOK_TABLE_OR_COL rating) 5)))))
STAGE DEPENDENCIES:
  Stage-1 is a root stage
```

```
    Stage-0 is a root stage

STAGE PLANS:
  Stage: Stage-1
    Map Reduce
      Alias -> Map Operator Tree:
        ratings
          TableScan
            alias: ratings
            Filter Operator
              predicate:
                  expr: ((movieid = 1) and (rating = 5))
                  type: boolean
              Filter Operator
                predicate:
                    expr: ((movieid = 1) and (rating = 5))
                    type: boolean
                Select Operator
                  Group By Operator
                    aggregations:
                          expr: count()
                    bucketGroup: false
                    mode: hash
                    outputColumnNames: _col0
                    Reduce Output Operator
                      sort order:
                      tag: -1
                      value expressions:
                            expr: _col0
                            type: bigint
      Reduce Operator Tree:
        Group By Operator
          aggregations:
                expr: count(VALUE._col0)
          bucketGroup: false
          mode: mergepartial
          outputColumnNames: _col0
          Select Operator
            expressions:
                  expr: _col0
                  type: bigint
            outputColumnNames: _col0
            File Output Operator
              compressed: false
              GlobalTableId: 0
              table:
                  input format: org.apache.hadoop.mapred.TextInputFormat
                  output format:
org.apache.hadoop.hive.ql.io.HiveIgnoreKeyTextOutputFormat

  Stage: Stage-0
    Fetch Operator
      limit: -1


Time taken: 0.093 seconds
```

If you need additional information on physical files include EXTENDED between EXPLAIN and the query.

Next, a simple use case of data partitioning is shown.

Partitioned Table

Partitioning a table enables you to segregate data into multiple namespaces and filter and query the data set based on the namespace identifiers. Say a data analyst believed that ratings were impacted when the user submitted them and wanted to split the ratings into two partitions, one for all ratings submitted between 8 p.m. and 8 a.m. and the other for the rest of the day. You could create a virtual column to identify this partition and save the data as such.

Then you would be able to filter, search, and cluster on the basis of these namespaces.

SUMMARY

This chapter tersely depicted the power and flexibility of Hive. It showed how the old goodness of SQL can be combined with the power of Hadoop to deliver a compelling data analysis tool, one that both traditional RDBMS developers and new big data pioneers can use.

Hive was built at Facebook and was open sourced as a subproject of Hadoop. Now a top-level project, Hive continues to evolve rapidly, bridging the gap between the SQL and the NoSQL worlds. Prior to Hive's release as open source, Hadoop was arguably useful only to a subset of developers in any given group needing to access "big data" in their organization. Some say Hive nullifies the use of the buzzword, NoSQL, the topic of this book. It almost makes some forcefully claim that NoSQL is actually an acronym that expands out to Not Only SQL.

13
Surveying Database Internals

WHAT'S IN THIS CHAPTER?

➤ Peeking under the hood of MongoDB, Membase, Hypertable, Apache Cassandra, and Berkeley DB

➤ Exploring the internal architectural elements of a few select NoSQL products

➤ Understanding the under-the-hood design choices

Learning a product or a tool involves at least three dimensions, namely:

➤ Understanding its semantics and syntax

➤ Learning by trying and using it

➤ Understanding its internals and knowing what is happening under the hood

In the preceding chapters, you were exposed to a considerable amount of syntax, especially in the context of MongoDB, Redis, CouchDB, HBase, and Cassandra. Many of the examples illustrated the syntax and explained the concepts so trying them out would have given you a good hands-on head start to learning the NoSQL products. In some chapters, you had the opportunity to peek under the hood. In this chapter you dive deeper into in-depth discovery by exploring the architecture and the internals of a few select NoSQL products. As with the other chapters, the set of products I chose represents different types of NoSQL products. The products discussed in this chapter made it to the list for various reasons, some of which are as follows:

➤ **MongoDB** — MongoDB has been featured in many chapters of this book. The book has already covered a few aspects of MongoDB internals and adding to that information base provides a comprehensive enough coverage of the product.

➤ **Membase** — As far as key/value in-memory, with the option to persist to disk data stores go, Redis has been the example of choice so far. Many Redis features and internals have been illustrated through multiple chapters. This chapter steps out of the Redis umbrella to cover a competing product, Membase. Membase has gained popularity because its performance characteristics are notable and adoption of the Memcached protocol makes it a drop-in replacement for Memcached.

➤ **Hypertable** — As far as sorted ordered column-family stores go, much has been covered with HBase in mind. Although HBase is a popular Google Bigtable clone, a couple of alternatives are built on the same model. The alternatives are Hypertable and Cloudata. Cloudata is the newest of the open-source options but Hypertable is a well-established player. Hypertable is deployed as a scalable data store for many large Internet applications and services. Hypertable is written in C++ and provides superior performance metrics as compared to HBase. So I cover a few aspects of Hypertable in this chapter.

➤ **Apache Cassandra** — Google Bigtable and Amazon Dynamo are the two popular blueprints for architecting large-scale NoSQL stores. Apache Cassandra tries to bring together the ideas from both products. Apache Cassandra has been much talked about and its fast writes have created enough excitement. The chapter covers some bits of what Cassandra is made up of.

➤ **Berkeley DB** — Berkeley DB is a powerful key/value store that forms the underlying storage of leading NoSQL products like Amazon Dynamo, LinkedIn, Voldemort, and GenieDB.

The coverage of the topics in this chapter is by no means exhaustive or uniform across products. However, the chapter provides enough information to pique your curiosity to explore the internals further, to unwrap the underlying code of these products, to use these products gainfully, and to possibly contribute to making these products better. In addition, the chapter may also inspire you to explore the internals of other NoSQL products. Some of these other NoSQL products may have been mentioned only in passing in this book. Even others may not even have been mentioned.

MONGODB INTERNALS

Many MongoDB commands and usage patterns have been covered in the book so far. Storage and querying mechanisms have been explored and the topic of replication has been touched upon. A few details about the wire format, BSON, have also been introduced. This section illustrates a few important additional aspects of MongoDB. The illustration builds on top of what you already know.

MongoDB follows client-server architecture, commonly found in traditional RDBMSs. Client-server architecture involves a single server and multiple clients connecting to the server. In a sharded and replicated scenario, multiple servers — instead of only one — form the topology. In a standalone mode or in a clustered and sharded topology, data is transported from client to server and back, and among the nodes.

> ### BSON SPECIFICATION
>
> MongoDB encodes the documents it stores in a JSON-like binary format called BSON, which was introduced in Chapter 2 of this book. I briefly review a few BSON characteristics here.
>
> A BSON document is a collection of zero or more binary key/value pairs. The basic binary types that make up BSON representations are as follows:
>
> ➤ **byte** — 1 byte
>
> ➤ **int32** — 4 bytes
>
> ➤ **int64** — 8 bytes
>
> ➤ **double** — 8 bytes
>
> int32 and int64 correspond to the 32-bit and 64-bit signed integers, respectively. Double corresponds to a 64-bit IEEE 754 floating-point value. A possible example document could be as follows:
>
> ```
> { "hello": "world" }
> ```
>
> Such a document could be represented using BSON as follows:
>
> ```
> "\x16\x00\x00\x00\x02hello\x00 \x06\x00\x00\x00world\x00\x00"
> ```
>
> The BSON notations shown here use the familiar C semantics for binary value representation, using Hexadecimal equivalents. If you were to map the readable document to the binary notation, it would be as follows:
>
> ```
> { and }—"\x16\x00\x00\x00 and \x00
> "hello":—x02hello\x00
>  "world"—\x06\x00\x00\x00world\x00
> ```
>
> You can read more about the BSON specification at http://bsonspec.org/.

MongoDB Wire Protocol

Clients speak to a MongoDB server using a simple TCP/IP-based socket connection. The wire protocol used for the communication is a simple request-response-based socket protocol. The wire protocol headers and payload are BSON encoded. The ordering of messages follows the little endian format, which is the same as in BSON.

In a standard request-response model, a client sends a request to a server and the server responds to the request. In terms of the wire protocol, a request is sent with a message header and a request payload. A response comes back with a message header and a response payload. The format for the message header between the request and the response is quite similar. However, the format of the request and the response payload are not the same. Figure 13-1 depicts the basic request-response communication between a client and a MongoDB server.

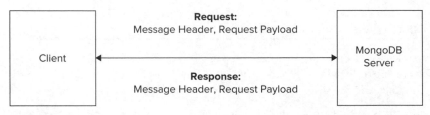

FIGURE 13-1

The MongoDB wire protocol allows a number of operations. The allowed operations are as follows:

 RESERVED *is also an operation, which was formerly used for* OP_GET_BY_OID. *It's not listed in the list of opcodes as it's not actively used.*

➤ **OP_INSERT** (code: 2002) — Insert a document. The "create" operation in CRUD jargon.

 CRUD, *which stands for Create, Read, Update and Delete, are standard data management operations. Many systems and interfaces that interact with data facilitate the CRUD operations.*

➤ **OP_UPDATE** (code: 2001) — Update a document. The update operation in CRUD.

➤ **OP_QUERY** (code: 2004) — Query a collection of documents. The "read" operation in CRUD.

➤ **OP_GET_MORE** (code: 2005) — Get more data from a query. Query response can contain a large number of documents. To enhance performance and avoid sending the entire set of documents, databases involve the concept of a cursor that allows for incremental fetching of the records. The OP_GET_MORE operation facilitates fetching additional documents via a cursor.

➤ **OP_REPLY** (code: 1) — Reply to a client request. This operation sends responses in reply to OP_QUERY and OP_GET_MORE operations.

➤ **OP_KILL_CURSORS** (code: 2007) — Operation to close a cursor.

➤ **OP_DELETE** (code: 2006) — Delete a document.

➤ **OP_MSG** (code: 1000) — Generic message command.

Every request and response message has a header. A standard message header has the following properties:

➤ **messageLength** — The length of the message in bytes. Paradoxically, the length includes 4 bytes to hold the length value.

➤ **requestID** — A unique message identifier. The client or the server, depending on which is initiating the operation, can generate the identifier.

➤ **responseTo** — In the case of OP_QUERY and OP_GET_MORE the response from the database includes the requestID from the original client request as the responseTo value. This allows clients to map requests to responses.

➤ **opCode** — The operation code. The allowed operations are listed earlier in this subsection.

Next, you walk through a couple of simple and common request-response scenarios.

Inserting a Document

When creating and inserting a new document, a client sends an OP_INSERT operation via a request that includes:

➤ **A message header** — A standard message header structure that includes messageLength, requestID, responseTo, and opCode.

➤ **An int32 value** — Zero (which is simply reserved for future use).

➤ **A cstring** — The fully qualified collection name. For example, a collection named aCollection in a database named aDatabase will appear as aDatabase.aCollection.

➤ **An array** — This array contains one or more documents that need to be inserted into a collection.

The database processes an insert document request and you can query for the outcome of the request by calling the getLastError command. However, the database does not explicitly send a response corresponding to the insert document request.

Querying a Collection

When querying for documents in a collection, a client sends an OP_QUERY operation via a request. It receives a set of relevant documents via a database response that involves an OP_REPLY operation.

An OP_QUERY message from the client includes:

➤ **A message header** — A standard header with messageLength, requestID, responseTo, and opCode elements in it.

➤ **An int32 value** — Contains flags that represent query options. The flags define properties for a cursor, result streaming, and partial results when some shards are down. For example, you could define whether cursors should close after the last data is returned and you could specify whether idle cursors should be timed out after a certain period of inactivity.

➤ **A cstring** — Fully qualified collection name.

➤ **An int32 value** — Number of documents to skip.

➤ **Another int32 value** — Number of documents to return. A database response with an OP_REPLY operation corresponding to this request receives the documents. If there are more documents than returned, a cursor is also usually returned. The value of this property sometimes varies depending on the driver and its ability to limit result sets.

➤ **A query document in BSON format** — Contains elements that must match the documents that are searched.

➤ **A document** — Representing the fields to return. This is also in BSON format.

In response to a client OP_QUERY operation request, a MongoDB database server responds with an OP_REPLY. An OP_REPLY message from the server includes:

➤ **A message header** — The message header in a client request and a server response is quite similar. Also as mentioned earlier, the responseTo header property for an OP_REPLY would contain the requestID value of the client request for a corresponding OP_QUERY.

➤ **An int32 value** — Contains response flags that typically denote an error or exception situation. Response flags could contain information about query failure or invalid cursor id.

➤ **An int64 value** — Contains the cursor id that allows a client to fetch more documents.

➤ **An int32 value** — Starting point in the cursor.

➤ **Another int32 value** — Number of documents returned.

➤ **An array** — Contains the documents returned in response to the query.

So far, only a sample of the wire protocol has been presented. You can read more about the wire protocol online at www.mongodb.org/display/DOCS/Mongo+Wire+Protocol. You can also browse through the MongoDB code available at https://github.com/mongodb.

The documents are all stored at the server. Clients interact with the server to insert, read, update, and delete documents. You have seen that the interactions between a client and a server involve an efficient binary format and a wire protocol. Next is a view into the storage scheme.

MongoDB Database Files

MongoDB stores database and collection data in files that reside at a path specified by the --dbpath option to the mongod server program. The default value for dbpath is /data/db. MongoDB follows a predefined scheme for storing documents in these files. I cover details of the file allocation scheme later in this subsection after I have demonstrated a few ways to query for a collection's storage properties.

You could query for a collection's storage properties using the Mongo shell. To use the shell, first start mongod. Then connect to the server using the command-line program. After you connect, query for a collection's size as follows:

```
> db.movies.dataSize();
327280
```

mongodb_data_size.txt

The collection in this case is the movies collection from Chapter 6. The size of the flat file, movies .dat, that has the movies information for the University of Minnesota group lens movie ratings data set is only 171308 but the corresponding collection is much larger because of the additional metadata the MongoDB format stores. The size returned is not the storage size on the disk. It's just the size of data. It's possible the allocated storage for this collection may have some unused space. To get the storage size for the collection, query as follows:

```
> db.movies.storageSize();
500480
```

mongodb_data_size.txt

The storage size is 500480, whereas the data size is much smaller and only 327280. This collection may have some associated indexes. To query for the total size of the collection, that is, data, unallocated storage, and index storage, you can query as follows:

```
> db.movies.totalSize();
860928
```

mongodb_data_size.txt

To make sure all the different values add up, query for the index size. To do that you need the collection names for the indexes associated with the collection named movies. To get fully qualified names and database and collection names of all indexes related to the movies collection, query for all namespaces in the system as follows:

```
> db.system.namespaces.find()
```

mongodb_data_size.txt

I have a lot of collections in my MongoDB instance so the list is long, but the relevant pieces of information for the current example are as follows:

```
{ "name" : "mydb.movies" }
{ "name" : "mydb.movies.$_id_" }
```

mydb.movies is the collection itself and the other one, mydb.movies.$_id_, is the collection of elements of the index on the id. To view the index collection data size, storage size, and the total size, query as follows:

```
> db.movies.$_id_.dataSize();
139264
> db.movies.$_id_.storageSize();
655360
> db.movies.$_id_.totalSize();
655360
```

mongodb_data_size.txt

You can also use the collection itself to get the index data size as follows:

```
> db.movies.totalIndexSize();
360448
```

mongodb_data_size.txt

The `totalSize` for the collection adds up to the `storageSize` and the `totalIndexSize`. You can also get size measurements and more by using the `validate` method on the collection. You could run `validate` on the `movies` collection as follows:

```
> db.movies.validate();
{
    "ns" : "mydb.movies",
    "result" : "\nvalidate\n  firstExtent:0:51a800 ns:mydb.movies\n
    lastExtent:0:558b00 ns:mydb.movies\n  # extents:4\n
    datasize?:327280 nrecords?:3883 lastExtentSize:376832\n
    padding:1\n  first extent:\n    loc:0:51a800 xnext:0:53bf00
    xprev:null\n    nsdiag:mydb.movies\n    size:5888
    firstRecord:0:51a8b0 lastRecord:0:51be90\n  3883 objects found,
    nobj:3883\n  389408 bytes data w/headers\n  327280 bytes
    data wout/headers\n  deletedList: 1100000000001000000\n
    deleted: n: 3 size: 110368\n  nIndexes:2\n
    mydb.movies.$_id_ keys:3883\n    mydb.movies.$title_1 keys:3883\n",
    "ok" : 1,
    "valid" : true,
    "lastExtentSize" : 376832
}
```

mongodb_data_size.txt

The `validate` command provides more information than just the size. Information on records, headers, extent sizes, and keys is also included.

MongoDB stores the database and its collections in files on the filesystem. To understand the size allocation of the storage files, list them with their sizes. On Linux, Unix, Mac OS X, or any other Unix variant, you can list the sizes as follows:

```
ls -sk1 ~/data/db
total 8549376
      0 mongod.lock
  65536 mydb.0
 131072 mydb.1
 262144 mydb.2
 524288 mydb.3
1048576 mydb.4
2096128 mydb.5
2096128 mydb.6
2096128 mydb.7
  16384 mydb.ns
```

```
     65536 test.0
    131072 test.1
     16384 test.ns
```

mongodb_data_size.txt

The output is from my /data/db directory and will be different for you. However, the size pattern of the database files should not be different. The files correspond to a database. For each database, there is one namespace file and multiple data storage files. The namespace file across databases is the same size: 16384 bytes or 16 MB on my 64-bit Snow Leopard Mac OS X. The data files themselves are numbered in a sequential order, starting with 0. For mydb, the pattern is as follows:

➤ mydb.0 is 65536 bytes or 64 MB in size.

➤ mydb.1 is double the size of mydb.0. Its size is 131072 bytes or 128 MB.

➤ mydb.2, mydb.3, mydb.4, and mydb.5 are 256 MB, 512 MB, 1024 MB (1 GB), and ~2047 MB (2 GB).

➤ mydb.6 and mydb.7 are each 2 GB, the same size as that of mydb.5.

MongoDB incrementally allocates larger fixed blocks for data file storage. The size is capped at a predetermined level, 2 GB being the default, beyond which each file is the same size as the largest block. MongoDB's storage file allocation is based on an algorithm that optimizes minimal unused space and fragmentation.

There are many more nuances to MongoDB, especially around memory management and sharding. I leave it to you to explore on your own. This book covers a number of products and covering every little detail about multiple products is beyond the scope of this book.

Next, I cover a few essential architectural aspects of Membase.

MEMBASE ARCHITECTURE

Membase supports the Memcached protocol and so client applications that use Memcached can easily include Membase in their application stack. Behind the scenes, though, Membase adds capabilities like persistence and replication that Memcached does not support.

Each Membase node runs an instance of the ns_server, which is sort of a node supervisor and manages the activities on the node. Clients interact with the ns_server using the Memcached protocol or a REST interface. The REST interface is supported with the help of a component called Menelaus. Menelaus includes a robust jQuery layer that maps REST calls down to the server. Clients accessing Membase using the Memcached protocol reach the underlying data through a proxy called Moxi. Moxi acts as an intermediary that with the help of vBuckets always routes clients to the appropriate place. To understand how vBuckets route information correctly, you need to dig a bit deeper into the consistent hashing used by vBuckets.

The essence of vBuckets-based routing is illustrated in Figure 13-2.

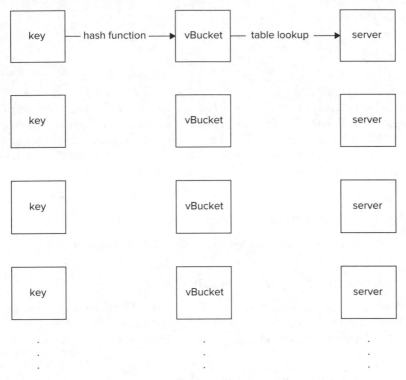

FIGURE 13-2

As shown in Figure 13-2, client requests for data identified with keys are mapped to vBuckets and not servers. The vBuckets in turn are mapped to servers. The hash function maps keys to vBuckets and allows for rebalancing as the number of vBuckets changes. At the same time, vBuckets themselves map to servers via a lookup table. Therefore, the vBuckets-to-server mapping is sort of stationary and the real physical storage of the data is not moved when vBuckets are reallocated.

Membase consists of the following components:

➤ **ns_server** — The core supervisor.

➤ **Memcached and Membase engine** — Membase builds on top of Memcached. The networking and protocol support layer is straight from Memcached and included in Membase. The Membase engine adds additional features like asynchronous persistence and support for the Telocator Alphanumeric Protocol (TAP).

➤ **Vbucketmigrator** — Based on how ns_server starts one or more vbucketmigrator processes, data is either replicated or transferred between nodes.

➤ **Moxi** — Memcached proxy with support for vBuckets hashing for client routing.

There is a lot more to Membase but hopefully you understand the very basics from this subsection so far. More of Membase architecture and performance is included in the following chapters.

In addition, bear in mind that Membase is now part of CouchBase, a merged entity created by the union of Membase and CouchDB. This union is likely to impact the Membase architecture in significant ways in the next few releases.

HYPERTABLE UNDER THE HOOD

Hypertable is a high-performance alternative to HBase. The essential characteristics of Hypertable are quite similar to HBase, which in turn is a clone of the Google Bigtable. Hypertable is actually not a new project. It started around the same time as HBase in 2007. Hypertable runs on top of a distributed filesystem like HDFS.

In HBase, column-family-centric data is stored in a row-key sorted and ordered manner. You also learned that each cell of data maintains multiple versions of data. Hypertable supports similar ideas. In Hypertable all version information is appended to the row-keys. The version information is identified via timestamps. All data for all versions for each row-key is stored in a sorted manner for each column-family.

Hypertable provides a column-family-centric data store but its physical storage characteristics are also affected by the notion of access groups. Access groups in Hypertable provide a way to physically store related column data together. In traditional RDBMS, data is sorted in rows and stored as such. That is, data for two contiguous rows is typically stored next to each other. In column-oriented stores, data for two columns is physically stored together. With Hypertable access groups you have the flexibility to put one or more columns in the same group. Keeping all columns in the same access group simulates a traditional RDBMS environment. Keeping each column separate from the other simulates a column-oriented database.

Regular Expression Support

Hypertable queries can filter cells based on regular expression matches on the row-key, column qualifier, and value. Hypertable leverages Google's open-source regular expression engine, RE2, for implementing regular expression support. Details on RE2 can be accessed online at `http://code.google.com/p/re2/`. RE2 is fast, safe, and thread-friendly regular expression engine, which is written in C++. RE2 powers regular expression support in many well known Google products like Bigtable and Sawzall.

RE2 syntax supports a majority of the expressions supported by Perl Compatible Regular Expression (PCRE), PERL, and VIM. You can access the list of supported syntax at `http://code.google.com/p/re2/wiki/Syntax`.

Some tests (`http://blog.hypertable.com/?p=103`) conducted by the Hypertable developers reveal that RE2 was between three to fifty times faster than `java.util.regex.Pattern`. These tests were conducted on a 110 MB data set that had over 4.5 million unique IDs. The test results can vary depending on the data set and its size but the results are indicative of the fact that RE2 is fast and efficient.

Many concepts in Hypertable and HBase are the same and so repeating those same concepts here is not beneficial. However, a passing reference to an idea that is important in both places but not discussed yet is that of a Bloom Filter.

Bloom Filter

Bloom Filter is a probabilistic data structure used to test whether an element is a member of a set. Think of a Bloom Filter as an array of m number of bits. An empty Bloom Filter has a value of 0 in all its m positions. Now if elements a, b, and c are members of a set, then they are mapped via a set of k hash functions to the Bloom Filter. This means each of the members, that is a, b, and c are mapped via the k different hash functions to k positions on the Bloom Filter. Whenever a member is mapped via a hash function to a specific position in the m bit array the value in that particular position is set to 1. Different members, when passed through the hash functions, could map to the same position in the Bloom Filter.

Now to test if a given element, say w, is a member of a set, you need to pass it through the k hash functions and map the outcome on the Bloom Filter array. If the value at any of the mapped positions is 0, the element is not a member of the set. If the value at all the positions is 1, then either the element is a member of the set or the element maps to one or more position where the value was set to 1 by another element. Therefore, false positives are possible but false negatives are not.

Learn more about Bloom Filter, explained in the context of PERL, at `www.perl.com/pub/2004/04/08/bloom_filters.html`.

APACHE CASSANDRA

Apache Cassandra is simultaneously a very popular and infamous NoSQL database. A few examples that used Cassandra in the early part of the book introduced the core ideas of the store. In this section, I review Cassandra's core architecture to understand how it works.

Peer-to-Peer Model

Most databases, including the most popular of NoSQL stores, follow a master-slave model for scaling out and replication. This means for each set, writes are committed to the master node and replicated down to the slaves. The slaves provide enhanced read scalability but not write scalability.

Cassandra moves away from the master-slave model and instead uses a peer-to-peer model. This means there is no single master but all the nodes are potentially masters. This makes the writes and reads extremely scalable and even allows nodes to function in cases of partition tolerance. However, extreme scalability comes at a cost, which in this case is a compromise in strong consistency. The peer-to-peer model follows a weak consistency model.

Based on Gossip and Anti-entropy

Cassandra's peer-to-peer scalability and eventual consistency model makes it important to establish a protocol to communicate among the peers and detect node failure. Cassandra relies on a gossip-based protocol to communicate among the nodes. Gossip, as the name suggests, uses an idea similar to the concept of human gossip. In the case of gossip a peer arbitrarily chooses to send messages to other nodes. In Cassandra, gossip is more systematic and is triggered by a `Gossiper` class that runs on the basis of a timer. Nodes register themselves with the `Gossiper` class and receive updates as gossip propagates through the network. Gossip is meant for large distributed systems and is not particularly reliable. In Cassandra, the `Gossiper` class keeps track of nodes as gossip spreads through them.

In terms of the workflow, every timer-driven Gossiper action requires the Gossiper to choose a random node and send that node a message. This message is named GossipDigestSyncMessage. The receiving node, if active, sends an acknowledgment back to the Gossiper. To complete gossip, the Gossiper sends an acknowledgment in response to the acknowledgment it receives. If the communication completes all steps, gossip successfully shares the state information between the Gossiper and the node. If during gossip the communication fails, it indicates that possibly the node may be down.

To detect failure, Cassandra uses an algorithm called the Phi Accrual Failure Detection. This method of detection converts the binary spectrum of node alive or node dead to a level in the middle that indicates the suspicion level. The traditional idea of failure detection via periodic heartbeats is therefore replaced with a continuous assessment of suspicion levels.

Whereas gossip keeps the nodes in sync and repairs any temporary damages, more severe damages are identified and repaired via an anti-entropy mechanism. In this process, data in a column-family is converted to a hash using the Merkle tree. The Merkle tree representations compare data between neighboring nodes. If there is a discrepancy, the nodes are reconciled and repaired. The Merkle tree is created as a snapshot during a major compaction operation.

This reconfirms that the weak consistency in Cassandra may require reading from a Quorum to avoid inconsistencies.

Fast Writes

Writes in Cassandra are extremely fast because they are simply appended to commit logs on any available node and no locks are imposed in the critical path. A write operation involves a write into a commit log for durability and recoverability and an update into an in-memory data structure. The write into the in-memory data structure is performed only after a successful write into the commit log. Typically, there is a dedicated disk on each machine for the commit log because all writes into the commit log are sequential and so we can maximize disk throughput. When the in-memory data structure crosses a certain threshold, calculated based on data size and number of objects, it dumps itself to disk.

All writes are sequential to disk and also generate an index for efficient lookup based on a row-key. These indexes are also persisted along with the data. Over time, many such logs could exist on disk and a merge process could run in the background to collate the different logs into one log. This process of compaction merges data in SSTables, the underlying storage format. It also leads to rationalization of keys and combination of columns, deletions of data items marked for deletion, and creation of new indexes.

Hinted Handoff

During a write operation a request sent to a Cassandra node may fail if the node is unavailable. A write may not reconcile correctly if the node is partitioned from the network. To handle these cases, Cassandra involves the concept of hinted handoff. Hinted handoff can best be explained through a small illustration so let's consider two nodes in a network, X and Y. A write is attempted on X but X is down so the write operation is sent to Y. Y stores the information with a little hint, which says that the write is for X and so please pass it on when X comes online.

Basho Riak (see `www.basho.com/products_riak_overview.php`) is another Amazon Dynamo inspired database that also leverages the concept of hinted handoff for write reconciliation.

Besides the interesting and often talked about Cassandra features and the underlying internals, I also need to mention that Cassandra is built on Staged Event-Driven Architecture (SEDA). Read more about SEDA at `www.eecs.harvard.edu/~mdw/proj/seda/`.

The next product I cover is a good old key/value store, Berkeley DB. Berkeley DB is the underlying storage for many NoSQL products and Berkeley DB itself can be used as a NoSQL product.

BERKELEY DB

Berkeley DB comes in three distinct flavors and supports multiple configurations:

- ➤ **Berkeley DB** — Key/value store programmed in C. This is the original flavor.
- ➤ **Berkeley DB Java Edition (JE)** — Key/value store rewritten in Java. Can easily be incorporated into a Java stack.
- ➤ **Berkeley DB XML** — Written in C++, this version wraps the key/value store to behave as an indexed and optimized XML storage system.

Berkeley DB, also referred to as BDB, is a key/value store deep in its guts. Simple as it may be at its core, a number of different configurations are possible with BDB. For example, BDB can be configured to provide concurrent non-blocking access or support transactions. It can be scaled out as a highly available cluster of master-slave replicas.

BDB is a key/value data store. It is a pure storage engine that makes no assumptions about an implied schema or structure to the key/value pairs. Therefore, BDB easily allows for higher-level API, query, and modeling abstractions on top of the underlying key/value store. This facilitates fast and efficient storage of application-specific data, without the overhead of translating it into an abstracted data format. The flexibility offered by this simple, yet elegant design, makes it possible to store structured and semi-structured data in BDB.

BDB can run as an in-memory store to hold small amounts of data or it can be configured as a large data store, with a fast in-memory cache. Multiple databases can be set up in a single physical install with the help of a higher-level abstraction, called an environment. One environment can have multiple databases. You need to open an environment and then a database to write data to it or read data from it. You should close a database and the environment when you have completed your interactions to make optimal use of resources. Each item in a database is a key/value pair. The key is typically unique but you could have duplicates. A value is accessed using a key. A retrieved value can be updated and saved back to the database. Multiple values are accessed and iterated over using a cursor. Cursors allow you to loop through the collection of values and manipulate them one at a time. Transactions and concurrent access are also supported.

The key of a key/value pair almost always serves as the primary key, which is indexed. Other properties within the value could serve as secondary indexes. Secondary indexes are maintained separately in a secondary database. The main database, which has the key/value pairs, is therefore also sometimes referred to as the primary database.

BDB runs as an in-process data store, so you statically or dynamically link to it when accessing it using the C, C++, C#, Java, or scripting language APIs from a corresponding program.

Storage Configuration

Key/value pairs can be stored in four types of data structures: B-tree, Hash, Queue, and Recno.

B-Tree Storage

A B-tree needs little introduction but if you do need to review its definition, read a freely available resource on B-tree online at `www.bluerwhite.org/btree/`. It's a balanced tree data structure that keeps its elements sorted and allows for fast sequential access, insertions, and deletions. Keys and values can be arbitrary data types. In BDB the B-tree access method allows duplicates. This is a good choice if you need complex data types as keys. It's also a great choice if data access patterns lead to access of contiguous or neighboring records. B-tree keeps a substantial amount of metadata to perform efficiently. Most BDB applications use the B-tree storage configuration.

Hash Storage

Like the B-tree, a hash also allows complex types to be keys. Hashes have a more linear structure as compared to a B-tree. BDB hash structures allow duplicates.

Whereas both a B-tree and a hash support complex keys, a hash database usually outperforms a B-tree when the data set far exceeds the amount of available memory because a B-tree keeps more metadata than a hash, and a larger data set implies that the B-tree metadata may not fit in the in-memory cache. In such an extreme situation the B-tree metadata as well as the actual data record itself must often be fetched from files, which can cause multiple I/Os per operation. The hash access method is designed to minimize the I/Os required to access the data record and therefore in these extreme cases, may perform better than a B-tree.

Queue Storage

A queue is a set of sequentially stored fixed-length records. Keys are restricted to logical record numbers, which are integer types. Records are appended sequentially allowing for extremely fast writes. If you are impressed by Apache Cassandra's fast writes by appending to logs, give BDB with the queue access method a try and you won't be disappointed. Methods also allow reading and updating effectively from the head of the queue. A queue has additional support for row-level locking. This allows effective transactional integrity even in cases of concurrent processing.

Recno Storage

Recno is similar to a queue but allows variable-length records. Like a queue, Recno keys are restricted to integers.

The different configurations allow you to store arbitrary types of data in a collection. There is no fixed schema other than those imposed by your model. In the extreme situation, you are welcome to store disparate value types for two keys in a collection. Value types can be complex classes, which could represent a JSON document, a complex data structure, or a structured data set. The only restriction really is that the value should be serializable to a byte array. A single key or a single value can be as large as 4 GB in size.

The possibility of secondary indexes allows filtering on the basis of value properties. The primary database does not store data in a tabular format and so non-existing properties are not stored for sparse data sets. A secondary index skips all key/value pairs that lack the property on which the index is created. In general, the storage is compact and efficient.

SUMMARY

Although only a few aspects of the internals of multiple databases were covered in this chapter, it's not inaccurate to apply the same ideas to other stores. Architecture and under-the-hood exploration can be done at multiple levels of depth, starting from conceptual overview to in-depth code tours. I am mostly restricted to conceptual levels to make the chapter accessible to all. But this overview should give you the tools and knowledge to begin your own explorations.

PART IV
Mastering NoSQL

14

Choosing Among NoSQL Flavors

WHAT'S IN THIS CHAPTER?

➤ Understanding the strengths and weaknesses of NoSQL products

➤ Comparing and contrasting the available NoSQL products

➤ Evaluating NoSQL products based on performance benchmarks

Not all NoSQL databases are similar, nor are they made to solve the same problems, so comparing them to choose one from among them is probably a fruitless exercise. However, understanding which database is appropriate for a given situation and context is important. This chapter presents the facts and opinions to help you compare and contrast the available NoSQL choices. It uses feature, performance, and context-based criteria to classify the NoSQL databases and to weigh them against each other.

The evolution of NoSQL and databases beyond RDBMS can be compared to the rapid evolution of multiple programming languages in the past few years. Availability of multiple programming languages allows the use of the right language for the right task, often leading a single developer to have more than one language in his or her repertoire. A single developer working with multiple languages is often compared to a person speaking more than one natural language. The knowledge of multiple languages makes a person a polyglot. Being a polyglot enables an individual to communicate effectively in situations where the lack of knowledge of a language could have been an impediment. Similarly, adopting multiple programming languages is termed as *polygot programming*. Often, polyglot programming is seen as a smart way of programming where an appropriate language is used for the task at hand. Along the same lines, it's becoming evident that one database does not fit all sizes and knowledge and adoption of more than one database is a wise strategy. The knowledge and use of multiple database products and methodologies is popularly now being called *polyglot persistence*.

NoSQL databases come in many shapes, sizes, and forms so feature-based comparison is the first way to logically group them together. Often, solutions for many problems easily map to desired features.

COMPARING NOSQL PRODUCTS

This section compares and contrasts the NoSQL choices on the basis of the following features:

➤   Scalability

➤   Transactional integrity and consistency

➤   Data modeling

➤   Query support

➤   Access and interface availability

Scalability

Although all NoSQL databases promise horizontal scalability they don't rise up equally to the challenge. The Bigtable clones — HBase and Hypertable — stand in front and in-memory stores, like Membase or Redis, and document databases, like MongoDB and Couchbase Server, lag behind. This difference is amplified as the data size becomes very large, especially if it grows over a few petabytes.

In the past several chapters, you gained a deep understanding of the storage architecture of most mainstream NoSQL database types. Bigtable and its clones promote the storage of large individual data points and large collections of data. The Bigtable model supports a large number of columns and an immensely large number of rows. The data can be sparse where many columns have no value. The Bigtable model, of course, does not waste space and simply doesn't store cells that have no value.

> *The number of columns and rows in an HBase cluster is theoretically unbound. The numbers of column-families are restricted to about 100. The number of rows can keep growing as long as newer nodes are available to save the data. The number of columns is rarely more than a few hundred. Too many columns could impose logical challenges in manipulating the data set.*

Google led the column-family-centric data store revolution to store the large and ever-growing web index its crawlers brought home. The Web has been growing in unbounded ways for the past several years. Google needed a store to grow with the expanding index. Therefore, Bigtable and its clones were built to scale out, limited only by the hardware available to spin off newer nodes in the cluster. Over the past few years, Google has successfully used the Bigtable model to store and retrieve a variety of data that is also very large in volume.

The HBase wiki lists a number of users on its Powered By page (`http://wiki.apache.org/hadoop/Hbase/PoweredBy`). Some users listed clearly testify to HBase's capability to scale.

> *Although the next paragraph or two demonstrate HBase's capabilities, Hypertable, being another Google Bigtable clone, also delivers the same promise.*

Meetup (www.meetup.com) is a popular site that facilitates user groups and interest groups to organize local events and meetings. Meetup has grown from a small, unknown site in 2001 to 8 million members in 100 countries, 65,000+ organizers, 80,000+ meetup groups, and 50,000 meetups each week (http://online.wsj.com/article/SB10001424052748704170404575624733792905708.html). Meetup is an HBase user. All group activity is directly written to HBase and is indexed per member. A member's custom feed is directly served from HBase.

Facebook is another big user of HBase. Facebook messaging is built on HBase. Facebook was the number one destination site on the Internet in 2010. It has grown to more than 500 million active users (www.facebook.com/press/info.php?statistics) and is the largest software application in terms of the number of users. Facebook messaging is a robust infrastructure that integrates chat, SMS, and e-mail. Hundreds of billions of messages are sent every month through this messaging infrastructure. The engineering team at Facebook shared a few notes on using HBase for their messaging infrastructure. Read the notes online at www.facebook .com/notes/facebook-engineering/the-underlying-technology-of-messages/454991608919.

HBase has some inherent advantages when it comes to scaling systems. HBase supports auto load balancing, failover, compression, and multiple shards per server. HBase works well with the Hadoop distributed filesystem (a.k.a. HDFS, which is a massively scalable distributed filesystem). You know from earlier chapters that HDFS replicates and automatically re-balances to easily accommodate large files that span multiple servers. Facebook chose HBase to leverage many of these features. HBase is a necessity for handling the number of messages and users they serve. The Facebook engineering notes also mention that the messages in their infrastructure are short, volatile, and temporal and are rarely accessed later. HBase, and in general Bigtable clones, are particularly suitable when ad-hoc querying of data is not important. From earlier chapters, you know that HBase supports the querying of data sets but is a weak replacement to an RBDMS as far as its querying capabilities are concerned. Infrastructures like Google App Engine (GAE) successfully expose a data modeling API, with advanced querying capabilities, on top of the Bigtable. More information on querying is covered in a section titled "Querying Support," later in this chapter.

So it seems clear that column-family-centric NoSQL databases are a good choice if extreme scalability is a requirement. However, such databases may not be the best choice for all types of systems, especially those that involve real-time transaction processing. An RDBMS often makes a better choice than any NoSQL flavor if transactional integrity is very important. Eventually consistent NoSQL options, like Cassandra or Riak, may be workable if weaker consistency is acceptable. Amazon has demonstrated that massively scalable e-commerce operations may be a use case for eventually consistent data stores, but examples beyond Amazon where such models apply well are hard to find. Databases like Cassandra follow the Amazon Dynamo paradigm and support eventual consistency. Cassandra promises incredibly fast read and write speeds. Cassandra also supports Bigtable-like column-family-centric data modeling. Amazon Dynamo also inspired Riak. Riak supports a document store abstraction in addition to being an eventually consistent store. Both Cassandra and Riak scale well in horizontal clusters but if scalability is of paramount importance, my vote goes in favor of HBase or Hypertable over the eventually consistent stores. Perhaps places where eventually consistent stores fare better than sorted ordered column-family stores is where write throughput and latency is important. Therefore, if both horizontal scalability and high write throughput are required, possibly consider Cassandra or Riak. Even in these cases, consider a hybrid approach where you can logically partition the data write process from the access and analytics and use two separate databases for each of the tasks.

If scalability implies large data becoming available at an incredibly fast pace, for example stock market tick data or advertisement click tracking data, then column-family stores alone may not provide a complete solution. It's prudent to store the massively growing data in these stores and manipulate them using MapReduce operations for batch querying and data mining, but you may need something more nimble for fast writes and real-time manipulation. Nothing is faster than manipulating the data in memory and so leveraging NoSQL options that keep data in memory and flush it to disk when it fills the available capacity are probably good choices. Both MongoDB and Redis follow this strategy. Currently, MongoDB uses mmap and Redis implements a custom mapping from memory to disk. However, both MongoDB and Redis, have actively been re-engineering their memory mapping feature and things will continue to evolve. Using MongoDB or Redis with HBase or Hypertable makes a good choice for a system that needs fast real-time data manipulation and a store for extensive data mining. Memcached and Membase can be used in place of MongoDB or Redis. Memcached and Membase act as a layer of fast and efficient cache, and therefore supplement well on top of column-family stores. Membase has been used effectively with Hadoop-based systems for such use cases. With the merger of Membase and CouchDB, a well integrated NoSQL product with both fast cache-centric features and distributed scalable storage-centric features is likely to emerge.

Although scalability is very important if your data requirements grow to the size of Google's or Facebook's, not all applications become that large. Scalable systems are probably relevant for cases much smaller than these widespread systems but sometimes an attempt to make things scalable can become an exercise in over-engineering. You certainly want to avoid unnecessary complexity.

In many systems, data integrity and transactional consistency are more important than any other requirements. Is NoSQL an option for such systems?

Transactional Integrity and Consistency

Transactional integrity is relevant only when data is modified, updated, created, and deleted. Therefore, the question of transactional integrity is not pertinent in pure data warehousing and mining contexts. This means that batch-centric Hadoop-based analytics on warehoused data is also not subject to transactional requirements.

Many data sets like web traffic log files, social networking status updates (including tweets or buzz), advertisement click-through imprints, road-traffic data, stock market tick data, and game scores are primarily, if not completely, written once and read multiple times. Data sets that are written once and read multiple times have limited or no transactional requirements.

Some data sets are updated and deleted, but often these modifications are limited to a single item and not a range within the data set. Sometimes, updates are frequent and involve a range operation. If range operations are common and integrity of updates is required, an RDBMS is the best choice. If atomicity at an individual item level is sufficient, then column-family databases, document databases, and a few distributed key/value stores can guarantee that. If a system needs transactional integrity but could accommodate a window of inconsistency, eventual consistency is a possibility.

Opponents of NoSQL take the lack of ACID support in many scalable and robust non-relational databases as a major weakness. However, many data sets need little or no transactional support. Such data sets gain immediately from the scalable and fluid architecture of the NoSQL options. The power of scalable parallel processing using MapReduce operations on these NoSQL databases can help manipulate and mine large data sets effectively. Don't let the unnecessary worry of transactional integrity worry you.

HBase and Hypertable offer row-level atomic updates and consistent state with the help of Paxos. MongoDB offers document-level atomic updates. All NoSQL databases that follow a master-slave replication model implicitly support transactional integrity.

Data Modeling

RDBMS offers a consistent way of modeling data. Relational algebra underlies the data model. The theory is well established and implementation is standardized. Therefore, consistent ways of modeling and normalizing data is well understood and documented. In the NoSQL world there is no such standardized and well-defined data model. This is because all NoSQL products do not intend to solve the same problem or have the same architecture.

If you need an RDBMS-centric data model for storage and querying and cannot under any circumstances step outside those definitions, just don't use NoSQL. If, however, you are happy with SQL-type querying but can accommodate non-relational storage models, you have a few NoSQL options to choose from.

Document databases, like MongoDB, provide a gradual adoption path from formal RDBMS models to lose document-centric models. MongoDB supports SQL-like querying, rudimentary relational references, and database objects that draw a lot of inspiration from the standard table- and column-based model. If relaxed schema is your primary reason for using NoSQL, then MongoDB is a great option for getting started with NoSQL.

MongoDB is used by many web-centric businesses. Foursquare is perhaps its most celebrated user. Shutterfly, bit.ly, etsy, and sourceforge are a few other users that add feathers to MongoDB's cap. In many of these use cases MongoDB is preferred because it supports a flexible data model and offers speedy reads and writes. Web applications often evolve rapidly and it often gets cumbersome for developers to continuously change underlying RDBMS models, especially when the changes are frequent and at times drastic. Added to the schema change challenges are the issues relating to data migration.

MongoDB has good support for web framework integration. Rails, one of the most popular web application frameworks, can be used effectively with MongoDB. The data from Rails applications can be persisted via an object mapper. Therefore, MongoDB can easily be used in place of an RDBMS. Read about Rails 3 integration at `www.mongodb.org/display/DOCS/Rails+3+-+Getting+Started`.

For Java web developers, Spring offers first-class support for MongoDB via its Spring Data project. Read more about the Spring Data Document release that supports MongoDB at `www.springsource .org/node/3032`. Spring Data project, in fact, adds support for a number of NoSQL products, and not just MongoDB. It integrates Spring with Redis, Riak, CouchDB, Neo4j, and Hadoop. Get more details online at the Spring Data project homepage, which is `www.springsource.org/spring-data`.

MongoDB acts like a persistent cache, where data is kept in memory and flushed to disk as required. Therefore, MongoDB could also be thought of as an intermediate option between an RDBMS and an in-memory store or a flat file structure. Many web applications like real-time analytics, comments system, ratings storage, content management software, user data system, and event logging applications benefit from the fluid schema that MongoDB offers. Added to that, such applications enjoy MongoDB's RDBMS-like querying capabilities and its ability to segregate data into collections that resemble tables.

Apache CouchDB is a document database alternative to MongoDB. Apache CouchDB is now available as Couchbase server, with the primary creators of CouchDB having recently merged their company, CouchOne, with Membase, Inc. Couchbase offers a packaged version of Apache CouchDB with GeoCouch and support in the form of Couchbase Server.

Couchbase Server epitomizes adherence to web standards. Couchbase's primary interface to the data store is through RESTful HTTP interactions and is more web-centric than any database has ever been. Couchbase includes a web server as a part of the data store. It is built on top of Erlang OTP. This means you could effectively create an entire application using Couchbase. Future versions of Couchbase will be adding access to the data store through the Memcached protocol, gaining from Membase's ability to manage speed and throughput with a working set. Couchbase also plans to scale up, growing from Membase's elastic capabilities to seamlessly span across more nodes. Although Couchbase is very powerful and feature-rich, it has a very small footprint. Its nimble nature makes it appropriate for installation on a smartphone or an embedded device. Read more about mobile Couchbase at `www.couchbase.com/products-and-services/mobile-couchbase`.

Couchbase models support REST-style data management. A database in CouchDB can contain JSON format documents, with additional metadata or supporting artifacts as attachments. All operations on data — create, retrieve, update, and delete — are performed via RESTful HTTP requests. Long-running complex queries across replicated Couchbase servers leverage MapReduce.

 REST, *which stands for Representational State Transfer, represents a style of software architecture suitable for distributed hypermedia systems like the world wide web. The term REST was introduced and defined by Roy Fielding as a part of his PhD thesis. Read more about REST at* `www.ics.uci.edu/~fielding/ pubs/dissertation/rest_arch_style.htm`.

Not Just a Map

In typical in-memory databases and caches, the most well-known data structure is a map or a hash. A map stores key/value pairs and allows for fast and easy access to data. In-memory NoSQL stores provide filesystem-backed persistence of in-memory data. This means that stored data survives a system reboot. Many NoSQL in-memory databases support data structures beyond just maps, making using them for more than simple cache data extremely attractive.

At the most basic level, Berkeley DB stores pairs of binary key/value pairs. The underlying store itself does not attach any metadata to the stored key/value pairs. Layers on top of basic storage, like the persistence API or the object wrappers, allow persistence of higher-level abstractions to a Berkeley DB store.

Membase, on the other hand, supports the Memcached protocol, both text and binary, and adds features around distributed replica management and consistent hashing on top of the basic key/value store. Membase also adds the ability to grow and shrink the number of servers as part of a cluster without interrupting client access. Redis takes a slightly different approach. It supports most popular data structures out of the box. In fact, it is defined as a "data structure" server. Redis supports lists, sets, sorted sets, and strings in addition to maps. Redis has even added transaction-like capabilities to specify atomicity across a number of discrete operations.

If your use case gains from using a file-backed in-memory NoSQL product, consider the supported data models to make a choice on the best fit. In many cases, a key/value storage is enough, but if you need more than that look at Berkeley DB, Membase, and Redis. If you need a powerful and stable distributed key/value store to support large user and activity load, you are not likely to go wrong with Membase.

What about HBase and Hypertable?

In the previous section on scalability, I gave my entire vote in favor of the column-family stores. When it comes to supporting the rich data models, though, these are generally not the most favorable choices. The upfront choice of row-keys for lookup and only column-family-centric model metadata support is usually considered inadequate. With a powerful abstraction layer on top of column-family stores, a lot becomes possible.

Google started the column-family store revolution. Google also created the data modeling abstraction on top of its column-family store for its very popular app engine. The GAE data modeling support provides rich data modeling using Python and Java. (Chapter 10 has details on this topic.) With the DataNucleus JDO and JPA support, you can use the popular object modeling abstractions in Java to persist data to HBase and Hypertable. You can also draw inspiration from the non-relational support in Django that works well on the app engine.

Querying Support

Storage is one part of the puzzle. The other is querying the stored data. Easily and effectively querying data is almost mandatory for any database to be considered seriously. It can be especially important when building the operational data store for applications with which people are interacting. An RDBMS thrives on SQL support, which makes accessing and querying data easy. Standardized syntax and semantics make it an attractive choice. The first chapter in this book talks about the quest for a SQL-like query language in the world of NoSQL and the subsequent chapters show how it is implemented.

Among document databases, MongoDB provides the best querying capabilities. Best is a relative term, and developers argue about what they consider superior to alternatives, but I base my judgment on three factors: similarity to SQL, an easy syntax, and an easy learning curve. CouchDB's querying capabilities are equally powerful and rather more straightforward once you understand the concepts of views and design documents. However, the concept of views as CouchDB defines it is new and can pose initial challenges to developers.

For key/value pairs and in-memory stores, nothing is more feature-rich than Redis as far as querying capabilities go. Redis has one of the most exhaustive sets of methods available for querying the data structures it stores. To add icing to the cake, it is all nicely documented. Read about the access methods at `http://redis.io/commands`.

Column-family stores like HBase have little to offer as far as rich querying capabilities go. However, an associated project called Hive makes it possible to query HBase using SQL-like syntax and semantics. Chapter 12 covers Hive. Hypertable defines a query language called HQL and also supports Hive.

Bringing Hive into the mix raises the question of manipulating data for operational usage versus accessing it for batch processing and business intelligence. Hive is not an interactive tool in a way SQL is to RDBMS. Hive resembles SQL in syntax but is really a way to abstract MapReduce-style manipulations. Hive allows you to use SQL like predicate-driven syntax instead of map and reduce function definitions to carry batch data manipulation operations on the data set.

Access and Interface Availability

MongoDB has the notion of drivers. Drivers for most mainstream libraries are available for interfacing and interacting with MongoDB. CouchDB uses web-standard ways of interaction and so you can connect to it using any programming language that supports the web idiom of communication. Wrappers for some languages make communication to CouchDB work like drivers for MongoDB, though CouchDB always has the RESTful HTTP interface available.

Redis, Membase, Riak, HBase, Hypertable, Cassandra, and Voldemort have support for language bindings to connect from most mainstream languages. Many of these wrappers use language-independent services layers like Thrift or serialization mechanisms like Avro under the hood. So it becomes important to understand the performance characteristics of the various serialization formats.

One good benchmark that provides insight into the performance characteristics of serialization formats on the JVM is the jvm-serializers project at `https://github.com/eishay/jvm-serializers/wiki/`. The performance measures via the efforts of this project relate to a number of data formats. The formats covered are as follows:

➤ **protobuf 2.3.0** — Google data interchange format. `http://code.google.com/p/protobuf/`

➤ **thrift 0.4.0** — Open sourced by Facebook. Commonly used by a few NoSQL products, especially HBase, Hypertable, and Cassandra. `http://incubator.apache.org/thrift/`

➤ **avro 1.3.2** — An Apache project. Replacing Thrift in some NoSQL products. `http://avro.apache.org/`

➤ **kryo 1.03** — Object graph serialization framework for Java. `http://code.google.com/p/kryo/`

➤ **hessian 4.0.3** — Binary web services protocol. `http://hessian.caucho.com/`

➤ **sbinary 0.3.1-SNAPSHOT** — Describing binary format for scala types. `https://github.com/harrah/sbinary`

➤ **google-gson 1.6** — Library to convert Java objects to JSON. `http://code.google.com/p/google-gson/`

➤ **jackson 1.7.1** — Java JSON-processor. `http://jackson.codehaus.org/`

➤ **javolution 5.5.1** — Java for real-time and embedded systems. `http://javolution.org/`

➤ **protostuff 1.0.0.M7** — Serialization that leverages protobuf. `http://code.google.com/p/protostuff/`

➤ **woodstox 4.0.7** — High-performance XML processor. `http://woodstox.codehaus.org/`

➤ **aalto 0.9.5** — Aalto XML processor. `www.cowtowncoder.com/hatchery/aalto/index.html`

➤ **fast-infoset 1.2.6** — Open-source implementation of Fast infoset for binary XML. `http://fi.java.net/`

➤ **xstream 1.3.1** — Library to serialize XML and back. `http://xstream.codehaus.org/`

The performance runs are on a JVM but the results may be as relevant to other platforms as well. The results show that protobuf, protostuff, kryo, and the manual process are among the most efficient for serialization and de-serialization. Kyro and Avro are among the formats that are most efficient in terms of serialized size and compressed size.

Having gained a view into the performance of formats, the next section segues into benchmarks of NoSQL products themselves.

BENCHMARKING PERFORMANCE

The Yahoo! Cloud Services Benchmark (YCSB) is the best known benchmarking infrastructure for comparing NoSQL products. It's not without its limitations but it does provide a well-rounded insight into how the different NoSQL products stack up. The YCSB toolkit contains two important utilities:

➤ A workload generator

➤ Sample load that the workload generator uses

The YCSB project is online at `https://github.com/brianfrankcooper/YCSB`. Yahoo! has run tests on a number of popular NoSQL products as a part of the benchmark. The last published results include the following:

➤ Sherpa/PNUT Bigtable-like systems (HBase, Hypertable, HTable, Megastore)

➤ Azure

➤ Apache Cassandra

➤ Amazon Web Services (S3, SimpleDB, EBS)

➤ CouchDB

➤ Voldemort

➤ Dynomite

➤ Tokyo Cabinet

➤ Redis

➤ MongoDB

The tests are carried out in a tiered manner, measuring latency and throughput at each tier. Tier 1 focuses on performance by maximizing workload on a given hardware. The hardware is kept constant and workload is increased until the hardware is saturated. Tier 2 focuses on scalability. This means hardware is added as workload increases. The tier 2 benchmarks measure latency as workload and hardware availability are scaled up proportionally.

Workloads have different configurations for measuring performance and scalability in a balanced and exhaustive manner. The popular test cases are illustrated next.

50/50 Read and Update

A 50/50 read and update scenario could be considered an update-heavy test case. Results show that under this test case Apache Cassandra outperforms the competition on both read and update latencies. HBase comes close but stays behind Cassandra. Cassandra is able to perform more than 10,000 operations (50/50 read and update) per second with an average of around 25 milliseconds of read latency. Updates seem to be better than even reads with an average latency of just over 10+ milliseconds for the same workload of more than 10,000 operations per second. YCSB includes MySQL in addition to the NoSQL products. Although I ignore the RDBMS vs. NoSQL benchmarks in this chapter, it's interesting to see that MySQL's read and update latencies are comparable until around 4,000 operations per seconds but latency tends to increase quickly as the numbers grow to more than 5,000 operations per second.

95/5 Read and Update

A 95/5 read and update test case is a read-heavy case. This test case reveals and concurs with a few of the theories stated in this book such as the ones that state the sorted ordered column-family stores perform best for contiguous range reads. HBase seems to deliver consistent performance for reads, irrespective of the number of operations per second. The 5 percent updates in HBase have practically no latency. MySQL delivers the best performance for read-only cases. This is possibly because data is returned from cache. Combining HBase with a distributed cache like Memcached or Membase could match MySQL read performance and scale better with increased workloads. Cassandra demonstrates impressive performance in a read-heavy case as well, outperforming HBase in the tests. Remember, though, that Cassandra follows an eventual consistency model and all writes are appended to the commit log.

Scans

HBase is meant to outperform other databases for scans, short 1–100 records and range scans, and the test confirms that. Cassandra shows unpredictable performance as far as scans go.

Scalability Test

As workloads are increased and hardware is added the performance is fairly consistent for Cassandra and HBase. Some results show HBase being unstable when there are less than three nodes. An important aspect of adding hardware is elasticity. Elasticity measures how data gets rebalanced as additional nodes get added. Cassandra seems to perform poorly and seems to take long periods of time to stabilize. HBase shows consistent performance per rebalancing is affected by compaction.

As mentioned earlier, the performance tests tell a story but basing decisions solely on the tests is possibly misleading. Also, products are continuously evolving and tests run on different versions of a product produce different results. Combining performance measures with feature-based comparison is likely a more prudent choice than depending on either alone.

The Hypertable tests are not part of the YCSB tests. The Hypertable tests and YCSB tests are separate and independent tests. YCSB tests are more broad-based and apply to a number of NoSQL and RDBMS products, whereas the Hypertable tests focus on testing the performance of sorted ordered column-family stores.

Hypertable Tests

The Hypertable team carried out a set of tests to compare and contrast HBase and Hypertable, two Google Bigtable clones. The tests provide interesting insights. The carried out tests were in line with what the research paper on Google Bigtable proposed. Read section 7 of the Bigtable research paper, available online at `http://labs.google.com/papers/bigtable.html` to understand the tests.

The results consistently demonstrated that Hypertable outperformed HBase in most measures. You can access details on the tests and the results at `www.hypertable.com/pub/perfeval/test1/`. Some significant findings are explained next.

Hypertable dynamically adjusts how much memory it allocates to each subsystem depending on the workload. For read-intensive cases, Hypertable allocates most of the memory to the block cache. HBase has a fixed cache allocation, which is 20 percent of the Java heap. Flipping the measure from the latency standpoint, it becomes clear that Hypertable consistently involves less latency than HBase does, but the difference is stark when the data size is smaller. In the lower limit case of only 2 GBs of data, all data can be loaded up in the cache.

The results of tests that compared Hypertable and HBase for random write, sequential read, and scan performance also showed that Hypertable performed better in each of these cases. When you run a clustered data store to manage your large data, sometimes performance differences like these can have cost ramifications. Better performance could translate to lower compute cycle and resource consumption, which could mean greater cost savings.

Numerous other benchmarks from various product vendors are available, including the following:

➤ **Tokyo Cabinet Benchmarks** — `http://tokyocabinet.sourceforge.net/benchmark.pdf`

➤ **How fast is Redis** — `http://redis.io/topics/benchmarks`

➤ **Riak benchmark** — `https://bitbucket.org/basho/basho_bench/`

➤ **VoltDB: Key/value benchmarking** — `http://voltdb.com/blog/key/value-benchmarking`

➤ **Sort benchmark** — `http://sortbenchmark.org/`

CONTEXTUAL COMPARISON

The previous two sections compared the NoSQL options on the basis of features and benchmarks. This section provides contextual information that relates a few NoSQL products to the conditions that led to their creation and evolution.

Not all NoSQL products are equal. Not all NoSQL products stack up equally either in terms of features or benchmarks. However, each NoSQL product has its own history, motivation, use case, and unique value proposition. Aligning yourself with these viewpoints, and especially with the product's history and evolution, will help you understand which NoSQL product is suitable for the job at hand.

For the popular document databases, explore the following online resources:

➤ **CouchDB** — Watch a video (`www.erlang-factory.com/conference/SFBayAreaErlangFactory2009/speakers/DamienKatz`) from an Erlang Factory's 2009 session, where CouchDB founder Damien Katz talks about the History of CouchDB development from a very personal point of view. He talks about the inspirations for CouchDB and why he decided to move his wife and kids to a cheaper place and live off savings to build the database. He talks about the decision to switch to Erlang and the transition to joining the Apache Foundation. The video brings to light the motivations and reasons for the product's existence.

➤ **MongoDB** — Read the unofficial history of MongoDB that Kristina Chodrow wrote on her blog: `www.snailinaturtleneck.com/blog/2010/08/23/history-of-mongodb/`.

For the established key/value-centric databases, explore these:

➤ **Redis** — Read a mailing list post (`http://groups.google.com/group/redis-db/browse_thread/thread/0c706a43bc78b0e5/17c21c48642e4936?#17c21c48642e4936`) by Antirez (Salavtore Sanfillippo) after he decided to eat his own dog food and switch lloogg.com to use Redis instead of MySQL.

➤ **Tokyo Cabinet** — Read the Tokyo Cabinet value proposition on the product homepage at `http://fallabs.com/tokyocabinet/`.

➤ **Kyoto Cabinet** — The Tokyo Cabinet folks created a new product called Kyoto Cabinet. Read details online at `http://fallabs.com/kyotocabinet/`.

The history of Bigtable and Dynamo clones — HBase, Hypertable, Cassandra, and Riak — is primarily that of an attempt to copy the success of Google and Amazon. Studying the initial history of evolution of these clones does not reveal anything substantially more than a quest to copy the good ideas that emerged at Google and Amazon. Certainly, copying the ideas wasn't easy and involved a process of discovery and innovation. As users leverage these products for newer and varied use cases, the products continue to rapidly evolve. Evolution of these products is likely to introduce many newer features beyond those implemented as a part of the original inspiration.

NoSQL is a young and emerging domain and although understanding the context of a product's evolution in the domain is beneficial, a lot of the history of many of the NoSQL products is still being written.

SUMMARY

This chapter provided a terse yet meaningful comparison of the popular NoSQL products. The chapter does not claim to be exhaustive or promise a panacea for all problems. Adoption of a NoSQL product needs to be done with care and only after understanding a product's features, performance characteristics, and history.

The chapter did not explain all the features or provide a model to choose a product. Instead it built on what has been covered in the previous chapters in this book. The illustration highlighted a few important facts and summarized essential viewpoints. The decision, as always, should and must be yours.

15

Coexistence

WHAT'S IN THIS CHAPTER?

➤ Getting ready for polyglot persistence

➤ Understanding the database technologies suitable for immutable data sets

➤ Choosing the right database to facilitate ease of application development

➤ Using both RDBMS and NoSQL products together

The emergence of NoSQL and the growing excitement around it is making developers wonder if NoSQL options are a replacement to RDBMS. This has led some to claim that RDBMS is dead and that NoSQL is the next predominant database technology. It has also spurred opposing reactions where arguments are being put forward to prove that NoSQL is a "flash in the pan." The truth is far removed from either of those radical claims. NoSQL and RDBMS are both important and have their place. Peaceful coexistence of the two technologies is reality. Plurality in technology has always been the norm and polyglot persistence is the present and the future. This chapter explains a few cases and the process required to get ready for polyglot persistence.

In the first situation, I explore a case of leveraging the NoSQL ideology within a popular open-source RDBMS product, MySQL. Subsequently, I explore the database requirements for immutable data sets and in the domain of data warehousing and business intelligence. I also present the situations where the choice of an appropriate database technology makes the task of application development easier.

USING MYSQL AS A NOSQL SOLUTION

So far, this book has treated RDBMS and NoSQL as two distinct technologies. This separation of concerns is important for understanding the NoSQL concepts as opposed to SQL and relational tables. However, the two schools of thought are not completely removed from each other. The two share many underlying ideas. One little glimpse of that appears in the context of the structure of indexes in RDBMS and in some of the NoSQL products, which often use B-tree and B-tree-like structures for storage. Even so, the support for schema and SQL provides a unique identity to RDBMS.

One of the most popular open-source relational databases is MySQL. MySQL is modular in design, provides pluggable storage engines, and allows pluggable modules to support additional features as desired. At a conceptual level a MySQL server, accessed from a client, could be depicted as in Figure 15-1.

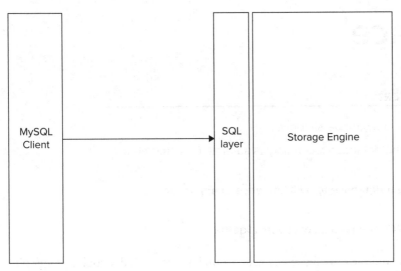

FIGURE 15-1

MySQL is a fast database server. Its typical read and write response times for a few thousand rows are impressive and sufficient for most use cases. As the amount of data increases, you can boost MySQL performance by running the server on a machine that has ample memory at its disposal. MySQL, like most RDBMS products, caches fetched rows in its storage engine's buffer pool, thereby providing improved performance on subsequent fetches of the same rows. However, with increased data the SQL overheads become substantial. Each fetch, especially when frequent and concurrently issued by multiple clients, leads to several expensive actions:

- ➤ Parsing SQL statements
- ➤ Opening tables
- ➤ Locking tables
- ➤ Making SQL execution plans
- ➤ Unlocking tables
- ➤ Closing tables
- ➤ Managing concurrent access using mutexes and threads

Therefore, to boost performance under heavy loads, you need to cache as much data as possible. Memcached is a typical in-memory caching solution that works well with MySQL. Rows are cached and served to clients exclusively from memory. When large amounts of memory — say over 32 GB — is available, MySQL with Memcached works well to serve more than 400,000 queries per second. These queries of course are primary key lookups and not ad-hoc joins or such. The assumption also is that the entire relevant data set can fit in memory and does not need to be read from the disk. Disk I/O is very expensive as compared to in-memory access and can impose a large overhead.

Memcached was presented earlier in this book as a viable key/value-pair store. Alternatives like Membase, Redis, Tokyo Cabinet, and Kyoto Cabinet could be used in conjunction with MySQL to achieve similar performance characteristics. This is a case where an RDBMS — MySQL — is used effectively in conjunction with a NoSQL solution, such as Memcached to serve get lookups by primary key. Figure 15-2 depicts a typical MySQL with the Memcached data store being accessed by a client.

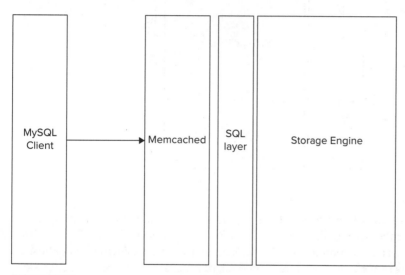

FIGURE 15-2

Using Memcached with MySQL is beneficial but the architecture has its drawbacks:

➤ Data is in-memory in two places: the storage engine buffer and Memcached.

➤ Replication of data between the storage engine and Memcached can have inconsistent states of data.

➤ The data is fetched into Memcached via the SQL layer and so the SQL overhead is still present, even if it's minimized.

➤ Memcached performance is superior only until all relevant data fits in memory. Disk I/O overheads can be high and can make the system slow.

An alternative to using MySQL with Memcached is to bypass the SQL layer and get directly to the storage engine. This is exactly what the HandlerSocket plugin for MySQL does. The HandlerSocket plugin for MySQL is an open-source plugin that allows the bypassing of the SQL layer to access

the underlying MySQL storage engine. The project is hosted online on github at `https://github`
`.com/ahiguti/HandlerSocket-Plugin-for-MySQL`.

The HandlerSocket plugin can be loaded into an existing MySQL server. Loading HandlerSocket
does not switch the SQL layer off. In fact both layers become available. HandlerSocket provides a
NoSQL-like interface to MySQL allowing faster access, especially for primary key-based fetches.
Figure 15-3 shows what a MySQL configuration with HandlerSocket looks like.

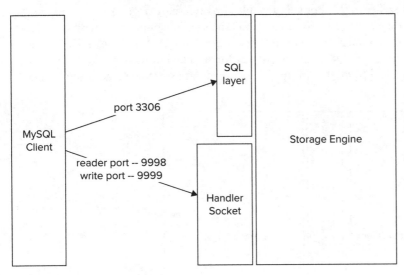

FIGURE 15-3

HandlerSocket implements network protocol, API, and a lightweight connection to interface
directly with a MySQL storage engine, like InnoDB. It allows you to query the MySQL store in the
same flexible and high-performance manner that NoSQL databases offer. Benchmarks published
online at `http://yoshinorimatsunobu.blogspot.com/2010/10/using-mysql-as-nosql-story-`
`for.html` show that up to 750,000 primary key lookup queries per second could be performed with
HandlerSocket. This seems extremely impressive.

HandlerSocket's API does not involve the overhead of opening, locking, unlocking, and closing
tables. Its API is very lightweight and NoSQL-centric as compared to the SQL layer. HandlerSocket
has C++ and Perl APIs available with the distribution. Additional implementations of the
HandlerSocket API for PHP, Java, Python, Ruby, JavaScript, and Scala are available from sources
other than the core distribution. You can get a list of sources of these additional libraries at
`https://github.com/ahiguti/HandlerSocket-Plugin-for-MySQL`. HandlerSocket's network
packets are small and can support several concurrent connections.

Using HandlerSocket is better than using Memcached with the SQL layer, because it not only avoids the
SQL layer but also avoids duplicate caches and the possible inconsistencies in replication. HandlerSocket
interfaces directly with the storage engine, so there are not two replicas but a single store.

The HandlerSocket-based NoSQL solution is especially suitable for high-performance reads. The
base MySQL storage engine provides transactional support and recovery from a crash. You can also

use all the tools and utilities that come with MySQL to monitor and manage the queries. Last but not least, HandlerSocket can easily be plugged into an existing MySQL server, which makes it an extremely flexible solution.

In addition to this NoSQL way of accessing MySQL, MySQL also can be used as the underlying storage of a popular eventually consistent NoSQL data store, Voldemor. The InnoDB storage engine can also be plugged in as the storage engine for Riak.

In some cases, using MySQL as a NoSQL solution is not an option because specific storage schemes offered by document databases, column-family stores, or key/value pairs may be desirable. In such cases you could let RDBMS run the transactional systems and move over much of the rest to NoSQL.

MOSTLY IMMUTABLE DATA STORES

RDBMS offers transactional support and the consistency that NoSQL frequently lacks. Interestingly, this often becomes one of the major reasons for not adopting NoSQL. However, you need to consider the transactional and mutable nature of the data set even before you start evaluating transactional support (or the lack of it) in a database.

Contrary to many developer's beliefs, a lot of modern-day applications have little or no need for transactional support. This is mainly because the data is often written once and read and manipulated many times. If you are wondering what kind of data falls into this category, just open your e-mail or your social media application and verify how many of these systems are about updates or even deletes. Many social media applications, for example those that send messages or tweets or publish and propagate status updates, are primarily written once and consumed many times. A few systems that manage such activity streams may allow updates, but even in such cases updates are usually the result of compensating transactions and not inline updates. Deletes also may be allowed but not necessarily propagated to all recipients in a transactional manner. This means tweets or messages that are deleted might be deleted from the originating service but might not be deleted from all consuming applications. Deletion is usually sent by such services as a compensating message.

The write-once and read-many-times paradigm is also prevalent for RSS updates, e-mails, SMS messages, or feedback. Applications that solicit responses to polls, feedback, ratings, and comments are also often write-once and read-multiple-times type cases. If updates are allowed on such applications, they are usually infrequent.

> *You have seen in the previous chapters that NoSQL databases like HBase, Hypertable, and MongoDB provide row-level atomic updates. These and other databases don't assure ACID transactions over ranges. However, row-level updates are sufficient for many cases where updates are isolated and not applied to groups of data items.*
>
> *A few NoSQL databases like Apache Cassandra, Riak, and LinkedIn Voldemort are eventually consistent databases. This means these eventually consistent databases do not offer a Paxos or any similar algorithm-based, strong consistency but have a window of inconsistency as updates spread through the replicated nodes. Even such databases are consistent within a short time frame and many applications are comfortable with an inconsistent state for short periods of time.*

Many large social media venues like Facebook, Twitter, and LinkedIn are big users of NoSQL and RDBMS.

Polyglot Persistence at Facebook

Facebook in particular uses MySQL for many mission-critical features. Facebook is also a big HBase user. Facebook's optimizations to MySQL were presented in a Tech Talk, the recordings of which are available online at `www.livestream.com/facebookevents/video?clipId=flv_cc08bf93-7013-41e3-81c9-bfc906ef8442`. Facebook is about large volume and superior performance and its MySQL optimizations are no exception to that. Its work is focused on maximizing queries per second and controlling the variance of the request-response times. The numbers presented in the November 2010 presentation are very impressive. Some of the key metrics shared in the context of its online transaction processing system were as follows:

➤ Read responses were an average of 4ms and writes were 5ms.

➤ Maximum rows read per second scaled up to a value of 450 million, which is obviously very large compared to most systems.

➤ 13 million queries per second were processed at peak.

➤ 3.2 million row updates and 5.2 million InnoDB disk operations were performed in boundary cases.

Facebook has focused on reliability more than maximizing queries per second, although the queries-per-second numbers are very impressive too. Active sub-second-level monitoring and profiling allows Facebook database teams to identify points of server performance fractures, called stalls. Slower queries and problems have been progressively identified and corrected, leading to an optimal system. You can get the details from the presentation.

Facebook is also the birthplace of Cassandra. Facebook has lately abandoned Cassandra and gone in favor of HBase. The current Facebook messaging infrastructure is built on HBase. Facebook's new messaging system supports storage of more than 135 billion messages a month. As mentioned earlier, the system is built on top of HBase. A note from the engineering team, accessible online at `www.facebook.com/note.php?note_id=454991608919`, explains why Facebook chose HBase over other alternatives. Facebook chose HBase for multiple reasons. First, the Paxos-based strong consistency model was favored. HBase scales well and has the infrastructure available for a highly replicated setup. Failover and load balancing come out of the box and the underlying distributed filesystem, HDFS provides an additional level of redundancy and fault tolerance in the stack. In addition, ZooKeeper, the co-ordination system, could be reused with some modifications to support a user service.

Therefore, it's clear that companies like Facebook have adopted polyglot persistence strategies that enable them to use the right tool for the job. Facebook engineering teams have not shied away from making changes to the system to suit their needs, but they have demonstrated that choosing either DBMS or NoSQL is not as relevant as choosing an appropriate database. Another theme that has emerged time and again from Facebook is that it has used a tool that it is familiar with the most. Instead of chasing a trend, it has used tools that its engineers can tweak and work with. For example, sticking with MySQL and PHP has been good for Facebook because it has managed to tweak them to suit its needs. Some have argued that legacy has stuck, but clearly performance numbers show that Facebook has figured out how to make it scalable.

Like Facebook, Twitter and LinkedIn have adopted polyglot persistence. Twitter, for example, uses MySQL and Cassandra actively. Twitter also uses a graph database, named FlockDB, for maintaining relationships, such as who's following whom and who you receive phone notifications from. Twitter's popularity and data volume have grown immensely over the years. Kevin Weil's September 2010 presentation (`www.slideshare.net/kevinweil/analyzing-big-data-at-twitter-web-20-expo-nyc-sep-2010`) claims tweets and direct messages now add up to 12 TB/day, which when linearly scaled out imply over 4 petabytes every year. These numbers are bound to continue to grow and become larger and larger as more people adopt Twitter and use tweets to communicate with the world. Manipulating this large volume of data is a huge challenge. Twitter uses Hadoop and MapReduce functionality to analyze the large data set. Twitter leverages the high-level language Pig (`http://pig.apache.org/`) for data analysis. Pig statements lead to MapReduce jobs on a Hadoop cluster. A lot of the core storage at Twitter still depends on MySQL. MySQL is heavily used for multiple features within Twitter. Cassandra is used for a select few use cases like storing geocentric data.

LinkedIn, like Twitter, relies on a host of different types of data stores. Jay Kreps at the Hadoop Summit provided a preview into the large data architecture and manipulation at LinkedIn last year. The slides from that presentation are available online at `www.slideshare.net/ydn/6-data-applicationlinkedinhadoopsummmit2010`. LinkedIn uses Hadoop for many large-scale analytics jobs like probabilistically predicting people you may know. The data set acted upon by the Hadoop cluster is fairly large and usually in the range of more than 120 billion relationships a day. It is carried out by around 82 Hadoop jobs that require over 16 TB of intermediate data. The probabilistic graphs are copied over from the batch offline storage to a live NoSQL cluster. The NoSQL database is Voldemort, an Apache Dynamo clone that represents data in key/value pairs. The relationship graph data is read-only and Voldemort's eventual consistency model doesn't cause any problems. The relationship data is processed in a batch mode but filtered through a faceted search in real time. These filters may lead to the exclusion of people who a person has indicated they don't know.

Looking at Facebook, Twitter, and LinkedIn it becomes clear that polyglot persistence has its benefits and leads to an optimal stack, where each data store is appropriately used for the use case in hand.

Data Warehousing and Business Intelligence

An entire category of applications is built to store and manipulate archived data sets. Usually, these data warehouses are built out of old transactional data, which is typically referred to as fact data. Data, in the data warehouse, is then analyzed and manipulated to uncover patterns or decipher trends. All such archived and warehoused data is read-only and the transactional requirements for such data stores is minimal. These data sets have traditionally been stored in special-purpose data stores, which have the capability to store large volumes of data and analyze the data on the basis of multiple dimensions.

With the advent of Hadoop, some of the large-scale analytics is done by MapReduce-based jobs. The MapReduce-based model of analytics is being enriched by the availability of querying tools like Hive and workflow definition high-level languages like Pig. Added to this, the innovation in the MapReduce space is ever expanding. The Apache Mahout project builds a machine learning infrastructure on top of Hadoop. Therefore, you could run collaborative filtering algorithms or Naive Bayes classifiers over a Hadoop MapReduce infrastructure using Mahout.

WEB FRAMEWORKS AND NOSQL

Building scalable web applications can be a very challenging experience. Requirements keep changing and data keeps evolving. In such situations traditional RDBMSs tend to be a little less flexible. Document databases are a good fit for some of these use cases.

Using Rails with NoSQL

Ruby on Rails needs no introduction. It is by far the most popular agile web development framework. Adhering to convention over configuration, Rails make web development easy and fun. Rails implements a Model-View-Controller (MVC) framework, where RESTful verbs are the primary and default operations on underlying models. The use of ActiveRecord enables automatic mapping of model objects to data persisted in relational tables. Views provide the user interface to manipulate the underlying data and controllers facilitate the coordination between the model and the view.

If you are an agile web developer and use Rails to get your job done, you can easily swap in MongoDB for MySQL, PostgreSQL, or any other RDBMS. First-class support for MongoDB with the help of mongo_mapper does the trick.

To use MongoDB with Rails, first switch ActiveRecord off. You don't need ActiveRecord, the ORM layer when using MongoDB. If you have Rails installed successfully, which on most platforms implies running the following command after Ruby and RubyGems are set up:

```
gem install rails
```

you can easily create an app and instruct it to avoid ActiveRecord. You create a Rails app without ActiveRecord as follows:

```
rails new sample_app -skip-active-record
```

Next, install mongo_mapper, which is distributed as a gem and can be installed using a familiar syntax, which is as follows:

```
gem install mongo_mapper
```

After mongo_mapper is installed add it to the gemfile so that the bundler can make it available to a Rails application. Modify the gemfile to the following:

```
require 'rubygems'
require 'mongo'
source 'http://gemcutter.org'

gem "rails", "3.0.0"
gem "mongo_mapper"
```

Mongo and rubygems are required before gem definitions to serve as a workaround for a bson_ext issue.

Next, run bundle install to download and install the required gems.

After the bundler is ready, create a file in `config/initializers` and add the following content to that initializer file:

```
MongoMapper.connection = Mongo::Connection.new('localhost', 27017)
MongoMapper.database = "#sample_app-#{Rails.env}"

if defined?(PhusionPassenger)
    PhusionPassenger.on_event(:starting_worker_process) do |forked|
        MongoMapper.connection.connect if forked
    end
end
```

A simple `Model` class that leverages mongo_mapper could be as follows:

```
class UserData
    include MongoMapper::Document

    key :user_id, Integer
    key :user_name, String
end
```

Now a model object can be persisted using a controller like so:

```
class MyActionController < ApplicationController
  def create_user

    @auser = UserData.create(
            {
              :user_id => 1,
              :user_name => "John Doe",
              :updated_at => Time.now
            })
    @auser.save()
  end
end
```

This action can be invoked by a REST-style URL as follows:

```
get 'my_action/create_user'
```

Rails is not the only web framework; others include Django (Python) and Spring (Java).

Using Django with NoSQL

Django is to the Python community what Rails is to Ruby developers. Django is a lightweight web framework that allows for rapid prototyping and fast development. The Django idiom is also based on an ORM to map models to databases. The SQL standard and the presence of a dis-intermediating ORM layer makes it possible for Django applications to swap one RDBMS for another. However, doing the same for the NoSQL world is not common. In fact, often code written to work with one NoSQL product is so proprietary that it cannot be used with an alternative NoSQL product. Application sources that work seamlessly across NoSQL products and with both SQL and NoSQL products are desirable.

In the NoSQL world the concept of indexes and the ways of joining data sets varies widely from one product to another. Making Django applications work with multiple NoSQL products involves writing custom hooks for index management and data aggregation and joins for each NoSQL product.

Last but not least, NoSQL is a popular choice for cloud platforms but portability across these platforms is a very challenging issue. For example, Google App Engine (GAE) provides a modeling abstraction on top of the Google Bigtable, whereas Amazon Web Services provides a hosted document database in SimpleDB. Django applications for the GAE or the Amazon SimpleDB get tightly coupled to the platform and migrating applications between these two platforms or to another cloud service provider becomes extremely difficult. Sometimes, such moves almost require a complete rewrite, creating vendor lock-in and increasing costs and effort required for migrating from one platform to another.

The django-nonrel independent open-source project was put together to address all these issues and to provide a common level of abstraction for Django to work with multiple NoSQL products. The project source is available online at `https://bitbucket.org/wkornewald/django-nonrel/src`. Waldemar Kornewald and Thomas Wanschik are the creators of and core contributors to this project.

The django-nonrel project patches the core Django distribution only enough to make it work with databases other than RDBMS. The heavy lifting is done by django-dbindexer, which takes care of denormalizing and joining data sets in the NoSQL world.

Django-dbindexer is an early stage open-source project. It's hosted online at `https://bitbucket.org/wkornewald/django-dbindexer/src`. Django-dbindexer serves as the layer that sits on top of NoSQL databases. It's the level that takes care of the differences among the NoSQL products, so case-sensitive queries and support for joins (or the lack of them) is taken care of at this level. For example, case-insensitive filters on MongoDB can't use indexes. Complete scans as opposed to indexes are inefficient. In the django-dbindexer layer, such inefficient filters can be treated as case-sensitive filters and therefore an index can be leveraged.

The lack of a common powerful query language, like SQL in RDBMS, also poses challenges when supporting certain queries across NoSQL platforms. Django-dbindexer simplifies and standardizes the query API as well. So a workaround code in the GAE as follows:

```
# models.py:

class MyModel(models.Model):
    name = models.CharField(max_length=64)
    lowercase_name = models.CharField(max_length=64, editable=False)
    last_modified = models.DateTimeField(auto_now=True)
    month_last_modified = models.IntegerField(editable=False)

    def save(self, *args, **kwargs):
        self.lowercase_name = self.name.lower()
        self.month_last_modified = self.last_modified.month
        super(MyModel, self).save(*args, **kwargs)
```

```
def run_query(name, month):
    MyModel.objects.filter(lowercase_name=name.lower(),
                           month_last_modified=month)
```

models.py

gets replaced by more elegant, clean, and reusable code like this:

Available for download on Wrox.com

```
# models.py:

class MyModel(models.Model):
    name = models.CharField(max_length=64)
    last_modified = models.DateTimeField(auto_now=True)

    def run_query(name, month):
        MyModel.objects.filter(name__iexact=name, last_modified__month=month)

# dbindexes.py:

from models import MyModel
from dbindexer.api import register_index
register_index(MyModel, {'name': 'iexact', 'last_modified': 'month'})
```

models_with_dbindexer.py

You can read more about django-nonrel by accessing the documentation, available online at `www.allbuttonspressed.com/projects/django-nonrel`.

Using Spring Data

Though Rails and Django are popular web frameworks for agile development, a lot of enterprise developers still use Java to build their new-generation applications. Spring is a popular Java dependency injection framework that has been widely adopted around the world. Spring has included NoSQL support via its Spring Data project. You can access information on the Spring Data project at `www.springsource.org/spring-data`. Spring Data not only provides an abstraction layer for many NoSQL products but also facilitates MapReduce-based processing and access to cloud platforms.

In the following section, I put together a small example using Spring Data to access and interact with Redis. Spring Data supports Redis via a sub-project. It supports other NoSQL products using a similar mechanism. Java client libraries to interface and interact with Redis exist today. One such library is JRedis, `http://code.google.com/p/jredis/`. Another is jedis, `https://github.com/xetorthio/jedis`. Spring Data abstracts out these Java client libraries under RedisTemplate much the same way as Spring abstracts out JDBC access via JdbcTemplate or Hibernate access via HibernateTemplate. The objective of the template is to shield the user from the low-level details of the API.

To get started, download and build the Spring Data Redis sub-project from `https://github .com/SpringSource/spring-data-keyvalue`. For simplicity and faster development, you can use the SpringSource Tool Suite (STS), `www.springsource.com/developer/sts`, and create a new Spring project using a project template. STS uses Maven to configure and build a project so the definitions are specified in a project's project object model (POM). You can read more about Maven at `http://maven.apache.org/`. Modify the `pom.xml` file to configure it to use the Redis Spring Data sub-project. A typical `pom.xml` is shown in Listing 15-1.

LISTING 15-1: Spring Data Redis project POM

```xml
<?xml version="1.0" encoding="UTF-8"?>
xmlns="http://maven.apache.org/POM/4.0.0"
xmlns:xsi="http://www.w3.org/2001/XMLSchema-instance"
xsi:schemaLocation="http://maven.apache.org/POM/4.0.0
http://maven.apache.org/maven-v4_0_0.xsd">
  <modelVersion>4.0.0</modelVersion>
  <groupId>com.treasuryofideas.pronosql</groupId>
  <artifactId>redis</artifactId>
  <name>redis-dictionary</name>
  <packaging>war</packaging>
  <version>1.0.0-BUILD-SNAPSHOT</version>
  <properties>
    <java-version>1.6</java-version>
    <org.springframework-version>3.0.5.RELEASE</org.springframework-version>
    <org.springframework.roo-version>1.0.2.RELEASE</org.springframework.roo-version>
    <org.aspectj-version>1.6.9</org.aspectj-version>
    <redis.version>1.0.0.M2-SNAPSHOT</redis.version>
  </properties>
  <dependencies>
    <!-- Spring -->
    <dependency>
      <groupId>org.springframework</groupId>
      <artifactId>spring-context</artifactId>
      <version>${org.springframework-version}</version>
      <exclusions>
        <!-- Exclude Commons Logging in favor of
SLF4j -->
        <exclusion>
          <groupId>commons-logging</groupId>
          <artifactId>commons-logging</artifactId>
        </exclusion>
      </exclusions>
    </dependency>

    <!-- AspectJ -->
    <dependency>
      <groupId>org.aspectj</groupId>
      <artifactId>aspectjrt</artifactId>
      <version>${org.aspectj-version}</version>
    </dependency>

    <dependency>
      <groupId>log4j</groupId>
      <artifactId>log4j</artifactId>
      <version>1.2.15</version>
      <exclusions>
```

```xml
          <exclusion>
            <groupId>javax.mail</groupId>
            <artifactId>mail</artifactId>
          </exclusion>
          <exclusion>
            <groupId>javax.jms</groupId>
            <artifactId>jms</artifactId>
          </exclusion>
          <exclusion>
            <groupId>com.sun.jdmk</groupId>
            <artifactId>jmxtools</artifactId>
          </exclusion>
          <exclusion>
            <groupId>com.sun.jmx</groupId>
            <artifactId>jmxri</artifactId>
          </exclusion>
        </exclusions>
        <scope>runtime</scope>
    </dependency>

    <!-- @Inject -->
    <dependency>
        <groupId>javax.inject</groupId>
        <artifactId>javax.inject</artifactId>
        <version>1</version>
    </dependency>

    <!-- Test -->
    <dependency>
        <groupId>junit</groupId>
        <artifactId>junit</artifactId>
        <version>4.8.1</version>
        <scope>test</scope>
    </dependency>

    <dependency>
        <groupId>org.springframework.data</groupId>
        <artifactId>spring-data-redis</artifactId>
        <version>${redis.version}</version>
    </dependency>

    <dependency>
        <groupId>org.springframework.data</groupId>
        <artifactId>spring-data-keyvalue-core</artifactId>
        <version>${redis.version}</version>
    </dependency>

    <dependency>
        <groupId>org.springframework</groupId>
        <artifactId>spring-aop</artifactId>
        <version>${org.springframework-version}</version>
    </dependency>
    <dependency>
        <groupId>org.springframework</groupId>
        <artifactId>spring-aspects</artifactId>
```

```xml
          <version>${org.springframework-version}</version>
      </dependency>

      <dependency>
        <groupId>org.apache.commons</groupId>
        <artifactId>commons-io</artifactId>
        <version>1.3.2</version>
      </dependency>

      <dependency>
        <groupId>org.springframework</groupId>
        <artifactId>spring-test</artifactId>
        <version>${org.springframework-version}</version>
        <scope>test</scope>
        <exclusions>
          <exclusion>
            <groupId>commons-logging</groupId>
            <artifactId>commons-logging</artifactId>
          </exclusion>
        </exclusions>
      </dependency>
    </dependencies>
    <repositories>
      <repository>
        <id>spring-maven-milestone</id>
        Springframework Maven Repository
        <url>http://maven.springframework.org/milestone</url>
      </repository>
      <repository>
        <id>spring-maven-snapshot</id>
        <snapshots>
          <enabled>true</enabled>
        </snapshots>
        Springframework Maven SNAPSHOT Repository
        <url>http://maven.springframework.org/snapshot</url>
      </repository>
    </repositories>
    <build>
      <plugins>
        <plugin>
          <groupId>org.apache.maven.plugins</groupId>
          <artifactId>maven-compiler-plugin</artifactId>
          <configuration>
            <source>${java-version}</source>
            <target>${java-version}</target>
          </configuration>
        </plugin>
        <plugin>
          <groupId>org.apache.maven.plugins</groupId>
          <artifactId>maven-dependency-plugin</artifactId>
          <executions>
            <execution>
              <id>install</id>
              <phase>install</phase>
              <goals>
                <goal>sources</goal>
```

```
            </goals>
          </execution>
        </executions>
      </plugin>
    </plugins>
  </build>
</project>
```

Maven makes it elegant and easy to build a project, define its dependencies, and manage these dependencies. The POM file in the preceding listing defines all dependencies on external libraries required to build the project. External libraries are downloaded and set up when the POM file is used to manage the project life cycle.

Next, I build a simple key/value example using Redis and Spring Data. In this very rudimentary example I build a tag synonyms store. Such a store would have a tag as the key. All tags that have similar or the same meaning as the key tag would constitute the value. For example, a tag like "web" may be the key and tags like "internet" and "www" could be values. You can easily store such data structure using a Redis list. To access this tag synonyms data store from Spring you will need to build a DAO class as shown in Listing 15-2.

Available for download on Wrox.com

LISTING 15-2: TagSynonymsDao

```
import org.springframework.data.keyvalue.redis.core.RedisTemplate;

public class TagSynonymsDao {

  private RedisTemplate<String, String> template;

  public TagSynonymsDao(RedisTemplate template) {
    this.template = template;
  }

  public Long addSynonymTag(String keyTag, String synonymTag) {
    Long index = template.opsForList().rightPush(keyTag, synonymTag);
    return index;
  }

  public List getAllSynonymTags(String keyTag) {
    List<String> synonymTags = template.opsForList().range(word, 0, -1);
    return synonymTags;
    }

    public void removeSynonymTags(String... synonymTags) {
      template.delete(Arrays.asList(synonymTags));
}


  }
```

The listing above demonstrates RedisTemplate in the context of the TagSynonyms example. The data access class interacts with Redis via the template and uses the methods defined in the RedisTemplate to push an element, run a range query, and delete an element.

That's all for this rudimentary example but I hope you get a sense of the available and emerging abstractions that would allow you to work smoothly among NoSQL products and between RDBMS and NoSQL options.

MIGRATING FROM RDBMS TO NOSQL

Migrating from a structured schema to a schema-less form is not very hard. In many cases you could simply export the data from RDBMS tables and move them into NoSQL collections. However, things get complicated when the NoSQL database is a column-family, sorted ordered, or a key/value store. Changes in paradigm often lead to redesign efforts.

The greater impedance mismatch is around ad-hoc querying and secondary indexes, which are often difficult to support in a NoSQL environment. NoSQL looks at the data store from a query perspective and not from a generic storage viewpoint.

To facilitate data importation from RDBMS to Hadoop for NoSQL-style manipulations, Cloudera has created an open-source product called Sqoop. Sqoop is a command-line tool with the following capabilities:

➤ Imports individual RDBMS tables or entire databases to files in HDFS

➤ Generates Java classes to allow you to interact with your imported data

➤ Provides the ability to import from SQL databases straight into your Hive data warehouse

You can learn more about Sqoop at `https://github.com/cloudera/sqoop`.

SUMMARY

This chapter presented a case for polyglot persistence. It showed the path to using RDBMS and NoSQL side-by-side. Examples of large popular social media venues were cited to draw inspiration. Facebook, Twitter, and LinkedIn examples were included.

Subsequently, the chapter provided a brief overview of the products that bridge the gap between the RDBMS and the NoSQL world. Popular frameworks like Rails, Django, and Spring and their support for both RDBMS and NoSQL were illustrated with the help of a few examples.

Last but not least, a brief conversation on migrating data from RDBMS to NoSQL was included to show how data can be moved from tables to structures that are more amenable to MapReduce-style analytics.

The next chapter covers a few topics that pertain to performance tuning.

16

Performance Tuning

WHAT'S IN THIS CHAPTER?

➤ Understanding the factors that affect parallel scalable applications

➤ Optimizing scalable processing, especially when it leverages the MapReduce model for processing

➤ Presenting a set of best practices for parallel processing

➤ Illustrating a few Hadoop performance tuning tips

Today, much of the big data analysis in the world of NoSQL rests on the shoulders of the MapReduce model of processing. Hadoop is built on it and each NoSQL product supporting huge data sizes leverages it. This chapter is a first look into optimizing scalable applications and tuning the way MapReduce-style processing works on large data sets. By no means does the chapter provide a prescriptive solution. Instead, it provides a few important concepts and good practices to bear in mind when optimizing a scalable parallel application. Each optimization problem is unique to its requirements and context and so providing one universally applicable general solution is probably not feasible.

GOALS OF PARALLEL ALGORITHMS

MapReduce makes scalable parallel processing easier than it had been in the past. By adhering to a model where data is not shared between parallel threads or processes, MapReduce creates a bottleneck-free way of scaling out as workloads increase. The underlying goal at all times is to reduce latency and increase throughput.

The Implications of Reducing Latency

Reducing latency simply means reducing the execution time of a program. The faster a program completes — that is, the less time a program takes to produce desired results for a given set of inputs — the better it fares on the latency metrics. Under a given set of inputs and outputs, latency reduction usually involves choosing the most optimal algorithms for producing the output and parallelizing the execution of sub-tasks. If a task can be broken down into a number of parallel and independent sub-tasks, running them in parallel can reduce the overall time taken to complete the task. Therefore, in parallel programs, latency effectively is a measure of the time taken to execute the smallest 'atomic' sub-task. The word 'atomic' here denotes the smallest unit of work that cannot be further broken down into parallel sub-tasks. In a case, where parallelization is not feasible, latency is a measure of the time taken to execute the entire program.

As far as optimizing algorithms go, you need to keep in mind that the given algorithm needs to fit within the model of map and reduce functions. Of course, you can have multiple passes through these functions, if required.

How to Increase Throughput

Throughput refers to the amount of input that can be manipulated to generate output within a given process. In many large data sets, throughput takes center stage, sometimes even at the expense of increased latency. This is because analyzing large amounts of data is not trivial. For example, Kevin Weil of Twitter, in a presentation at Web2.0 Expo in 2010 (www.slideshare.net/kevinweil/analyzing-big-data-at-twitter-web-20-expo-nyc-sep-2010) revealed that Tweets added up to 12 Terabytes per day. This amount of data needs around 48 hours to be written to a disk at a speed of about 80 Mbps. The same story appears in all venues, for example Facebook and Google, where heavy user traffic generates large amounts of user data every day.

Hadoop provides the capability to analyze large sets of data, even data that is spread beyond a single machine. In traditional single large systems, the throughput was often constrained by the available resources. For example, the amount of RAM in a system or the number and power of CPU(s) determined the amount of processing a machine could do. As data grew, even the most powerful machines seemed to reach their limits. In a horizontally scaled Hadoop environment that leverages the Hadoop distributed filesystem (HDFS) such limits have become lesser problems. Adding nodes to a cluster enables Hadoop to take on more processing as data grows. Also as a side effect the parallelization allows for commodity hardware with limited capabilities, as compared to powerful machines, to contribute effectively and help in increasing throughput.

Linear Scalability

In a typical horizontally scaled MapReduce-based model, the processing is parallel but the scalability is often linear. This means if one node of a cluster can process x megabytes of data every second, then n nodes can process x multiplied by n amounts of data. Flipping the argument the other way as data grows by every multiple of x, you need another node to keep the same rate of processing. Also, if all n nodes are equally balanced in terms of load, the time could be kept constant as long as a newer node is available to take on the additional load. Alternatively, time could be proportionately reduced for processing a given amount of data by adding more nodes to the cluster.

Simple math to demonstrate this could be as follows:

➤ Time taken to process y amounts of data on a single node = t seconds

➤ Time taken to process y amounts of data on n nodes = t/n seconds

These simple mathematical formulas assume that tasks can be parallelized into equally balanced units and that each unit takes about the same time to process the given data set.

INFLUENCING EQUATIONS

Milind Bhandarkar, a key contributor to Hadoop, in a presentation on Scaling Hadoop Applications (www.slideshare.net/hadoop/scaling-hadoopapplications) nicely summarizes the influencing theory using three important and well-known equations:

➤ Amdahl's Law

➤ Little's Law

➤ Message Cost Model

Amdahl's Law

Amdahl's Law provides a formula for finding the maximum improvement in performance of an overall system when only a part of the system is improved. Amdahl's Law is named after Gene Amdahl, www.computer.org/portal/web/awards/amdahl, a well-known computer architect who contributed to the making of the IBM mainframes.

Amdahl's Law can succinctly be explained using a simple example. Say you have a process that runs for 5 hours and this process can be divided into sub-tasks that can be parallelized. Assume that you can parallelize all but a small part of the program that takes 25 minutes to run. Then this part of the program, the one that takes 25 minutes to complete, ends up defining the best speeds that the overall program can achieve. Essentially, the linear part of the program limits the performance.

In mathematical terms this example could be seen as follows:

➤ Total time taken for the program to run: 5 hours (300 minutes)

➤ Time taken for the serial part of the program: 25 minutes

➤ Percentage of the overall program that can be parallelized: ~91.6

➤ Percentage that cannot be parallelized (or is serial in nature): 8.4

➤ Therefore, maximum increase in speed of the parallelized version compared to the non-parallelized version is $1 / (1 - 0.916) = ~11.9$

In other words, the completely parallelized version could be more than 11 times faster than the non-parallel version of the same program.

Amdahl's Law generalizes this calculation of speed improvement in an equation, which is as follows:

$$1 / ((1 - P) + P/S)$$

where P represents the proportion that is parallelized and S the times the parallelized part performs as compared to the non-parallelized one.

This generalized equation takes into account different levels of speed increase for different parts of a program. So, for example, a program can be parallelized into four parts, $P1$, $P2$, $P3$, and $P4$, where

P1, P2, P3, and P4 are 10%, 30%, 40%, and 20%, respectively. If P1 can speed up by $2x$, P2 by $3x$, and P3 by $4x$, but P4 cannot be speeded up, then the overall running time is as follows:

0.10/2 + 0.30/3 + 0.40/4 + 0.20/1 = 0.45

Therefore, the maximum speed increase is 1/0.45 or 2.22, more than double that of the non-parallel program.

You can read more about Amdahl's Law at `www-inst.eecs.berkeley.edu/~n252/paper/Amdahl.pdf`.

Amdahl's Law applies as much to MapReduce parallelization as it does to multi-core programming.

> *Gustafson's Law,* `http://citeseerx.ist.psu.edu/viewdoc/summary?doi=10.1.1.85.6348`, *reevaluates Amdahl's Law. It states that given more computing power, more complex problems can be solved in the same time as a simpler problem takes, when lesser computing power is used. Therefore, Gustafson's Law contradicts the scalability limits imposed by the linear part of the program, especially when large complex repetitive tasks are carried out using more computing resources.*

Little's Law

Little's Law applies to parallel computing but has its origins in the world of economics and queuing theory. The law appears deceptively simple but provides a probability distribution independent way of analyzing the load on stable systems. The law states that the average number of customers in a stable system is the product of the average arrival rate and the time each customer spends in the system. In terms of a formula, it appears as follows:

➤ $L = kW$

➤ L is the average number of customers in a stable system

➤ k is the average arrival rate

➤ W is the time a customer spends in the system

To understand this a bit further, consider a simple system, say a small gas station with cash-only payments over a single counter. If four customers arrive every hour at this gas station and each customer takes about 15 minutes (0.25 hours) at the gas station, there should be an average of only one customer at any point in time at this station. If more than four customers arrive at the same station, it becomes clear that it would lead to bottlenecks in the system. If gas station customers get frustrated by waiting longer than normal and leave without filling up, you are likely to have higher exit rates than arrival rates and in such a situation the system would become unstable.

Viewing a system in terms of Little's Law, it becomes evident that if a customer or an active process, when translated to parallel programs, takes a certain amount of time, say W, to complete and the maximum capacity for the system allows handling of only L processes at any time, then the arrival rate cannot be more than L/W per unit of time. If the arrival rate exceeds this value, the system would be backed up and the computation time and volume would be impacted.

Message Cost Model

The third equation is the Message Cost Model. The Message Cost Model breaks down the cost of sending a message from one end to the other in terms of its fixed and variable costs. Simply put, the Message Cost Model equation is as follows:

$$C = a + bN$$

➤ C is the cost of sending the message from one end, say A, to the other, say B

➤ a is the upfront cost for sending the message

➤ b is the cost per byte of the message

➤ N is the number of bytes of the message

This equation is simple to understand and there are two key takeaways from this model:

➤ Transfer of a message irrespective of its size involves an upfront fixed cost. In terms of messages, the overhead around connection establishment, handshake, and setup are quite common.

➤ The cost of a message transfer is directly and linearly co-related to the message size.

The Message Cost Model provides some interesting insights into costs associated with transmission of messages across a network. On a gigabit Ethernet, a is about 300 micro-seconds, which is 0.3 milliseconds, and b is 1 second per 125 MB. 1 Gigabit is 1000 Mb or 125 MB. A gigabit Ethernet implies a transmission rate of 125 MBps. A cost of 1 second per 125 MB is the same as 1 ms per 125 KB because 1000 ms make up a second and 1000 KB make up an MB. This means 100 messages of 10 KB each take 100 multiplied by (0.3 + 10/125) ms, which is 38 ms, whereas 10 messages of 100 KB take only 10 multiplied by (0.3 + 100/125) ms, which is 11 ms. Therefore, a way to optimize message cost is to send as big a packet as possible each time, thereby amortizing the upfront cost over a much larger size.

 In a theoretical calculation a, the fixed cost, in the Message Cost Model is considered fixed for all message sizes but usually that's not the case. The value of a varies depending on the message size.

PARTITIONING

Partitioning is a very important aspect of parallelization. In the MapReduce method of processing, each reducer forms a partition. During the map phase key/value pairs are emitted. The reducers consume these key/value pairs. The MapReduce method prefers a share-nothing model of processing so it's necessary that all key/value pairs that have the same key go to the same partition and get manipulated by the same reducer.

In the Hadoop MapReduce framework, a default partitioner is defined. The default partitioner is `HashPartitioner`. `HashPartitioner` uses the `hashCode` function value of the keys. Therefore, '*hashCode value*' modulo '*number of partitions*' = n (where n is the number used to distribute the key/value pairs across the partitions).

Hadoop uses an interface called Partitioner to determine which partition a key/value pair emitted by a map task goes to. The number of partitions, and therefore the number of reduce tasks, are known when a job starts. The Partitioner interface is as follows:

```
public interface Partitioner<K, V> extends JobConfigurable {
    int getPartition(K key, V value, int numPartitions);
```

The `getPartition` method takes the key, value, and the number of partitions as arguments and returns the partition number, which identifies the partition the key/value is sent to. For any two keys, $k1$ and $k2$, if $k1$ and $k2$ are equal then the partition number returned by `getPartition` is the same.

If partitioning is not balanced using emitted key/value pairs there could be a load imbalance or over partitioning, both of which are not efficient. When a few reducers take on most of the load and others remain idle, load imbalance occurs. Imbalance leads to increased latency. Machines and disks under full load also tend to become slower and hit boundary conditions where efficiency is reduced. Load imbalance causes some reducers to reach these full states.

You know from the earlier illustration of Amdahl's Law that any parallel process optimization is limited by the longest serial task. In partitioned MapReduce processing, a serial longer running execution can form a bottleneck. It can also lead to sequential waits because reduce and grouping tasks complete the entire process only when all constituent key/value pairs are processed.

SCHEDULING IN HETEROGENEOUS ENVIRONMENTS

Hadoop's default simple scheduling algorithm compares each task's progress to the average progress to schedule jobs. The default scheduler assumes the following:

➤ Nodes perform work at about the same rate

➤ Tasks progress at a constant rate throughout

In heterogeneous environments, this default simple speculative algorithm does not perform optimally. Therefore, improvements have been made specifically to address the problems in heterogeneous environments.

The Longest Approximate Time to End (LATE) scheduler is an improvement on the default Hadoop scheduler. The LATE scheduler launches speculative tasks only on fast nodes. It also puts a speculative cap by limiting the number of tasks that are speculated. Also, a slow task threshold determines whether a task is slow enough to get speculated.

Although the LATE scheduler is an improvement on the default Hadoop scheduler, both these schedulers compute the progress of tasks in a static manner. SAMR, a self-adaptive MapReduce scheduling algorithm, outperforms both the default and LATE schedulers in heterogeneous environments. You can read more about SAMR in a paper titled "SAMR: A Self-adaptive MapReduce Scheduling Algorithm in Heterogeneous Environment" authored by Quan Chen, Daqiang Zhang,

Minyi Guo, Qianni Deng, and Song Guo. The paper is catalogued online at `http://portal.acm` `.org/citation.cfm?id=1901325`.

ADDITIONAL MAPREDUCE TUNING

A number of configuration parameters that affect MapReduce can be configured appropriately to achieve better performance.

Communication Overheads

When the data sets are too large the algorithmic complexity of MapReduce is the least of the concerns. The focus is often on processing the large data set in the first place. However, you must bear in mind that some of the communication overhead and the associated algorithmic complexity can be minimized by simply getting rid of the reduce task if possible. In such cases, map does everything. In cases where eliminating the reduce task is not an option, launching the reduce tasks before all map tasks have completed can improve performance.

Compression

Compressing data as it gets transmitted between nodes and between map and reduce jobs improves performance dramatically. Essentially, the communication overhead is reduced and avoidable bandwidth and network usage is removed. For large clusters and large jobs, compression can lead to substantial benefits.

 Some data sets aren't easily compressible or do not compress enough to provide substantial benefits.

Turning compression on is as simple as setting a single configuration parameter to true. This single parameter is:

```
mapred.compress.map.output
```

The compression codec can also be configured. Use `mapred.map.output.compression.codec` to configure the codec.

 LZO is a compression algorithm that is suitable for real-time compression. It favors speed over compression ratio. Read more about LZO at `www.oberhumer.com/opensource/lzo/`.

A further improvement could be to use splittable LZO. Most MapReduce tasks are I/O bound. If files on HDFS are compressed into a format that can be split and consumed by the MapReduce tasks directly, it improves I/O and overall performance. Under normal gzip-based compression algorithms, parallelizing spilt gzip segments poses a problem and so these spilt portions need to be processed by a single mapper. If a single mapper is used the parallelization effort is affected. With bzip2, this can be avoided and split portions can be sent to different mappers but the decompression is very CPU intensive and therefore the gains in I/O are lost in CPU time. LZO comes as a good optimal middle ground where the sizes and decompression speeds are optimal. Learn more about splittable LZO online at `https://github.com/kevinweil/hadoop-lzo`.

File Block Size

HDFS, the underlying distributed filesystem in Hadoop, allows the storage of very large files. A default block size in HDFS is about 64 MB in size. If your cluster is small and the data size is large, a large number of map tasks would be spawned for the default block size. For example, 120 GBs of input would lead to 1,920 map tasks. This can be derived by a simple calculation as follows:

$$(120 * 1024)/64$$

Thus, increasing block size seems logical in small clusters. However, it should not be increased to a point that all nodes in a cluster are not used.

Parallel Copying

Maps outputs are copied over to reducers. In cases where the output of the map task is large, the copying over of values can be done in parallel by multiple threads. Increasing the threads increases the CPU usage but reduces latency. The default number of such threads is set to 5. You can increase the number by setting the following property:

```
mapred.reduce.parallel.copies
```

HBASE COPROCESSORS

HBase coprocessors are inspired by the idea of coprocessors in Google Bigtable. A few simple processes like counting, aggregating, and such can be pushed up to the server to enhance performance. The idea of coprocessors achieves this.

Three interfaces in HBase — Coprocessor, RegionObserver, and Endpoint — implement the coprocessor framework in a flexible manner. The idea behind Coprocessor and RegionObserver is that you can insert user code by overriding upcall methods from these two related interfaces. The coprocessor framework handles the details of invoking the upcalls. More than one Coprocessor or RegionObserver can be loaded to extend function. They are chained to execute sequentially. These sequential coprocessors are ordered on the basis of assigned priorities.

Through an endpoint on the server side and dynamic RPC provided by the client library, you can define your own extensions to HBase RPC transactions exchanged between clients and the region servers.

LEVERAGING BLOOM FILTERS

Bloom Filters were introduced in Chapter 13. Please review the definition if you aren't sure what they are.

A get row call in HBase currently does a parallel N-way get of that row from all StoreFiles in a region. This implies N reads requests from disk. Bloom Filters provide a lightweight in-memory structure to reduce those N disk reads to only the files likely to contain that row.

Reads are in parallel and so the performance gains on an individual get is minimal. Also, read performance is dominated by disk read latency. If you replace parallel get with serial get you would see an impact of Bloom Filters on read latency.

Bloom Filters can be more heavyweight than your data. This is one big reason why they aren't enabled by default.

SUMMARY

This chapter presented a few perspectives on tuning the performance of parallel MapReduce-based processes. The MapReduce algorithm enables the processing of large amounts of data using commodity hardware. Scaling MapReduce algorithms requires some clever configuration. Optimal configuration of MapReduce tasks can tune performance.

The chapter presented a few generic performance-tuning tips but used Hadoop and the associated set of tools for illustration.

17

Tools and Utilities

WHAT'S IN THIS CHAPTER?

➤ Examining popular tools and utilities for monitoring and managing NoSQL products

➤ Surveying log processing, MapReduce management, and search related tools

➤ Demonstrating a few scalable and robust manageability related utilities

This book is about NoSQL and the objective from the very beginning was to get you familiar with the topic. The intent was not to make you an expert in a specific NoSQL product. The book exposed you to as many underlying concepts as possible and to the rich diversity offered by the different NoSQL products. I have achieved that initial goal and given you enough material on NoSQL so that you feel confident and comfortable about the basic building blocks of this ever-growing domain. This final chapter continues that effort to enhance your learning of NoSQL. Instead of focusing on more concepts though, this chapter presents a few interesting and important tools and utilities that you are likely to leverage as you adopt NoSQL in your technology stack. The list is by no means exhaustive or a collection of the best available products. It's just a representative sample.

The chapter is structured around 14 different open-source and freely available use cases, tools, and utilities. Although each of these is related to NoSQL, they are independent of each other. This means you can read linearly through this chapter or choose to go to a specific page that covers a specific product as required.

The first couple of tools, especially RRDTool and Nagios, are relevant beyond NoSQL systems. They are useful for monitoring and managing all types of distributed systems.

RRDTOOL

RRDTool is a leading open-source tool for high-performance logging and the graphing of time series data. It integrates easily with shell scripts and many different scripting languages, including Python, Ruby, Perl, Lua, and Tcl. RRDTool is written in C and compiles to most platforms. It can easily run on Linux, Windows, and Mac OS X. You can download RRDTool from http://oss.oetiker.ch/rrdtool/.

RRDTool includes a database and a graph generation and rendering environment. The RRDTool database is unlike a traditional RDBMS. It's more like a rolling log file. RRDTool serves as a very helpful monitoring tool because it can be used to capture and graph performance, usage, and utilization metrics.

Here I present a simple example to help you understand RRDTool. Say you need to capture a metric like CPU utilization on a machine that runs a NoSQL database node. You may decide to capture the utilization metric every 60 seconds (once every minute). In addition, you may want to average the utilization metric for every hour and save such calculations for a day (24 hours). You can easily store such data and graph the saved values for easy analysis.

The RRDTool database can be thought of as a storage scheme around the perimeter of a circle. This means as data gets written around a circle you eventually come back to the starting point. When you come back to the start, newer data values overwrite the old ones. This means the amount of data you store is determined up front by the total storage allocated for the database. Continuing with the circle analogy, the circumference of the circle is determined up front.

The easiest way to create an RRDTool database is via its command-line interface (CLI), which for the rudimentary CPU utilization metric example could be as follows:

```
rrdtool create myrrddb.rrd \
        --start 1303520400 \
        --step 60 \
        DS:cpu:GAUGE:120:0:100 \
        RRA:AVERAGE:0.5:60:24 \
        RRA:AVERAGE:0.5:1440:31
```

This command creates an RRDTool database named `myrrddb.rrd`. It creates the database by initializing it with a set of properties that define the metric it captures and how this metric gets aggregated. Parsing the command line by line is a good idea to understand all the parameters.

The `start` and `step` parameters define the start time and the interval of capture for the database. The time value passed, as a parameter to the `start` argument, is a time value represented in terms of number of seconds since epoch, which in the case of RRDTool is 1/1/1970. The `step` value in seconds specifies the frequency of recording and saving a metric. Because the intent is to save CPU utilization values once every minute, the `step` value is specified as 60 (60 seconds).

The line right after the `step` argument defines the metric being captured. The value `DS:cpu:GAUGE:120:0:100` follows this format:

DS:variable_name:data_source_type:heartbeat:min:max

DS is a keyword that stands for *data source*. DS is essentially what I have been calling metric so far. *variable_name* identifies the data source. In the example, cpu is a variable name for holding the CPU utilization value. data_source_type defines the type of value stored for a data source. The value in this example is GAUGE. The possible values for a data_source_type are as follows:

➤ **COUNTER** — Records the rate of change over a period. The values in this case are always increasing.

➤ **DERIVE** — Similar to a COUNTER but can accept negative values.

➤ **ABSOLUTE** — Also records rate of change but the current value stored is always in relation to the last value. The current value is different from the last value. In math terms, it's always the "delta."

➤ **GAUGE** — Records actual value and not rate of change.

RRDTool records values at a defined interval. In the example, myrrddb.rrd would expect a CPU utilization value to be available every 60 seconds. The RRDTool database, unlike an RDBMS, expects a value to be made available at a predefined interval. This means that if it doesn't get a value, it records it as UNDEFINED. The heartbeat value, which in the example is 120 seconds, is when the database thinks the value is not present and then records it as UNDEFINED. If values don't come exactly as defined, RRDTool has the capability to interpolate values if the record still arrives within the heartbeat interval. The last two values, min and max, are boundary conditions for values. Data source values outside these values are recorded as UNDEFINED. In the example, I assume the CPU utilization is a percentage utilization value and therefore 0 and 100 mark the boundary conditions for such a measure.

The last two lines depict the aggregation functions on the time series data. In the database create statement in the example, the last two lines are as follows:

```
RRA:AVERAGE:0.5:60:24 \
RRA:AVERAGE:0.5:1440:31
```

RRA, like DS, is another keyword. RRA stands for Round Robin Archive. The RRA definitions follow this format:

```
RRA:consolidation_function:xff:step:rows
```

consolidation_function is an aggregation function. AVERAGE, MINIMUM, MAXIMUM, and LAST could be possible consolidation_function values. In the example, two RRA definitions are included. Both average data points. Consolidation functions operate on the values captured from the data source. Therefore, in the example of CPU utilization, RRA values will be aggregates of the per-minute CPU utilization recordings. step defines the aggregation bundle and rows specifies the number of aggregated records to be saved. In the example, a value of 60 for steps implies that the average is calculated on the basis of 60 data points of the data source recordings. The recordings are every minute so this means the averages are for every hour, because an hour has 60 minutes. The number of rows to be archived is 24. Therefore, the first RRA records average CPU utilization on a per-hour basis and keeps records for a day.

The second RRA definition is an average CPU utilization for a day, and 31 days (or a month's worth) of data is stored for this consolidation function.

RRDTool has the ability to graph the time series data it records. You can manipulate the database from shell script or from one of the popular scripting languages. You can learn about RRDTool's capabilities and configurations at `www.mrtg.org/rrdtool/`. Covering all the details is certainly beyond the scope of this book.

RRDTool is a handy tool for monitoring the health of a cluster of NoSQL nodes. As an example, Hypertable leverages RRDTool for its monitoring UI. Read more about the Hypertable monitoring UI at `http://code.google.com/p/hypertable/wiki/HypertableManual#Appendix_A._Monitoring_UI`.

NAGIOS

Nagios is a leading open-source hosts and services monitoring software. This powerful software application leverages a plugin architecture to provide extremely flexible and extensible monitoring infrastructure. The core of Nagios includes a monitoring process that monitors hosts or services of any type. The core process is totally unaware of what is being monitored or the meaning of the captured metrics. A plugin framework sits on top of the core process. Plugins can be compiled executables or scripts (Perl scripts and shell scripts). The plugins contain the core logic of reaching out to services and monitored entities, and measuring a specific property of that system.

A plugin checks a monitored entity and returns the results to Nagios. Nagios can process the result and take any necessary action, such as run an event handler or send a notification. Notifications and altering mechanisms serve an important function and facilitate on-time communication.

Figure 17-1 depicts the Nagios architecture.

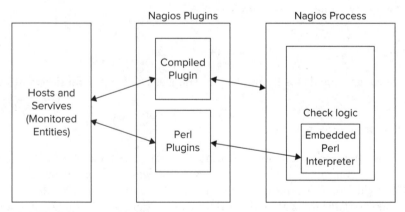

FIGURE 17-1

Nagios can be used very effectively to monitor NoSQL databases and Hadoop clusters. A few plugins have already emerged for Hadoop and MongoDB, and Nagios can monitor Membase due to its Memcached compatibility. Plugins for other databases can also be added. Learn all about writing plugins at `http://nagios.sourceforge.net/docs/nagioscore/3/en/pluginapi.html`.

A GPL-licensed HDFS check plugin for Nagios is available online at `www.matejunkie.com/hadoop-dfs-check-plugin-for-nagios/`. A Nagios plugin to monitor MongoDB is available online at `https://github.com/mzupan/nagios-plugin-mongodb`.

A number of robust plugins for Nagios can help check CPU load, disk health, memory usage, and ping rates. Most protocols, including HTTP, POP3, IMAP, DHCP, and SSH can be monitored. Services in most operating systems, including Linux, Windows, and Mac OS X can be checked for their health. Read more about Nagios at www.nagios.org/.

SCRIBE

Scribe is an open-source real-time distributed log aggregator. Created at Facebook and generously open sourced by them, Scribe is a very robust and fault-tolerant system. You can download Scribe from https://github.com/facebook/scribe. Scribe is a distributed system. Each node in a cluster runs a local Scribe server and one of the nodes runs a Scribe central or master server. Logs are aggregated at the local Scribe server and sent to the central server. If the central server is down, logs are written to the local files and later sent to the central server when it's up and running again. To avoid heavy loads on central server startup the synch is delayed for a certain time after the central server comes up.

Scribe log messages and formats are configurable. It is implemented as a Thrift service using the non-blocking C++ server.

Scribe provides a very configurable option for log writing. Messages are mapped to categories and categories are mapped to certain store types. Stores themselves can have a hierarchy. The different possible types of stores are as follows:

➤ **File** — Local file or NFS.

➤ **Network** — Send to another Scribe server.

➤ **Buffer** — Contains a primary and a secondary store. Messages are sent to primary. If primary is down, messages are sent to secondary. Messages are finally sent to primary once it's up again.

➤ **Bucket** — Contains a large number of other stores. Creates a store hierarchy. Decides which messages to send to which stores based on a hash.

➤ **Null** — Discards all messages.

➤ **Thriftfile** — Writes messages into a Thrift TFileTransport file.

➤ **Multi** — Acts as a forwarder. Forwards messages to multiple stores.

The Thrift interface for Scribe is as follows:

```
enum ResultCode
{
  OK,
  TRY_LATER
}

struct LogEntry
{
  1:  string category,
  2:  string message
}
```

```
service scribe extends fb303.FacebookService
{
  ResultCode Log(1: list<LogEntry> messages);
}
```

A sample PHP client message could be like this:

```
$messages = array();
$entry = new LogEntry;
$entry->category = "test_bucket";
$entry->message = "a message";
$messages []= $entry;
$result = $conn->Log($messages);
```

scribe_client.php

Log parsing and management is a very important job in the world of big data and its processing. Flume is another solution like Scribe.

FLUME

Flume is a distributed service for efficiently collecting, aggregating, and moving large amounts of log data. It is based on streaming data flows. It is robust and fault tolerant and allows for flexible configurations. Flume documentation is available online at `http://archive.cloudera .com/cdh/3/flume/`.

Flume consists of multiple logical nodes, through which the log data flows. The nodes can be classified into three distinct tiers, which are as follows:

➤ **Agent tier** — The agent tiers usually are on nodes that generate the log files.

➤ **Collector tier** — The collector tier aggregates log data and forwards the log to the storage tiers.

➤ **Storage tier** — This could be HDFS.

The Agent tier could listen to log data from multiple tiers and sources. For example, Flume agents could listen to log files from syslog, a web server log, or Hadoop JobTracker.

Flume can be thought of as a network of logical nodes that facilitate the flow of log data from the source to the final store. Each logical node consists of a source and a sink definition. Optionally, logical nodes can have decorators. The logical node architecture allows for per-flow data guarantees like compression, durability, and batching. Each physical node is a separate Java process but multiple logical nodes can be mapped to a single physical node.

CHUKWA

Chukwa is a Hadoop subproject devoted to large-scale collection and analysis. Chukwa leverages HDFS and MapReduce to provide a scalable infrastructure to aggregate and analyze log files.

Unlike Scribe and Flume, Chukwa adds an additional powerful toolkit for monitoring and analysis, beyond log collection and aggregation. For collection and aggregation, it's quite similar to Flume.

The Chukwa architecture is shown in Figure 17-2.

Chukwa's reliance on the Hadoop infrastructure is its strength but it also is its weakness. As it's currently structured, it's meant to be a batch-oriented tool and not for real-time analysis.

Read more about Chukwa in the following presentations and research papers:

➤ "Chukwa: a scalable log collector" — www.usenix.org/event/lisa10/tech/slides/rabkin.pdf

➤ "Chukwa: A large-scale monitoring system" — www.cca08.org/papers/Paper-13-Ariel-Rabkin.pdf

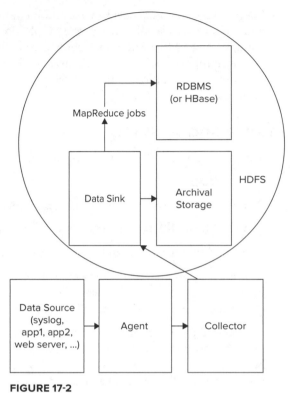

FIGURE 17-2

PIG

Pig provides a high-level data flow definition language and environment for large-scale data analysis using MapReduce jobs. Pig includes a language, called Pig Latin, which has a simple and intuitive syntax that makes it easy to write parallel programs. The Pig layer manages efficient execution of the parallel jobs by invoking MapReduce jobs under the seams.

The MapReduce framework forces developers to think of every algorithm in terms of map and reduce functions. The MapReduce method of thinking breaks every operation into very simple operations, which go through the two steps of map and reduce. The map function emits key/value pairs of data and the reduce function runs aggregation or manipulation functions on these emitted key/value pairs. The net result of this exercise is that every join, group, average, or count operation needs to be defined every time in terms of its MapReduce equivalents. This hampers developer productivity. In terms of the Hadoop infrastructure, it also involves writing a lot of Java code. Pig provides a higher-level abstraction and provides a set of ready-to-use functions. Therefore, with Pig you no longer need to write MapReduce jobs for join, group, average, and count from the ground up. Also, the number of lines of code typically gets reduced from 100s of lines of Java code to 10s of lines of Pig Latin script.

Not only does Pig reduce the number of lines of code, but the terse and easy syntax makes it possible for non-programmers to run MapReduce jobs. As Pig evolves it becomes possible for data scientists and analysts to run complex parallel jobs without directly using a programming language.

Pig provides a language and an execution engine. The execution engine not only translates and passes over the job down to the MapReduce infrastructure but also manages the Hadoop configuration. Most often, such configuration is optimal and, therefore, Pig takes away the responsibility of optimizing configuration from you as well. This provides an extra optimization boost with no additional effort. Such optimizations involve choosing the right number of reducers or appropriate partitioning.

Interfacing with Pig

You can access the Pig engine using any of the following four mechanisms:

➤   Via a script

➤   Using the command-line interface, grunt

➤   Through a Java interface, the `PigServer` class

➤   With the help of an Eclipse plugin

Commands can be written using the Pig Latin scripts and then the scripts can be submitted to the Pig engine. Alternatively, you can start a Pig command-line shell, called grunt, and then use the command-line shell to interact with the Pig engine.

Although Pig takes away the effort of writing a Java program to run Hadoop MapReduce tasks, you may need to interface Pig from your Java application. In such cases, the Pig Java library classes can be used. The `PigServer` class allows a Java program to interface with the Pig engine via a JDBC-type interface. The usage of a Java library as opposed to an external script or program can reduce complexity, when leveraging Pig with a Java application.

Last but not least, the Pig team has created an Eclipse plugin, called PigPen, that provides a powerful IDE. The Eclipse plugin allows for graphical definition of data flow, in addition to a script development environment.

Pig Latin Basics

Pig Latin supports the following data types:

➤   Int

➤   Long

➤   Double

➤   Chararray

➤   Bytearray

➤   Map (for key/value pairs)

➤   Tuple (for ordered lists)

➤   Bag (for a set)

The best way to learn Pig Latin and how to execute Pig scripts is to work through a few examples. The Pig distribution comes with an example, complete with data and scripts. It's available in the tutorial folder in the distribution. That is probably the best first example to start with.

The contents of the tutorial folder within the Pig distribution are as follows:

- `build.xml` — The ANT build script.
- `data` — Sample data. Contains sample data from the Excite search engine log files.
- `scripts` — Pig scripts.
- `src` — Java source.

It's beyond the scope of this chapter or the book to get into the detailed syntax and semantics of all the Pig commands. However, I will walk through a few steps in one of the scripts in the tutorial. That should give you a flavor of Pig scripts.

You will find four scripts in the tutorial/scripts directory. These files are as follows:

- `script1-hadoop.pig`
- `script1-local.pig`
- `script2-hadoop.pig`
- `script2-local.pig`

The `*-local` scripts run jobs locally and the `*-hadoop` scripts run the job on a Hadoop cluster. The tutorial manipulates sample data from the Excite search engine log files. In `script1-local.pig` you will find a script that finds search phrases of a higher frequency at certain times of the day. The initial lines in this script register variables and load data for Pig. Soon after, the data is manipulated to count the frequency of n-grams. A snippet from the example is as follows:

```
-- Call the NGramGenerator UDF to compose the n-grams of the query.
ngramed1 = FOREACH houred GENERATE user, hour,
  flatten(
  org.apache.pig.tutorial.NGramGenerator(query))
  as ngram;

-- Use the DISTINCT command to get the unique n-grams for all records.
ngramed2 = DISTINCT ngramed1;

-- Use the GROUP command to group records by n-gram and hour.
hour_frequency1 = GROUP ngramed2 BY (ngram, hour);

-- Use the COUNT function to get the count (occurrences) of each n-gram.
hour_frequency2 = FOREACH hour_frequency1 GENERATE flatten($0), COUNT($1) as count;
```

The snippet shows sample Pig script lines. In the first of the lines, the FOREACH function helps loop through the data to generate the n-grams. In the second line, DISTINCT identifies the unique n-grams. The third line in the snippet groups the data by hour using the GROUP function. The last line in the snippet loops over the grouped data to count the frequency of occurrence of the n-grams. The FOREACH function helps loop through the data set. From the snippet it becomes evident that higher-level functions like FOREACH, DISTINCT, GROUP, and COUNT allow for easy data manipulation, without the need for detailed MapReduce functions.

Pig imposes small overheads over writing directly to MapReduce. The overhead is as low as 1.2x and so is acceptable for the comfort it offers. PigMix (http://wiki.apache.org/pig/PigMix) is a benchmarking tool that compares a task performance via Pig to direct MapReduce-based jobs.

At Yahoo!, Pig, along with Hadoop streaming is the preferred way to interact with a Hadoop cluster. Yahoo! runs one of the largest Hadoop clusters in the world and leverages this cluster for a number of mission critical features. The usage of Pig at Yahoo! testifies in favor of Pig's production readiness.

Learn more about Pig at http://pig.apache.org/.

NODETOOL

Apache Cassandra is a popular eventually consistent data store. Its distributed nature and replication under an eventually consistent model makes it susceptible to possible complexities at run time. Having a few tools to manage and monitor the Cassandra clusters therefore comes in handy. One such command-line utility is nodetool. The nodetool utility can be run as follows:

```
bin/nodetool
```

Running it without any parameters prints out the most common choices available as command-line options. Cassandra's distributed nodes form a ring where each node in the ring contains data that maps to a certain set of ordered tokens. All keys are hashed to tokens via MD5. To get the status of a Cassandra ring, simply run the following command:

```
bin/nodetool -host <host_name or ip address> ring
```

The *host_name* or *ip address* could be of any node in the ring. The output of this command contains the status of all nodes in a ring. It prints out the status, load, range, and an ascii art.

To get information about a particular node, run the following command:

```
bin/nodetool -host <host_name or ip address> info
```

This output of this command includes the following:

➤ Token

➤ Load info — Number of bytes of storage on disk

➤ Generation no — Number of times the node was started

➤ Uptime in seconds

➤ Heap memory usage

Nodetool has a number of other commands, which are as follows:

➤ **ring** — Print information on the token ring

➤ **info** — Print node information (uptime, load, and so on)

➤ **cfstats** — Print statistics on column-families

➤ **clearsnapshot** — Remove all existing snapshots

➤ **version** — Print Cassandra version

➤ **tpstats** — Print usage statistics of thread pools

➤ **drain** — Drain the node (stop accepting writes and flush all column-families)

➤ **decommission** — Decommission the node

➤ **loadbalance** — Loadbalance the node

➤ **compactionstats** — Print statistics on compactions

➤ **disablegossip** — Disable gossip (effectively marking the node dead)

➤ **enablegossip** — Reenable gossip

➤ **disablethrift** — Disable Thrift server

➤ **enablethrift** — Reenable Thrift server

➤ **snapshot [snapshotname]** — Take a snapshot using optional name `snapshotname`

➤ **netstats [host]** — Print network information on provided host (connecting node by default)

➤ **move <new token>** — Move node on the token ring to a new token

➤ **removetoken status|force|<token>** — Show status of current token removal, force completion of pending removal, or remove provisioned token

Learn more about nodetool at `http://wiki.apache.org/cassandra/NodeTool`.

OPENTSDB

As data grows and you expand your infrastructure by adding nodes to your storage and compute clusters, soon enough you have a large number of hosts, servers, and applications to manage. Most of these hosts, servers, and applications provide hooks that make them monitorable. You can ping these entities and measure their uptime, performance, usage, and other such characteristics. Capturing these metrics, especially on a frequent basis, collating them, and then analyzing them can be a complex task.

OpenTSDB is a distributed scalable time series data store that provides a flexible way to manage and monitor a vast number of hosts, servers, and applications. It uses an asynchronous way of collecting, storing, and indexing the metrics from a large number of machines. OpenTSDB is an open-source tool. The team at StumbleUpon created it. It uses HBase to store the collected data. The application allows for real-time plotting and analysis.

A high-level look at the architecture of OpenTSDB is depicted in Figure 17-3.

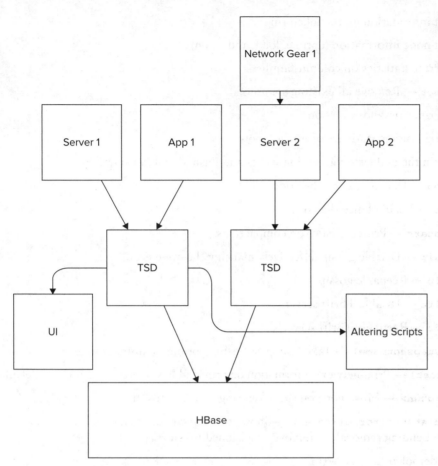

FIGURE 17-3

OpenTSDB has the capacity to store billions of records and so you don't need to worry about deleting metrics and log data. Analysis can be run on this large data set to reveal interesting correlated measures, which can provide interesting insight into the working of your systems. OpenTSDB is distributed; it also avoids a single point of failure.

Learn more about OpenTSDB at `http://opentsdb.net/index.html`.

SOLANDRA

Lucene is a popular open-source search engine. It is written in Java and has been in use in many products and organizations for the past few years. Solr is a wrapper on top of the Lucene library. Solr provides an HTTP server, JSON, XML/HTTP support, and a bunch of other value-added features on top of Lucene. Under the seams, all of Solr's search facility is powered by Lucene. You can learn more about Lucene at `http://lucene.apache.org/java/docs/index.html` and learn more about Solr at `http://lucene.apache.org/solr/`.

Solandra is an interesting experimental project by Jake Luciani. The Solandra project was originally introduced under the name of Lucandra, which integrated Lucene with Cassandra and used Cassandra as the data store for Lucene indexes and documents. Later, the project was moved over to support Solr, which builds on top of Lucene.

Lucene is a simple and elegant search library that can be easily integrated into your application. Its core facility manages indexes. Documents are parsed and indexed and stored away into a storage scheme, which could be a filesystem, memory, or any other store. Queries for documents are parsed by Lucene and translated into corresponding index searches. The index reader reads indexes and builds a response, which is returned to the calling party.

Solandra uses Cassandra as the storage scheme and so implements `IndexWriter` and `IndexReader` interfaces for Lucene to write indexes and documents to Cassandra. Figures 17-4 and 17-5 depict the logical architecture around index reader and writer in Solr (and Lucene) and Solandra.

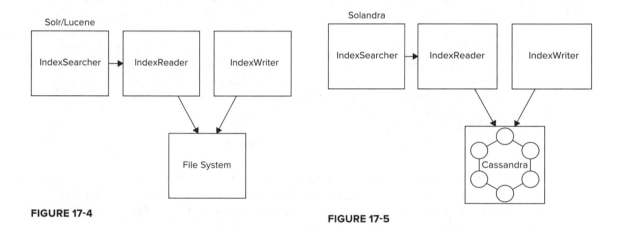

FIGURE 17-4   **FIGURE 17-5**

Solandra defines two column-families to store the index and the documents. The search term column-family, the one that stores index, has a key of the form *indexName/field/term* and the values stored in the column-family against the term are *{ documentId , positionVector }*. The document itself is also stored, but in a separate column-family. The document column-family has a key of the form *indexName/documented* and the values stored against a key of this form are *{ fieldName , value }*.

Solandra runs a Solr and Cassandra instance together on a node within the same JVM. Solandra index reader and writer performance has been observed to be slower than regular Solr, but Solandra adds the capability to scale easily. If you already use Cassandra or are having trouble scaling Solr by other means, give Solandra a try. The Solandra project is online at `https://github .com/tjake/Solandra`.

Similar experiments have also been carried out with HBase as the underlying storage instead of Cassandra. One such experimental project is lucehbase, which is online at `https://github .com/thkoch2001/lucehbase`.

If scaling Lucene is your concern and you are not a Cassandra user, I would not recommend using Solandra. I would recommend using Katta instead. Katta (`http://katta.sourceforge.net/`) enables storage of Lucene indexes on the Hadoop distributed filesystem, therefore providing scalable and distributed search software. It also allows you to leverage the scalable Hadoop infrastructure.

HUMMINGBIRD AND C5T

Hummingbird is actively developed real-time web traffic visualization software that uses MongoDB. It's in the early stages of development but is so interesting and impressive that it's worth a mention as one of the tools and utilities to watch out for.

Hummingbird is built on top of node.js and leverages web sockets to push data up to your browser. As a fallback option, Hummingbird uses Flash sockets to send the data up to the server. Twenty updates are sent per second providing a real-time view of the activity on your website. The project is open source and liberally licensed using the MIT license. It's online at `https://github.com/mnutt/hummingbird`.

> *Node.js is an event-driven I/O framework for the V8 JavaScript engine on Linux and Unix platforms. It is intended for writing scalable network programs such as web servers. It is similar in design to and influenced by systems like Ruby's Event Machine or Python's Twisted. Learn more about node.js at* `http://nodejs.org/`.

Hummingbird stores its real-time web traffic data in MongoDB, which provides fast read and write capabilities. A node.js-based tracking server records user activity on a website and stores it in a MongoDB server. A number of metrics like hits, locations, sales, and total views are implemented. As an example, the hits metric is defined as follows:

```
var HitsMetric = {
  name: 'Individual Hits',
  initialData: [],
  interval: 200,
  incrementCallback: function(view) {
    var value = {
      url: view.env.u,
      timestamp: view.env.timestamp,
      ip: view.env.ip
    };
    this.data.push(value);
  }
}

for (var i in HitsMetric)
  exports[i] = HitsMetric[i];
```

Learn more about Hummingbird at `http://projects.nuttnet.net/hummingbird/`.

C5t is another interesting piece of software built using MongoDB. It's content management software written using TurboGears, a Python web framework, and MongoDB. The source is available online at `https://bitbucket.org/percious/c5t/wiki/Home`.

Typing in the desired URL can create pages. Pages can be public or private. It offers built-in authentication and authorization and full text search.

GEOCOUCH

GeoCouch is an extension to CouchDB that provides spatial index for Apache CouchDB. The project is hosted at `https://github.com/couchbase/geocouch` and it is included with Couchbase by Couchbase, Inc. who sponsor its development. The first version of GeoCouch used Python and SpatiaLite and interacted with CouchDB via `stdin` and `stdout`. The current version of GeoCouch is written in Erlang and integrates more elegantly with CouchDB.

Spatial indexes bring in the perspective of location to a data point. With the emergence of GPS, location-based sensors, mapping, and local searches, geospatial indexing is becoming an important part of many applications.

GeoCouch supports a number of geospatial index types:

- ➤ Point
- ➤ Polygon
- ➤ LineString
- ➤ MultiPoint
- ➤ MultiPolygon
- ➤ MultiLineString
- ➤ GeometryCollection

GeoCouch uses an R-tree data structure to store the geospatial index. R-tree (`http://en.wikipedia.org/wiki/R-tree`) is used in many geospatial products like PostGIS, SpatiaLite, and Oracle Spatial. The R-tree data structure uses a bounding box as an approximation to a geolocation. It is good for representing most geometries.

A good case study of GeoCouch is the PDX API (`www.pdxapi.com/`) that leverages GeoCouch to provide a REST service for the open geodatasets offered by the city of Portland. The city of Portland published its geodatasets as shapefiles. These shapefiles were converted to GeoJSON using PostGIS. CouchDB supports JSON and was able to easily import GeoJSON and help provide a powerful REST API with no extra effort.

ALCHEMY DATABASE

Alchemy database (`http://code.google.com/p/alchemydatabase/`) is a split personality database. It can act as an RDBMS and as a NoSQL product. It is built on top of Redis and Lua. Alchemy embeds a Lua interpreter as a part of the product. Because of its reliance on Redis, the database is very fast and tries to do most operations in memory. However, this also means it shares the limitations of Redis when it comes to having a big divergence between the working set in memory and the entire data set on disk.

Alchemy achieves impressive performance because:

➤ It uses an event-driven network server that leverages memory as much as possible.

➤ Efficient data structures and compression help store a lot of data efficiently in RAM.

➤ The most relevant SQL statements for OLTP are supported, keeping the system lightweight and still useful. Every complex SQL statement is not supported. The list of supported SQL commands is available online at `http://code.google.com/p/alchemydatabase/wiki/CommandReference#Supported_SQL`.

WEBDIS

Webdis (`http://webd.is`) is a fast HTTP interface for Redis. It's a simple HTTP web server that sends requests down to Redis and sends responses back to the client. By default, Webdis supports JSON but it also supports other formats, which are as follows:

➤ Text, served as text/plain

➤ HTML, XML, PNG, JPEG, PDF served with their extensions

➤ BSON, served as application/bson

➤ Raw Redis protocol format

Webdis acts like a regular web server, but of course with a few modifications it supports all those commands that Redis can respond to. Regular requests are responded to with a 200 ok code. If access control doesn't allow a response to a request, the client receives a 403 forbidden HTTP response. GET, POST, and OPTIONS are not allowed and so return 405 Method Not Allowed. Webdis supports HTTP PUT and value can be set with a command as follows:

```
curl --upload-file my-data.bin http://127.0.0.1:7379/SET/akey
```

SUMMARY

As I write the summary to this last chapter, I hope you had an enjoyable and enriching experience learning the details of an emerging and important technology. This chapter presents a few use cases, tools, and utilities that relate to NoSQL.

Tools like RRDTool and Nagios are general purpose and are valuable additions to any monitoring and management software. Tools like nodetool add value when it comes to specifically managing and monitoring Cassandra.

Scribe, Flume, and Chukwa provide powerful capabilities around distributed log processing and aggregation. They provide a very robust function to help manage the large number of log files that are generated in any distributed environment. OpenTSDB provides a real-time infrastructure for monitoring hosts, services, and applications.

Pig is a valuable tool for writing smart MapReduce jobs on a Hadoop cluster. The chapter gets you started with it. Interesting applications like Solandra, Hummingbird, c5t, GeoCouch, Alchemy database, and Webdis demonstrate what you can do when you combine the flexibility and power of NoSQL products with your interesting ideas. The list of use cases, tools, and utilities covered in this chapter are not exhaustive but only a small sample. After reading through this book, I hope you are inspired to learn more of the specific NoSQL products that seem most interesting and most appropriate for your context.

APPENDIX

Installation and Setup Instructions

WHAT'S IN THIS APPENDIX?

➤ Installing and setting up a few popular NoSQL products

➤ Understanding the minor installation differences between platforms

➤ Compiling products from source, where applicable

➤ Configuring some of the NoSQL products

Software installation and setup instructions usually vary depending on the underlying operating system. Most instructions work on Linux, Unix, and Mac OS X. Instructions specific to installation and setup on Windows OS are included in a few select places. The installation instructions are not exhaustive.

Note that these instructions frequently refer to installing different software components in the /opt directory. By default, this directory is not usually writable by users other than root. If the directions refer to extracting archives or other operations in the /opt directory and it is not writable by the user extracting the archive, run the commands under the sudo(8) command or use the chmod(1) command to make the /opt directory writable.

INSTALLING AND SETTING UP HADOOP

This section contains the instructions for installing and configuring Hadoop Common, Hadoop Distributed File System (HDFS), and Hadoop MapReduce.

The following software is required:

➤ **Java 1.6.x** — Hadoop is tested against the Sun (now Oracle) JDK.

➤ **SSH and sshd** — SSH must be installed and sshd must be running. Hadoop scripts use sshd to connect to remote Hadoop daemons.

Hadoop can be installed and run as a single-node or as a multi-node cluster. A single-node installation can also be configured to run in a pseudo-distributed mode. In this section, the focus is on Hadoop setup for a single-node, with configuration for pseudo-distributed mode. Cluster setup and configuration is not covered here but references to external documentation on the subject are provided.

Installing Hadoop

To install Hadoop, follow these steps:

1. Download a stable Hadoop distribution release from `http://hadoop.apache.org/common/releases.html`. Currently, the latest release is version 0.21.0 but go in favor of version 0.20.2. Using Hadoop 0.20.2 avoids a set of inconsistencies that version 0.21.0 imposes, especially when used with HBase.

2. Unpack, untar, and unzip the downloaded distribution.

3. Move the unpacked distribution to a desired place in the filesystem. I prefer moving the unpacked distribution to `/opt`.

4. (Optional) Create a symbolic link named `hadoop` to point to the unpacked distribution folder. A symbolic link can be created as follows: `ln -s hadoop-0.20.2 hadoop`. This command assumes you are in the directory in which you've extracted the archive.

After Hadoop is installed, follow these essential configuration steps:

1. Edit `conf/hadoop-env.sh`. Set `JAVA_HOME` to the relevant JDK. On Ubuntu, with OpenJDK, `JAVA_HOME` could be `/usr/lib/jvm/java-1.6.0-openjdk`. On Mac OS X `JAVA_HOME` is most likely `/System/Library/Frameworks/JavaVM.framework/Versions/1.6.0/Home`.

2. Run `bin/hadoop`. All is good, if you see an output like so:

```
Usage: hadoop [--config confdir] COMMAND
where COMMAND is one of:
  namenode -format format the DFS filesystem
  secondarynamenoderun the DFS secondary namenode
  namenode           run the DFS namenode
  datanode           run a DFS datanode
  dfsadmin           run a DFS admin client
  mradmin            run a Map-Reduce admin client
  fsck               run a DFS filesystem checking utility
  fs                 run a generic filesystem user client
  balancer           run a cluster balancing utility
  jobtracker         run the MapReduce job Tracker node
  pipes              run a Pipes job
  tasktracker        run a MapReduce task Tracker node
  job                manipulate MapReduce jobs
  queue              get information regarding JobQueues
  version            print the version
  jar <jar>          run a jar file
  distcp <srcurl> <desturl> copy file or directories recursively
  archive -archiveName NAME <src>* <dest> create a hadoop archive
```

```
   daemonlog          get/set the log level for each daemon
or
   CLASSNAME          run the class named CLASSNAME
Most commands print help when invoked w/o parameters.
```

If you do not see the Hadoop command options, ensure that the JAVA_HOME is pointing to the correct JDK.

Configuring a Single-node Hadoop Setup

By default, Hadoop is configured to run in single-node mode. To test whether Hadoop is working properly, take HDFS for a test drive as follows:

➤ `$ mkdir input`

➤ `$ cp bin/*.sh input`

➤ `$ bin/hadoop jar hadoop-examples-*.jar grep input output 'start[a-z.]+'`

This command should kick-off MapReduce tasks, which create verbose output that would start as follows:

```
<date time>INFO jvm.JvmMetrics: Initializing JVM Metrics with
 processName=JobTracker, sessionId=
<date time>INFO mapred.FileInputFormat: Total input paths to process : 12
<date time> INFO mapred.JobClient: Running job: job_local_0001
<date time> INFO mapred.FileInputFormat: Total input paths to process : 12
<date time> INFO mapred.MapTask: numReduceTasks: 1
<date time> INFO mapred.MapTask: io.sort.mb = 100
<date time> INFO mapred.MapTask: data buffer = 79691776/99614720
<date time> INFO mapred.MapTask: record buffer = 262144/327680
<date time> INFO mapred.MapTask: Starting flush of map output
<date time> INFO mapred.TaskRunner: Task:attempt_local_0001_m_000000_0 is done.
And is in the process of commiting
<date time> INFO mapred.LocalJobRunner: file:/opt/hadoop-0.20.2/input/hadoop-
config.sh:0+1966
...
```

Verify the output by listing its contents with **cat output/***.

While it may vary based on the release you've installed, the output should be similar to:

```
2    starting
1    starts
1    startup
```

Configuring a Pseudo-distributed Mode Setup

An important prerequisite for configuring Hadoop in a pseudo-distributed mode setup is to have the ability to SSH to localhost without a passphrase.

Try the following:

```
ssh localhost
```

If you are prompted to accept the authenticity of localhost, answer **yes** to the prompt.

If you are logged in successfully without having to enter your password, you are ready to proceed. Otherwise, you will need to run the following commands to set up key-based authentication, without the need of a password:

```
$ ssh-keygen -t rsa -P '' -f ~/.ssh/id_rsa
$ cat ~/.ssh/id_rsa.pub >> ~/.ssh/authorized_keys
```

Hadoop can be run on a single-node in pseudo-distributed mode. In the pseudo-distributed mode, each Hadoop daemon runs as a separate Java process.

Here are the essential installation steps:

1. Edit `conf/core-site.xml` by replacing the empty `<configuration></configuration>` tags with:

```
<configuration>
  <property>
      <name>fs.default.name</name>
      <value>hdfs://localhost:9000</value>
  </property>
</configuration>
```

    (This configures the HDFS daemon.)

2. Edit `conf/hdfs-site.xml` by replacing the empty `<configuration></configuration>` tags with:

```
<configuration>
  <property>
      <name>dfs.replication</name>
      <value>1</value>
  </property>
</configuration>
```

    (This configures the replication factor. A replication factor of 1 means no replication. You need more than a single node to have a higher replication factor.)

3. Edit `conf/mapred-site.xml` by replacing the empty `<configuration></configuration>` tags with:

```
<configuration>
  <property>
      <name>mapred.job.tracker</name>
      <value>localhost:9001</value>
  </property>
</configuration>
```

    (This configures the MapReduce daemon.)

4. Test the pseudo-distributed setup by formatting the Hadoop Distributed File System (HDFS) on this single system:

```
bin/hadoop namenode -format
```

All is good if you see output similar to the following (your hostname will be different):

```
11/05/26 23:05:36 INFO namenode.NameNode: STARTUP_MSG:
/************************************************************
STARTUP_MSG: Starting NameNode
STARTUP_MSG:   host = treasuryofideas-desktop/127.0.1.1
STARTUP_MSG:   args = [-format]
STARTUP_MSG:   version = 0.20.2
STARTUP_MSG:   build =
https://svn.apache.org/repos/asf/hadoop/common/branches/branch-0.20 -r 911707;
 compiled by 'chrisdo' on Fri Feb 19 08:07:34 UTC 2010
************************************************************/
11/05/26 23:05:37 INFO namenode.FSNamesystem:
 fsOwner=treasuryofideas,treasuryofideas,adm,dialout,
cdrom,plugdev,lpadmin,admin,sambashare
11/05/26 23:05:37 INFO namenode.FSNamesystem: supergroup=supergroup
11/05/26 23:05:37 INFO namenode.FSNamesystem: isPermissionEnabled=true
11/05/26 23:05:37 INFO common.Storage: Image file of size 105 saved in 0 seconds.
11/05/26 23:05:37 INFO common.Storage: Storage directory /tmp/hadoop-
treasuryofideas/dfs/name has been successfully formatted.
11/05/26 23:05:37 INFO namenode.NameNode: SHUTDOWN_MSG:
/************************************************************
SHUTDOWN_MSG: Shutting down NameNode at treasuryofideas-desktop/127.0.1.1
************************************************************/
```

5. Start all Hadoop daemons:

```
bin/start-all.sh
```

6. Verify all of the expected components are running by checking for the log files, which are available by default in the logs directory of the Hadoop distribution.

You should see the following log files with your username in place of username and your system's hostname in place of hostname:

```
$ ls logs/
hadoop-username-datanode-hostname.log
hadoop-username-datanode-hostname.out
hadoop-username-jobtracker-hostname.log
hadoop-username-jobtracker-hostname.out
hadoop-username-namenode-hostname.log
hadoop-username-namenode-hostname.out
hadoop-username-secondarynamenode-hostname.log
hadoop-username-secondarynamenode-hostname.out
hadoop-username-tasktracker-hostname.log
hadoop-username-tasktracker-hostname.out
history/
```

7. Access the Namenode and JobTracker web interface at http://localhost:50070/ and http://localhost:50030/, respectively.

8. Run jps, which lists the Java processes. You should see the following output, along with other Java processes you may have running:

```
2675 JobTracker
2442 DataNode
2279 NameNode
3027 Jps
2828 TaskTracker
2603 SecondaryNameNode
```

(The process IDs will in all probability be different on your machine.)

9. Next, re-run the HDFS test drive like so:

```
bin/hadoop fs -put bin input
bin/hadoop jar hadoop-*-examples.jar grep input output 'start[a-z.]+'

11/06/04 11:53:07 INFO mapred.FileInputFormat: Total input paths to process : 17
11/06/04 11:53:08 INFO mapred.JobClient: Running job: job_201106041151_0001
11/06/04 11:53:09 INFO mapred.JobClient: map 0% reduce 0%
11/06/04 11:53:24 INFO mapred.JobClient: map 11% reduce 0%
(...)
11/06/04 11:54:58 INFO mapred.JobClient: map 100% reduce 27%
11/06/04 11:55:10 INFO mapred.JobClient: map 100% reduce 100%
11/06/04 11:55:15 INFO mapred.JobClient: Job complete: job_201106041151_0001
(...)
11/06/04 11:55:48 INFO mapred.JobClient: Combine output records=0
11/06/04 11:55:48 INFO mapred.JobClient: Reduce output records=4
11/06/04 11:55:48 INFO mapred.JobClient: Map output records=4
```

10. To verify the output, copy the output from HDFS to the local filesystem and then concatenate and print the contents to standard output:

```
bin/hadoop fs -get output
pseudo-output
cat pseudo-output/*
cat: psuedo-output/_logs: Is a directory
5       starting
1       started
1       starts
1       startup
```

11. Concatenate and print the MapReduce job directly from HDFS. This should match what you see from getting the output on your local filesystem previously.

```
bin/hadoop fs -cat output/part*
5       starting
1       started
1       starts
1       startup
```

That completes the essential pseduo-distributed setup. For Hadoop cluster setup and configuration start at http://hadoop.apache.org/common/docs/r0.20.2/cluster_setup.html.

INSTALLING AND SETTING UP HBASE

To install and configure HBase in standalone mode, do the following:

1. Download the latest stable HBase distribution from an Apache Mirror (`www.apache.org/dyn/closer.cgi/hbase/`). Currently, the latest stable version is hbase-0.90.3. You should double-check compatibility with the version of Hadoop you are using, as there are often specific dependencies from HBase.

2. Unpack, untar, and unzip the HBase distribution:

```
tar zxvf hbase-0.90.3.tar.gz.
```

3. Move the unpacked distribution to a desired place in the filesystem. I moved it to `/opt`.

4. Create a symbolic link as follows: `ln -s hbase-0.90.3 hbase`.

5. Edit `conf/hbase-site.xml` by replacing the empty `<configuration.</configuration>` tags with:

```
<configuration>
  <property>
      <name>hbase.rootdir</name>
      <value>file:///opt/hbase_rootdir</value>
  </property>
</configuration>
```

(The `hbase.rootdir` is the directory HBase writes to. I have set `hbase.rootdir` to `/opt/hbase_rootdir`. You can choose any other location on your filesystem. The default `hbase.rootdir` value is `/tmp/hbase-${user.name}`, which may be deleted every time the server reboots.)

6. Verify by starting HBase:

```
bin/start-hbase.sh
```

7. Connect to HBase via the shell:

```
bin/hbase shell
```

INSTALLING AND SETTING UP HIVE

The following software is required to set up Hive:

➤ **Java 1.6.x** — Hadoop is tested against the Sun (now Oracle) JDK.

➤ **Hadoop 0.20.2** — Hive works with Hadoop versions between 0.17.x to 0.20.x.

To install and configure Hive, do the following:

1. Download the stable binary distribution from an Apache Mirror (`www.apache.org/dyn/closer.cgi/hive/`). The current stable release version is hive-0.70.0. The binary distributions have `-bin` in the filename, and are cross-platform since they are written in Java.

2. Unpack, untar, and unzip the Hive distribution:

```
tar zxvf hive-0.7.0-bin.tar.gz.
```

3. Move the unpacked distribution to a desired place in the filesystem. I moved it to `/opt`.

4. Create a symbolic link:

```
ln -s hive-0.7.0-bin hive
```

5. Set the `HIVE_HOME` environment variable:

```
export HIVE_HOME=/opt/hive
```

(Point to the directory that contains Hive distribution.)

6. Add the hive executable to the `PATH` environment variable:

```
export PATH=$HIVE_HOME/bin:$PATH
```

7. Verify that it is set correctly by running `which hive`. You should see the path you've configured.

```
which hive
/opt/hive/bin/hive
```

Configuring Hive

Make sure to have either Hadoop in your path or set the `HADOOP_HOME` environment variable to point to the Hadoop folder. You can set `HADOOP_HOME` as follows:

1. Set the environment variable:

```
export  HADOOP_HOME=/opt/hadoop
```

(Point to the directory that contains the HADOOP distribution.)

2. Create `/tmp directory` on HDFS:

```
$HADOOP_HOME/bin/hadoop fs -mkdir        /tmp
```

(Note that this may already exist.)

3. Give write permission on the `/tmp` HDFS directory to the group:

```
$HADOOP_HOME/bin/hadoop fs -chmod g+w    /tmp\
```

4. Create `hive.metastore.warehouse.dir` directory (default value: `/user/hive/warehouse`) on HDFS:

```
$HADOOP_HOME/bin/hadoop fs -mkdir        /user/hive/warehouse
```

5. Give write permission on HDFS `/user/hive/warehouse` directory to the group:

```
$HADOOP_HOME/bin/hadoop fs -chmod g+w    /user/hive/warehouse
```

Overlaying Hadoop Configuration

Hive configuration lays on top of the Hadoop configuration. The default Hive configuration is included in the `conf/hive-default.xml` file in the Hive distribution. You can override the default Hive configuration by redefining configuration variables and their values in `conf/hive-site.xml`. You can also change the Hive configuration directory by pointing the `HIVE_CONF_DIR` variable to the new configuration directly. In addition to redefining variables in `conf/hive-site.xml`, you can also redefine the configuration variables using any of the following:

➤ **Hive Command Line Interface (CLI) SET command** — For example, `hive > SET mapred.job.tracker=hostName.organizationName.com:50030;` sets the MapReduce cluster to the one specified.

➤ **hiveconf configuration variable and value pair** — Pass the `hiveconfig` variable and value pair to the hive executable.

For example, `bin/hive -mapred.job.tracker=hostName.organizationName.com:50030` sets the MapReduce cluster exactly the same way as the earlier `SET` command does. Multiple `hiveconf` variable and value pairs can be passed to the hive executable. Sometimes passing a number of configuration parameters can be a little difficult to maintain. In such cases, concatenate all configuration variable and value pairs and set it as the value of the `HIVE_OPTS` environment variable.

To verify the Hive installation and setup, run `$HIVE_HOME/bin/hive`.

INSTALLING AND SETTING UP HYPERTABLE

The easiest way to install Hypertable is to use the binary downloads. Hypertable binaries are compliant with all systems built with glibc 2.4+. If your system is built with a version of glibc older than 2.4, compile and package Hypertable manually using the instructions at `http://code.google.com/p/hypertable/wiki/HowToPackage`.

Hypertable offers binaries for both 64-bit and 32-bit platforms. Packages are available in `.rpm`, `.deb`, and `.dmg` formats. A binary distribution is also available in `.tar.bz2` format. To try to be package-agnostic, I usually choose the `.tar.bz2` format.

Follow these steps to install the Hypertable 64-bit `.tar.bz2` platform:

1. Download the latest release distribution from `www.hypertable.com/download/`. The latest release distribution version is 0.9.5.0.pre5.

2. Unpack, untar, and unzip the distribution:

```
tar jxvf hypertable-0.9.5.0.pre5-linux-x86_64.tar.bz2.
```

3. Move the contents of the unpacked distribution to a desired directory on your filesystem. The unpacked distribution content is in a directory structure like so:

```
/opt/hypertable/<version>
```

Therefore, making the distribution available at `/opt/hypertable/<version>` is recommended. It can be achieved using:

```
cd hypertable-0.9.5.0.pre5-linux-x86_64/opt, and
mv hypertable /opt
```

4. Create a symbolic link, named **current**, to point to the release distribution:

```
ln -s /opt/hypertable/0.9.5.0.pre5 /opt/hypertable/current
```

5. Optionally, make the distribution compliant with the Filesystem Hierarchy Standard (FHS).

Making the Hypertable Distribution FHS-Compliant

FHS is a recommended way to organize the files in a Linux/Unix filesystem. The standard recommends that host-specific configuration files for add-on software packages be stored in `/etc/opt`. The standard also suggests that variable data for such software should be in `/var/opt`.

To make the Hypertable distribution FHS-compliant, do the following:

1. Replace *<userName>:<groupName>* with your user and group (available from the `id` command) and run the following commands:

```
sudo mkdir /etc/opt/hypertable /var/opt/hypertable
sudo chown <userName>:<groupName> /etc/opt/hypertable /var/opt/hypertable
```

2. Run the following:

```
$ bin/fhsize.sh:
Setting up /var/opt/hypertable
Setting up /etc/opt/hypertable
fshize /opt/hypertable/current:  success
```

Making Hypertable FHS-compliant avoids re-creation of the config, log, hyperspace, and localBroker root directory when Hypertable is upgraded.

3. Verify that Hypertable is FHS-compliant by listing the contents of `/opt/hypertable/current` and to verify the symbolic links. The listing should be as follows:

```
$ cd /opt/hypertable/current
$ ls -l
bin
```

```
conf -> /etc/opt/hypertable
examples
fs -> /var/opt/hypertable/fs
hyperspace -> /var/opt/hypertable/hyperspace
include
lib
log -> /var/opt/hypertable/log
Monitoring
run -> /var/opt/hypertable/run
```

Configuring Hadoop with Hypertable

If you configured Hadoop according to the instructions earlier in this chapter, you have the HDFS daemon configured by putting the following in the Hadoop `conf/core-site.xml` as follows:

```
<configuration>
  <property>
      <name>fs.default.name</name>
      <value>hdfs://localhost:9000</value>
  </property>
</configuration>
```

(contents of `conf/core-site.xml`)

Now you need to edit `conf/hypertable.cfg`:

1. Verify that the configuration for HDFS in `hypertable.cfg`, by ensuring the following `HdfsBroker.fs.default.name` is

```
# HDFS Broker
HdfsBroker.fs.default.name=hdfs://localhost:9000
matches with the HDFS daemon configuration in Hadoop conf/core-site.xml
Create /hypertable directory on HDFS:
$HADOOP_HOME/bin/hadoop fs -mkdir        /hypertable
```

2. Give write permission on the HDFS `/hypertable` directory to the group with this command:

```
$HADOOP_HOME/bin/hadoop fs -chmod g+w    /hypertable
```

INSTALLING AND SETTING UP MONGODB

Download the latest release distribution from `www.mongodb.org/downloads`. Binary distributions for most mainstream operating systems are available via the MongoDB download link. I download and install 1.8.2-rc2 for 64-bit Linux. If you choose any other distribution, the following steps of installing and setting up will still largely be the same.

1. Unpack, untar, and unzip the `.tgz` format as follows:

```
tar zxvf mongodb-osx-x86_64-1.8.2-rc2.tgz
```

2. Move the extracted package to a desired place on your filesystem. I prefer to move it to `/opt` as follows:

```
mv mongodb-osx-x86_64-1.8.2-rc2 /opt
```

3. Create a symbolic link named `mongodb` to point to the directory that contains the MongoDB distribution:

```
ln -s mongodb-osx-x86_64-1.8.2-rc2 mongodb
```

Configuring MongoDB

By default, MongoDB stores the data files in the `/data/db` directory. If you want to use the default directory, create the directory and set the appropriate permissions as follows:

```
$ sudo mkdir -p /data/db
$ sudo chown `id -u` /data/db
```

If you would like an alternative directory like `/opt/data/db` to store the MongoDB data files, change the directory creation and permission setting commands as follows:

```
$ sudo mkdir -p /opt/data/db
$ sudo chown `id -u` /opt/data/db
```

When you use a data directory other than the default value, remember to pass it in as the value of the `--dbpath` argument of the mongodb server executable program. For example:

```
bin/mongod --dbpath /opt/data/db
```

INSTALLING AND CONFIGURING COUCHDB

To install CouchDB, Erlang and Erlang OTP are required.

It's easy to install Erlang on Linux and Unix. On Mac OS X you can leverage brew (`http://mxcl.github.com/homebrew/`) to install Erlang. On Windows, the easiest way to install CouchDB is to install Couchbase's Couchbase Server 1.1, which is available at `www.couchbase.com/downloads` and includes both an Erlang Windows distribution and CouchDB with some additional features. There are instructions for installing Apache CouchDB on Windows from components online at `http://wiki.apache.org/couchdb/Installing_on_Windows`; include the steps involved in installing Erlang.

Apache CouchDB has installers for most platforms. Access the installers and instructions on how to use them at `http://wiki.apache.org/couchdb/Installation`. Couchbase, the company behind CouchDB, provides binary installations for many platforms.

So far, most of the installation instructions included in this appendix have focused on installing the binaries. All the software programs listed in this appendix are open source. The source of these products is freely available and you can choose to build and install the software programs from source. As an example, the following section demonstrates how to build and install CouchDB from source on Unbuntu 10.04.

Installing CouchDB from Source on Ubuntu 10.04

CouchDB can be installed from source on Ubuntu Linux using the following steps:

1. Install the dependencies:

```
sudo apt-get build-dep couchdb
sudo apt-get install xulrunner-1.9.2-dev libicu-dev libcurl4-gnutls-dev libtool
```

2. Get the xulrunner version as follows:

```
xulrunner -v
```

The output on Ubunutu 10.04 on my machine was `Mozilla XULRunner 1.9.2.17 - 20110424212116`.

3. Create an xulrunner shared library loading configuration. This is needed because there may be many xulrunner versions, and the OS:

```
sudo vi /etc/ld.so.conf.d/xulrunner.conf
```

4. Add the following lines:

```
/usr/lib/xulrunner-1.9.2.17
/usr/lib/xulrunner-devel-1.9.2.17
```

5. Run `ldconfig`:

```
sudo /sbin/ldconfig
```

6. Get the source code from the code repository. You can use either SVN or Git.

```
git clone git://git.apache.org/couchdb.git
```

7. Change to the source directory:

```
cd couchdb
```

8. Bootstrap the build:

```
./bootstrap
```

Note that if you get an error here, you may have to install dependencies, which are covered in the `INSTALL.Unix` file included in the distribution. `aclocal` may also need to be installed with `sudo apt-get install automake`.

9. Configure the build:

```
./configure
```

10. Build and install:

```
make && sudo make install
```

11. Create a user name `couchdb`:

```
useradd couchdb
```

12. Change permissions on CouchDB directories to user `couchdb`.

13. Change ownership on CouchDB directories to user `couchdb`:

```
chown -R couchdb:couchdb /usr/local/etc/default/couchdb
chown -R couchdb:couchdb /usr/local/etc/init.d/couchdb
chown -R couchdb:couchdb /usr/local/etc/couchdb
chown -R couchdb:couchdb /usr/local/etc/logrotate.d/couchdb
chown -R couchdb:couchdb /usr/local/lib/couchdb
chown -R couchdb:couchdb /usr/local/bin/couchdb
chown -R couchdb:couchdb /usr/local/var/lib/couchdb
chown -R couchdb:couchdb /usr/local/var/run/couchdb
chown -R couchdb:couchdb /usr/local/var/log/couchdb
chown -R couchdb:couchdb /usr/local/share/doc/couchdb
chown -R couchdb:couchdb /usr/local/share/couchdb
```

INSTALLING AND SETTING UP REDIS

To begin the Redis installation process, follow these steps:

1. Download the latest stable release from `http://redis.io/download`. Version 2.2.8 is the latest version.

2. Unpack, untar, and unzip the Redis distribution: `tar zxvf redis-2.2.8.tar.gz`.

3. Move the Redis unpacked distribution to a desired location on the filesystem. I usually move it to `/opt` using `mv redis-2.2.8 /opt`.

4. Create a symbolic link to point to the Redis distribution:

```
ln -s redis-2.2.8 redis
```

5. To build, change to the directory that contains Redis and run `make`:

```
cd redis
make
```

6. To verify, run `make test`.

INSTALLING AND SETTING UP CASSANDRA

To begin the process of installing Cassandra, follow these steps:

1. Download a binary development release version from `http://cassandra.apache.org/download/`. The latest version is 0.8.0-rc1. The downloaded file is `apache-cassandra-0.8.0-rc1-bin.tar.gz`.

2. The distribution is available in the `.tar.gz` format. Unpack, untar, and unzip the distribution:

   ```
   tar zxvf apache-cassandra-0.8.0-rc1-bin.tar.gz
   ```

3. Move the extracted distribution to a desired location on the filesystem:

   ```
   mv apache-cassandra-0.8.0-rc1 /opt
   ```

4. Create a symbolic link named `apache-cassandra` to point to the directory that contains Cassandra:

   ```
   ln -s apache-cassandra-0.8.0-rc1 apache-cassandra
   ```

Configuring Cassandra

Cassandra can be configured by defining a configuration variable in `conf/cassandra.yaml`. Most default configurations are good for a single-node setup. Simply make sure that all the paths to the directories specified in `cassandra.yaml` exist.

The following configurations point to a file on the filesystem:

```
# directories where Cassandra should store data on disk.
data_file_directories:
    - /var/lib/cassandra/data

# commit log
commitlog_directory: /var/lib/cassandra/commitlog

# saved caches
saved_caches_directory: /var/lib/cassandra/saved_caches
```

Then create `/var/lib/cassandra` using **sudo mkdir -p /var/lib/cassandra**. Make sure to set appropriate permissions on this directory so the user that runs the Cassandra process can write to these directories.

Configuring log4j for Cassandra

The log4j server properties are specified in `log4j-server.properties`. The log4j appender file is specified in this file as follows:

```
log4j.appender.R.File=/var/log/cassandra/system.log
```

Make sure the directory `/var/log/cassandra` exists and is set with appropriate permissions so that the user running the Cassandra process can write to it.

Installing Cassandra from Source

The following sources are required:

➤ Java 1.6.x

➤ Ant 1.8.2

Build Cassandra from source using the following steps:

1. Download the source of the latest development release from `http://cassandra.apache.org/download/`. The current version is 0.8.0.rc1.

2. Unpack, untar, and unzip the downloaded source:

```
tar zxvf apache-cassandra-0.8.0-rc1-src.tar.gz.
```

3. Run the Ant build task:

```
ant
```

INSTALLING AND SETTING UP MEMBASE SERVER AND MEMCACHED

Download the relevant edition from `www.couchbase.com/downloads`. Three different distributions are available to download and install:

➤ Membase server

➤ Memcached server

➤ Couchbase server

To install Membase server, download a copy for your operating system from `www.couchbase.com/downloads`. Binaries are easy to install. A sample walk through for Mac OS X illustrates how you could install the binaries.

The next few steps relate to Mac OS X:

1. The Membase version on Mac OS X is packaged as a zip file. The specific file is `membase-server-community-1.6.5.3.zip`.

2. Unzip the file:

```
unzip membase-server-community-1.6.5.3.zip.
```

The unzipped application is available in a Mac OS X distribution format folder `Membase.app`.

3. Move `Membase.app` to `/Applications` or any other folder that you save the applications in.

INSTALLING AND SETTING UP NAGIOS

This section only covers instructions that will help you install Nagios from source on Ubuntu. For additional details, read the Nagios documentation, available online at www.nagios.org/documentation.

The following software is required:

- ➤ Apache 2
- ➤ PHP
- ➤ The GNU Compiler Collection (GCC), http://gcc.gnu.org/, compiler and development libraries
- ➤ GD development libraries

You can install these required pieces of software as follows:

1. Install Apache 2:

```
sudo apt-get install apache2
```

2. Install PHP:

```
sudo apt-get install libapache2-mod-php5
```

3. Install GCC and development libraries:

```
sudo apt-get install build-essential
```

4. Install GD development libraries:

```
sudo apt-get install libgd2-xpm-dev
```

It's recommended that a user named nagios be created and that the Nagios process be owned and run by this user. Create a user named nagios on Ubuntu as follows:

```
sudo /usr/sbin/useradd -m -s /bin/bash nagios
sudo passwd nagios
```

(Set a password. I default it to nagios. You will be prompted to enter a password and will be prompted to confirm the password.)

Create a nagcmd group and add both the nagios and the apache user to this group:

```
sudo /usr/sbin/groupadd nagcmd
sudo /usr/sbin/usermod -a -G nagcmd nagios
sudo sudo /usr/sbin/usermod -a -G nagcmd nagios
```

Downloading and Building Nagios

If all the required pieces of software are installed, download and build Nagios as follows:

1. Download Nagios Core and Nagios Plugins from www.nagios.org/download/. The current release version of Nagios Core is 3.2.3 and the current release version of Nagios Plugins is 1.4.15.

2. Unpack, untar, and unzip the Nagios distribution:

```
tar zxvf nagios-3.2.3.tar.gz
```

3. Change to the nagios-3.2.3 directory:

```
cd nagios-3.2.3
```

4. Configure Nagios:

```
./configure --with-command-group=nagcmd
```

5. Build Nagios:

```
make all
```

6. Install the binaries:

```
sudo make install
```

7. Install the init script:

```
sudo make install-init
```

The output of this command should be as follows:

```
/usr/bin/install -c -m 755 -d -o root -g root /etc/init.d
/usr/bin/install -c -m 755 -o root -g root daemon-init /etc/init.d/nagios
```

```
*** Init script installed ***
```

8. Install sample config files:

```
sudo make install-config.
```

The output of this command would be as follows:

```
/usr/bin/install -c -m 775 -o nagios -g nagios -d /usr/local/nagios/etc
/usr/bin/install -c -m 775 -o nagios -g nagios -d /usr/local/nagios/etc/objects
/usr/bin/install -c -b -m 664 -o nagios -g nagios sample-config/nagios.cfg
/usr/local/nagios/etc/nagios.cfg
/usr/bin/install -c -b -m 664 -o nagios -g nagios sample-config/cgi.cfg
/usr/local/nagios/etc/cgi.cfg
/usr/bin/install -c -b -m 660 -o nagios -g nagios sample-config/resource.cfg
```

```
/usr/local/nagios/etc/resource.cfg
/usr/bin/install -c -b -m 664 -o nagios -g nagios sample-config/template-
object/templates.cfg /usr/local/nagios/etc/objects/templates.cfg
/usr/bin/install -c -b -m 664 -o nagios -g nagios sample-config/template-
object/commands.cfg /usr/local/nagios/etc/objects/commands.cfg
/usr/bin/install -c -b -m 664 -o nagios -g nagios sample-config/template-
object/contacts.cfg /usr/local/nagios/etc/objects/contacts.cfg
/usr/bin/install -c -b -m 664 -o nagios -g nagios sample-config/template-
object/timeperiods.cfg /usr/local/nagios/etc/objects/timeperiods.cfg
/usr/bin/install -c -b -m 664 -o nagios -g nagios sample-config/template-
object/localhost.cfg /usr/local/nagios/etc/objects/localhost.cfg
/usr/bin/install -c -b -m 664 -o nagios -g nagios sample-config/template-
object/windows.cfg /usr/local/nagios/etc/objects/windows.cfg
/usr/bin/install -c -b -m 664 -o nagios -g nagios sample-config/template-
object/printer.cfg /usr/local/nagios/etc/objects/printer.cfg
/usr/bin/install -c -b -m 664 -o nagios -g nagios sample-config/template-
object/switch.cfg /usr/local/nagios/etc/objects/switch.cfg

*** Config files installed ***
```

9. Set permission on the directory for holding the external command file:

```
sudo make install-commandmode
```

The output of the command is as follows:

```
/usr/bin/install -c -m 775 -o nagios -g nagcmd -d /usr/local/nagios/var/rw
chmod g+s /usr/local/nagios/var/rw

*** External command directory configured ***
```

Configuring Nagios

1. Configure email address.

2. Edit the contacts config file:

```
sudo vi /usr/local/nagios/etc/objects/contacts.cfg.
```

Change the email field from `nagios@localhost` to your email address.

The next couple of steps help configure the Nagios web interface.

3. Install Nagios web config file in the Apache config.d directory: `sudo make install-webconf`

```
/usr/bin/install -c -m 644
sample-config/httpd.conf /etc/apache2/conf.d/nagios.conf
*** Nagios/Apache conf file installed ***
```

4. Create an account for logging in to the Nagios web interface:

```
sudo htpasswd -c /usr/local/nagios/etc/htpasswd.users nagiosadmin
```

You will be prompted for a password and be asked to confirm it.

5. Restart Apache:

```
sudo /etc/init.d/apache2 reload
```

Compiling and Installing Nagios Plugins

In an earlier step you downloaded the Nagios Plugin from `www.nagios.org/download/`. The latest release file version is 1.4.15.

Nagios Plugins can be compiled and installed as follows:

1. Unpack, untar, and unzip the Nagios Plugins distribution:

```
tar zxvf nagios-plugins-1.4.15.tar.gz
```

2. Change to the Nagios Plugins extracted distribution:

```
cd nagios-plugins-1.4.15
```

3. Configure Nagios Plugins:

```
./configure --with-nagios-user=nagios --with-nagios-group=nagios
```

4. Build Nagios Plugins:

```
make
```

5. Install Nagios Plugins:

```
sudo make install
```

Nagios and Nagios Plugins are now installed and you can start Nagios. Additional configuration is not covered in this document but you can read the official documentation, available at `www.nagios.org/documentation` to get all the details.

INSTALLING AND SETTING UP RRDTOOL

Instructions for installing RRDtool on Linux and Unix are covered in this section.

SVN client, automake, autoconf, and libtool are required to install RRDtool.

RRDtool can be installed from source as follows:

```
svn checkout svn://svn.oetiker.ch/rrdtool/trunk/program
mv program rrdtool-trunk
cd rrdtool-trunk
./autogen.sh
./configure --enable-maintainer-mode
make
sudo make install
```

INSTALLING HANDLER SOCKET FOR MYSQL

Handler Socket for MySQL works with MySQL server 5.x. Handler Socket for MySQL can be installed as follows:

```
git clone git://github.com/ahiguti/HandlerSocket-Plugin-for-MySQL.git
cd HandlerSocket-Plugin-for-MySQL
./autogen.sh
./configure --with-mysql-source=/root/install/mysql-<version number>
--with-mysql-bindir=/usr/bin
make
make install
```

INDEX

D

Try Safari Books Online FREE
for 15 days + 15% off
for up to 12 Months*

Read this book for free online—along with thousands of others—
with this 15-day trial offer.

With Safari Books Online, you can experience
searchable, unlimited access to thousands of
technology, digital media and professional
development books and videos from dozens of
leading publishers. With one low monthly or yearly
subscription price, you get:

- Access to hundreds of expert-led instructional
  videos on today's hottest topics.

- Sample code to help accelerate a wide variety
  of software projects

- Robust organizing features including favorites,
  highlights, tags, notes, mash-ups and more

- Mobile access using any device with a browser

- Rough Cuts pre-published manuscripts

START YOUR FREE TRIAL TODAY!
Visit **www.safaribooksonline.com/wrox5** to get st

*Available to new subscribers only. Discount applies to the
Safari Library and is valid for first 12 consecutive monthly
billing cycles. Safari Library is not available in all countries.

An Imprint of
Now you k